Fodor's

TORONTO

T0034421

Welcome to Toronto

Cultured and cosmopolitan, Toronto neverthe-less manages to remain relaxed, livable, and fun all at the same time. Canada's center of the arts and media has plenty of pleasant tree-lined streets in Yorkville for window-shopping and wandering; a host of independent galler-ies in West Queen West with edgy works; big-name music festivals year-round; and an adventurous, constantly evolving food scene. Toronto's impressive sights may be what pull you in, but its vibrant neighborhoods, artistic happenings, and friendly locals will make you want to return.

TOP REASONS TO GO

★ **CN Tower:** Rising 1,815 feet in the air, this icon has stupendous panoramic views.

★ **Foodie paradise:** Sophisticated restaurants, excellent ethnic spots, and markets.

★ **Nonstop shopping:** High-end designer flagships and a plethora of vintage shops.

★ **Festival city:** A star-studded film festival, the Nuit Blanche all-nighter, and more.

★ **Hip and happening:** Urbanites flock to West Queen West, Old Town, and beyond.

★ **The Waterfront:** The Beach's boardwalk and car-free Toronto Islands help you unwind.

Contents

1 **EXPERIENCE TORONTO** 6

   20 Ultimate Experiences 8

   What's Where 18

   Best Parks and Public
   Spaces in Toronto 20

   What to Eat and Drink in Toronto . 22

   Best Music Venues in Toronto.... 24

   The Best Thing to Do in Every
   Toronto Neighborhood 26

   Toronto Today 30

   Top Sports Experiences 32

   Toronto With Kids 34

2 **TRAVEL SMART** 35

   Know Before You Go 36

   Getting Here and Around 38

   Essentials 43

   Best Tours in Toronto 46

   Great Itineraries 52

   Toronto's Best Festivals 54

   Contacts 56

3 **HARBOURFRONT, ENTERTAINMENT
DISTRICT, AND THE FINANCIAL
DISTRICT** 57

   Harbourfront and the Islands..... 58

   Neighborhood Snapshot 60

   Harbourfront 61

   Entertainment District 71

   Financial District 81

4 **OLD TOWN AND THE
DISTILLERY DISTRICT** 89

   Neighborhood Snapshot 90

   Old Town 91

   Distillery District 98

5 **YONGE-DUNDAS
SQUARE AREA** 103

   Neighborhood Snapshot 104

6 **CHINATOWN, KENSINGTON
MARKET, AND QUEEN WEST**... 113

   Neighborhood Snapshot 114

   Chinatown 115

   Kensington Market 121

   Queen West 125

7 **WEST QUEEN WEST,
OSSINGTON, AND PARKDALE**.. 133

   Neighborhood Snapshot 134

   West Queen West 135

   Ossington 141

   Parkdale 145

8 **LESLIEVILLE, GREEKTOWN,
LITTLE INDIA, AND THE BEACH** 149

   Neighborhood Snapshot 150

   Leslieville 151

   Greektown 155

   Little India 158

   The Beach 159

9 **QUEEN'S PARK, THE ANNEX, AND
LITTLE ITALY** 163

   Neighborhood Snapshot 164

   Queen's Park 165

   The Annex 169

   Little Italy 174

10 **YORKVILLE, CHURCH AND
WELLESLEY, ROSEDALE, AND
CABBAGETOWN** 179

   Toronto's Film Scene 180

   Neighborhood Snapshot 182

Yorkville 183
Church and Wellesley 193
Rosedale 196
Cabbagetown 199

11 GREATER TORONTO 201
Neighborhood Snapshot 202
North Toronto 203
Northern and Eastern Suburbs .. 207
Pearson International
Airport Area.................. 210

12 SIDE TRIPS FROM TORONTO ... 211
Welcome to Side Trips
from Toronto 212
Niagara Falls.................. 214
Wine Region Know-How 216
Planning 218
Niagara Falls.................. 220
Niagara-on-the-Lake 232
The Niagara Escarpment 241
Stratford...................... 245
Midland and Penetanguishene .. 253
Gravenhurst................... 256
Huntsville..................... 259

INDEX 263

ABOUT OUR WRITERS 271

MAPS

Toronto Area Orientation........ 47
Toronto 48–49
Canada 50–51
Harbourfront, Entertainment
District, and the
Financial District 62–63
PATH Underground City.......... 82
Old Town and the Distillery
District 94
Yonge-Dundas Square Area..... 106
Chinatown, Kensington Market,
and Queen West 118
West Queen West, Ossington,
and Parkdale.................. 137
Leslieville, Greektown,
Little India, and The Beach...... 152
Queen's Park, the Annex,
and Little Italy................. 166
Yorkville, Church and Wellesley,
Rosedale, and Cabbagetown.... 186
Greater Toronto 205
Niagara Falls, Ontario 224
Niagara-on-the-Lake 234
Niagara Escarpment........... 243
Stratford, Ontario.............. 247
TTC Subway Routes 272

Chapter 1

EXPERIENCE TORONTO

20 ULTIMATE EXPERIENCES

Toronto offers terrific experiences that should be on every traveler's list. Here are Fodor's top picks for a memorable trip.

1 Set sail for the Toronto Islands

Located just a scenic 15-minute ferry ride away from downtown, Toronto Island Park is an idyllic getaway hidden just off the shoreline of Lake Ontario. *(Ch. 3)*

2 Tour the Distillery District

Once the site of the world's largest whiskey distillery, this cobblestone-paved neighborhood still oozes Victorian industrial character. *(Ch. 4)*

3 See the city from the CN Tower

Ride the glass-bottom elevator up 1,220 feet to the observation deck, or try the EdgeWalk, where you stroll around on the top of the tower. *(Ch. 3)*

4 Soak in the city's film scene

Many hotly anticipated movies debut at the Toronto International Film Festival, with stars and directors flying in to walk the red carpet and appear for panels and Q&As. *(Ch. 3)*

5 Eat your way around the globe

The city is home to a wealth of global cuisines—everything from Sri Lankan to Salvadorean to Ethiopian. Chinese, Korean, and Japanese food all have a strong foothold here. *(Ch. 5–11)*

6 Stroll along Queen West

One of the world's coolest neighborhoods, Queen Street West is at the heart of Toronto's cultural and independent retail scene. *(Ch. 6)*

7 Hang with dinosaurs at the ROM

The Royal Ontario Museum—the biggest museum in Canada—is a must-visit for history buffs and culture vultures alike. *(Ch. 10)*

8 Explore Kensington Market

Kensington, a bohemian, multicultural neighborhood, has fought to maintain its unique local character, including a patchwork of independent stores, grocers, and cafés. *(Ch. 6)*

9 Browse and snack at St. Lawrence Market

Once home to Toronto's first city hall and then a prison, this sprawling indoor market has become one of the city's must-hit destinations for food lovers. *(Ch. 4)*

10 Take in some contemporary art

As the country's cultural capital, Toronto is home to a number of top-shelf art museums, including the Power Plant and the Art Gallery of Toronto. *(Ch. 3, 6)*

11 Laugh through Toronto's comedy clubs

Toronto clubs like Yuk Yuk's, Second City, and Comedy Bar are hotbeds for future comedy megastars, many of whom have gone on to *Saturday Night Live* and movie stardom. *(Ch. 10)*

12 Feel the spray of Niagara Falls

One of the continent's most beautiful and thrilling natural wonders is a short trip away. *(Ch. 12)*

13 Take a public art walk

See some of Toronto's best art outside any museum. Step outside into the colorful Graffiti Alley or the Bentway, or stay up all night at the annual Nuit Blanche. *(Ch. 3, 6)*

14 Attend the Stratford Shakespeare Festival

Nearby Stratford hosts around a half-million visitors per year for its world-famous Shakespeare Festival, running from April through the fall. *(Ch. 12)*

15 Shop in high fashion in Yorkville

Once a hippie haven, Yorkville is now the city's home to high-fashion retailers like Burberry, Gucci, and Chanel and plenty of bougie boutiques. *(Ch. 10)*

16 Go kayaking along the lake or rivers

It may be a big city, but you can see it by paddle by renting a kayak along the Humber River, at The Beach, or on the Toronto Islands. *(Ch. 3, 8, 11)*

17 Grab a beer from a local brewery

Toronto is home to an enviable craft brewing scene, including Bellwoods Brewery and Steam Whistle Brewery, where you can grab a fresh pint to stay or a few bottles to go. *(Ch. 3, 7)*

18 Catch a play

With mega-productions from companies like Mirvish and a thriving independent scene at Soulpepper and Theatre Passe Muraille, Toronto's theater scene rivals New York's or London's. *(Ch. 3-6)*

19 Tour Ontario's wine country

Toronto is the perfect gateway to a ton of gorgeous wineries around Prince Edward County and the Niagara Peninsula, which produce some of the world's best ice wines, among others. *(Ch. 12)*

20 Enjoy the nightlife

Toronto's nightlife is bumping again, from the hip bars of Ossington to the LGBTQ+ scene of Church–Wellesley, with clubs and fun spots everywhere between. *(Ch. 7, 10)*

WHAT'S WHERE

1 Harbourfront, the Entertainment District, and the Financial District. Between the Waterfront and Queen Street, many of the city's main attractions are packed in this epicenter of Canadian financial power, as well as the restaurants, theaters, and clubs of King Street West.

2 Old Town and the Distillery District. Stroll through the Old Town past Victorian buildings to the foodie paradise St. Lawrence Market. Farther east, the Distillery District offers great shopping and cafés.

3 Yonge-Dundas Square Area. The square hosts frequent performances in summer, and the surrounding neighborhood has Broadway-style theaters and department stores.

4 Chinatown, Kensington Market, and Queen West. Busy and bustling, the sidewalks here are overflowing. Wander through the much-loved hippie-punk hangout of Kensington Market and scarf down dumplings in Chinatown.

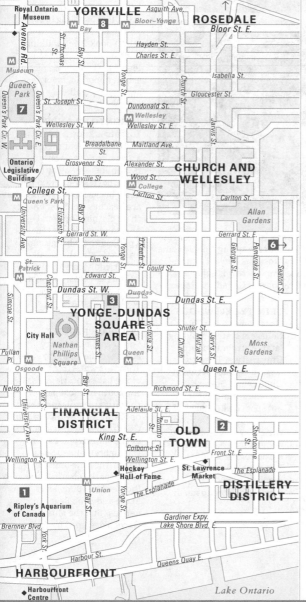

5 **West Queen West, Ossington, and Parkdale.** West Queen West and Ossington step up the city's hip quotient, and Parkdale is North America's largest Tibetan community.

6 **Leslieville, Greektown, Little India, and The Beach.** Here, the leafy residential streets and boardwalk of The Beach beckon, while funkified Leslieville offers boho shopping and great brunch spots.

7 **Queen's Park, the Annex, and Little Italy.** Stately Queen's Park is home to the University of Toronto. Farther west lies Little Italy, packed with cool cafés. North of the campus you'll hit the Annex, the city's academic and artsy haunt.

8 **Yorkville, Church–Wellesley, Rosedale, and Cabbagetown.** Yorkville itself is refined and classy. North of here is the moneyed residential neighborhood of Rosedale. A nudge east and south is Toronto's queer-friendly Church–Wellesley neighborhood.

9 **Greater Toronto.** Attractions such as Canada's Wonderland and the Toronto Zoo lure visitors from downtown.

Best Parks and Public Spaces in Toronto

HIGH PARK

The biggest public park in Toronto, High Park is perfect for a picnic, nature hike, or dog walk. In the spring, people come to see the beautiful pink cherry blossoms flower from the park's sakura trees, and in the summer crowds enjoy Shakespeare productions and music as part of Canadian Stage.

TOMMY THOMPSON PARK

One of the strangest natural phenomena in Toronto is Tommy Thompson Park, a long peninsula jutting into Lake Ontario on the Leslieville Spit. An "accidental wilderness" formed from bricks and rubble, its unique makeup has created the perfect breeding ground for birds and mammals you'll rarely find elsewhere. Despite its popularity among cyclists, joggers, and walkers, dogs are not allowed.

TRINITY BELLWOODS

Once home to Trinity College, a stately building later incorporated into University of Toronto, this large, hilly park between Dundas and Queen has become a summer hipster hot spot rivaling most of the nearby bars. Dogs and their Wayfairer-wearing owners congregate and sip on cold beers (not fully legal, but it happens anyway), slackline between trees, and listen to music.

ROSEDALE RAVINES

You'd never know that this system of lovely nature trails exists just underneath the mostly residential neighborhoods of midtown Toronto. Down a flight of stairs, the ravines are full of babbling brooks and shady spots to sit and read a book. Keep walking and you'll end up in Mount Pleasant Cemetery, a picturesque, if morbid, favorite among city walkers.

TORONTO ISLANDS

Toronto is known for glass and concrete, but there's a green park oasis only a 15-minute ferry away (or an even shorter water taxi for a few bucks more). There are beaches—at least one of them clothing-optional—plus tandem bicycle rentals, a petting zoo, a hedge maze, an artist retreat, a small and friendly community of Island residents, and signs encouraging you to "please walk on the grass."

THE WATERFRONT

You don't have to ferry across to the Island to enjoy Toronto's waterfront. All along Lake Ontario, across the southernmost part of the city, are trails for hiking or biking. Follow the Martin Goodman trail to see most of the waterfront, passing the umbrella-lined Sugar Beach, the now-unused theme park Ontario Place (home of the Budweiser Stage and Echo Beach music venues), and the Music Garden designed by Yo-Yo Ma.

Rouge National Urban Park

THE BENTWAY

One of the most creative reuses of public space, the Bentway repurposes a stretch of land underneath the elevated Gardiner Expressway. Like New York's High Line but under a bridge instead of on top of it, the shaded walk is now home to public art projects, concerts, and communal food events. You can follow it into nearby Fort York. In the winter, the whole trail becomes a public skating rink.

RIVERDALE PARK

This sprawling east-end park crosses over the Lower Don River and offers plenty of spots to lounge around, play a game of baseball or a tennis match, or take your kids to play. You can stretch the trip out to visit Riverdale Farm, a working farm filled with sheep and goats, and the infamous, now-decommissioned Don Jail. The east-side top of the hill offers one of the best views of the city, especially around sundown.

WOODBINE BEACH

One of the top sites of the east-end Beach neighborhood, Woodbine spans 37.5 acres along the coast of Lake Ontario. The boardwalk is a popular place for a stroll, and there's plenty of places to sunbathe, take a dip, fly a kite, or play a game of beach volleyball. It's also the go-to spot for fireworks on long holiday weekends in May (Victoria Day) and July (Canada Day).

ROUGE NATIONAL URBAN PARK

If you trek outside of downtown into the suburb of Scarborough, you'll be rewarded with a huge, amazing park full of some of the city's best hikes, marshes, a beach on Lake Ontario, and Toronto's only campground within city limits. The Rouge includes some of Canada's oldest known Indigenous sites dating back over 10,000 years. You don't need a car to get there, as it is accessible via the GO Train system.

What to Eat and Drink in Toronto

SPICE THINGS UP WITH INDIAN CUISINE

If you find yourself craving a good tikka masala while in Toronto, your first stop should be Banjara, which offers a broad, universally delicious menu. In Little India, the raucous, always-busy Lahore Tikka House specializes in grilled kebabs and tandoori chicken.

BROWSE THE WORLD'S CULTURES IN KENSINGTON MARKET

The bohemian Kensington Market is one of Toronto's most unique and vibrant neighborhoods, with a diversity that's reflected in its mix of shops and restaurants. You'll find Latin, Caribbean, and Asian influences in the shops here.

SAMPLE THE LATEST IN JAPANESE SNACKS

Toronto has enjoyed a Japanese food boom in recent years, spurred by the viral success of Uncle Tetsu's Japanese Cheesecake. You can find Japanese pancakes, *izakaya* bar food, and matcha-flavored ice cream. A stretch of Dundas Street has even picked up the nickname Little Tokyo.

EXPERIENCE INDIGENOUS CUISINE

In recent years, Toronto has become home to several restaurants serving traditional dishes from the area's First Nations, which serve an important dual function as local hubs for Indigenous culture. The longest-running is Tea N Bannock, a Little India café with a menu that puts staples like bison, fry bread, and arctic char front and center.

TRY SOME REGIONAL CHINESE DISHES

Toronto is home to a sizable Chinese population, so it's no surprise that a number of China's local cuisines are represented. Start at Yueh Tung for a variety of Hakka dishes. In Chinatown, Rol San is an always-busy, no-frills spot for Cantonese. Heading north on Spadina, Mother's Dumplings has northeastern eats like pork-and-chive dumplings and scallion pancakes. Dim sum is a must-try experience in Chinatown and in the suburbs of Markham and Scarborough, especially if you can find an old-school spot bringing around dishes on carts.

GO ON A MOMO CRAWL IN PARKDALE

The west-end stretch of Queen Street is home to a large Tibetan population, which is reflected in the proliferation of eateries serving *momos*, Tibetan dumplings stuffed with a variety of meats and veggies and served steamed or fried. If you want to sample the whole local smorgasbord, Students for a Free Tibet hosts a Momo Crawl food event every summer.

Northern Thai at Pai

DIVE INTO NORTHERN THAI
The family behind Pai runs several of Toronto's most beloved Thai joints, including tried-and-true Sukhothai, genteel, marble-swathed Kiin, and the psychedelic Selva. You can't go wrong with a meal at any of them—but Pai just might be the most memorable.

STOP BY MARKET 707 FOR AN INTERNATIONAL SMORGASBORD
It might not look like much, but Market 707, a row of shipping-container food stalls on a quiet stretch of Dundas, is an incubator for some of Toronto's most interesting new food businesses, playing host to everything from Ethiopian to Filipino food. The offerings change as businesses come and go.

FEEL THE HEAT WITH CARIBBEAN EATS
Toronto's thriving Caribbean population fuels a vibrant dining scene. Many of the old-school Caribbean roti joints have fallen victim to rising rents, but mom and pops like Ali's Roti in Parkdale are still holding strong. Most of the best Caribbean dining is in the suburbs these days.

TRY JAMAICAN-CHINESE FUSION
The Chinese-Jamaican-Southern mishmash you see at hip Dundas West joint Patois is unlike any other in town. The party-ready spot is fueled by dishes from the chef's Jamaican-Chinese upbringing, with plenty of tropical cocktails to wash it all down.

Best Music Venues in Toronto

MASSEY HALL

This grand concert hall was made famous by artists like Neil Young, but a 2021 renovation modernized the space without affecting its midsize intimacy or pin-drop acoustics. There are both big-ticket shows and more affordable showcases for up-and-coming artists.

HORSESHOE TAVERN

This storied Queen West tavern has been around since 1947 and has had multiple lives as a hotbed of country music and punk rock. Stepping past the barflies into the dark back room, it still feels like a working-class watering hole, but nowadays it's more likely to hold an indie rock concert than a whiskey hoedown (though they have been known to happen).

KOERNER HALL

Koerner Hall is an eye-catching, sculptural concert hall within the TELUS Centre for Performance and Learning at the Royal Conservatory of Music next to the ROM. The 1,135-seat room is both gorgeous and sophisticated, with rich acoustics and rollicking wood "strings" floating overhead. It's a favorite of the (mostly classical) musicians who play there.

THE REX HOTEL & JAZZ BAR

An unpretentious room on Queen Street, the Rex Hotel is one of the top spots to catch jazz music in Toronto. With two shows every night, you can stop in any time and know you'll catch something good without having to spend a fortune. A favorite among touring musicians, working locals, and even students showcasing their skills for an attentive audience, the venue books an eclectic mix of jazz styles.

DANFORTH MUSIC HALL

This east-end spot on the Danforth is constantly booked with big-name artists not quite big enough for an arena show. Built as a cinema in 1919, it's now a home for both seated and general admission concerts (though the balcony seats stay put) of all sorts of genres: rock, hip-hop, electronic, and even the occasional comedy show. Although no longer a movie house, popcorn is still for sale in the concession stands.

BUDWEISER STAGE

The outdoor amphitheater at Ontario Place on the waterfront, Budweiser Stage has a big-show feel throughout its summer concert season. With a capacity of thousands, it's a spot for both big touring bands and local rap hero Drake, who's hosted his annual, star-studded OVO Fest at the venue for years. The nearby Echo Beach is a

El Mocambo

slightly smaller non-seated venue where you can watch concerts with sand underfoot.

THE GARRISON
In the decade-plus it's been in business, this Dundas West venue (once a Portuguese sports bar) has become a local institution for buzzy Toronto acts and up-and-coming touring bands. It's also a popular spot for DJ'd dance parties. The Garrison and its smaller sister bar the Baby G down the street both frequently have an extended 4 am last call, so it's a good place to spend a late night.

LULA LOUNGE
A Latin and world music hot spot on Dundas West, Lula Lounge is your spot for Afro-Cuban, Brazilian, and all sorts of other sounds from around the globe. Especially popular are its Sunday drag brunches and weekend salsa nights, which include both lessons and a full food menu. Musicians also take to the street for the annual Do West Fest, where Lula curates an outdoor stage.

HISTORY
Mega-promoters Live Nation partnered with local music hero and international superstar Drake for this flashy venue in The Beach, a 2,500-capacity general admission venue designed to make any big artist of any genre sound good. A superb sound system and lighting setup makes the artist onstage the main attraction, though there are all sorts of VIP food, drink, and seating options if you spring for them.

EL MOCAMBO
A historic Spadina venue best known for legendary concerts by the Rolling Stones and Elvis Costello, El Mocambo is now owned by eccentric celebrity investor Michael Wekerle. After a long and expensive renovation, he's turned it into a splashy, neon-colored ode to rock history. Come here for the perfect Instagram shot, or to see bigger bands looking for an intimate show they can live-stream.

The Best Thing to Do in Every Toronto Neighborhood

HARBOURFRONT

One of downtown Toronto's best experiences isn't in the downtown core at all, but a short ferry ride away. The Toronto Islands are a conveniently located getaway just off the shore of Lake Ontario, offering peaceful beaches (including the fabled clothing-optional section of Hanlan's Point), beautiful parks, and an amazing view of the Toronto skyline. Families will enjoy the Centreville amusement park; if you're hungry, stop on the giant patio at Island Cafe, at the Riviera, or grab a pint at Toronto Island BBQ and Beer.

ENTERTAINMENT DISTRICT

This downtown district's biggest draw is its collection of theaters. The Royal Alexandra, built in 1907, has played host to major touring musicals like *Kinky Boots*; down the street is sister theater the Princess of Wales, a modern glass-walled space that's hosted *Mamma Mia!* and *The Book of Mormon*. Across the street is Roy Thomson Hall, home to the Toronto Symphony Orchestra. If film is more your scene, check out what's screening at the TIFF Bell Lightbox, which serves as the main hub for the Toronto International Film Festival in September but spotlights both classics and indie flicks year-round.

FINANCIAL DISTRICT

Unsurprisingly, Toronto's main office district is home to a lot of top-shelf restaurants ready to give those expense accounts a hearty workout. Canoe, one of the city's best-known fine dining destinations, could coast on the views from its 54th-floor perch—but instead, it offers a vibrant menu that highlights Canada's seasonal bounty. Down at street level in the same building, Bymark specializes in luxe comfort foods like lobster grilled cheese sandwiches.

OLD TOWN

A must-visit for history buffs and foodies alike, the St. Lawrence Market started its storied life as Toronto's first city hall, then as a prison. Now, the sprawling space is jammed with vendors offering all manner of meats, cheeses, breads, produce, and artisanal foods. Be sure to pick up a peameal (aka Canadian) bacon sandwich at Carousel Bakery, and check out the farmers' market on Saturday and flea market on Sunday.

THE DISTILLERY DISTRICT

Once the site of the biggest distillery in the world, this historic neighborhood's industrial Victorian architecture has been carefully preserved; instead of pumps and stills, the rows of rough-hewn brick buildings now hold cute boutiques and cafés. Be sure to stop at Brick Street Bakery for a fresh croissant, or at Mill Street Brewery for a pint; pick up chocolates at Soma and scout for fashions at Gotstyle or John Fluevog.

YONGE-DUNDAS SQUARE AREA

Referred to (accurately, if somewhat quaintly) as Toronto's answer to Times Square, Dundas Square is best known as a busy shopping area, flanked by the Eaton Centre—but its array of stores, with few exceptions, can be found in most big U.S. cities. Be sure to take a little time to check out the square itself, which frequently plays host to outdoor shows (including bigger names during Luminato and Pride, both in June), cultural events, food festivals, and more. Even if nothing's going on, it's a good place to take a breather and people-watch.

CHINATOWN

Toronto's largest Chinatown has been going strong since a wave of Chinese immigration in the 1960s, and though rents are rising and hip cafés and streetwear boutiques have been creeping into the area, this stretch of Spadina Avenue is still home to some of the city's best Chinese food. Among your options are dumplings at Dumpling House, dim sum at Sky Dragon, and seafood specialties at Wah Sing. Not craving Chinese food? There's all-night Vietnamese at Pho Pasteur, modernized bar snacks at R&D, and artistic French-Canadian dishes at AGO Bistro.

KENSINGTON MARKET

Kensington Market is an oasis of bohemian weirdness in the heart of downtown, a neighborhood of colorful homes, ramshackle shops, and often-inexpensive (and delicious) multicultural eats. Vintage hounds should check the shops that line Kensington Avenue for leather jackets and vintage Levi's, while foodies can dig into Indigenous cuisine (Pow Wow Cafe), amazing Baja-style fish tacos (Seven Lives), and vegan versions of Middle Eastern classics (Eat Nabati).

QUEEN WEST

Queen West has become increasingly corporate as the years pass and rents rise, but this mazelike array of back alleys is a homegrown outdoor shrine to street art. The result of a city revitalization project launched in 2011, Graffiti Alley (sometimes referred to as Rush Lane) serves as an ever-changing museum of work by some of the city's foremost street artists, and is a perennially popular setting for music videos and photo shoots. Once you've walked up an appetite, head around the corner to Queen and grab some great cheap eats at Banh Mi Boys or 416 Snack Bar.

WEST QUEEN WEST

This hip district is home to a wealth of eclectic independent shops of all stripes. Hunt for locally made leather bags at Zane, or give your wardrobe a boost at Horses Atelier, read some local literature at Type Books, catch up on comics and nerd culture at Silver Snail, or check out locally made blown glass and pottery at Craft Ontario. If you've got time to spare, head up to Dundas West for more indie boutiques.

OSSINGTON

If your Toronto travel plans include a bar crawl, odds are you'll end up on the Ossington strip, one of the city's hottest nightlife destinations. Bellwoods Brewery is a low-key spot with the most sought-after beers in town, while Reposado is a candlelit shrine to tequila and mescal. Where Ossington meets Dundas, you'll find the Dakota Tavern, a bar that hosts folk, country, and bluegrass shows, while the Communist's Daughter is a tiny booze-can stuffed with locals.

PARKDALE

Take a break and sip a coffee in Parkdale, home to some of the city's homiest independent cafés. The clock seems to tick a little slower here among the tattoo-covered caffeine lovers. Start early in the morning with a rich cappuccino from Sam James Coffee Bar, one of the pioneers of so-called third wave coffee. Finish the day at Skyline, a beloved old-school diner that turns into a friendly and beery neighborhood haunt after dark.

LESLIEVILLE

This low-key neighborhood has plenty of hidden-gem restaurants, stores, and cafés, but it's also become an epicenter of the city's recent brewery boom. Avling is a gorgeous, pastel-washed new space with a rooftop garden that fuels the kitchen. Eastbound and Radical Road are low-key brewpubs with some unusual specialties. Veer north toward Little India for Left Field, a baseball-themed brewery that turns out some of the city's finest sours and IPAs, and Godspeed, which offers a novel mash-up of Japanese and German styles.

GREEKTOWN

This east-end neighborhood (also known as the Danforth) is the place to get your feta fix, from hole-in-the-wall bakeries to sit-down spots with live entertainment. On the take-out side, there's quick and reliable spots like Messini or the slightly grungy Alexandros (which stays open until 4 am). For something more elaborate, there's Christina's—home to some great Greek dips, plus belly dancers and a Greek band on weekends—and Mezes, a lively spot with a heated patio. Summer festivals like Thrill of the Grill and Taste of the Danforth bring the party outdoors.

LITTLE INDIA

Largely off the tourist beaten path, this east-end neighborhood is still lined with mom-and-pop businesses selling saris, bangles, and delicious eats. Lahore Tikka House, which splits its menu between North Indian and Pakistani, is the undisputed go-to for tandoori, kebabs, and biryani, while Udupi Palace has the vegetarian market cornered. If you're not in the mood for Indian, pop by Lake Inez, a modern pan-Asian snack bar with a mosaic mural of Kate Bush and Virginia Woolf.

THE BEACH

The sandy shores that lend this largely residential east-end neighborhood its name are without a doubt its top selling point for visitors. The beach, which is quite clean and certified safe for swimming, is divided into two main chunks. Woodbine, a long, sandy stretch that plays host to volleyball courts, paddleboards, and canoe rentals, is popular with families and beach partiers alike. Meanwhile, a 10-minute boardwalk stroll to the east, Kew-Balmy is rockier and less crowded, the perfect spot for a quiet beach read or a dip in the lake.

QUEEN'S PARK

To locals, Queen's Park refers to not only the neighborhood but the historic Ontario Legislative Building that serves as the seat of the provincial government. Built in 1893, the pink sandstone building takes its cues from British architecture, with a hefty collection of artwork from Canada and abroad. Just a few blocks west, you'll hit the edge of the University of Toronto's sprawling campus, which is packed with stately buildings, including the neo-Gothic Hart House.

THE ANNEX

The sprawling Casa Loma, a Gothic revival–style mansion, was built in the 1910s as the home of ultra-wealthy financier Henry Pellatt, at a cost of C$3.5 million (yep, that's in 1913 dollars). The lushly decorated 98-room estate now serves as a museum and event venue, complete with stables, a 60-foot-tall ballroom, a pipe organ, a collection of vintage cars, and 5 acres of gardens.

LITTLE ITALY

Little Italy has had its share of identities: it was first a stronghold for Portuguese and Italian families, then a burgeoning nightclub district, and now, finally, it seems to have found a way to balance the two. There are plenty of classic dining destinations like Cafe Diplomatico, an Italian spot known for its popular side patio. But a new generation of Italian restaurants, like sleekly modern Giulietta, have also settled in. Of course, it's not all checkered tablecloths: you can also get a serious fried chicken sandwich at PG Clucks, or try some Belgian brews at Birreria Volo.

YORKVILLE

Toronto's "Mink Mile" is home to some excellent cultural institutions, like the Royal Ontario Museum—but what the area is really known for is its shopping. Hermès, Prada, Gucci, and many other boldface names maintain storefronts along Bloor Street; you can find even more at Holt Renfrew, Canada's fanciest department store, which packs in bags, clothing, shoes, and beauty products and has a separate men's store down the block. Head north into the heart of the neighborhood to find the ritzy Yorkville Village mall and a number of independent boutiques catering to the well-heeled.

CHURCH–WELLESLEY

The Village, as the locals call it, is the epicenter of gay life in Toronto. Glad Day, the world's oldest LGBTQ+ bookstore, is a must-visit; you can check out the latest voices in queer lit while sipping on a coffee or digging into brunch at the on-site café. Crews & Tangos hosts dancing and drag shows, while Woody's is home to some very fun events (the weekly "Best Butt" contest is a favorite) and nightly DJs. If you're around in June, the Pride festivities are among some of the biggest in the world; don't miss the Pride parade at the end of the month.

ROSEDALE

Though it's no less moneyed, Rosedale is a lot less splashy than Yorkville, and the shopping is a lot more subdued. Grab a cute, homespun-looking beanie or throw pillow at Tuck Shop Trading Co., or stock up on fancy condiments at Summerhill Market. If your souvenir-shopping tastes run toward hard-to-find wines and spirits, the Summerhill location of the provincially run LCBO liquor store—located inside a historic train station—is a must-visit; things appear on the shelves here that you just can't find anywhere else.

Toronto Today

It can be hard to define a city like Toronto. It's culturally diverse, to be sure, but that's not exactly a unifying characteristic. So what exactly is Toronto all about? Americans call Torontonians friendly and the city clean, while other Canadians say its locals can be rude and egocentric. Toronto is often touted simply as a "livable" city, a commendable but dull virtue. Toronto might not be quite as exciting as New York City, as quaint as Montréal, as outdoorsy as Vancouver, or as historic as London, but instead it's a patchwork of *all* these qualities. And rest assured that Toronto *is* clean, safe, and just all-around nice. Torontonians say "sorry" when they jostle you. They recycle and compost. They obey traffic laws. For many, Toronto is like the boy next door you eventually marry after fooling around with New York or Los Angeles. Why not cut the charade and start the love affair now?

DIVERSITY

Toronto is one of the most immigrant-friendly cities on the planet, and the city's official motto, "Diversity Our Strength," reflects this hodgepodge of ethnicities. More than half its population is foreign-born, and half of all Torontonians are native speakers of a foreign language. (The "other" Canadian national language of French, however, is not one of the most commonly spoken languages here, trailing Chinese, Portuguese, Punjabi, and Tagalog.) In a few hours in Toronto you can travel the globe, from Little India to Little Italy, Koreatown to Greektown— or at least eat your way around it, from Polish pierogi to Chinese dim sum to Portuguese salt-cod fritters.

NEIGHBORHOODS

Every city has neighborhoods, but Toronto's are particularly diverse, distinctive, and walkable. Some were once their own villages, and many, such as Greektown (the Danforth), Little Portugal, and Chinatown, are products of the ethnic groups who first settled there. For the most part, boundaries aren't fixed and are constantly evolving: on a five-minute walk down Bloor Street West you can pass a Portuguese butcher, an Ethiopian restaurant, a hip espresso bar, and a Maltese travel agency. In the 1970s and '80s, areas such as Yorkville and Queen West were transformed by struggling-artist types and have since grown into affluent retail powerhouses. In the last decade once run-down neighborhoods, including West Queen West and Leslieville, have blossomed into funky, boho areas with enviable shopping and eating options with housing prices to match. Barring a change in fortune, gentrification is set to continue to more areas.

CULTURE

The Toronto International Film Festival, the Art Gallery of Ontario, Canada's center for magazine and book publishing, national ballet and opera companies, the Toronto Symphony Orchestra—these are just a handful of the many reasons Toronto attracts millions of arts and culture lovers each year to live, work, and play. On any given day or night, you'll find events to feed the brain and the spirit: art gallery openings, poetry readings, film screenings, concerts, dance performances, and festivals showcasing the arts, from the focused Toronto Jazz Festival and the North by Northeast indie rock extravaganza to events marrying visual and performing arts, like Nuit Blanche and Luminato.

THE WATERFRONT

Lake Ontario forms Toronto's very obvious southern border, but residents who live out of its view often forget it's there until they attend an event at the Canadian National Exhibition or the Harbourfront Centre. It's one of the city's best features, especially in the summer, providing opportunities for boating, ferrying to the Toronto Islands, or strolling, biking, or jogging beside the water. The lakeshore is more of an attraction than ever, with ongoing initiatives to revitalize the waterfront and create more parks, beaches, and walkways.

FOOD

There's no shortage of amazing restaurants in this city, and local and fresh produce is all the rage. Celebrity chefs like Lynn Crawford, Susur Lee, and Matty Matheson always seem to have something new and buzzy, while Toronto's cornucopia of cultures means you can sample almost any cuisine, from Abyssinian to Yemeni. Nowhere is the Toronto love of food more apparent than at St. Lawrence Market, where you can pick up nonessentials like fiddlehead ferns, elk burgers, truffle oil, and mozzarella *di bufala*. In warm weather, farmers' markets bring the province's plenty to the city.

Top Sports Experiences

Toronto has a love-hate relationship with its professional sports teams, and fans can sometimes be accused of being fair-weather—except when it comes to hockey, which always attracts rabid, sell-out crowds whether the Maple Leafs win or lose (mostly lose). In other words, don't count on getting Leafs tickets, but take heart that sports bars will be filled with fired-up fans. The Raptors (basketball) are also a hot commodity following their 2019 championship win, but it can be easier to score tickets to Blue Jays (baseball), Argos (football), and Toronto FC (soccer) games, depending on who they play.

If you prefer to work up a sweat yourself, consider golf at one of the GTA's courses, ice-skating at a city rink in winter, shooting some hoops at a local basketball course, or exploring the many parks and beaches.

Ticketmaster. This outlet is a good resource for game tickets. ☎ *416/345–9200* ⊕ *www.ticketmaster.ca.*

BASEBALL

Toronto Blue Jays. Toronto's professional baseball team plays late March through September. They won consecutive World Series championships in 1992 and 1993, and had playoff runs in 2015, 2016, 2020, and nearly in 2021 as well. The Rogers Centre (formerly the SkyDome) has a fully retractable roof; some consider it one of the world's premier entertainment centers, but the concrete behemoth is starting to show its age and is rumored to be replaced in the near future. Enjoy it while you can. ⊠ *Rogers Centre, 1 Blue Jays Way, Harbourfront* ☎ *416/341–1234 ticket line, 888/654–6529 toll-free ticket line* ⊕ *www.bluejays.com* Ⓜ *Union.*

BASKETBALL

Toronto Raptors. The city's NBA franchise, this popular basketball team played its first season in 1995–96. For several years they struggled mightily to win both games and fans in this hockey-mad city, but the Raptors have finally come into their own, particularly after winning the 2019 NBA Championship. Single-game tickets are available beginning in September; the season is from October through May. ⊠ *Scotiabank Arena, 40 Bay St., at Gardiner Expwy., Harbourfront* ☎ *416/366–3865* ⊕ *www.nba.com/raptors* Ⓜ *Union.*

FOOTBALL

Toronto Argonauts. The Toronto Argonauts Canadian Football League (CFL) team has a healthy following. American football fans who attend a CFL game often discover a faster, more unpredictable and exciting contest than the American version. The longer, wider field means quarterbacks have to scramble more. Tickets for games (June–November) are usually a cinch to get. ⊠ *BMO Field, 170 Princes' Blvd., Harbourfront* ☎ *416/341–2746* ⊕ *www.argonauts.ca.*

GOLF

The golf season lasts only from April to late October. Discounted rates are usually available until mid-May and after Canadian Thanksgiving (early October). All courses are best reached by car.

Angus Glen Golf Club. This club has remained one of the country's best places to play since it opened in 1995, hosting the Canadian Open in 2002 and 2007 on its par-72 South and North courses, respectively, and the 2015 Pan Am Games. It's a 45-minute drive north of downtown. ⊠ *10080 Kennedy Rd., Markham* ☎ *905/887–0090, 905/887–5157 reservations* ⊕ *www.angusglen.com.*

Don Valley Golf Course. About a 20-minute drive north of downtown, this is a par-72, 18-hole municipal course. Despite being right in the city, it's a lovely, hilly course with water hazards and tree-lined fairways. ⊠ *4200 Yonge St., North York* ☎ *416/392–2465* ⊕ *www.toronto.ca/ parks/golf.*

Glen Abbey Golf Club. This Jack Nicklaus–designed 18-hole, par-73 club is considered to be Canada's top course. It's in the affluent suburb of Oakville, about 45 minutes west of the city. ⊠ *1333 Dorval Dr., just north of QEW, Oakville* ☎ *905/844–1800* ⊕ *glenabbey.clublink.ca.*

HOCKEY

Toronto Maple Leafs. Hockey is as popular here as you've heard, and Maple Leafs fans are particularly ardent. Even though the Leafs haven't won a Stanley Cup since 1967, they continue to inspire fierce devotion in Torontonians. If you want a chance to cheer them on, you'll have to get on the puck. No matter the stats, Leafs tickets are notoriously the toughest to score in the National Hockey League. The regular hockey season is October–April. ■TIP→ **Buy tickets at least a few months in advance or risk the game being sold out.** ⊠ *Scotiabank Arena, 40 Bay St., at Gardiner Expwy., Harbourfront* ☎ *416/703–5323* ⊕ *www.mapleleafs.com* Ⓜ *Union.*

Toronto Marlies. If you're keen to see some hockey while you're in town, go to a Toronto Marlies game at Coca-Cola Coliseum. The level of play is very high, and tickets are cheaper and easier to come by than those of the Marlies' NHL big brother, the Toronto Maple Leafs. ⊠ *Coca-Cola Coliseum, 45 Manitoba Dr., Harbourfront* ☎ *416/597–7825* ⊕ *www. marlies.ca* Ⓜ *Union or Bathurst.*

SOCCER

Toronto's British roots combined with a huge immigrant population have helped make the Toronto Football Club (Toronto FC), the newest addition to the city's pro sports tapestry, a success. And during international soccer events like the FIFA World Cup, UEFA European Championship, and Copa América (America Cup), sports bars and cafés with TVs are teeming.

Toronto FC. Canada's first Major League Soccer team and Toronto's first professional soccer team in years, Toronto FC kicked off in 2006 in a stadium seating more than 25,000 fans. They get seriously pumped up for these games, singing fight songs, waving flags, and throwing streamers. Games sometimes sell out; single-game tickets go on sale a few days before the match. The season is February–October. ⊠ *BMO Field, 170 Princes' Blvd., Harbourfront* ☎ *855/985– 5000 Ticketmaster* ⊕ *www.torontofc.ca* Ⓜ *Union.*

ICE-SKATING

★ **Nathan Phillips Square Rink.** Winter skaters flock to this local favorite rink in the heart of the city, right next to the futuristic looking City Hall building and in front of the distinctive Toronto sign. ⊠ *100 Queen St. W, Queen West* ☎ *311 Toronto Parks, Forestry and Recreation rink hotline* ⊕ *nathanphillipssquareskaterentals.com* Ⓜ *Osgoode.*

Natrel Rink. This spacious, outdoor rink at Harbourfront Centre is often voted the best in the city due to its lakeside location and DJ skate nights. Skate rentals are C$13. ⊠ *235 Queens Quay W, Harbourfront* ☎ *416/973–4000* ⊕ *www. harbourfrontcentre.com* Ⓜ *Union.*

Toronto With Kids

Toronto is one of the most livable cities in the world, and many families reside downtown with plenty of activities to keep them busy.

Always check what's on at **Harbourfront Centre,** a cultural complex with shows and workshops for all ages. On any given day you could find a circus, clown school, musicians, juggling, storytelling, or acrobat shows. Even fearless kids' (and adults') eyes bulge at the 1,465-foot glass-elevator ride up the side of the **CN Tower,** and once they stand on the glass floor, their minds are officially blown. Next door, **Ripley's Aquarium** lets the little ones pet horseshoe crabs and gawk at neon-colored jellyfish.

Kids won't realize they're getting schooled at the **ROM,** with its Bat Cave and dinosaur skeletons, or the **Ontario Science Centre,** with interactive exhibits exploring the brain, technology, and outer space; documentaries are shown in the massive OMNIMAX dome. Out at the eastern end of the suburb of Scarborough, the well-designed **Toronto Zoo** is home to giraffes, polar bears, and gorillas. Less exotic animals hang at **Riverdale Farm,** in the more central Cabbagetown: get nose-to-nose with sheep, cows, and pigs.

Spending a few hours on the **Toronto Islands** is a good way to decompress. The Centreville Amusement Park and petting zoo is geared to the under-12 set, with tame rides such as the log flume and an antique carousel. Alternatively, pile the whole family into a surrey to pedal along the carless roads, or lounge at the beach at Hanlan's Point (warning: clothing-optional) or Ward's Island (clothes generally worn). The **Canadian National Exhibition (CNE),** aka "the Ex," is a huge three-week fair held in late August with carnival rides and games, puppet shows, a daily parade, and horse, dog, and cat shows. Kids can also pet and feed horses at the horse barn or tend to chickens and milk a cow on the "farm." But the mother of all amusement parks is a half-hour drive north of the city at **Canada's Wonderland,** home of Canada's tallest and fastest roller coaster. In winter, ice-skating at the Harbourfront Centre is the quintessential family activity.

Young sports fans might appreciate seeing a **Blue Jays** (baseball), **Maple Leafs** (hockey), **Raptors** (basketball), or **Toronto FC** (soccer) game. To take on hockey greats in a virtual game and see the original Stanley Cup, head to the **Hockey Hall of Fame**.

Intelligent productions at the **Young People's Theatre** don't condescend to kids and teens, and many are just as entertaining for adults.

For the latest on upcoming shows and events, plus an overwhelming directory of stores and services, go to ⊕ *Toronto4Kids.com*.

Chapter 2

TRAVEL SMART

2

Updated by
Daniel Otis

★ **CAPITAL:**
Toronto (capital of the
province of Ontario)

♔ **POPULATION:**
2.79 million (2021)

💬 **LANGUAGE:**
English

$ **CURRENCY:**
Canadian dollars

☎ **AREA CODES:**
416, 647, 437, 905

⚠ **EMERGENCIES:**
911

🚗 **DRIVING:**
On the right

⚡ **ELECTRICITY:**
120–220 v/60 cycles;
plugs have two or three
rectangular prongs

🕓 **TIME:**
EST (same as New York City)

🌐 **WEB RESOURCES:**
destinationtoronto.com,
destinationontario.com

✈ **AIRPORTS:**
YYZ, YTZ

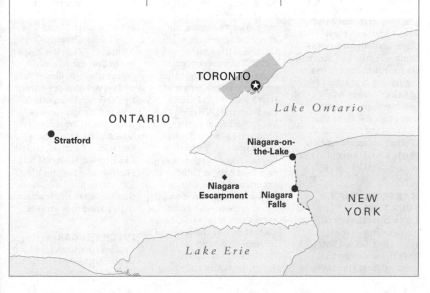

Know Before You Go

To get a sense of Toronto's culture, start by familiarizing yourself with the rituals of daily life. Decide on your priorities, and don't overbook. Allow time for wandering. Schedule coffee (or Ontario microbrew) breaks, and be realistic about your sightseeing style. Plan your days geographically.

CONSIDER WEATHER AND SEASON

Toronto is most pleasant from late spring through early fall, when there are outdoor concerts, frequent festivals, and open-air dining. On the other hand, some hotels drop their prices up to 50% during the off-season. Fall through spring is prime viewing time for dance, opera, theater, classical music, and sports like hockey and basketball. The temperature frequently falls below freezing from late November into March, when snowstorms can wreak havoc on travel plans, although Toronto's climate is mild by Canadian standards thanks to the regulating properties of Lake Ontario. A few underground shopping concourses, such as the PATH in the Financial District downtown, allow you to avoid the cold in the winter months.

MAKE THE MOST OF YOUR TIME

Planning is the key to maximizing your experience. First, book a hotel near the activities that most interest you. If you're here to see a Broadway-style show, get the view from the CN Tower, stroll the lakefront, stomp your feet at a Raptors game, or soak up some culture at the ballet, opera, or symphony, then you should look for a room in or near Harbourfront. If food, shopping, or museums are your passion, affluent Yorkville might be better suited.

GET ORIENTED

The boundaries of what Torontonians consider downtown, where most of the city sights are located, are subject to debate, but everyone agrees Lake Ontario is the southern cutoff. The other coordinates of the rectangle that compose the main part of the city are High Park to the west, the DVP (Don Valley Parkway) to the east, and Eglinton Avenue to the north. A few sights beyond these borders make excellent half- or full-day excursions. Most city streets are organized on a grid system: with some exceptions, street numbers start at zero at the lake and increase as you go north. On the east–west axis, Yonge (pronounced "young") Street, Toronto's main north–south thoroughfare, is the dividing line: you can expect higher numbers the farther away you get from Yonge.

PLAN YOUR ROUTE INTO THE CITY

Getting from the airport to the downtown core isn't tricky if you plan your route in advance. Most flights arrive and depart from Toronto Pearson International Airport (YYZ), a 30-minute drive or more northwest of the city center. Cabs, limos, Ubers, and Lyfts are a C$50–C$75 flat rate (varies by destination) to most downtown locations. The UP Express train to downtown's Union Station can be a faster and cheaper option at C$12.35; it also connects with the Bloor–Danforth subway line near Dundas West station. The Toronto Transit Commission (TTC) operates the 900 Airport Express, a shuttle bus to Kipling subway station; the ride downtown takes more time, but only costs C$3.25. The Billy Bishop Toronto City Airport (YTZ), better known as the Toronto Island Airport, is right downtown and served almost entirely by Porter Airlines, which flies to Chicago, Newark (NJ), Boston, Washington, D.C., and cities across Ontario and eastern Canada like Ottawa, Montréal, and Halifax. Amtrak and VIA Rail trains pull into Union Station, at the intersection of Bay and Front Streets.

DITCH THE CAR

Traffic is dense and parking expensive within the city center. If you have a car, leave it at your hotel. A car is helpful to access some farther-flung destinations, but in the city, take taxis or use the reliable TTC subway, streetcar, and bus system. Taxis are easy to hail, or you can call ☎ 416/829–4222 for pickup. The meter starts at C$4.25 and you are charged C$1.75 for each additional kilometer (roughly 6/10 mile) after the first 0.143 km. Ubers and Lyfts are also an option, and are usually a bit cheaper. As for public transit, the TTC operates the subway, streetcars, and buses that easily take you to most downtown attractions. The subway is clean and efficient, with trains arriving every few minutes; streetcars and buses are a bit slower. A single transferable fare is C$3.25; day passes are C$13.50.

HAVE AN INTERNATIONAL OUTLOOK

Just over half of Toronto's inhabitants were born outside Canada, and even more have foreign roots. Ethnic enclaves—Little Portugal, Greektown, Corso Italia (the "other Little Italy," on St. Clair West), and Koreatown—color downtown. Explore Toronto's multiculturalism in its food or its many international festivals: the glittering Toronto Caribbean Carnival (aka Caribana) along the waterfront; the Taste of the Danforth (Greek); the raucous celebration of Mexican Independence Day in Nathan Phillips Square; and the annual Festival of India.

EXPLORE THE GREAT OUTDOORS

You don't need a car to escape Toronto's bustle and summer heat and indulge in a calm, cool day by the lake. A rite of passage for every Torontonian is a warm-weather trip to the Islands—a 15-minute ferry trip from downtown—for a beach day, barbecue, picnic, bike ride, or the Centreville Amusement Park. Or head to the east side of the city for strolls along the boardwalk in The Beach neighborhood.

ORDER A COFFEE

You should experience (or at least observe) the ritual of caffeine and sugar intake at Tim Hortons, a coffee chain with a distinctly Canadian image and affordable prices. Go for a "double-double" (two cream, two sugar) and a box of Timbits (doughnut holes). But plenty of Torontonians eschew "Tim's" for more upscale brews, and the city has no shortage of independently owned cafés with stellar espresso and exquisitely steamed milk, especially along Queen Street (east of Broadview or west of Spadina) and in the Annex and Little Italy.

BE PREPARED TO CHEER

Leafs fans—or "Leafs Nation" as they are known collectively—are accustomed to jokes, rooting as they do for a team that hasn't won the Stanley Cup since 1967. If the opportunity arises to attend a game (though nearly every one has been sold out for six decades), count yourself luckier than most Torontonians. If not, try a Marlies AHL game at the Coca-Cola Coliseum. For hockey fans, the Hockey Hall of Fame is a must. Seeing a hockey game at a sports bar is a true Canadian pastime: grab a brewski and join locals in heckling the refs on bad calls. When the Leafs score, the mirth is contagious. If hockey isn't your thing, Toronto has basketball (the Raptors won the 2019 NBA Championship), baseball (Blue Jays), soccer (Toronto FC), and Canadian football (Argos).

SAVE A BUCK

Not everything in this large city has to be expensive. The Toronto CityPASS saves money and time as it lets you bypass ticket lines. Admission fees to the CN Tower, Casa Loma, the Royal Ontario Museum (ROM), Ripley's Aquarium, and the Ontario Science Centre or the Toronto Zoo are included for a one-time fee of C$106 plus tax— savings of C$56, valid for nine days. Many events listed on the city's website are free. Harbourfront Centre hosts numerous free concerts, cultural programs and festivals year-round. Some museums and art collections have free (or pay-what-you-can) admission all the time, like the Textile Museum of Canada and the Power Plant Contemporary Art Gallery. Even larger museums have days or evenings when they offer free entry, including the Bata Shoe Museum (Sunday), the Gardiner Museum (Wednesday after 4), the ROM (third Tuesday of each month after 5:30), and the Art Gallery of Ontario (Wednesday after 6).

Getting Here and Around

Air

AIRPORTS

Most flights into Toronto land at Terminals 1 and 3 of Lester B. Pearson International Airport (YYZ), 29 km (18 miles) northwest of downtown. The automated Terminal Link shuttle system moves passengers almost noiselessly between Terminals 1 and 3 and Viscount Station, which is close to Value Park Garage and ALT Hotel.

Porter Airlines—which flies to destinations in eastern Canada and the northeastern United States, including Boston, Chicago, Halifax, Montréal, Newark, Ottawa, Québec City, and Washington, D.C.—is the primary airline operating from Billy Bishop Toronto City Airport (YTZ), often called Toronto Island Airport, which is much smaller than Pearson and offers easier access to downtown Toronto.

GROUND TRANSPORTATION

The drive from Pearson can take well over an hour during weekday rush hours from 6:30 to 10 am and 3:30 to 7 pm. The most time-effective and cost-efficient way to get downtown from Pearson is the Union Pearson Express train (also referred to as the UP Express), which connects Pearson's Terminal 1 with Union Station, making stops at the Bloor (a quick transfer to the Dundas West subway station) and Weston GO stations. A trip from Pearson to Union Station takes only 25 minutes and costs C$12.35. Trains currently leave Union Station between 4:55 am and 11:00 pm, and depart Pearson from 5:27 am to 11:27 pm; every 15 minutes during peak morning and afternoon hours, and every 30 minutes at other times, weekends and holidays. Buy tickets at the terminal or online at ⊕ *upexpress.com*.

Taxis from Pearson have various fixed rates and most downtown destinations cost between C$50 and C$75; ask to see a rate map or check prices at ⊕ *torontopearson.com*. It's illegal for city cabs to pick up passengers at the airport, unless they're called. Likewise, airport taxis can't pick up passengers going to the airport; only regular taxis can be hailed or called to go to the airport. Uber and Lyft are also available in both directions.

From the arrivals levels at Pearson, GO Transit interregional buses transport passengers to the Yorkdale, Sheppard-Yonge, and Finch subway stations. Departures are at least once an hour, and luggage space limited, but at C$7 it's one of the least expensive ways to get to the city's northern sections.

Two TTC buses run from Pearson to the subway system. The 900 Airport Express bus connects to Kipling subway station; Bus 52A links to the Lawrence West station. Luggage space is limited and the ride can be slow, but the price is only C$3.25 in exact change.

From Toronto Island Airport, an underground pedestrian tunnel with moving sidewalks connects the airport to the terminal at the foot of Bathurst Street in six minutes. The airport also operates a free 90-second ferry from the island to the mainland that departs every 15 minutes. Taxis, rideshares and TTC streetcars can be found by the airport, which also offers a free shuttle service to Union Station.

Bicycle

Outside of winter months, a bicycle is a great way to explore Toronto. The city has an excellent network of designated bicycle lanes that can get you around faster than cars and buses when traffic is heavy. Plentiful park and ravine paths also make for great urban escapes.

Bike Share Toronto (⊕ *www.bikesharetoronto.com*) provides easy 24/7 access to thousands of bikes at over 600 stations across the city. Single trips cost C$3.25; passes are C$7 for 24 hours and C$15 for 72 hours. After the first half hour, you are charged C$4 for each additional 30 minutes; if you have a pass, watch the clock and swap bikes to avoid extra fees. You can pay with a credit card at bike share kiosks, or via the Public Bike System Company (PBSC) app.

Many bike shops and tour operators also offer rentals. Located downtown, Toronto Bicycle Tours (⊕ *www.torontobicycletours.com*) and Wheel Excitement (⊕ *www.wheelexcitement.ca*) both rent bikes starting at C$40 a day. Hourly rentals are also available on the Toronto Islands (⊕ *www.torontoislandbicyclerental.com*). Bike thefts are very common in the city, so be sure to use a strong lock and secure removeable parts like quick-release wheels when parking.

○ Boat

Frequent ferries connect downtown Toronto with the Toronto Islands. In summer, ferries leave the terminal at Queens Quay and Bay Street every 30 to 60 minutes for Ward's Island, Centre Island, and Hanlan's Point. Ferries begin operating between 6:30 and 8 am and end between 10 and 11:45 pm. Fares are C$8.70 round-trip and available in person and online. Smaller water taxis also operate along the waterfront between Spadina Avenue and Yonge Street; one-way trips to the island start at C$10.

 ## Bus

ARRIVING AND DEPARTING

Most long-distance buses arrive at the Union Station Bus Terminal, which serves a number of lines, including Greyhound, Megabus, and Coach Canada. Greyhound services Toronto via Buffalo (3 hours) and New York City (11 to 13 hours), and offers connections to other U.S. destinations. A low-cost bus company, Megabus, runs service to and from Montréal, Niagara Falls, and U.S. cities like Buffalo, Baltimore, Philadelphia, New York City, and Washington, D.C. During busy times, border crossings can add an hour or more to your trip.

WITHIN TORONTO

Toronto Transit Commission buses and streetcars link with every subway station to cover all points of the city. See the Public Transportation section for more information.

 ## Car

You don't need a car to get around downtown Toronto, but one comes in handy if visiting attractions beyond the city center in the Greater Toronto Area, Stratford, or Niagara Region. Traffic and parking within Toronto can be a nuisance. In Canada, U.S. and many other driver's licenses can be used for stays of up to three months.

ARRIVING FROM THE UNITED STATES BY CAR

Expect waits of up to an hour or more at major border crossings. If you can, avoid crossing on weekends and holidays at Detroit–Windsor, Buffalo–Fort Erie, and Niagara Falls, New York–Niagara Falls, Ontario.

Getting Here and Around

Highway 401 is the major link between Windsor (and Detroit) and Montréal. There are no tolls, but it can become very crowded from about 6:30 to 10 am each weekday morning and from 3:30 to 7 pm each afternoon; plan your trip to avoid rush hours. A toll highway, the 407, offers quicker travel; there are no tollbooths, but cameras photograph license plates and the system bills you. The 407 runs roughly parallel to the 401 for a 65-km (40-mile) stretch immediately north of Toronto.

If you're driving from Niagara Falls or Buffalo take the Queen Elizabeth Way (QEW), which curves along the western shore of Lake Ontario and eventually turns into the Gardiner Expressway, which flows right into downtown.

CAR RENTALS

In Ontario, you usually must be 20 to rent a car, and there may be a surcharge if you are under 25. Rates vary widely depending on the time of year, usually peaking during summer and holidays. Expect to pay at least C$60 a day and C$400 a week for an economy car with unlimited mileage. If you prefer manual transmission, check whether the rental agency of your choice offers it. All the major chains have branches both downtown and at Pearson International Airport; rates are often comparable. Your existing U.S. car insurance coverage can typically be applied to rentals in Canada.

DRIVING

Toronto is mostly arranged on a grid. Important thoroughfares include Yonge Street going north and south, and Bloor Street going east and west. Street numbers generally start low at the lake and increase as you go north. With east–west streets, numbers typically increase the farther you travel from Yonge. The major highways leading into the city are Highway 401, the Don Valley Expressway, and the Gardiner Expressway. If possible, avoid driving during weekday rush hours between 6:30 to 10 am and 3:30 to 7 pm.

GASOLINE

Gasoline is usually more expensive in Canada than the United States, so fill up before crossing the border. There are a handful of stations in downtown Toronto; most offer three octane grades and diesel by the liter. One U.S. gallon is nearly 3.8 liters.

PARKING

Parking can be expensive and difficult in the downtown core. Street parking is available on some thoroughfares and many residential streets. Be sure to carefully read signs outlining parking rules and fees; they can be confusing, and enforcement is swift and strict. Known as "Green P" for its round green signs, Toronto's parking authority operates meters, lots, and garages across the city that accept coins and major credit cards. Rates vary widely. The Green P app makes payments and time extensions easier.

Free parking can be found on some city streets, but generally a permit is required overnight. Temporary 24-hour, 48-hour, and weekly on-street parking permits are available from the City of Toronto website, ⊕ www.toronto.ca. Private companies also operate numerous lots and garages throughout the city. Parking in Toronto is usually safe, but as in any big city, lock your doors and keep valuables out of view.

ROAD CONDITIONS

Be extra cautious while driving in winter; roads can be slippery. Luckily most rental cars are equipped with snow tires. Give snow plows plenty of space. Toronto's seasonal temperature swings create thousands of potholes each year; watch out, especially on smaller streets.

ROADSIDE EMERGENCIES

Dial 911 for emergencies. There are many options for roadside service. The Canadian Automobile Association (CAA) is a popular choice, and coverage is included with an American Automobile Association (AAA) membership; call ☎ *1-800-CAA-HELP* for assistance.

RULES OF THE ROAD

Canadians drive on the right and road rules are similar to those in the United States. Speed limits and distances are posted in kilometers and kilometers per hour (one mile equals 1.6 km); your vehicle's speedometer likely displays both. Highways leading in and out of the city can get very busy during rush hour, summer weekends, and holidays.

Canadian drivers are typically polite and honking is rare. You must yield to pedestrians at crosswalks. While on major downtown routes like Queen, Dundas, College, and Bathurst Streets, you must stop whenever a streetcar (aka trolley or tram) opens its doors in front of you. Many downtown streets don't allow left turns at busier times; be sure to check posted signs. Most streets are two-way, but there are some exceptions. Always keep your eyes open for cyclists, especially while turning right or opening your doors after street parking.

Ⓜ Public Transportation

The Toronto Transit Commission operates buses, streetcars, and subways. There are three main subway lines with more than 70 stations along the way: the Bloor–Danforth line, which crosses Toronto about 5 km (3 miles) north of the lakefront from east to west; the Yonge–University line, which loops north and south like a giant "U," with the bottom of the "U" at Union Station; and the Sheppard line, which covers the northeastern section of the city. A light rapid transit (LRT) line extends service to Harbourfront along Queens Quay.

Buses and streetcars link with every subway station to cover all points of the city. Service is generally excellent, with buses and streetcars covering major city thoroughfares about every 10 minutes; suburban service is less frequent. Real-time bus arrival and occupancy info is available online at ⊕ *www.ttc.ca.* The Rocketman app is also handy for schedules and route planning.

FARES

The single fare for subways, buses, and streetcars is C$3.25; children 12 and under ride free. You can get change for your fare at subway turnstiles, but buses and streetcars typically require exact change. An all-day unlimited-use day pass (valid until 5:30 am the next day) costs C$13.50 and can be purchased at TTC stations.

Depending on the length of your stay, you may want to pick up a reloadable PRESTO fare card that can be purchased at stations for C$6. A major bonus to PRESTO is that TTC fares paid with the card are valid for two hours, so you can hop on and off without paying twice. The PRESTO card also works on inter-city GO trains and buses and the UP Express airport train. There is a slight discount on most PRESTO fares.

Subway trains run from approximately 6 am to 2 am Monday through Saturday and from 8 am to 2 am Sunday; trains arrive every two to five minutes. Most buses and streetcars run on similar hours. On weekdays the subways get very crowded from 8 to 10 am and 4 to 7 pm—avoid if possible.

Getting Here and Around

Late-night buses along Bloor and Yonge Streets, and as far north on Yonge as Steeles Avenue, run from about 1 am to 5 am. Streetcars that run 24 hours include those on King Street, Queen Street, College Street, and Spadina Avenue, though late-night service is much less frequent. All-night transit-stop signs are marked with blue bands.

STOPS AND INFORMATION

Streetcar stops have a red pole with a picture of a streetcar on it. Bus stops usually have shelters and gray poles with bus numbers and route information. Both buses and streetcars have their final destination and their number on the front, back, and side windows. Drivers are generally helpful and can answer questions.

The TTC's free *Ride Guide* is available in most subways, buses, and streetcars. The guide shows nearly every major place of interest in the city and how to reach it by public transit.

🚕 Taxi and Rideshare

Taxis can be hailed on the street, but outside of the city center it's smart to call ahead. Taxi fares are C$4.25 for the first 0.143 km, plus C25¢ for each 29 seconds not in motion and for each additional 0.143 km. A C$2 surcharge is added for each passenger in excess of four. The average fare to take a cab across downtown is about C$15, plus a 15% tip. The largest companies are Beck, Co-op, Diamond, and Royal.

■ TIP→ **Call** ☎ *416/829–4222* **to be connected to taxi companies via a free automated system.**

Uber and Lyft are the most popular rideshare apps in Toronto. Both are available day and night, but beware of price surges during rush hour, in bad weather, and toward last call at 2 am. Set up payment details in advance and be sure to download both apps to compare pricing. Standard vehicles are typically a bit less expensive than taxis; a trip across downtown usually costs less than C$15, plus tip. Premium rides are also available.

Uber and Lyft both service Toronto Pearson International Airport. Terminal 1 pickups are on the ground level at door Q or P; Terminal 3 pickups are at the arrivals level, on the outer curb near door D. Premium vehicles service door A at both terminals. There is an additional fee of C$4 to C$5 to take a standard Uber or Lyft to or from the airport.

🚆 Train

Amtrak has service from New York to Toronto (12½ hours), providing connections between its own network and VIA Rail's Canadian routes. VIA Rail runs trains to many major Canadian cities. Amtrak and VIA Rail operate from Union Station on Front Street between Bay and York Streets.

GO Transit is the Greater Toronto Area's commuter rail. The double-decker trains are comfortable and have restrooms.

Essentials

Embassy/Consulate

All international embassies are in Ottawa; there are some consulates in Toronto, including a U.S. consulate. The consulate offers services between 8:30 am and noon by appointment.

Health and Safety

Toronto does not have any unique health concerns. Pollution in the city is generally rated Good to Moderate on the international Air Quality Index. Smog advisories are listed by the Ontario Ministry of the Environment at ⊕ *www.airqualityontario. com.*

As in the United States, the phone number for emergency services is 911. The Dental Emergency Clinic operates from 8 am to midnight. Many branches of Shoppers Drug Mart are open until 10 pm, with some open 24 hours. Select Rexall drugstores are open until midnight.

Hotels

Much of Toronto's downtown hotel market is geared toward business travelers. But these same chain hotels are close to tourist attractions, so they are good picks for all kinds of travelers. There are also upscale boutique hotels, such as the Hotel Le Germain, and ultraluxe chains like the Shangri-La and Ritz-Carlton. Within a 15-minute drive of downtown are High Park and the Humber River, served by bed-and-breakfasts and the lovely Old Mill Inn. West Queen West has some unique places to stay, such as the restored Gladstone and Drake hotels. Lester B. Pearson International Airport is 29 km (18 miles) northwest

of downtown; staying in this neighborhood means quick connections to areas beyond.

Prices are for two people in a standard double room in high season, excluding service and 13% tax.

What It Costs in Canadian Dollars			
$	$$	$$$	$$$$
LODGING FOR TWO			
under C$150	C$150–C$250	C$251–C$350	over C$350

Money

ATMS AND BANKS

ATMs are available in most bank, trust company, and credit union branches across the country, as well as in many convenience stores, malls, and gas stations. The major banks in Toronto are Scotiabank, CIBC, HSBC, Royal Bank of Canada, the Bank of Montréal, and TD Canada Trust.

CREDIT CARDS

It's a good idea to inform your credit card company before you travel, especially if you're going abroad and don't travel internationally very often. Otherwise, the credit card company might put a hold on your card owing to unusual activity—not a good thing halfway through your trip. Record all your credit card numbers—as well as the phone numbers to call if your cards are lost or stolen—in a safe place, so you're prepared should something go wrong. Both MasterCard and Visa have general numbers you can call (collect if you're abroad) if your card is lost, but you're better off calling the number of your issuing bank as MasterCard and Visa usually just transfer you to your bank;

Essentials

your bank's number is usually printed on your card.

If you plan to use your credit card for cash advances, you'll need to apply for a PIN at least two weeks before your trip. Although it's usually cheaper and safer to use a credit card abroad for large purchases (so you can cancel payments or be reimbursed if there's a problem), note that some credit card companies *and* the banks that issue them add substantial percentages to all foreign transactions, whether they're in a foreign currency or not. Check on these fees before leaving home so there won't be any surprises when you get the bill.

Before you charge something, ask the merchant whether they plan to do a dynamic currency conversion (DCC). In such a transaction the credit card processor (the shop, restaurant, or hotel, not Visa or MasterCard) converts the currency and charges you in U.S. dollars. In most cases you'll pay the merchant a 3% fee for this service in addition to any credit card company and issuing-bank foreign-transaction surcharges.

Dynamic currency conversion programs are becoming increasingly widespread. Merchants who participate in them are supposed to ask whether you want to be charged in U.S. dollars or the local currency, but they don't always do so. And even if they do offer you a choice, they may well avoid mentioning the additional surcharges. The good news is that you *do* have a choice. And if this practice really gets your goat, you can avoid it entirely thanks to American Express; with its cards, DCC simply isn't an option.

CURRENCY AND EXCHANGE

U.S. dollars are sometimes accepted—more commonly in the Niagara region close to the border than in Toronto.

Some hotels, restaurants, and stores are skittish about accepting Canadian currency over C$20 due to counterfeiting, so be sure to get small bills when you exchange money or visit an ATM. Major U.S. credit cards and debit or check cards with a credit card logo are accepted in most areas. Your credit-card-logo debit card will be charged as a credit card.

The units of currency in Canada are the Canadian dollar (C$) and the cent, in almost the same denominations as U.S. currency ($5, $10, $20, 5¢, 10¢, 25¢, etc.). The $1 and $2 bill are no longer used; they have been replaced by $1 and $2 coins (known as a "loonie," because of the loon that appears on the coin, and a "toonie," respectively). Canada stopped producing 1¢ pennies in 2012; cash purchases are rounded to the nearest five cents. The exchange rate is currently US79¢ to C$1, but this fluctuates often.

Even if a currency-exchange booth has a sign promising "no commission," expect some kind of huge, hidden fee. And as for rates, you're almost always better off getting foreign currency at an ATM or exchanging money at a bank.

Google displays currency conversions—just type in the amount you want to convert and an explanation of how you want it converted (e.g., "14 Swiss francs in dollars"), and voilà. ⊕ *Oanda.com* also allows you to print out a handy table with the current day's conversion rates. ⊕ *XE. com* is another good currency conversion website.

📷 Packing

The weather is often unpredictable in Toronto, so pack a lot of layers. Summers tend to be sweltering, so pack loose-fitting clothing, sunscreen, and a hat.

A light sweater for cooler evenings isn't a bad idea. Rain gear is a good idea, especially in spring and fall. A parka, hat, and gloves are a must in winter, as is warm, waterproof footwear for navigating snowdrifts piled up by the city's plows.

Jeans are as popular in Toronto as they are elsewhere and are perfectly acceptable for most restaurants. Men may need a jacket and tie for higher-end restaurants and nightspots.

🌐 Passport and Visa

Anyone who is not a Canadian citizen or Canadian permanent resident must have a passport to enter Canada. Passport requirements apply to minors as well. Anyone under 18 traveling alone or with only one parent should carry a signed and notarized letter from both parents or from all legal guardians authorizing the trip. It's also a good idea to include a copy of the child's birth certificate, custody documents if applicable, and death certificates of one or both parents, if applicable.

Anyone flying into Canada (other than Canadian and U.S. citizens and lawful permanent residents) is now asked to acquire a temporary visa, called an Electronic Travel Authorization (or eTA), online through the Government of Canada website. The authorization costs C$7 and applications generally take up to 72 hours to approve (with most being approved in just a few minutes), but applications are still encouraged in advance in case of any unforeseen issues. After approval, the eTA is valid for six months. To learn more and apply, visit ⊕ www.cic.gc.ca/english/ visit/eta-start.asp.

🍽 Restaurants

Toronto's calling card—its ethnic diversity—offers up a potent mix of cuisines. The city's chefs are now pushing into new territory, embracing trends from all over the world. Top-notch Spanish tapas, Japanese ramen, and Korean fusion fare have all enjoyed trend status, and farm-to-table dining is a staple. The city's growing cachet has lured in world-famous chefs such as Daniel Boulud and David Chang, who have landed in Toronto with Café Boulud and Momofuku. And as locals will tell you, first come the chefs, then come the foodie travelers, always snapping photos at the city's newest hot spots.

Prices in the reviews are the average cost of a main course at dinner or, if dinner is not served, at lunch.

What It Costs in Canadian Dollars			
$	$$	$$$	$$$$
AT DINNER			
under C$12	C$12– C$20	C$21– C$30	over C$30

💲 Tipping

Tips and service charges aren't usually added to a bill in Toronto. In general, tip 15% to 20% of the total bill. This goes for food servers, barbers and hairdressers, and taxi drivers. Porters and doormen should get about C$2 a bag. For maid service, leave C$2 to C$5 per person a day.

Best Tours in Toronto

BOAT TOURS

If you want to get a glimpse of the sky-line, try a boat tour. There are many boat tour companies operating all along the downtown waterfront.

Great Lakes Schooner Company. To further your appreciation for man-made beauty, this company lets you see Toronto's sky-line from the open deck of the 165-foot three-masted *Kajama*. Two-hour tours are available early May to the end of Sep-tember. ✉ *Harbourfront* ☎ *416/203–2322* ⊕ *www.greatlakesschooner.com* ✉ *From C$34.75.*

BUS TOURS

For a look at the city proper, take a bus tour around the city. If you want the free-dom to get on and off the bus when the whim strikes, take a hop-on, hop-off tour.

City Sightseeing Toronto. City Sightseeing Toronto has a fleet of London-style dou-ble-decker hop-on, hop-off buses. It also runs tours to Niagara Falls. ✉ *1 Dundas St. E, Dundas Square Area* ☎ *416/410–0536* ⊕ *www.citysightseeingtoronto.com* ✉ *From C$60.*

SPECIAL-INTEREST TOURS

Toronto Field Naturalists. More than 140 guided tours are scheduled throughout the year, each focusing on an aspect of nature, such as geology or wildflowers, and with starting points accessible by public transit. ✉ *2-2449 Yonge St., Toronto* ☎ *416/593–2656* ⊕ *www.torontofieldnat-uralists.org* ✉ *Free.*

Toronto Bruce Trail Club. This hiking club arranges day and overnight hikes around Toronto and its environs. ✉ *2938 Dundas St. W, Toronto* ☎ *416/763–9061* ⊕ *www.torontobrucetrailclub.org* ✉ *From C$32.*

Toronto Society of Architects. The Toronto Society of Architects offers two-hour walking tours on Saturday and Sunday from early June to October for C$15. ✉ *20 Bloor St. E, Hudson Bay Centre, Toronto* ⊕ *www.torontosocietyofarchi-tects.ca/tours* ✉ *C$15.*

WALKING TOURS

Heritage Toronto. To get a feel for Toronto's outstanding cultural diversity, check out one of about 50 walking tours offered from June to mid-October. They last one and a half to two hours and cover one neighborhood or topic, such as music history on Yonge Street or historical architecture downtown. ✉ *157 King St. E, 3rd fl., Toronto* ✛ *Inside St. Lawrence Hall* ☎ *416/338–0684* ⊕ *www.heritage-toronto.org* ✉ *Some free, some starting at C$20.*

Royal Ontario Museum. The museum offers 1½-hour ROMWalks tours on such topics as Cabbagetown, a now-trendy, heritage neighborhood with many houses dating to the 1850s. Several free walks are giv-en weekly. ✉ *100 Queens Park, Toronto* ☎ *416/586–8097* ⊕ *www.rom.on.ca/en/whats-on/romwalks* ✉ *Free.*

Tasty Tours. Tasty Tours runs foodie walk-ing tours that mostly focus on Toronto's diverse and colorful Kensington Market neighborhood. ✉ *178 Baldwin St., Toronto* ☎ *416/871–7133* ⊕ *www.tastytourstoron-to.com* ✉ *C$69.*

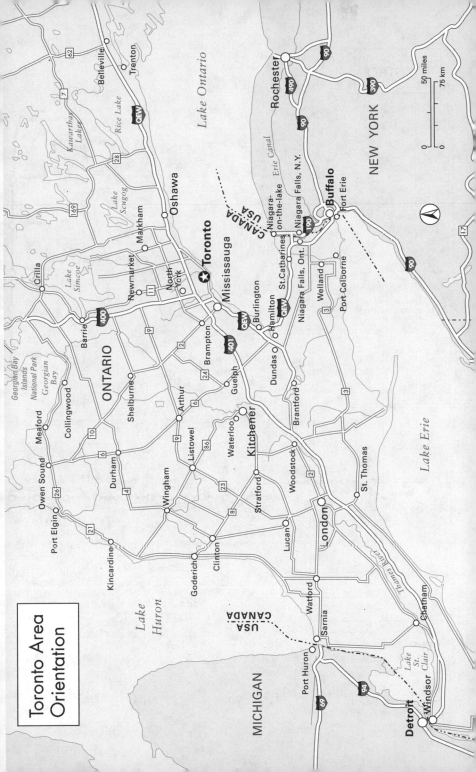

Toronto Area
Orientation

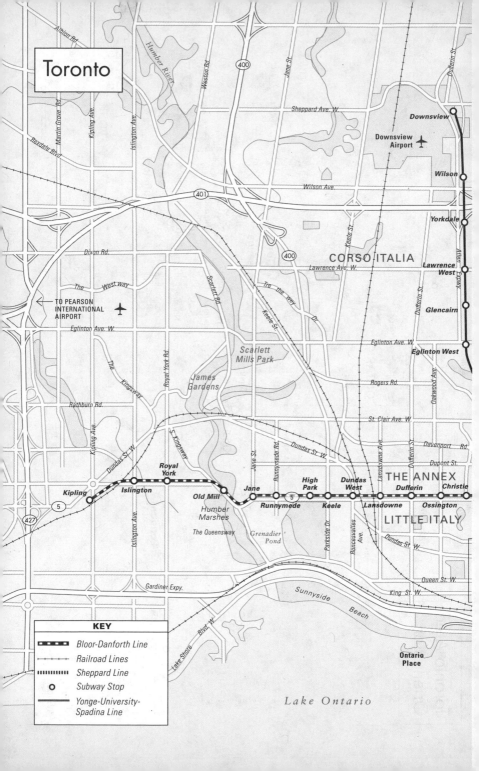

Toronto

Downsview

Downsview Airport

Sheppard Ave. W.

Wilson

Wilson Ave.

Yorkdale

CORSO ITALIA

Lawrence West

Lawrence Ave. W.

Glencairn

TO PEARSON INTERNATIONAL AIRPORT

West way

Eglinton Ave. W.

Eglinton West

Eglinton Ave. W.

Scarlett Mills Park

Rogers Rd.

James Gardens

St. Clair Ave. W.

Rathburn Rd.

Davenport Rd.

Dupont St.

Dundas St. W.

THE ANNEX

Royal York

High Park

Dundas West

Dufferin

Christie

Kipling

Islington

Old Mill

Jane

Keele

Lansdowne

Ossington

LITTLE ITALY

Runnymede

Humber Marshes

The Queensway

Grenadier Pond

Gardiner Expy.

Queen St. W.

King St. W.

Sunnyside Beach

Ontario Place

Lake Ontario

KEY

- ■■■■ Bloor-Danforth Line
- ┼┼┼┼ Railroad Lines
- ▥▥▥▥ Sheppard Line
- ○ Subway Stop
- ── Yonge-University-Spadina Line

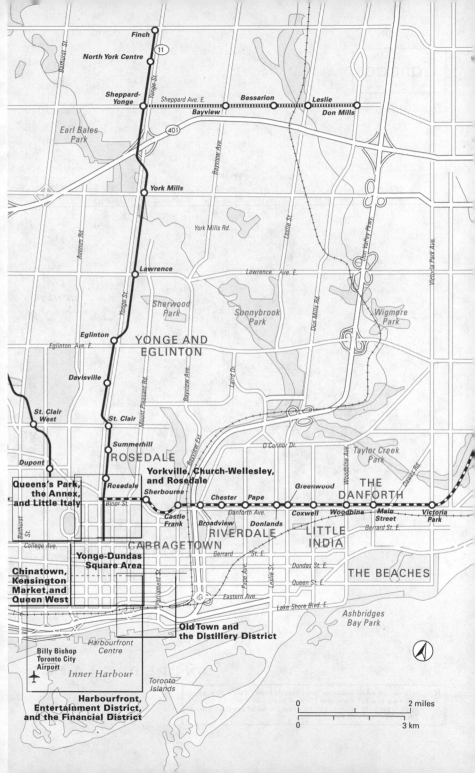

Finch

North York Centre

11

Sheppard-Yonge   Sheppard Ave. E.   Bessarion   Leslie
                                    Bayview   Don Mills

401

York Mills

York Mills Rd.

Lawrence   Lawrence   Ave. E.

Eglinton
Eglinton Ave. E.

YONGE AND
EGLINTON

Davisville

St. Clair
West

St. Clair

Summerhill

Dupont

Queens's Park,
the Annex,
and Little Italy

ROSEDALE

Rosedale

Yorkville, Church-Wellesley,
and Rosedale

Sherbourne   Chester   Pape   Greenwood   THE
                                                                              DANFORTH
Bloor St.

Castle   Danforth Ave.   Coxwell
Frank   Woodbine   Main
                    Broadview   Donlands   Street   Victoria
CABBAGETOWN   RIVERDALE   Park
                                                              LITTLE
College Ave.   INDIA   Gerrard St. E.

Chinatown,   Yonge-Dundas   Gerrard   St. E.
Kensington   Square Area
Market, and   Dundas St. E.
Queen West   Queen St. E.   THE BEACHES

                                          Eastern Ave.

Old Town and   Lake Shore Blvd. E.
the Distillery District   Ashbridges
                                                              Bay Park

Billy Bishop
Toronto City
Airport   Harbourfront
                    Centre

Inner Harbour   Toronto
                          Islands

Harbourfront,
Entertainment District,
and the Financial District

0   2 miles

0   3 km

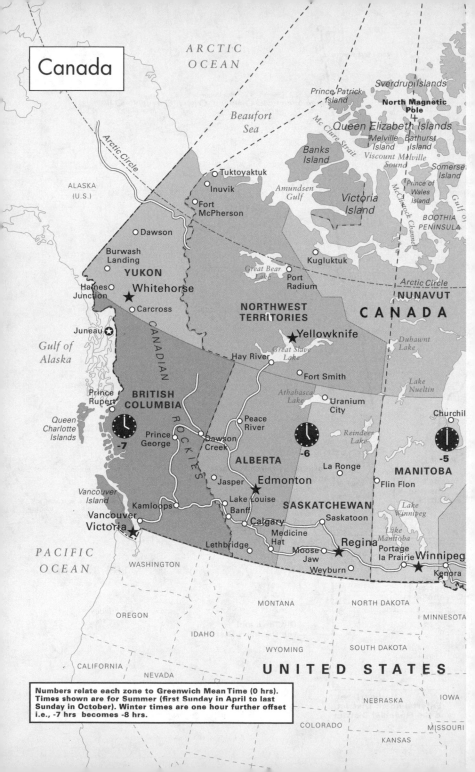

Canada

ARCTIC
OCEAN

Sverdrup Islands

Beaufort
Sea

Prince Patrick
Island

**North Magnetic
Pole**

Queen Elizabeth Islands

Melville
Island

Bathurst
Island

Viscount Melville
Sound

Somerset
Island

Banks
Island

Amundsen
Gulf

Victoria
Island

Prince
of
Wales
Island

BOOTHIA
PENINSULA

Arctic Circle

ALASKA
(U.S.)

Tuktoyaktuk

Inuvik

Fort
McPherson

McClure Strait

McClintock Channel

Gulf
of
Boothia

Dawson

Kugluktuk

Burwash
Landing

Great Bear
Lake

Port
Radium

Arctic Circle

YUKON

Whitehorse

NORTHWEST
TERRITORIES

NUNAVUT

CANADA

Haines
Junction

Carcross

Yellowknife

Dubawnt
Lake

CANADIAN

Juneau

Hay River

Great Slave
Lake

Gulf of
Alaska

Prince
Rupert

BRITISH
COLUMBIA

Fort Smith

Lake
Nueltin

Athabasca
Lake

Uranium
City

ROCKIES

Queen
Charlotte
Islands

-7

Prince
George

Dawson
Creek

Peace
River

Reindeer
Lake

-6

Churchill

La Ronge

-5

ALBERTA

MANITOBA

Jasper

Edmonton

Flin Flon

Vancouver
Island

Kamloops

Lake Louise
Banff

SASKATCHEWAN

Lake
Winnipeg

Vancouver

Calgary

Saskatoon

Lake
Manitoba

Victoria

Lethbridge

Medicine
Hat

Moose
Jaw

Regina

Portage
la Prairie

Winnipeg

PACIFIC
OCEAN

WASHINGTON

Weyburn

Kenora

MONTANA

NORTH DAKOTA

MINNESOTA

OREGON

IDAHO

WYOMING

SOUTH DAKOTA

CALIFORNIA

NEVADA

UNITED STATES

NEBRASKA

IOWA

COLORADO

KANSAS

MISSOURI

**Numbers relate each zone to Greenwich Mean Time (0 hrs).
Times shown are for Summer (first Sunday in April to last
Sunday in October). Winter times are one hour further offset
i.e., -7 hrs becomes -8 hrs.**

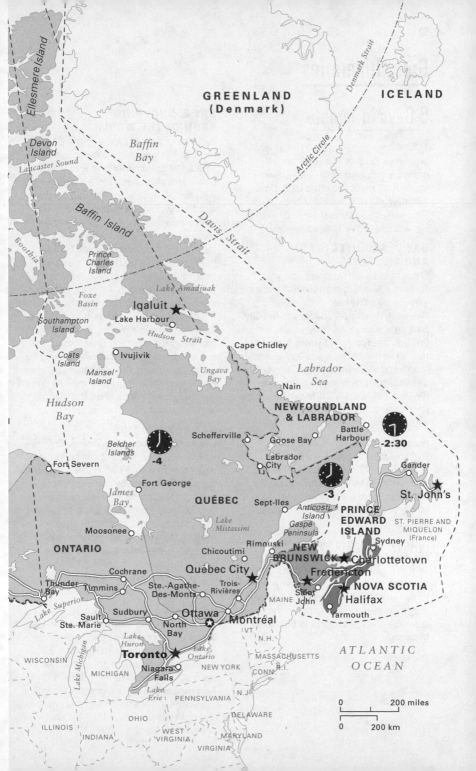

Great Itineraries

5 Days in Toronto

To really see Toronto, a stay of at least one week is ideal. However, these itineraries are designed to inspire thematic tours of some of the city's best sights, whether you're in town for one day or five. We've also included a two- to three-day escape to the Niagara region.

DAY 1: ARCHITECTURE AND MUSEUMS

There's no better spot to begin your Toronto adventure than Finnish architect Viljo Revell's **City Hall,** at Queen and Bay, with its regal predecessor, **Old City Hall,** right across the street. Take a stroll through the **Financial District,** looking up to admire the skyscrapers above you, and then head west along Front Street. You'll see your next destination before you reach it: the soaring **CN Tower.** Take a trip to the top to experience its glass floor and amazing views.

Next, grab a streetcar going east to Parliament, then head south toward the water to find the **Distillery District,** filled with restored Victorian industrial buildings. Here's a great place to stop for lunch, with plenty of delicious restaurants and bistros.

After lunch, head to the **Royal Ontario Museum**—even if you just admire the still controversial modern Crystal gallery from the outside. Across the street is the smaller **Gardiner Museum,** filled with gorgeous ceramics, and down the street is a shoe lover's dream, the **Bata Shoe Museum.**

DAY 2: SHOPPING AROUND THE WORLD

Eager shoppers should begin in **China-town,** at the wonderfully chaotic intersection of Spadina Avenue and Dundas Street, for shops and stalls overflowing with exotic vegetables, fragrant herbs, and flashy Chinese baubles. Go all out with a heaping bowl of steaming noodles, or just grab a snack at an empanada stand in nearby **Kensington Market** (head west on Dundas to Augusta and turn right). Take your time browsing the market; quirky grocery stores, modern cafés, hip bars, and funky clothing boutiques all beckon. Then grab the College streetcar across town to Gerrard Street (between Coxwell and Greenwood) to see the **Gerrard India Bazaar** and shop for some bejeweled saris and shiny bangles. Finish the day with a spicy madras curry washed down with a soothing mango lassi (yogurt drink).

DAY 3: WITH KIDS

Get an early start at the **Toronto Zoo,** where 700-plus acres of dense forests are home to over 5,000 animals and 460 species from Canada and around the world, including polar bears, red pandas, giraffes, and kangaroos. Little science enthusiasts might prefer the equally exciting (and indoor air-conditioned) exhibits at the **Ontario Science Centre.** Sports fans can see the original Stanley Cup at the **Hockey Hall of Fame,** right downtown at Yonge and Front.

Kid-friendly adventures vary by season. In the sweltering summer, **Harbourfront Centre** is full of activities and performances along the cooler waterfront. In winter, bundle kids up for a skate on the Centre's ice rink, which has rentals. **Ripley's Aquarium of Canada** is a great way for kids to stay warm or stay cool in any season, and get to learn about 450-plus species of sea creatures.

DAY 4: ISLAND LIFE

Start with picnic supplies from **St. Lawrence Market** (closed Sunday and Monday) for a cornucopia of imported delicacies. It's a short walk from the market to catch the ferry, at the foot of Bay Street and Queens Quay, to the **Toronto Islands**. There, besides a city skyline view you can't get anywhere else, beaches include **Hanlan's Point** (infamous for its nudists, so be warned) and **Ward's Island**, with its sandy beach and sprawling patio at the Riviera restaurant. Island life has an alluring slow pace, but anyone who'd rather cover more ground can rent a bicycle at the pier on **Centre Island.** Winter options include cross-country skiing, snowshoeing, and skating on the frozen lagoons.

DAY 5: NEIGHBORHOOD EXPLORING

Window-shoppers should begin along the rows of restored Victorian homes of **Yorkville**—in the 1960s, a hippie haven of emerging Canadian artists like Joni Mitchell and Neil Young. These days, the country's most exclusive shops and hottest designers have all moved in and spilled over onto Bloor Street West, between Yonge Street and Avenue Road, which is so swanky it's sometimes called Toronto's 5th Avenue. But in traditional Torontonian style, walk a few blocks west for a stark contrast in the eclectic shops along Bloor in crumbling turn-of-the-20th-century homes. Take a rest to recharge at **Future Bistro,** a student favorite for affordable comfort food, or splurge at **Sotto Sotto** or at **Café Boulud.** In the evening, catch a play, concert, or comedy show downtown at **Second City.**

DAYS 6–7: NIAGARA GETAWAY

If you have a few days to spare, don't miss the glory of **Niagara Falls,** about 80 miles south of Toronto. It's easiest to get there by car, or else hop on a VIA train, seasonal GO train, or Megabus from Union Station. When you arrive, see the falls best via a ride on a **Voyage to the Falls** boat tour. In the afternoon, and especially if you've got energetic kids to tire out, try the kitschy **Clifton Hill** for the midway, **SkyWheel,** and mini-putt. For a more relaxing day, try the **Botanical Gardens, Butterfly Conservatory,** or **White Water Walk** along the scenic Niagara Parkway. Get dressed up for dinner at the **Skylon Tower** or another restaurant overlooking the falls and tuck in for a night at the slots. Look to the skies for fireworks at 10 every night from late May to early October from either your falls-view hotel room or the **Table Rock Center.** The next day, a good breakfast is essential to prepare for a day of wine tasting and strolling in bucolic **Niagara-on-the-Lake.** You'll need a car to follow the beautiful Niagara Parkway north to Niagara-on-the-Lake's **Queen Street** for shopping. Wine and dine the day away along the **Wine Route,** which follows Highway 81 as far west as Grimsby. Dinner at one of the wineries or excellent area restaurants, then a night in a boutique hotel or luxurious B&B, is a great way to end your trip. If visiting during the **Shaw Festival** (usually between April and October, but with events in other months too), be sure to book a theater ticket.

Toronto's Best Festivals

Festivals keep Toronto lively even when cold winds blow in off Lake Ontario in winter. Themes range from art to food, Caribbean culture to gay pride. Most national championship sports events take place in and around Toronto.

THROUGHOUT THE YEAR

Shaw Festival. Typically held from late spring until fall in quaint Niagara-on-the-Lake, this festival presents plays by George Bernard Shaw and his contemporaries. Niagara-on-the-Lake is a two-hour drive south of Toronto. ⊠ *Niagara-on-the-Lake* ☎ *905/468–2172, 800/511–7429* ⊕ *www.shawfest.com.*

Stratford Festival. One of the best-known Shakespeare festivals in the world, this event was created in the 1950s to revive a little town two hours west of Toronto that happened to be called Stratford (and its river called the Avon). The festival includes Shakespeare plays as well as other classical and contemporary productions. Respected actors from around the world participate. ☎ *519/273–1600, 800/567–1600* ⊕ *www.stratfordfestival. ca.*

JANUARY AND FEBRUARY

Winterlicious. The winter culinary event offers discount prix-fixe menus at top restaurants as well as themed tastings and food-prep workshops. ⊕ *winterlicious.ca.*

APRIL AND MAY

Contact Photography Festival. Sponsored by Scotiabank, this photography festival features over 100 exhibits in art spaces and galleries across the city throughout the month of May. ⊠ *Toronto* ☎ *416/539–9595* ⊕ *www.scotiabankcontactphoto. com.*

Hot Docs. North America's largest documentary film fest, Hot Docs takes over independent cinemas for 10 days in late April and early May. ☎ *416/203–2155* ⊕ *www.hotdocs.ca.*

TIFF Next Wave Film Festival. Taking place in April, this youth-focused film festival screens new movies free for anyone under 25. ⊠ *Toronto* ☎ *416/599–2033* ⊕ *www.tiff.net/nextwave.*

JUNE

Luminato Festival. Running for about two weeks, this citywide arts festival combines visual arts, music, theater, dance, literature, and more in hundreds of events, many of them free. ☎ *416/368–4849* ⊕ *www.luminatofestival.com.*

Pride Toronto. Rainbow flags fly high during Pride Toronto, the city's best-known LGBTQ+ event. It includes cultural and political programs, concerts, a street festival, and a few parades (including the massive closing parade on the final Sunday of the festival), and is centered around the Church–Wellesley area. ☎ *416/927–7433* ⊕ *www.pridetoronto. com.*

Toronto Jazz Festival. This festival brings big-name jazz artists to city jazz clubs and other indoor and outdoor venues for 10 days from late June to early July. ⊠ *Toronto* ☎ *416/928–2033* ⊕ *www. torontojazz.com.*

JULY AND AUGUST

Beaches International Jazz Festival. In the east-end Beach neighborhood, this free event covers jazz, blues, Latin music, and more with concerts and a street festival that run throughout July. ⊠ *The Beach* ☎ *416/698–2152* ⊕ *www.beachesjazz. com.*

Canadian National Exhibition. With carnival rides, concerts, an air show, a dog show, a garden show, inventive carnival eats, and a "Mardi Gras" parade, this two-and-a-half-week-long fair is the biggest in Canada. Also known as "the Ex," it's been held at the eponymous fairgrounds on the Lake Ontario waterfront since

1879. ✉ *Toronto* ☎ *416/263–3800* ⊕ *www.theex.com.*

Honda Indy. At this summer fixture, cars speed around an 11-turn, 1,786-mile track that goes through the Canadian National Exhibition grounds and along Lake Shore Boulevard. ✉ *Toronto* ☎ *416/588–7223* ⊕ *www.hondaindy.com.*

National Bank Open. Founded in 1881, this is an ATP Masters 1000 event for men and a WTA 1000 tournament for women. Previously known as the Rogers Cup, it's held at Sobeys Stadium on the York University campus, with the men's and women's events alternating between Toronto and Montréal each year. ✉ *Toronto* ☎ *416/665–9777* ⊕ *www.nationalbankopen.com.*

Summerlicious. Each summer in July or August, around 200 restaurants in Toronto create prix-fixe menus—some at bargain prices—for this two-week culinary event. ✉ *Toronto* ⊕ *www.summerlicious.ca.*

SummerWorks Performance Festival. Plays, concerts, and performances are mounted at local theaters during this 11-day festival. ✉ *Toronto* ☎ *416/597–8594* ⊕ *www.summerworks.ca.*

Toronto Caribbean Carnival. One of the largest carnival festivals in North America, the Toronto Caribbean Carnival (commonly called Caribana) is a days-long pan-Caribbean celebration featuring calypso, steel pan, soca, and reggae music, along with dazzling dancers, fiery cuisine, and plenty of revelry that culminates in a massive Saturday parade in late July or early August. ✉ *Toronto* ☎ *416/391–5608* ⊕ *www.torontocarnival.ca.*

Toronto Fringe Festival. This 10-day event is the city's largest theater festival. It features new and developing plays by emerging artists. ✉ *Toronto* ☎ *416/966–1062* ⊕ *www.fringetoronto.com.*

SEPTEMBER
Toronto International Film Festival. Renowned worldwide, this festival is considered more accessible to the public than Cannes, Sundance, or other major film festivals. A number of films make their world or North American premieres at this 11-day festival each year, some at red-carpet events attended by Hollywood stars. ✉ *Toronto* ☎ *416/599–2033, 888/258–8433* ⊕ *www.tiff.net.*

Toronto International BuskerFest. No ordinary street festival, aerialists, fire-eaters, dancers, contortionists, musicians, and more perform here in Woodbine Park around the first weekend of September. ✉ *The Beach* ⊕ *www.torontobuskerfest.com.*

OCTOBER
Nuit Blanche. Concentrated in Toronto's downtown, this free all-night street festival has interactive contemporary art installations and performances at multiple venues. ✉ *Toronto* ⊕ *www.nbto.com.*

NOVEMBER AND DECEMBER
The Distillery Winter Village. Taking over the Distillery District from late November until just before Christmas, this festive outdoor market features local vendors, warm drinks, and dazzling light displays. ✉ *Distillery District* ⊕ *www.thedistillerywintervillage.com.*

Royal Agricultural Winter Fair. Held since 1922 at the Ex, this 10-day fair is a highlight of Canada's equestrian season each November, with jumping, dressage, and harness-racing competitions. ✉ *Toronto* ☎ *416/263–3400* ⊕ *www.royalfair.org.*

Contacts

✈ Air

AIRLINE SECURITY ISSUES Canadian Transportation Agency. ☎ 888/222–2592 ⊕ www.otc-cta.gc.ca. **Transportation Security Administration.** ☎ 855/289–9673 ⊕ www.tsa.gov.

AIRLINES Air Canada. ☎ 888/247–2262 ⊕ www.aircanada.com. **Air Transat.** ☎ 877/872–6728 ⊕ www.airtransat.com. **American Airlines.** ☎ 800/433–7300 ⊕ www.aa.com. **Delta Airlines.** ☎ 800/221–1212 for U.S. and Canadian reservations, 800/241–4141 for international reservations ⊕ www.delta.com. **Porter Airlines.** ☎ 888/619–8622 toll free, 416/619–8622 ⊕ www.flyporter.com. **United Airlines.** ☎ 800/864–8331 ⊕ www.united.com. **WestJet.** ☎ 888/937–8538 ⊕ www.westjet.com.

AIRPORT INFORMATION Billy Bishop Toronto City Airport. ✉ Toronto ☎ 416/203–6942 ⊕ www.billybishopairport.com. **Lester B. Pearson International Airport.** ✉ Toronto ☎ 416/247–7678, 866/207–1690 toll free ⊕ www.torontopearson.com.

GROUND TRANSPORTATION GO Transit. ☎ 416/869–3200, 888/438–6646 toll free ⊕ www.gotransit.com. **Toronto Transit Commission (TTC).** ☎ 416/393–4636

⊕ www.ttc.ca. **Union Pearson Express.** ☎ 416/869–3300, 844/438–6687 ⊕ www.upexpress.com.

⚓ Boat

Toronto Islands Ferries. ☎ 416/392–8193 ⊕ www.toronto.ca/parks/island.

🚲 Bicycle

BICYCLE RENTALS Bike Share Toronto. ✉ Toronto ☎ 855/898-2378 ⊕ www.bikesharetoronto.com. **Toronto Bicycle Tours.** ✉ Toronto ☎ 416/477-2184 ⊕ www.torontobicycletours.com. **Wheel Excitement.** ✉ Toronto ☎ 416/260-9000 ⊕ www.wheelexcitement.ca.

🚌 Bus

Coach Canada. ☎ 866/488-4452 ⊕ www.coachcanada.com. **Greyhound.** ☎ 800/661-8747 ⊕ www.greyhound.ca. **Megabus.** ☎ 866/488-4452 ⊕ ca.megabus.com.

⚠ Emergencies

DOCTORS AND DENTISTS Dental Emergency Services. ✉ 1650 Yonge St., Greater Toronto ☎ 416/485-7121 ⊕ www.dentalemergencyservices.ca.

FOREIGN CONSULATES U.S. Consulate General Toronto. ✉ 360 University Ave., Queen West ☎ 416/595-1700, 416/595-6506 emergency line, 416/201-4056 after hrs ⊕ ca.usembassy.gov.

GENERAL EMERGENCIES Ambulance, fire, and police. ☎ 911.

🚗 Rideshares

Lyft. ✉ Toronto ⊕ www.lyft.com. **Uber.** ✉ Toronto ⊕ www.uber.com.

🚕 Taxi

Beck Taxi. ☎ 416/751-5555 ⊕ www.becktaxi.com. **Co-op Cabs.** ☎ 416/504-2667 ⊕ www.co-opcabs.com. **Diamond Taxi.** ☎ 416/366-6868 ⊕ www.diamondtaxi.ca.

📍 Visitor Information

City of Toronto. ☎ 311 ⊕ www.toronto.ca. **Destination Canada.** ⊕ www.destinationcanada.com. **Destination Ontario.** ☎ 800/668-2746 ⊕ www.destinationontario.com. **Destination Toronto.** ☎ 800/499-2514 toll free ⊕ www.www.destinationtoronto.com.

Chapter 3

HARBOURFRONT, ENTERTAINMENT DISTRICT, AND THE FINANCIAL DISTRICT

3

Updated by
Jesse Ship

👁 Sights
★★★★★

🍴 Restaurants
★★★★☆

🛏 Hotels
★★★★★

🛍 Shopping
★★★★☆

🍸 Nightlife
★★★★★

HARBOURFRONT AND THE ISLANDS

Enjoy the skyline from one of Toronto's ferries.

The Harbourfront area is appealing for waterfront strolls or bike rides. Its myriad recreational and amusement options make it ideal for first-timers getting to know the lay of the land or longtime residents looking to get reacquainted with the city. The nearby Toronto Islands provide a perfect escape from the sometimes stifling summer heat of downtown.

One of downtown Toronto's most unique experiences isn't in the downtown core at all, but a short, skyline-filled ferry ride away. The Toronto Islands are a conveniently located getaway just off the shore of Lake Ontario, offering peaceful beaches (including the notorious clothing-optional section of Hanlan's Point) and beautiful parks.

BEST TIME TO GO

If you're looking for sun and sand, visit in June, July, or August. The cool breeze coming off Lake Ontario can be the perfect antidote to one of Toronto's hot and humid summer days, but in the off-season it can make things a little chilly if you aren't wearing an extra layer.

WAYS TO EXPLORE

BOAT

The best way to enjoy the waterfront is to get right onto Lake Ontario. There are many different boat tours—take your pick from the vendors lining the Harbourfront's lakeside boardwalk—but most offer the same deal: a pleasant, hour-long jaunt around the harbor for about C$25. Sunset dinner cruises are also offered.

To soak up the sun and skyline views, use the public ferry to head for the Toronto Islands. The best beaches are those on the southeast tip of Ward's Island, Centre Island Beach, and Hanlan's Point Beach. This last one is the most secluded, natural beach on the islands, backed by a small dunes area, a portion of which is clothing-optional. Most families with kids head for Centre Island Beach.

BIKE AND STROLL

To get away from busy downtown and stretch your legs, the Toronto Islands are the perfect destination. This car-free open space has paved trails for biking or strolling; miles and miles of green space to explore; and picture-perfect vistas of the surrounding lake and skyline.

Bicyclists, power-walkers, and Sunday strollers all enjoy the **Martin Goodman Trail,** the Toronto portion of the 450-km (280-mile) Lake Ontario Waterfront Trail. The string of beaches along the eastern waterfront (east of Coxwell Avenue) is connected by a continuous boardwalk that parallels the path. At the western end of the walking and biking trail is **Sunnyside Park Beach,** a favorite place for a swim in the "tank" (a huge heated pool) or a snack at the small restaurant inside the handsomely restored 1923 Sunnyside Bathing Pavilion.

FESTIVALS AND EVENTS

The **Canadian National Exhibition** (known as "the Ex") takes place the last two weeks of August and Labor Day weekend, attracting more than 1.5 million people each year. It began in 1879 primarily as an agricultural show and today is a collection of midway rides and games, carnival food, free concerts, horticultural and technological exhibits, and parades. It also hosts the Canadian International Air Show.

Throughout the year, **Harbourfront Centre** hosts a dizzying array of festivals, covering cultural celebrations such as Kuumba (February) and the Mexican Day of the Dead (November); foodie-friendly fetes like the Hot & Spicy Festival (August) and Vegetarian Food Fair (September); and literary events such as the International Festival of Authors (October).

A Toronto ferry

NEIGHBORHOOD SNAPSHOT

TOP EXPERIENCES

■ **Hit the trail:** Walk or bike the edge of Lake Ontario along the Martin Goodman Trail, the Toronto portion of the 450-km (280-mile) Lake Ontario Waterfront Trail.

■ **Explore the Waterfront:** If you want to take in the most marvelous views of the city skyline, hop aboard one of the public ferries for a scenic urban escape on the Toronto Islands.

■ **Cheer the home team:** This is a great city for sports fans. Depending on the time of year, catch a Jays (baseball), Raptors (basketball), or Leafs (hockey) game.

■ **Head straight to the top:** It's a thrilling ride to the observation deck of the CN Tower, the tallest freestanding tower in the Western Hemisphere.

■ **Have a night out:** They call it the Entertainment District for a reason: you can't beat this neighborhood for after-dark excitement.

GETTING HERE

To get to the Harbourfront, take the 509 Queens Quay streetcar from Union Station. The Entertainment District is around St. Andrew and Osgoode subway stations. The Financial District is at Queen, King, and Union stations. There is parking in these areas, but it's expensive and traffic is congested. Try walking or taking transit whenever possible.

PLANNING YOUR TIME

If you have kids in tow, plan on spending a whole day in the Harbourfront area. If you're going to the Toronto Islands, add 20 minutes total traveling time each way to cross the bay by ferry. Depending on what you're planning at the TIFF Bell Lightbox, you could spend an hour browsing an exhibit or several taking in curated films. The Hockey Hall of Fame and the Design Exchange are each good for about an hour.

FUN FACT

■ Toronto's waterfront has seen a massive revitalization in the last 40 years thanks to Prime Minister Pierre Elliott Trudeau's 1970s initiative. The bombastic federal leader spearheaded its transformation from industrial wasteland to sprawling hub of arts, culture, and walkable green space, which the city plans to develop further into the eastern Port Lands for generations to come.

In the last 20 years, Toronto's Harbourfront has been completely transformed. Cranes dot the skyline as condominium buildings seemingly appear overnight. Some of the area's best chefs have made this a culinary destination, and trendy boutique retail establishments have drawn shoppers of all types. Lovers of the outdoors head to the lakefront to take in the expansive views. Suddenly everyone wants to be overlooking, facing, or playing in Lake Ontario.

During the day, the warehouses in the Entertainment District might look deserted, but when the sun goes down, this neighborhood is party central. The bustle and excitement generated by Toronto's clubbers, theatergoers, and night owls keep the show alive until the wee hours of the morning.

On the other hand, while the sidewalks of the Financial District are brimming with suits and cell phones during the day, the area quiets down after the sun sets. Still, there are a few notable attractions here, such as the Hockey Hall of Fame and the Design Exchange. As for the Harbourfront area, many of its most popular attractions are outdoors, so it's especially appealing during warm weather.

Should a sudden downpour catch you off guard, shelter can be found in the area's museums and the network of underground shopping.

Harbourfront

In fair weather, the Harbourfront area is appealing for strolls, and myriad recreational and amusement options make it ideal for those traveling with children. The nearby Toronto Islands provide a perfect escape from the sometimes stifling summer heat of downtown.

 Sights

The Bentway
PROMENADE | FAMILY | Built under the Gardiner Expressway, the Bentway is part of the city's efforts to reclaim public spaces. The sprawling stretch of land houses whimsical art installations,

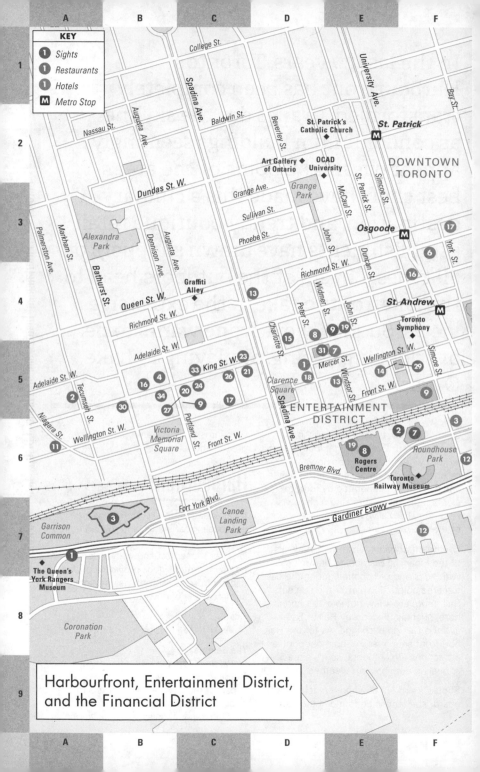

KEY

- **1** Sights
- **1** Restaurants
- **1** Hotels
- **M** Metro Stop

College St.

Spadina Ave.

Baldwin St.

Nassau St.

Augusta Ave.

Beverley St.

St. Patrick's
Catholic Church

St. Patrick M

University Ave.

Bay St.

**DOWNTOWN
TORONTO**

Art Gallery
of Ontario

OCAD
University

Dundas St. W.

Grange Ave.

Grange
Park

Markham St.

Palmerston Ave.

Dennison Ave.

Augusta Ave.

Sullivan St.

McCaul St.

John St.

St. Patrick St.

Simcoe St.

Osgoode M

17

Alexandra
Park

Phoebe St.

Richmond St. W.

Duncan St.

6

16

York St.

Bathurst St.

Graffiti
Alley

Queen St. W.

13

Richmond St. W.

Peter St.

Widmer St.

John St.

St. Andrew M

**Toronto
Symphony**

Richmond St. W.

Charlotte St.

Adelaide St. W.

15

8

9 **19**

Wellington St. W.

Simcoe St.

King St. W. **23**

31 **7**

1

Mercer St.

29

33

26

21

18

14

Adelaide St. W.

16

4

20 **24**

9

17

Clarence
Square

13

Windsor St.

Front St. W.

9

Tecumseh St.

34

27

Portland St.

Front St. W.

**ENTERTAINMENT
DISTRICT**

2 **7**

3

30

Spadina Ave.

Wellington St. W.

Victoria
Memorial
Square

11

Niagara St.

19 **8**

Roundhouse
Park

12

Bremner Blvd.

**Rogers
Centre**

Fort York Blvd.

Canoe
Landing
Park

Gardiner Expwy

**Toronto
Railway Museum**

12

3

Garrison
Common

1

The Queen's
York Rangers
Museum

Coronation
Park

Harbourfront, Entertainment District,
and the Financial District

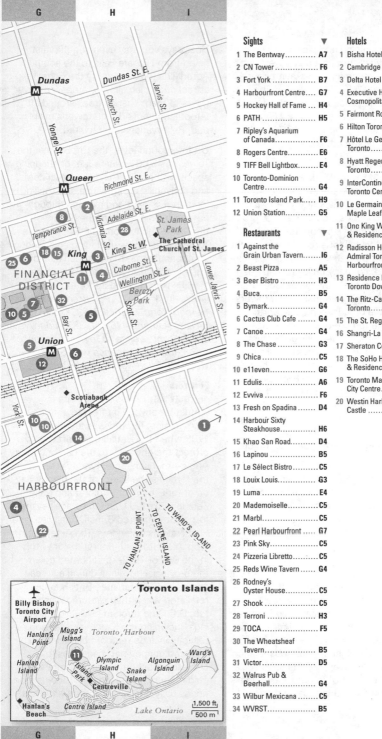

Sights ▼

1 The Bentway A7
2 CN Tower F6
3 Fort York B7
4 Harbourfront Centre.... G7
5 Hockey Hall of Fame ... H4
6 PATH H5
7 Ripley's Aquarium
   of Canada................ F6
8 Rogers Centre........... E6
9 TIFF Bell Lightbox........ E4
10 Toronto-Dominion
   Centre.................... G4
11 Toronto Island Park..... H9
12 Union Station........... G5

Restaurants ▼

1 Against the
   Grain Urban Tavern.......I6
2 Beast Pizza A5
3 Beer Bistro H3
4 Buca...................... B5
5 Bymark................... G4
6 Cactus Club Cafe G4
7 Canoe G4
8 The Chase G3
9 Chica C5
10 e11even................. G6
11 Edulis................... A6
12 Evviva F6
13 Fresh on Spadina D4
14 Harbour Sixty
   Steakhouse.............. H6
15 Khao San Road......... D4
16 Lapinou B5
17 Le Sélect Bistro.......... C5
18 Louix Louis.............. G3
19 Luma E4
20 Mademoiselle........... C5
21 Marbl.................... C5
22 Pearl Harbourfront G7
23 Pink Sky................. C5
24 Pizzeria Libretto.......... C5
25 Reds Wine Tavern G4
26 Rodney's
   Oyster House............ C5
27 Shook C5
28 Terroni H3
29 TOCA..................... F5
30 The Wheatsheaf
   Tavern.................. B5
31 Victor................... D5
32 Walrus Pub &
   Beerhall................ G4
33 Wilbur Mexicana C5
34 WVRST................... B5

Hotels ▼

1 Bisha Hotel Toronto D5
2 Cambridge Suites....... H3
3 Delta Hotel Toronto...... F6
4 Executive Hotel
   Cosmopolitan........... H4
5 Fairmont Royal York G5
6 Hilton Toronto F3
7 Hôtel Le Germain
   Toronto.................. E5
8 Hyatt Regency
   Toronto.................. D4
9 InterContinental
   Toronto Centre F5
10 Le Germain Hotel
   Maple Leaf Square G6
11 One King West Hotel
   & Residence............. H4
12 Radisson Hotel
   Admiral Toronto–
   Harbourfront F7
13 Residence Inn
   Toronto Downtown E5
14 The Ritz-Carlton,
   Toronto.................. E5
15 The St. Regis Toronto... G3
16 Shangri-La Toronto...... F4
17 Sheraton Centre F3
18 The SoHo Hotel
   & Residences............ D5
19 Toronto Marriott
   City Centre.............. E6
20 Westin Harbour
   Castle H6

communal dining and picnic spaces, a gloriously smooth paved pathway built for roller-skating and ice-skating (rentals available at C$10) depending on the season, and various community events, festivals, and concerts. ⊠ *250 Fort York Blvd., King West* ☎ *416/304–0222* ⊕ *www.thebentway.ca.*

★ CN Tower

OBSERVATORY | **FAMILY** | The tallest free-standing tower in the Western Hemisphere, this landmark stretches 1,815 feet and 5 inches high and marks Toronto with its distinctive silhouette. The CN Tower is this tall for a reason: prior to the opening of the telecommunications tower in 1976, so many buildings had been erected over the previous decades that lower radio and TV transmission towers had trouble broadcasting. It's worth a visit to the top if the weather is clear, despite the steep fee. Six glass-front elevators zoom up the outside of the tower at 15 miles per hour, and the ride takes less than a minute. Each elevator has one floor-to-ceiling glass wall—three opaque walls make the trip easier on anyone prone to vertigo—and most have glass floor panels for the dizzying thrill of watching the earth disappear before your eyes.

There are four observation decks. The Glass Floor Level is 1,122 feet above the ground. This may be the most photographed indoor location in the city—lie on the transparent floor and have your picture taken from above like countless visitors before you. Don't worry—the glass floor can support more than 48,000 pounds. Above is the LookOut Level, at 1,136 feet; one more floor above, at 1,151 feet, is the excellent 360 Restaurant. If you're here to dine, your elevator fee is waived. At 1,465 feet, the SkyPod is the world's highest public observation gallery. All the levels provide spectacular panoramic views of Toronto, Lake Ontario, and the Toronto Islands, and on really

clear days you may even see the mist rising from Niagara Falls to the south. Adrenaline junkies can try the EdgeWalk attraction, which allows harnessed tower goers to roam "hands free" around a 5-foot ledge outside the tower's main pod. Reservations are required.

On the ground level, the Gift Shop at the Tower has 5,000 square feet of shopping space with quality Canadian travel items and souvenirs, along with a shop selling Inuit art. Displays and exhibits throughout the building feature the history of the Tower and its construction; how the Tower works today, including engineering components that make it such a unique attraction; and a dynamic weather display. Peak visiting hours for the stunning views are 11 to 4. ⊠ *290 Bremner Blvd., Harbourfront* ☎ *416/868–6937, 416/362–5411 restaurant, 416/601–3833 EdgeWalk* ⊕ *www.cntower.ca* ⊠ *Tower Experience C$43, Tower Experience with SkyPod C$50.50, EdgeWalk C$195* Ⓜ *Union.*

Fort York

MILITARY SIGHT | This historic site is a must for anyone interested in the city's origins. Toronto was founded in 1793 when the British built Fort York to protect the entrance to the harbor during Anglo-American strife. Twenty years later, the fort was the scene of the bloody Battle of York, in which explorer and general Zebulon Pike led U.S. forces against the fort's outnumbered British, Canadian, and First Nations defenders. The Americans won this battle—their first major victory in the War of 1812—and burned down the provincial buildings during a six-day occupation. A year later, British forces retaliated when they captured Washington, D.C., and torched its public buildings, including the Executive Mansion. Exhibits include restored barracks, kitchens, and gunpowder magazines, plus changing museum displays. There are guided tours, marching drills, and cannon firings daily during the summer months.

Did You Know?

In 1995, the American Society of Civil Engineers named Toronto's CN Tower one of the Seven Wonders of the Modern World. The tower's enormous antenna was built in 36 sections that were delivered to the top by helicopter, shaving months off the construction time.

More than 450 species of marine life are on display at Ripley's Aquarium of Canada.

The Fort York Visitor Center has been highly praised for its modern architectural design and exhibits on the founding of York, the changing harbor, and the War of 1812, plus an area displaying rare artifacts related to Toronto and Fort York's history. The grounds of the fort have also become a popular venue for music festivals during spring and summer. ✉ *250 Fort York Blvd., between Bathurst St. and Strachan Ave.* ☎ *416/392–6907* ⊕ *www. fortyork.ca* ✉ *Free* Ⓜ *Bathurst.*

Harbourfront Centre
ARTS CENTER | FAMILY | Stretching from just west of York Street to Spadina Avenue, this culture-and-recreation center is a match for San Francisco's Pier 39 and Baltimore's Inner Harbor. The original Harbourfront opened in 1974, rejuvenating more than a mile of city; today a streamlined 10-acre version draws more than 3 million visitors each year. Queens Quay Terminal is a former Terminal Warehouse building that was transformed in 1983 into a magnificent, eight-story building with specialty shops, eateries, and the 450-seat Fleck Dance Theatre. Exhibits of contemporary arts are mounted at the Power Plant, which can be spotted by its tall red smokestack; it was built in 1927 as a power station for the Terminal Warehouse's ice-making plant.

Developed by renowned cellist Yo-Yo Ma and garden designer Julie Moir Messervy, the Music Garden on the south side of Queens Quay is Ma's interpretation of J. S. Bach's Cello Suite No. 1 (which consists of six movements—Prelude, Allemande, Courante, Sarabande, Minuet, and Gigue). Each movement is reflected in the park's elaborate design: undulating riverscape, a forest grove of wandering trails, a swirling path through a wildflower meadow, a conifer grove, a formal flower parterre, and giant grass steps. York Quay Centre hosts concerts, theater, readings, and ateliers. The Craft Studio, for example, has professional craftspeople working in ceramics, glass, metal, and textiles from February to December, in full view of the public. A shallow pond outside is used for canoe lessons in warmer months and as the largest artificial ice-skating rink in North America in winter. At the nearby Nautical Centre, many private firms rent boats and give sailing and canoeing lessons. Seasonal events include the Ice Canoe Race in late January, Winterfest in February, a jazz festival in June, Canada Day celebrations and the Parade of Lights in July, the Authors' Festival and Harvest Festival in October, and the Swedish Christmas Fair in November. ⊠ *235 Queens Quay W, Harbourfront* 🕾 *416/973–4000 event hotline, 416/973–4600 offices* ⊕ *www. harbourfrontcentre.com* Ⓜ *Union.*

★ Ripley's Aquarium of Canada

AQUARIUM | FAMILY | North America's largest aquarium contains more than 450 species of marine life spread out between 45 exhibit spaces. Maintaining their philosophy to "foster environmental education, conservation, and research," Ripley's also lives up to its reputation as a wow-inducing entertainment venue. One exhibit simulates a Caribbean scuba diving experience, complete with bountiful tropical fish, coral reefs, and a bright blue sky above. Sharks are a dominant theme: you can wind your way through tunnels that take you right into the almost 80,000-gallon shark tank, which houses three species of sharks and more than 5,000 other aquatic animals. The shark pattern on the roof is an unexpected treat for visitors peering down on the aquarium from the top of the CN Tower. ⊠ *288 Bremner Blvd.* 🕾 *647/351–3474* ⊕ *www.ripleyaquariums.com/canada* 💺 *C$30* Ⓜ *Union or St. Andrew.*

Rogers Centre

SPORTS VENUE | FAMILY | The Rogers Centre is home to baseball's Blue Jays and was the world's first stadium with a fully retractable roof. Rogers Communications, the owner of the Blue Jays, bought the stadium, formerly known as the SkyDome, in February 2005 for a mere C$25 million. One way to see the 52,000-seat stadium is to buy tickets for a Blue Jays game or one of many other events and concerts. You can also take a one-hour guided walking tour: the route depends on what's going on at the stadium, so you may find yourself in the middle of the field, in a press box, in the dressing rooms, or, if a roof tour is available, 36 stories above home plate on a catwalk. ⊠ *1 Blue Jays Way, Harbourfront* 🕾 *416/341–2770 tours, 416/341–1234 ticket information* ⊕ *www.rogerscentre.com* 💺 *Tours C$17* Ⓜ *Union.*

★ Toronto Island Park

ISLAND | FAMILY | These 14 narrow, tree-lined islands in Lake Ontario provide a gorgeous green retreat with endless outdoor activities. The more than 230 hectares of parkland are hard to resist, especially in the summer, when they're usually a few degrees cooler than the city.

Sandy beaches fringe the islands; the best are on the southeast tip of Ward's Island, the southernmost edge of Centre Island, and the west side of Hanlan's Point. A portion of Hanlan's Beach is officially "clothing-optional"—Ontario's only legal nude beach. In the summer, Centre Island has bike and rowboat rentals. Bring picnic fixings or something to grill in one of the park's barbecue pits, or grab a quick (but expensive) bite at one of the snack bars or cafés. (Note that the consumption of alcohol in a public park is illegal in Toronto.) There are also supervised wading pools, baseball diamonds, volleyball nets, tennis courts, and even a disc-golf course. Winter can be bitterly cold on the islands, but snowshoeing and cross-country skiing with downtown Toronto over your shoulder are appealing activities.

All transportation on the islands is self-powered; no private cars are permitted. The boardwalk from Centre Island to Ward's Island is 2½ km (1½ miles) long. Bikes are allowed on all ferries, or you can rent one for an hour or so once you get there. Bike rentals can be found south of the Centre Island ferry docks on the Avenue of the Islands.

You may want to take one of the equally frequent ferries to Ward's Island or Hanlan's Point from Jack Layton Ferry Terminal. Both islands have tennis courts and picnic and sunbathing spots. Late May through early September, the ferries run between the docks at the bottom of Bay Street and the Ward's Island dock between 6:35 am and 11:45 pm; for Centre and Hanlan's islands, they begin at 8 am. Ward's Island Ferries run roughly at half-hour intervals most of the working day and at quarter-hour intervals during peak times such as summer evenings. In winter the ferries run only to Ward's Island on a limited schedule. Savvy travellers can also grab a ride from a water taxi along the waterfront. ⊠ *Ferries at foot of Bay St. and Queen's Quay, Harbourfront* ☎ *416/392–8186 island information, 311* ⊕ *www.toronto.ca/parks/island* ⊠ *Ferry C$8 round-trip* Ⓜ *Union.*

🍴 Restaurants

The vibe here in summer is decidedly beachy; take a stroll along the lake, stopping for lunch on one of the breezy patios. If you brought your bathing suit, head to Sugar Beach—an urban oasis where locals sunbathe. Or work off that lunch by renting one of the city's public bikes and pedal around until you're ready for dinner.

Against the Grain Urban Tavern
$$$ | CANADIAN | Making the most of its proximity to Sugar Beach, Against the Grain is a sunbathing destination minutes from downtown, with a stellar patio in full sunny view of the lake. Shareable apps like nachos and wings, plus a great craft beer selection, capitalize on the laid-back vibe. **Known for:** great water views; popularity with the after-work crowd; diverse comfort food menu. Ⓢ *Average main: C$21* ⊠ *Corus Bldg., 25 Dock-side Dr., Harbourfront* ☎ *647/344–1562* ⊕ *corusquay.atgurbantavern.ca* Ⓜ *Union.*

e11even
$$$ | AMERICAN | By day, e11even presents steak-house fare for the downtown business crowd; by night, concertgoers and sports fans slide into wooden booths for a refined meal or nightcap. The menu of North American classics includes savory-sweet maple-glazed bacon, salads flanked with seared tuna, filet mignon, and casual fare like burgers and kosher beef dogs. **Known for:** 3,200-bottle-long wine list; refined atmosphere; the steak, of course. Ⓢ *Average main: C$30* ⊠ *15 York St., Harbourfront* ☎ *416/815–1111* ⊕ *www.e11even.ca* ⊙ *Closed Sun. No lunch Sat.* Ⓜ *Union.*

Harbour Sixty Steakhouse
$$$$ | STEAKHOUSE | Bucking the trend toward relaxed fine dining, Harbour Sixty goes for sheer opulence, the drama of which is apparent from the get-go as you walk up stone steps to the grand entrance of the restored Harbour Commission building. The kitchen rises to the occasion with starters like blinis with beluga caviar and mains like bone-in rib steak and a shareable seafood tower. **Known for:** extravagant interior; extensive wine list; authentic fine dining experience. Ⓢ *Average main: C$60* ⊠ *60 Harbour St., Harbourfront* ☎ *416/777–2111* ⊕ *www.harboursixty.com* ⊙ *No lunch weekends* Ⓜ *Union.*

Pearl Harbourfront

$$$ | CHINESE | Ride the Queens Quay Terminal escalator to one of the city's hidden fine dim sum experiences. The view overlooking Lake Ontario is nearly as delicious as the restaurant's menu of traditional Cantonese classics like *har gao* shrimp dumplings, broad snow pea leaves decorated with chunks of king mushroom, and various fresh seafoods from the tank prepared with homemade sauces. **Known for:** excellent service; diverse tea selection; traditional handmade dim sum. $ *Average main: C$25* ✉ *207 Queens Quay W, Suite 200, Harbourfront* ☎ *416/203–1233* ⊕ *pearlharbourfront.ca.*

Hotels

Staying around here is convenient for exploring the greatest concentration of Toronto's must-see attractions—especially the kid-friendly ones—like the Rogers Centre, Ontario Place, and the CN Tower.

Delta Hotel Toronto

$$$$ | HOTEL | Just steps from the Rogers Centre, CN Tower, Ripley's Aquarium, and the waterfront, the Delta Toronto has rooms with great views. **Pros:** connected to the PATH, convention center, and Union Station; modern decor and clean, spacious rooms; attentive staff. **Cons:** rooms can fill up quickly; parking is expensive; no mini-refrigerator. $ *Rooms from: C$455* ✉ *75 Lower Simcoe St., Harbourfront* ☎ *416/849–1200, 888/890–3222* ⊕ *www.deltatoronto.com* 🛏 *541 rooms* �I⊙I *No Meals* Ⓜ *Union.*

Le Germain Hotel Maple Leaf Square

$$$$ | HOTEL | Inside the Maple Leaf Square complex, this ultrastylish hotel is perfectly poised to receive traffic from the Scotiabank Arena across the street and the Rogers Centre just minutes away. **Pros:** free cancellation; attached to PATH network; great service. **Cons:** area is boisterous when events are happening at nearby Scotiabank Arena; limited equipment in fitness center; no full-service restaurant. $ *Rooms from: C$429* ✉ *75 Bremner Blvd., Harbourfront* ☎ *416/649–7575, 888/940–7575* ⊕ *www.germainmapleleafsquare.com* 🛏 *167 rooms* ℐ⊙I *No Meals* Ⓜ *Union.*

Radisson Hotel Admiral Toronto–Harbourfront

$$$ | HOTEL | FAMILY | You can't get much closer to Toronto's waterfront than this hotel, where unobstructed Lake Ontario and Toronto Islands vistas come standard. **Pros:** easy access to local attractions; beautiful outdoor pool; excellent views. **Cons:** neighborhood seems out of the way; pool is open to the public; rates are pricey. $ *Rooms from: C$347* ✉ *249 Queens Quay W, at York St., Harbourfront* ☎ *416/203–3333, 800/395–7046* ⊕ *www.radisson.com* 🛏 *157 rooms* ℐ⊙I *No Meals* Ⓜ *Union.*

Westin Harbour Castle

$$$$ | HOTEL | FAMILY | On a clear day you can see the skyline of Rochester, New York, across the sparkling blue Lake Ontario from most rooms at this midrange, kid-friendly hotel. **Pros:** very comfortable beds; great kids' programs; pet friendly. **Cons:** not right in downtown; basic restaurant offerings; decor is rather dated. $ *Rooms from: C$400* ✉ *1 Harbour Sq., at Bay St., Harbourfront* ☎ *416/869–1600, 866/716–8101* ⊕ *www.marriott.com/yyzwi* 🛏 *977 rooms* ℐ⊙I *No Meals* Ⓜ *Union.*

ⓨ Nightlife

In general, this area is quiet after dark, but a nightlife scene is slowly emerging as more condos are built and the waterfront gets more and more developed. Waterfront concerts take place here in summer, and dinner cruises leave from the Harbourfront.

BARS
Real Sports Bar & Grill
BARS | No hole-in-the-wall sports bar, this sleek 25,000-square-foot space adjacent to the Scotiabank Arena lights up with almost 200 high-definition flat-screen TVs and amazing sightlines from every club-style booth, table, or stool at one of the three bars. Head to the second floor to watch a game on the biggest TV, an HDTV screen two stories high. For popular sporting events, or any day or night the Jays, Leafs, or Raptors play, it's best to make a reservation (accepted up to three weeks in advance), though the bar does keep a third of its seats for walk-in traffic an hour before face-off. ⊠ *15 York St., at Bremner Blvd., Harbourfront* ☎ *416/815–7325* ⊕ *www.realsports.ca* Ⓜ *Union.*

BREWERIES
Amsterdam BrewHouse
BREWPUBS | This brewpub features two massive bars with more than 10 local brews on tap, an open-concept kitchen with an imported Italian wood-burning pizza oven, and a sprawling patio with stunning views of the Toronto Islands. The building, a former 1930s boathouse, also houses a brewery; tours and beer tastings are available daily. Tours are free, but book in advance. ⊠ *245 Queens Quay W, Harbourfront* ☎ *416/504–1020* ⊕ *www.amsterdambeer.com* Ⓜ *Union:*

 Performing Arts

MAJOR VENUES
Budweiser Stage
MUSIC | When summer comes, this outdoor amphitheater at the waterfront becomes one of the most sought-after concert venues in town. With a capacity of 16,000, it's a spot for big touring acts of all genres, from classic rock like Santana to hip-hop artists like Kendrick Lamar. It's also a common venue for hometown hero Drake's headline-grabbing OVO Fest and an annual warm-weather blowout for local folk-rockers Blue Rodeo. It's a seated venue, partially covered, though open-air tickets on a back lawn are also available. Nearby venue Echo Beach also offers slightly smaller shows on sand. ⊠ *Harbourfront* ☎ *416/260–5600* ⊕ *livenation.com* Ⓜ *509 Harbourfront streetcar from Union subway station or 511 Bathurst streetcar from Bathurst subway station.*

Scotiabank Arena
CONCERTS | Most arena shows are held here rather than at the larger Rogers Centre due to superior acoustics. Past performances at the nearly 20,000-capacity arena have included Beyoncé, Rod Stewart, *American Idol Live!,* and Nine Inch Nails. ⊠ *40 Bay St., at Gardiner Expressway, Harbourfront* ☎ *416/815–5500* ⊕ *www.scotiabankarena.com* Ⓜ *Union.*

 Activities

BIKING
Martin Goodman Trail
BIKING | The Martin Goodman Trail is part of a larger Waterfront Trail route that spans over 3,000 km (1,850 miles) across Southern Ontario. You can walk (or cycle) the entire length of the city or just stick to the Harbourfront neighborhood, where you'll have nice views of the Toronto Islands and airplanes flying into Billy Bishop Toronto City Airport to your south and the city skyline to your north. Bike Share Toronto offers a convenient way to bike the trail (or the city) with 5,000 bicycles parked at various locations across the downtown core. You can pay by the hour or get a day pass at a discounted rate. ⊠ *Harbourfront* ⊕ *waterfronttrail.org/places/communities/toronto.*

tiff. | Bell Lightbox

The TIFF Bell Lightbox is the focal point for the annual Toronto International Film Festival.

Shopping

Shopping in the Harbourfront area is somewhat limited, but the Harbourfront Centre complex can be a good place to find interesting art or cultural items from festival vendors in the summer months.

SPECIALTY GIFTS

Merchant of York

HOUSEWARES | Discover a sensorial paradise of highly curated artisan crafts-manship and design pieces from across Asia, Scandinavia, and North America at this gift shop built into the Harbourfront Centre. Most popular are high-grade Japanese MD notebooks and stationery, delicate glass-blown homewares by HMM from Taipei, and heavenly scented soy wax candles from dilo Studio out of Philadelphia. ⊠ *235 Queens Quay W, Harbourfront* ☏ *416/546-9675* ⊕ *www. merchantofyork.com.*

Entertainment District

This downtown district's biggest draw is its collection of theaters. The Royal Alexandra, built in 1907, has played host to major touring musicals. Down the street is sister theater Princess of Wales, a modern glass-walled space. Across the street is the unmistakable Roy Thomson Hall, home to the Toronto Symphony Orchestra. If film's more your speed, check out what's screening at the TIFF Bell Lightbox, which serves as the main hub for the Toronto International Film Festival in September but spotlights curated classics and indie flicks year-round.

◉ Sights

TIFF Bell Lightbox

OTHER ATTRACTION | A five-story architec-tural masterpiece, this glass-paneled building houses the year-round head-quarters of the internationally acclaimed

Toronto International Film Festival, which takes place in September. Throughout the year visitors can attend film-related lectures, watch screenings, and enjoy smaller film festivals, including the TIFF Next Wave Film Festival, a film festival with free movies for anyone under 25 that takes place in April. A stellar educational program includes summer camps and ongoing workshops—on how to produce a stop-motion movie, for example. The TIFF Cinematheque, open to the public, plays world cinema classics and contemporary art house films. ✉ *Reitman Sq., 350 King St. W, at John St., Entertainment District* ☎ *416/599–8433, 888/599–8433* 🌐 *www.tiff.net* [M] *St. Andrew.*

🍴 Restaurants

The Entertainment District tends to be pretty laid-back during the day, but it comes to life at night and on weekends when throngs of well-dressed people head to the theater and out for dinner or drinks.

★ Beast Pizza

$$ | **INTERNATIONAL** | In a quiet dining room tucked into the first floor of a house just off King West, this adventurous pizza parlor serves New York–style pies with topping combos like braised beef tongue and smoked bacon, or anchovies and crispy chicken skin. While there are pasta offerings on the menu, diners can also slurp cheesy bone marrow and order decadent house-made Twinkies for dessert. **Known for:** cozy interior; adventurous menu items; daily specials. [$] *Average main: C$14* ✉ *96 Tecumseth St.* ☎ *647/352–6000* 🌐 *www.thebeastrestaurant.com* ⏲ *No lunch. Closed Mon.–Tues.* [M] *St. Andrew.*

★ Buca

$$$ | **ITALIAN** | With its refreshing roster of Italian classics, stylish Buca was a pioneer on this stretch of King Street, and its influence continues today. Tucked into an alley just off the main drag, the repurposed boiler room has exposed brick walls, metal columns, and wooden tables that reflect the philosophy behind the menu. **Known for:** consistently voted one of the best Italian restaurants in Toronto; wines meticulously chosen from Italian vintners; trendy decor. [$] *Average main: C$28* ✉ *604 King St. W, Entertainment District* ☎ *416/865–1600* 🌐 *www.buca.ca* ⏲ *No lunch* [M] *Osgoode.*

Toronto's Poutine 🍴

The Québécois classic, traditionally made from French fries, cheese curds, and gravy, tends to get dressed up in Toronto. Modern takes might include pulled pork and other meats, as well as different sauces and ethnic spices. NomNomNom and Smoke's Poutinerie are restaurants dedicated to the decadent dish.

Chica

$$$ | **SPANISH** | Transport yourself to an Old World, intimate Spanish wine cave while dining on highly creative tapas dishes. While the menu is frequently changing—like any tapas bar worth its salt—one can expect the flair of French choux a la crème filled with a salmon-like uni mousse; a scallop ceviche layered with green honeydew, topped with a floral crown; and mainstays like acorn-fed Iberico ham imported from Spain. **Known for:** elegant and inventive cocktails; late-night dining; locally foraged ingredients. [$] *Average main: C$24* ✉ *75 Portland St.* ☎ *416/479-9779* 🌐 *barchicatoronto.com* [M] *St. Andrew.*

★ Edulis

$$$$ | EUROPEAN | European bistro meets local forager is the theme at Edulis, where the five- and seven-course tasting menus are devoted to classic rustic dishes. Rough-hewn wood walls and burlap breadbaskets evoke a farmhouse feel, and the soft lighting adds to the intimate atmosphere. **Known for:** affordable lunchtime specials on weekends; standout seafood dishes; truffle menu. Ⓢ *Average main: C$180* ✉ *169 Niagara St., King West* ☎ *416/703–4222* ⊕ *www.edulisrestaurant.com* ☯ *Closed Mon.–Wed. No lunch Thurs.–Sat.* Ⓜ *St. Andrew.*

Evviva

$$ | CANADIAN | Don't let the opulent interior at this busy breakfast spot fool you: the meals here are affordable (and yummy). It's one of the closest brunch restaurants to the Rogers Centre, making it a good place to grab a cup of coffee and some pancakes before an afternoon Jays game. **Known for:** velvet chairs and grand chandeliers; small but cozy side patio; extensive vegan brunch menu. Ⓢ *Average main: C$16* ✉ *25 Lower Simcoe St., Entertainment District* ☎ *416/351–4040* ⊕ *evviva.ca* ☯ *No dinner* Ⓜ *Union.*

Fresh on Spadina

$$ | VEGETARIAN | FAMILY | This delicious restaurant has been a vegan mecca for over 20 years and will make even the most die-hard meat eaters happy. The menu has evolved far past their power shake and rice bowl origins, and while the Balance bowl still tops the charts with its jicama, tofu, and addictive peanut sauce, they now offer everything from pizzas to decadent breakfast items like a crispy, corn-flake-coated almond butter French toast. **Known for:** cold-pressed juices and smoothies; garden-like atmosphere; young, lively crowd. Ⓢ *Average main: C$17* ✉ *147 Spadina Ave., Entertainment District* ☎ *416/599–4442* ⊕ *freshplantpowered.com* Ⓜ *St. Andrew or Osgoode.*

★ Khao San Road

$$ | THAI | Named for a street in Bangkok bursting with nightlife and excellent street eats, Khao San Road lives up to its moniker. The squash fritters are a head-turning crispy delight that you'll want to order when you see them show up at another table. **Known for:** ingredients sourced directly from Thailand; busy, vibrant atmosphere; all of the noodle dishes are standouts. Ⓢ *Average main: C$14* ✉ *11 Charlotte St., Entertainment District* ☎ *647/352–5773* ⊕ *www.khaosanroad.ca* ☯ *No lunch Sun.* Ⓜ *St. Andrew.*

Lapinou

$$$ | MODERN FRENCH | *Lapinou* (bunny) is a French term of endearment you might hear lovers whisper between bites at Toronto's neo-bistro with a frequently rotating menu and 1920s flair. Every dish is a work of modern art, fusing French traditions with creative twists like grilled asparagus slathered with a bechamel-like sauce, dotted with puffed buckwheat. **Known for:** private patio seating; locally sourced seasonal ingredients; extensive wine list. Ⓢ *Average main: C$30* ✉ *642 King St. W, Entertainment District* ☎ *416/479–4414* ⊕ *www.lapinoubistro.com* Ⓜ *St. Andrew.*

Le Sélect Bistro

$$$$ | FRENCH | Le Sélect occupies a special place in the heart of Toronto's Parisian cuisine aficionados. The sprawling plush booths, zinc bar, and mosaic flooring create the ideal ambience for buttery escargots with pillowy *pain au lait* (milk buns), hearty bowls of saffron-tinged bouillabaisse, and an oversized apple tarte tatin for two, drizzled tableside with rich caramel sauce. **Known for:** seafood towers and whole-fish specialties; extensive wine list with over 1,200 bottles;

large front patio and private dining rooms. $ *Average main: C$35* ⊠ *432 Wellington St. W, Entertainment District* ☎ *416/626–6262* ⊕ *www.leselectbistro. com.*

★ Luma

$$$ | CANADIAN | Duck out of a double-feature at the TIFF Bell Lightbox to grab a meal at Luma, a mini-oasis on the second floor of the bustling glass-paneled film venue. Even if you're not going to a film, it's a great restaurant, complete with a patio overlooking the lively Entertainment District and the CN Tower. **Known for:** great spot for people-watching; globally inspired menu; fresh seafood dishes. $ *Average main: C$30* ⊠ *330 King St. W, Entertainment District* ☎ *647/288–4715* ⊕ *www.lumarestaurant.com* ⊙ *Closed Sun. No lunch Sat.* Ⓜ *St. Andrew.*

Mademoiselle

$$$$ | SEAFOOD | You'd never know this St. Tropez–inspired seafood restaurant and raw bar with an indoor garden decor was once an infamous lady bar. Full-fledged beluga caviar and blini experiences, a 45-ounce tomahawk steak served on enormous sharing platters, and extravagant sushi rolls layered with luxuries such as torched Wagyu beef, foie gras, truffles, lobster tempura, and gold flakes make up part of the menu. **Known for:** over-the-top boozy cocktails; Japanese-imported ingredients; private dining experiences. $ *Average main: C$40* ⊠ *563 King St. W, Entertainment District* ☎ *437/231-5057* ⊕ *mademoiselleto.com* Ⓜ *St. Andrew.*

Marbl

$$$$ | CONTEMPORARY | The game will always be playing but this upscale, airy establishment is not your average sports bar. Show up post-game and you're likely to spot at least one of the Toronto Raptors or visiting team members dining on a platter of decadent appetizers like thick, creamy Dungeness crab cakes, or mounds of steak tartare decorated with a layer of silver-dollar-sized truffle shavings. **Known for:** weekend brunch; intimate private patio; rapper Drake is a frequent patron. $ *Average main: C$40* ⊠ *455 King St. W, Entertainment District* ☎ *416/979–2660* ⊕ *marbltoronto.com* Ⓜ *St. Andrew.*

Pink Sky

$$$ | SEAFOOD | A pink sky at night makes for dining delights at this extravagant eatery with surrealist schooner elements and wall-sized wood carvings. The captain's bounty of a menu features a gooey eight-cheese lobster mac with oversized rigatoni, tuna tartare prepped tableside scooped into Bibb lettuce leaves, and succulent octopus that bursts in the mouth like pomegranate candy. **Known for:** charcoal-grilled seafood creations; playful twists on classic cocktails; DJs on the weekend. $ *Average main: C$30* ⊠ *480 King St. W, Entertainment District* ☎ *647/660–0999* ⊕ *pinkskytoronto.com* Ⓜ *St. Andrew.*

Pizzeria Libretto

$$ | ITALIAN | If you love Italian cuisine, this Toronto institution serves authentic sourdough Neapolitan pizzas and a selection of traditional antipasti to discerning locals. It caters to all dietary restrictions, including gluten-free, dairy-free, nut-free, vegetarian, and vegan. **Known for:** lunchtime specials; family-style menu options; outstanding negroni selection. $ *Average main: C$20* ⊠ *545 King St. W, Entertainment District* ☎ *647/352–1200* ⊕ *www. pizzerialibretto.com* Ⓜ *504 streetcar.*

Rodney's Oyster House

$$$ | SEAFOOD | A den of oceanic delicacies, this playful basement raw bar is frequented by solo diners and showbiz types. Among the options are soft-shell steamer clams, a variety of smoked fish, East Coast lobster rolls, plus a rotating list of more than 20 varieties of oysters (including perfect Malpeques from

Local Chains Worth a Taste

For those times when all you want is a quick bite, consider these local chains where you're assured of fresh, tasty food and good value.

Burger's Priest: The junk-food faithful flock to this local chain for old-school smash burgers, fries, and shakes. Their not-so-secret "secret menu" (find it on their website) features awe-inspiring items like the Four Horsemen of the Apocalypse: a double cheeseburger with two veggie patties, all stacked between two grilled-cheese sandwiches.

imPerfect Fresh Eats: This family-run pan-Asian themed build-a-bowl concept keeps fresh food affordable by sourcing "less than perfect"-looking produce, keeping them out of landfills. Customize your order with sweet potato noodles, Forbidden Black Rice, Kalbi steak, and vegan chicken.

Freshii: This is a healthier choice where baseball-capped salad artists get through the lunch rush like a championship team. The interior is all steely white and blond wood, and designer greens and custom-made sandwiches clearly appeal to the masses. The Cobb is a standout.

Harvey's: Harvey's says it makes a hamburger a beautiful thing, and we agree—whether it's a beef, chicken, or veggie burger. You get to choose your toppings, which is a boon for picky kids. The fries are a hit, too.

Pizza Pizza: The Toronto pizza franchise may appear a little on the dowdy side, but they're constantly surprising their diners with trendy new offerings like ketogenic pizza options with cauliflower-based crusts and heart-shaped pies.

Second Cup: You'll find coffee plain and fancy, as well as flavored hot chocolates, a variety of teas, Italian soft drinks, and nibbles that include muffins, bagels, and raspberry–white chocolate scones.

Swiss Chalet Rotisserie and Grill: This Canadian institution is well-known for its rotisserie chicken and barbecued ribs, in portions that suit every family member. Ask for extra sauce for your fries.

Tim Horton's: Most locations never close, and coffee is made fresh every 20 minutes. Check out the variety of fresh doughnuts, muffins, bagels, and soup-and-sandwich combos. The Canadian Maple doughnut is an obvious front-runner.

---

owner Rodney Clark's own oyster beds on Prince Edward Island). **Known for:** impressive wine list; maritime hospitality; fun, vibrant vibe. Ⓢ *Average main: C$28* ✉ *469 King St. W, Entertainment District* ☎ *416/363–8105* ⊕ *www.rodneysoysterhouse.com* ⊘ *Closed Mon.* Ⓜ *St. Andrew.*

Shook

$$ | **MODERN ISRAELI** | "Shook" means market in Hebrew, and the quality and creativity of the chefs will get your taste buds dancing. Weekday brunch apps like the *kibbeh* (stuffed buckwheat dumplings) create a minimalist explosion for the senses, plated with truffle honey and sour labneh. **Known for:** fluffy three-flour pitas that are baked in-house; creative

cocktails; separate weekday and week-end brunch menus. $\boxed{\$}$ *Average main: C\$15* ✉ *77 Portland St., Entertainment District* ☎ *647/484-7476* ⊕ *shookkitchen. com* Ⓜ *St. Andrew.*

TOCA

\$\$\$\$ | ITALIAN | The swanky Ritz-Carlton dining experience comes to Toronto in the form of TOCA, where the menu of elevated Italian food takes advantage of local ingredients. To really up the ante you can reserve seats at the chef's table, at a private dining nook in the kitchen. **Known for:** 30-minute "express" lunch option on weekdays for business diners; the Sunday Market Brunch; the cheese cave. $\boxed{\$}$ *Average main: C\$44* ✉ *181 Wellington St. W* ☎ *416/572–8008* ⊕ *www.tocarestaurant.ca* Ⓜ *St. Andrew.*

Victor

\$\$\$ | FRENCH | Just off King Street in the Hôtel Le Germain, Victor presents a French-themed menu in a swanky atmosphere with abstract industrial brass tube lighting, wood floors, and subdued teal banquettes. Start with fried artichokes or roasted mushrooms for the table; add a serving of buttery roasted scallops or a smoke-saturated blackened trout; and pair with a bottle of white from their extensive French, Italian, and Californian wine list. **Known for:** great spot for a pre-theater dinner or romantic date night; quiet location, unlike other busy spots in this neighborhood; carefully curated wine, beer, and cocktail list. $\boxed{\$}$ *Average main: C\$25* ✉ *Hôtel Le Germain Toronto, 30 Mercer St.* ☎ *416/883–3431* ⊕ *www. victorrestaurant.com* ⊙ *No lunch* Ⓜ *St. Andrew.*

The Wheatsheaf Tavern

\$\$ | AMERICAN | Toronto's oldest bar, established in 1849, has upscaled its traditional sports bar menu to gastronomic proportions. Grab a patio perch in warmer months to take the pulse of the bustling King and Bathurst, while dining on offerings like XL-sized marinara meatballs, thick and crispy battered fish-and-chips with requisite mushy peas, or a juicy prime-rib sando washed down with a local beer. **Known for:** friendly and attentive service; half-price wings on Tuesday; live rock bands Wednesday through Sunday. $\boxed{\$}$ *Average main: C\$20* ✉ *667 King St. W* ☎ *416/504–9912* ⊕ *www. wheatsheaftavern.com.*

Wilbur Mexicana

\$ | MEXICAN | This fun, lively counter-service joint serves up Southern California–style Mexican street food like burritos and tacos. It's more than the average fast-food joint, though, and patrons like to linger with friends over beers. **Known for:** the hot sauce bar; great value; outstanding guacamole. $\boxed{\$}$ *Average main: C\$10* ✉ *552 King St. W, Entertainment District* ☎ *416/792–1878* ⊕ *wilburmexicana.com* Ⓜ *504 streetcar, or St. Andrew and a 15-minute walk.*

WVRST

\$\$ | GERMAN | You don't need to wait around until Oktoberfest to drink great German beer and indulge in delicious bratwurst; just walk into WVRST, a modern beer hall on King West. Choose amid the selection of sausages, from the traditional pork to vegetarian, or get a little wild with selections such as pheasant, duck, or bison. **Known for:** dozens of craft beers and ciders on tap; the outstanding double-fried duck-fat fries; German beer-hall vibe. $\boxed{\$}$ *Average main: C\$13* ✉ *609 King St. W, King West* ☎ *416/703–7775* ⊕ *www.wvrst.com* ⊙ *No lunch weekdays* Ⓜ *St. Andrew.*

 Hotels

Bisha Hotel Toronto

\$\$\$\$ | HOTEL | Bisha earns top marks for its boutique design hotel, with its velveteen lobby, over 3,000 pieces of art (some Warhols even), and luxurious suites overseen by Toronto's highly sought-after Studio Munge and Rock and Roll Hall-of-Famer Lenny Kravitz. **Pros:** glamorous rooftop pool and dining; excellent service; complimentary Wi-Fi. **Cons:** expensive minibar; party atmosphere isn't for everyone; can get loud at night. [$] *Rooms from: C$585* ✉ *80 Blue Jays Way, Entertainment District* ☎ *437/370–8142* 🌐 *www.bishahoteltoronto.com* 🛏 *96 rooms* 🍴 *No Meals* [M] *St. Andrew.*

Hilton Toronto

$$$ | **HOTEL** | If you want to be close to the Entertainment and Financial Districts, this hotel offers one of the area's best locations, and its lobby restaurant, Tundra, serves stellar Canadian cuisine. **Pros:** across the street from the Four Seasons Centre for the Performing Arts; popular on-site steak house; connected to PATH. **Cons:** rooms can be small; service lags at times; Wi-Fi not free for everyone. [$] *Rooms from: C$289* ✉ *145 Richmond St. W, at University Ave., Entertainment District* ☎ *416/869–3456, 800/267–2281* 🌐 *www.hilton.com/en/hotels/torhi-hh-hilton-toronto* 🛏 *600 rooms* 🍴 *No Meals* [M] *Osgoode.*

★ **Hôtel Le Germain Toronto**

$$$$ | **HOTEL** | The retro, redbrick exterior of this chic hotel—conveniently located near the TIFF Bell Lightbox—blends seamlessly with the historic architecture of the surrounding Theater District. **Pros:** custom package tours and experiences through the hotel; attentive staff goes above and beyond; outdoor terrace on 11th floor. **Cons:** popular hotel fills up fast; neighborhood can get noisy on weekends; some rooms have views of alleys. [$] *Rooms from: C$375* ✉ *30 Mercer St., Entertainment District* ☎ *416/345–9500, 866/345–9501* 🌐 *www.germainhotels.com/en/le-germain-hotel/toronto-mercer* 🛏 *122 rooms* 🍴 *No Meals* [M] *St. Andrew.*

Hyatt Regency Toronto

$$$$ | **HOTEL** | Request views of the CN Tower at this luxury hotel smack in the middle of the pulsating Entertainment District. **Pros:** closest large hotel to King Street West theaters; dozens of excellent restaurants and cinemas nearby; outdoor swimming pool and 24-hour fitness center. **Cons:** rooms can be small; guest rooms on lower floors facing King Street may be noisy; hotel could use a renovation. [$] *Rooms from: C$399* ✉ *370 King St. W, Entertainment District* ☎ *416/343–1234, 800/633–7313 in U.S.* 🌐 *www.hyatt.com/en-US/hotel/canada/hyatt-regency-toronto/torrt* 🛏 *426 rooms* 🍴 *No Meals* [M] *St. Andrew.*

InterContinental Toronto Centre

$$$$ | **HOTEL** | Attached to the Metro Toronto Convention Centre, this large but unassuming hotel is a good bet for visiting business executives, and vacationers can often find deals on weekends. **Pros:** not as stuffy as your usual business hotel; bright and airy lobby restaurant; near theaters and dining. **Cons:** no shopping nearby; expensive parking; busy during conferences. [$] *Rooms from: C$465* ✉ *225 Front St. W, west of University Ave., Entertainment District* ☎ *416/597–1400, 877/660–8550* 🌐 *www.torontocentre.intercontinental.com* 🛏 *576 rooms* 🍴 *No Meals* [M] *Union.*

★ **Residence Inn Toronto Downtown**

$$$$ | **HOTEL** | **FAMILY** | A big hit with families and extended-stay visitors, the modern suites at the Residence Inn Toronto Downtown come with full kitchens, spacious living and dining rooms, and comfortable bedrooms. **Pros:** close to Toronto's major attractions; a smart choice for families; pool, gym, and other amenities. **Cons:** breakfast buffet gets extremely crowded during peak season; can get very crowded on game days; valet parking only. [$] *Rooms from: C$409* ✉ *255 Wellington St. W, at Windsor St.,*

Entertainment District ☎ 416/581–1800 🌐 www.residenceinn.marriott.com 🛏 256 suites 🍴 Free Breakfast [M] Union.

★ Shangri-La Toronto

$$$$ | HOTEL | The Shangri-La Toronto combines the attention to service for which the brand is known with an art-focused twist on its traditional East-meets-West aesthetic. **Pros:** stellar ambience; noted art collection; luxurious amenities. **Cons:** pricey rates; standard rooms are small; service can be inconsistent. [$] *Rooms from: C$700 ✉ 188 University Ave., Entertainment District ☎ 647/788–8888 🌐 www.shangri-la.com/toronto/shangrila 🛏 202 rooms 🍴 No Meals [M] Osgoode or St. Andrew.*

Sheraton Centre

$$$$ | HOTEL | Views from this hotel in the city center are marvelous—to the south are the CN Tower and the Rogers Centre; to the north, both new and old city halls. **Pros:** underground access to PATH network; swimming pool is open late; walk to Four Seasons Centre. **Cons:** expensive parking and online access; hotel is overwhelmingly large; not all rooms have complimentary breakfast. [$] *Rooms from: C$389 ✉ 123 Queen St. W, at Bay St., Entertainment District ☎ 416/361–1000, 866/716–8101 🌐 www.sheratontoronto.com 🛏 1,377 rooms 🍴 No Meals [M] Osgoode.*

The SoHo Hotel and Residences

$$$$ | HOTEL | Saturated in pampering detail, the SoHo Met conjures luxury with Frette linens, down duvets, walk-in closets, marble bathrooms with heated floors, and Molton Brown bath products. **Pros:** high-tech touches like electronic do-not-disturb signs; stylish but not showy; spa is excellent. **Cons:** lap pool only 3 feet deep; construction noise; can be pricey. [$] *Rooms from: C$452 ✉ 318 Wellington St. W, east of Spadina Ave., Entertainment District ☎ 416/599–8800, 866/764–6638 🌐 www.sohohotel.ca 🛏 91 rooms 🍴 No Meals [M] St. Andrew.*

★ Toronto Marriott City Centre

$$$$ | HOTEL | FAMILY | This hotel is completely integrated into the Rogers Centre—the sports and entertainment dome that serves as the home of the Toronto Blue Jays—and 70 of the choicest rooms overlook the stadium itself. **Pros:** best place to watch Blue Jays baseball games; reasonable parking fee; good restaurant. **Cons:** little natural light in guest rooms overlooking field; the best rooms book up fast on game days; pick somewhere else if you're not a sports fan. [$] *Rooms from: C$359 ✉ 1 Blue Jays Way, at Front St. W, Entertainment District ☎ 416/341–7100, 800/237–1512 🌐 www.marriott.com/yyzcc 🛏 346 rooms 🍴 No Meals [M] Union.*

🍸 Nightlife

Traditionally this was Toronto's center for dance clubs cranking out house music. A few of the more popular clubs are still going strong (especially along Richmond Street), but the area is becoming less ostentatious as condos are erected and professionals in their thirties and forties move in. It's also home to three of the big Broadway-style theaters and tourist-oriented preshow restaurants with bars. The King West neighborhood has experienced a surge of swanky lounges, bars, and restaurants since the Toronto International Film Festival moved its headquarters to the area from Yorkville.

BARS

Lobby Lounge at the Shangri-La Toronto

COCKTAIL LOUNGES | The Shangri-La's spacious Lobby Lounge is famed for its high tea service complete with decadent pastry selection. The vibe gets swish by night as it transforms with live music, trendy cocktails, and delicious bar bites. *✉ Shangri-La Hotel, 188 University Ave. ☎ 647/788–8888 🌐 www.shangri-la.com [M] Osgoode.*

With its circular shape and striking glass canopy, Roy Thomson Hall is a classic of Toronto architecture.

Steam Whistle Brewery

BREWPUBS | The Steam Whistle Brewery, located on historic railway premises, makes an authentically crafted pilsner. There's a tasting room with a full food menu, a Munich-styled biergärten, and special events like Oktoberfest and the biannual (winter and summer) Roundhouse Craft Beer Festival. It's a great place to stop before or after a Blue Jays game. ⊠ *The Roundhouse, 255 Bremner Blvd., Entertainment District* ☎ *416/362–2337* ⊕ *www.steamwhistle.ca* Ⓜ *Union.*

COMEDY CLUBS

Yuk Yuk's

COMEDY CLUBS | Part of a Canadian comedy franchise, this venue headlines stand-up comedians on the rise (Jim Carrey and Russell Peters performed here on their way up), with covers usually between C$11 and C$25. Admission is C$5 on Tuesday for amateur night. The small space is often packed; getting cozy with your neighbors and sitting within spitting distance of the comedians is part of the appeal. Booking a dinner-and-show package guarantees better seats. ⊠ *224 Richmond St. W, 1½ blocks west of University Ave., Entertainment District* ☎ *416/967–6431* ⊕ *www.yukyuks.com* Ⓜ *Osgoode.*

🎟 Performing Arts

CLASSICAL MUSIC

★ Toronto Symphony Orchestra

MUSIC | Since 1922 this orchestra has achieved world acclaim with music directors such as Sir Ernest MacMillan, Seiji Ozawa, and Sir Andrew Davis. Canadian-born Peter Oundjian reinvigorated the ensemble and significantly strengthened its presence in the world when he was musical director from 2004 until 2018. Guest performers have included pianist Lang Lang, violinist Itzhak Perlman, and singer-songwriter Rufus Wainwright. Each season the orchestra screens a classic film, such as *Star Wars* or *Singin'* *in the Rain,* and plays the score as it runs. The TSO also presents about three concerts weekly at Roy Thomson Hall from October through June. ✉ *Roy Thomson Hall, 60 Simcoe St.* ☎ *416/593–1285 TSO information and tickets, 416/593–4828 Roy Thomson Hall ticket line* ⊕ *www.tso. ca* Ⓜ *St. Andrew.*

MAJOR VENUES
★ Roy Thomson Hall
CONCERTS | Toronto's premier concert hall, home of the Toronto Symphony Orchestra, also hosts visiting orchestras, popular entertainers, and Toronto International Film Festival red-carpet screenings. The 2,630-seat auditorium opened in 1982 and is named after Roy Thomson, who was born in Toronto and founded the publishing empire Thomson Corporation (now Thomson Reuters). ✉ *60 Simcoe St., at King St., Entertainment District* ☎ *416/872–4255 tickets, 416/593–4822 tours* ⊕ *www.roythomson.com* Ⓜ *St. Andrew.*

THEATERS
Factory Theatre
THEATER | This is the country's largest producer of exclusively Canadian plays. Many of the company's shows are world premieres that have gone on to tour Canada and win prestigious awards. ✉ *125 Bathurst St., at Adelaide St.* ☎ *416/504–9971* ⊕ *www.factorytheatre.ca.*

Princess of Wales
THEATER | State-of-the-art facilities and wonderful murals by American artist Frank Stella grace this 2,000-seat theater, built by father-and-son producer team Ed and David Mirvish in 1993 to accommodate the technically demanding musical *Miss Saigon.* Big-budget musicals like *Come from Away* and *The Book of Mormon* and plays such as *War Horse* are also showcased. ✉ *300 King St. W, at John St., Entertainment District* ☎ *416/872–1212 tickets, 800/461–3333 tickets* ⊕ *www.mirvish.com* Ⓜ *St. Andrew.*

Royal Alexandra
THEATER | The most historic of the Mirvish theaters, the "Royal Alex" has been the place to be seen in Toronto since 1907 and is the oldest continuously operating legitimate theater in North America. The restored and reconfigured theater features 1,244 plush red seats, gold plasterwork, and baroque swirls and flourishes that make theatergoing a refined experience. Charlton Heston made his debut here and Lawrence Olivier, Edith Piaf, Mary Pickford, Alan Bates, and John Gielgud have also graced the stage. Programs are a mix of blockbuster musicals and dramatic productions, some touring before or after Broadway appearances. ✉ *260 King St. W, Entertainment District* ☎ *416/872–1212 tickets, 800/461–3333 tickets* ⊕ *www.mirvish. com* Ⓜ *St. Andrew.*

👜 Shopping

While there aren't a ton of shops between the theaters and restaurants of King Street West between Bay and Spadina, those that are here are some of the city's best.

ANTIQUES
★ Toronto Antiques on King
ANTIQUES & COLLECTIBLES | The 6,000 square feet of this shop provides ample opportunity for browsing among the cabinets, shelves, and bins overflowing with porcelain, silver tea sets, Majolica pottery, Lalique vases, collectibles, and antique maps. It's also Toronto's leading purveyor of vintage and estate jewelry, making it a popular stop for those seeking out engagement rings. ✉ *284 King St. W, 2nd fl., at John St., Entertainment District* ☎ *416/260–9057* ⊕ *www. cynthiafindlay.com* 🕑 *Closed Mon.* Ⓜ *St. Andrew.*

OUTDOOR EQUIPMENT AND CLOTHING

★ Mountain Equipment Co-op

SPORTING GOODS | MEC (rhymes with "check"), the much-beloved Toronto spot for anyone remotely interested in camping, sells wares for minor and major expeditions. It's also a go-to spot for cycling gear. The vast assortment of backpacks means you can shop here for anything from a schoolbag to something that will accompany you on travels around the world. For C$5, you get lifetime membership to the co-op. ✉ *300 Queen St. W, Entertainment District* 🕿 *416/340–2667* ⊕ *www.mec.ca* Ⓜ *Osgoode.*

SPAS

Hammam Spa

SPAS | At Hammam Spa devoted Entertainment District clients soak up eucalyptus-scented steam in a 500-square-foot marble-tile Turkish bath following a massage or detoxifying algae wrap. ✉ *602 King St. W, at Portland St., Entertainment District* 🕿 *416/366–4772* ⊕ *www.hammamspa.ca* Ⓜ *Spadina or St. Andrew.*

Othership

SPAS | Open your pores in a luxurious dry sauna to reap the health benefits of the icy plunge baths at this hip health spa. Friendly staff are there to coach you along on your journey, with complimentary tea in the lounge to relax in between stations. ✉ *425 Adelaide St. W., Entertainment District* 🕿 *416/361–0101* ⊕ *www.othership.us* Ⓜ *St. Andrew.*

SPECIALTY GIFTS

★ TIFF Shop

OTHER SPECIALTY STORE | This sleek little gift shop at the TIFF Bell Lightbox, the cinematic HQ of the Toronto International Film Festival, stocks an ever-changing selection of cinematic paraphernalia linked to TIFF's current programming.

The exhaustive inventory of film books includes many difficult-to-find titles, biographies of just about every director you can think of, and studies of even the most obscure film movements. There are also unusual gift items and cute items for children. ✉ *TIFF Bell Lightbox, 350 King St. W, at John St., Entertainment District* 🕿 *416/934–7959* ⊕ *shop.tiff.net* Ⓜ *St. Andrew.*

Financial District

Toronto's Financial District has a wonderful architectural variety of skyscrapers. Most of the towers have bank branches, restaurants, and retail outlets on their ground floors and are connected to the PATH, an underground city of shops and tunnels. Unsurprisingly, Toronto's main office district is home to a lot of top-shelf restaurants ready to give those expense accounts a hearty workout.

Sights

★ Hockey Hall of Fame

OTHER MUSEUM | FAMILY | Even if you aren't a hockey fan, it's worth a trip to see this shrine to Canada's favorite sport. Exhibits include the original 1893 Stanley Cup, as well as displays of goalie masks, skate and stick collections, players' jerseys, video displays of big games, and a replica of the Montréal Canadiens' locker room. Grab a stick and test your speed and accuracy in the *Goodyear Shoot Out* virtual experience, or strap on a goalie mask and field shots from big-name players with the Shut Out computer simulation. The grand building, a former Bank of Montréal branch designed by architects Darling & Curry in 1885, is covered with beautiful ornamental details—note the richly carved Ohio stone and the Hermès figure supporting the chimney near the back. At the corner of Front and Yonge

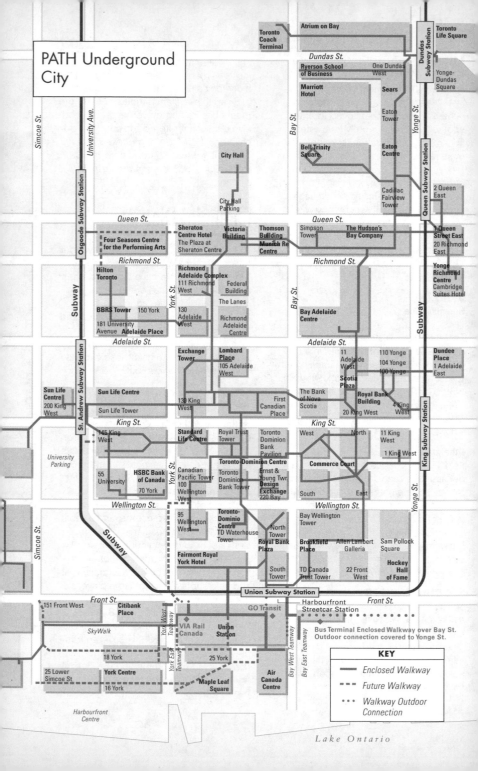

PATH Underground City

Simcoe St.

University Ave.

Osgoode Subway Station

Subway

St. Andrew Subway Station

Toronto Coach Terminal

Atrium on Bay

Dundas St.

Toronto Life Square

Dundas Subway Station

Yonge-Dundas Square

Ryerson School of Business

One Dundas West

Marriott Hotel

Sears

Bay St.

Eaton Tower

Yonge St.

Bell Trinity Square

Eaton Centre

Queen Subway Station

City Hall

City Hall Parking

Cadillac Fairview Tower

2 Queen East

Queen St.

Queen St.

Sheraton Centre Hotel The Plaza at Sheraton Centre

Victoria Building

Thomson Building

Munich Re Centre

Simpson Tower

The Hudson's Bay Company

1 Queen Street East

20 Richmond East

Four Seasons Centre for the Performing Arts

Subway

Richmond St.

Richmond St.

Yonge Richmond Centre Cambridge Suites Hotel

Hilton Toronto

York St.

Richmond Adelaide Complex 111 Richmond West

Federal Building

The Lanes

Richmond Adelaide Centre

Bay St.

Bay Adelaide Centre

BBRS Tower 181 University Avenue

150 York

130 Adelaide West

Adelaide Place

Adelaide St.

Adelaide St.

11 Adelaide West

110 Yonge

104 Yonge

100 Yonge

Dundee Place 1 Adelaide East

Exchange Tower

Lombard Place 105 Adelaide West

Scotia Plaza

King Subway Station

Sun Life Centre 200 King West

Sun Life Centre

Sun Life Tower

130 King West

First Canadian Place

The Bank of Nova Scotia

Royal Bank Building 20 King West

4 King West

King St.

King St.

145 King West

Standard Life Centre

Royal Trust Tower

Toronto Dominion Bank Pavilion

West

North

11 King West

1 King West

University Parking

55 University

HSBC Bank of Canada 70 York

Canadian Pacific Tower 100 Wellington West

Toronto-Dominion Bank Tower

Ernst & Young Twr. **Design Exchange** 220 Bay

Toronto-Dominion Centre

Commerce Court

South

East

Yonge St.

Wellington St.

Wellington St.

95 Wellington West

Toronto-Dominio Centre TD Waterhouse Tower

North Tower

Royal Bank Plaza

Bay Wellington Tower

Brookfield Place

Allen Lambert Galleria

Sam Pollock Square

Fairmont Royal York Hotel

South Tower

TD Canada Trust Tower

22 Front West

Hockey Hall of Fame

Simcoe St.

Subway

Front St.

Union Subway Station

Front St.

151 Front West

Citibank Place

York West Teamway

GO Transit

Harbourfront Streetcar Station

Bus Terminal Enclosed Walkway over Bay St.
Outdoor connection covered to Yonge St.

SkyWalk

VIA Rail Canada

Union Station

York East Teamway

Bay West Teamway

Bay East Teamway

18 York

25 York

25 Lower Simcoe St

York Centre

16 York

Maple Leaf Square

Air Canada Centre

Harbourfront Centre

KEY

—— Enclosed Walkway

- - - Future Walkway

••• Walkway Outdoor Connection

Lake Ontario

Streets, the impressive 17-foot bronze statue *Our Game* is a good photo op. ■ **TIP→ Entrance is through Brookfield Place on the lower level.** ✉ *Brookfield Place, 30 Yonge St., at Front St., Financial District* ☎ *416/360–7765* ⊕ *www.hhof. com* 🖼 *C$20* Ⓜ *Union.*

PATH

PEDESTRIAN MALL | This subterranean universe expanded from existing tunnels in the mid-1970s partly to replace the retail services in small buildings that were demolished to make way for the latest skyscrapers and partly to protect office workers from the harsh winter weather. As each major building went up, its developers agreed to connect their underground shopping areas with others and with the subway system. You can walk from beneath Union Station to the Fairmont Royal York hotel, the Toronto-Dominion Centre, First Canadian Place, the Sheraton Centre, The Bay and Eaton Centre, and City Hall without ever seeing the light of day, encountering everything from art exhibitions to buskers (the best are the winners of citywide auditions, who are licensed to perform throughout the subway system). According to Guinness World Records, the PATH is the biggest underground shopping complex in the world. Maps to guide you through the labyrinth are available in many downtown news and convenience stores. ⚠ **Be aware that large sections of the PATH may be closed on weekends when the office buildings are closed. This can cause particular problems for wheelchair users because not all sections of the underground are fully accessible.** ✉ *Financial District* Ⓜ *Queen's Park, St. Andrew, Osgoode, St. Andrew, Union, King, Queen, Dundas.*

Toronto-Dominion Centre

NOTABLE BUILDING | Ludwig Mies van der Rohe, a virtuoso of modern architecture, designed a significant portion of this six-building office complex, though he died before its completion in 1992. As with his acclaimed Seagram Building in New York, Mies stripped the TD Centre's buildings to their skin and bones of bronze-color glass and black-metal I-beams. The tallest building, the Toronto Dominion Bank Tower, is 56 stories high. The only architectural decoration consists of geometric repetition. Inside the low-rise square banking pavilion at King and Bay Streets is a virtually intact Mies interior. ✉ *66 Wellington St. W, Financial District* Ⓜ *St. Andrew.*

Union Station

TRAIN/TRAIN STATION | Historian Pierre Berton wrote that the planning of Union Station recalled "the love lavished on medieval churches." Indeed, this train depot can be regarded as a cathedral built to serve the god of steam. Designed in 1907 and opened by Edward, Prince of Wales, in 1927, it has a 40-foot-high coffered Guastavino tile ceiling and 22 pillars weighing 70 tons apiece. The floors are Tennessee marble laid in a herringbone pattern (the same that's in Grand Central Terminal in New York City). The main hall, with its lengthy concourse and light flooding in from arched windows at each end, was designed to evoke the majesty of the country that spread out by rail from this spot. The names of the towns and cities across Canada that were served by the country's two railway lines, Grand Trunk (incorporated into today's Canadian National) and Canadian Pacific, are inscribed on a frieze along the inside of the hall. As train travel declined, the building was nearly demolished in the 1970s, but public opposition proved strong enough to save it, and Union Station, a National Historic Site of Canada, is now a vital transport hub. Commuter, subway, and long-distance trains stop here. ✉ *65 Front St. W, between Bay and York Sts.* Ⓜ *Union.*

Did You Know?

The Skywalk connects
Union Station with the
Rogers Centre and the
CN Tower. It's also where
you'll find the station
for the Union Pearson
Express train to Pearson
Airport.

🍴 Restaurants

As one of the city's major business hubs, with plenty of hungry people at all times of the day, the Financial District has no shortage of places to eat. Venues cater to all the worker bees, from the assistant out on an espresso run to the executives with expense accounts.

Beer Bistro

$$ | EUROPEAN | A culinary tribute to beer, the creative menu here incorporates its star ingredient in every dish, but in subtle and clever ways without causing a malted-flavor overload. Start the hoppy journey with a taster flight of three draft beers, and follow that with a beer-bread pizza made with oatmeal stout or a bowl of mussels in a beer-based broth. **Known for:** cozy interior with an open kitchen; great patio in summer; delicious beer-focused desserts. $ *Average main: C$19* ✉ *18 King St. E, Financial District* ☎ *416/861–9872* ⊕ *www.beerbistro.com* Ⓜ *King.*

Bymark

$$$$ | CANADIAN | *Top Chef Canada* judge Mark McEwan has created a refined modern menu showcasing sophisticated seafood dishes, like whole roasted orata, and simply prepared meats, like the signature 6-ounce burger with molten Brie de Meaux, grilled porcini mushrooms, and shaved truffles. **Known for:** 5,000-bottle wine cellar; opulent interior; swank upstairs bar. $ *Average main: C$40* ✉ *66 Wellington St. W, Concourse Level, Financial District* ☎ *416/777–1144* ⊕ *www.mcewangroup. ca/bymark* ⊘ *Closed Sun. No lunch Sat.* Ⓜ *St. Andrew.*

Cactus Club Cafe

$$$ | STEAKHOUSE | The Toronto flagship of a Vancouver-based casual fine dining chain, this massive, modern Financial District spot is one of the district's trendiest dining destinations. Stellar dishes include butternut ravioli topped with sage, prawns, and truffle butter, and the "millionaire's cut"—a filet mignon with mashed potatoes and roasted asparagus. **Known for:** year-round patio; hip interior; fun appetizers to share. $ *Average main: C$25* ✉ *First Canadian Pl., 77 Adelaide St. W, Financial District* ☎ *647/748–2025* ⊕ *www.cactusclubcafe.com* Ⓜ *King.*

★ Canoe

$$$$ | CANADIAN | Huge dining-room windows frame breathtaking views of the Toronto Islands and the lake at this restaurant, on the 54th floor of the Toronto Dominion Bank Tower. Dishes like an appetizer of bison tartare with bannock bread and foie gras and entrées like crispy pork jowl roasted with chaga and an aged tournedos paired with truffled celeriac nod to both tradition and trend. **Known for:** classic desserts like a maple flan round out an exceptional meal; innovative tasting menus; food inspired by Canada. $ *Average main: C$44* ✉ *Toronto-Dominion Centre, 66 Wellington St. W, 54th fl., Financial District* ☎ *416/364–0054* ⊕ *www.canoerestaurant.com* ⊘ *Closed weekends* Ⓜ *King.*

The Chase

$$$$ | SEAFOOD | On the fifth floor of the historic Dineen Building, overlooking the Financial District, the Chase's marvelous lighting fixtures and floor-to-ceiling windows are a glamorous setting for the fish-and-oyster-focused menu. Dishes like whole fish or whole grilled octopus (also available as half) are meant for sharing, as are opulent seafood platters layered with shrimp, oysters, and king crab. **Known for:** elegant atmosphere; lovely rooftop patio; outstanding raw bar. $ *Average main: C$35* ✉ *10 Temperance St., 5th fl., Financial District* ☎ *647/348–7000* ⊕ *www.thechasetoronto.com* ⊘ *Closed Sun. No lunch Sat.* Ⓜ *King.*

★ Louix Louis
$$$$ | **FRENCH FUSION** | It's hard not to feel a little giddy sitting in the opulent whiskey-barrel-inspired dining room on the 31st floor of the St. Regis. Upward gazes are met with a swirling painted ceiling with floral glass chandeliers to mimic melting ice cubes. **Known for:** 400 brown spirits on the drink list, Canada's largest collection; 13-layer chocolate king's cake; salted brioche buns served straight from the pan. [$] *Average main: C$40* ✉ *325 Bay St., 31st fl., Financial District* ☎ *416/637–5550* 🌐 *louixlouis.com* [M] *Queen.*

Reds Wine Tavern
$$$ | **AMERICAN** | Repurposed wine bottles and wine glasses assembled as giant chandeliers hover above the tables at Reds Wine Tavern, offering a nod to the lengthy list of international wine picks. The menu is global, skipping from seared tuna tostadas with guacamole and daily curries to comfort foods like lobster grilled cheese and a variety of steaks. **Known for:** everything made from scratch; bread baked right on the premises; business lunches and after-work drinks. [$] *Average main: C$22* ✉ *77 Adelaide St. W, Financial District* ☎ *416/862–7337* 🌐 *www.redswinetavern.com* ⏲ *Closed Sat.–Sun.* [M] *King.*

Terroni
$$$ | **ITALIAN** | **FAMILY** | Open shelving lined with Italian provisions decorates this cool pizza joint, but it's the thin-crust pies, bubbled and blistered to perfection, that keep diners coming back. The menu suits all pizza lovers—from the simple Margherita to extravagant options like the Bruma, a white pizza with pancetta, egg, and black truffles. **Known for:** in addition to the pizza, the pastas are quite popular; the secluded back patio is lovely in good weather; stunning location inside a former courthouse. [$] *Average main: C$23* ✉ *57 Adelaide St. E, Financial District* ☎ *416/504–1992* 🌐 *www.terroni.ca* [M] *Queen.*

Walrus Pub & Beerhall
$$ | **CONTEMPORARY** | The Walrus brings life, and a hodgepodge of quirks, to the typically buttoned-up Financial District, giving young cubicle tycoons a space to blow off steam amid loud music, funky lighting, and stone-sculpted bar tables. Health-oriented gluten-free options like quinoa bowls topped with buttery grilled avocado even out the surf, turf, and Asian fusion–styled menu. **Known for:** selling 70–80 pizzas a day; happy hour specials from 2 to 5; ping-pong bar within a bar. [$] *Average main: C$20* ✉ *187 Bay St., Financial District* ☎ *416/363–7261* 🌐 *freehouse.co/walrus* [M] *King.*

Hotels

Cambridge Suites
$$$ | **HOTEL** | With just 12 suites per floor, this boutique hotel focuses on service: rooms are cleaned twice daily, and there's same-day dry cleaning and laundry, a rooftop gym with a view (and a whirlpool), and complimentary Wi-Fi. **Pros:** central location near many of the top attractions; social hour with discounted drinks; late checkout. **Cons:** parking is expensive; some dated decor; pets not allowed. [$] *Rooms from: C$297* ✉ *15 Richmond St. E, at Victoria St., Financial District* ☎ *416/368–1990, 800/463–1990* 🌐 *www.cambridgesuitestoronto.com* 🛏 *229 suites* 🍴 *No Meals* [M] *Queen.*

Executive Hotel Cosmopolitan
$$$ | **HOTEL** | Tucked away on a side street in the heart of Toronto, this ultra-boutique, all-suite hotel seamlessly blends a modern Eastern aesthetic with apartment-style amenities. **Pros:** central location; hipness factor; friendly staff. **Cons:** side streets dark at night; some rooms have so-so views; no on-site parking. [$] *Rooms from: C$289* ✉ *8 Colborne St.,*

at Yonge St. ☎ 416/350–2000, 888/388–3932 ⊕ www.cosmotoronto.com ⌁ 95 suites ⦿ No Meals Ⓜ King.

Fairmont Royal York

$$$$ | **HOTEL** | The Royal York, the tallest building in the British Commonwealth when it opened in 1929, remains one of the largest hotels in the city and a favorite of both royalty and Hollywood stars. **Pros:** lots of history; excellent health club (lap pool, whirlpool, saunas, well-appointed gym, and more); steps from Union Station. **Cons:** rooms can be small; charge for in-room Internet access; expensive parking. Ⓢ *Rooms from: C$499* ⊠ *100 Front St. W, at York St., Financial District* ☎ *416/368–2511, 866/540–4489* ⊕ *www.fairmont.com/royalyork* ⌁ *898 rooms* ⦿ *No Meals* Ⓜ *Union.*

One King West Hotel and Residence

$$$ | **HOTEL** | Made up entirely of suites, this 51-story tower is attached to the old Dominion Bank of Canada (circa 1914) in the city's downtown business and shopping core. **Pros:** great views from upper floors; central location; excellent service. **Cons:** not all suites have washer/dryer; parking is valet-only; pricey rates. Ⓢ *Rooms from: C$328* ⊠ *1 King St. W, at Yonge St., Financial District* ☎ *416/548–8100, 866/470–5464* ⊕ *www.onekingwest.com* ⌁ *340 suites* ⦿ *No Meals* Ⓜ *King.*

The Ritz-Carlton, Toronto

$$$$ | **HOTEL** | This Ritz has a great location—across from Roy Thomson Hall and smack-dab in the center of the Financial District—and a solid elegance, embellished with a Canadian motif of brass maple leaves and local woods. **Pros:** reliable Ritz service; top-of-the-line amenities; expansive rooms. **Cons:** five-star prices; expensive valet parking; pricey high tea. Ⓢ *Rooms from: C$469* ⊠ *181 Wellington St. W, Financial District*

☎ *416/585–2500* ⊕ *www.ritzcarlton.com/toronto* ⌁ *319 rooms* ⦿ *No Meals* Ⓜ *St. Andrew or Union.*

The St. Regis Toronto

$$$$ | **HOTEL** | Steeped in the glamour and tradition of the Astor family fortune, guests of both business and leisure class are greeted with a lobby adorned with cherry blossom ceiling panels and hyper-attentive check-in service. **Pros:** rooms with sleek dimmer switches and motorized curtains; saltwater infinity lap pool; meals at the opulent Louix Louis on the 31st floor. **Cons:** bathrobes lost their plushness; carpet in rooms need a good spot cleaning; loud air conditioners. Ⓢ *Rooms from: C$600* ⊠ *325 Bay St., Financial District* ☎ *416/306–5800* ⊕ *www.marriott.com/en-us/hotels/yyzxr-the-st-regis-toronto/overview* ⌁ *382 rooms* ⦿ *No Meals* Ⓜ *King.*

Nightlife

The bars and restaurants in the Financial District tend to be tony affairs, equally suited to schmoozing clients and blowing off steam after a long day at the office. After happy hour, this business- and high-rise-dense part of town quiets down.

BARS

Oliver and Bonacini Cafe Grill

BARS | If you want to "see and be seen" in the Financial District head to this vast restaurant and bar, which has a wraparound year-round patio facing both Front and Yonge Streets. The O&B has become the destination for Bay Street's movers and shakers. Check out the impressive cocktail menu. ⊠ *33 Yonge St., Financial District* ☎ *647/260–2070* ⊕ *www.oliverbonacini.com* Ⓜ *Union.*

● Shopping

Toronto's Financial District has a vast underground maze of shops—called the PATH—underneath its office towers. The tenants of this underground city are mostly the usual assortment of chain stores, with an occasional surprise. The network runs roughly from the Fairmont Royal York hotel near Union Station north to the Atrium at Bay and Dundas. The mall can be confusing for novices, so look for marked PATH signs.

CLOTHING

Moores Clothing For Men

MEN'S CLOTHING | This is the place to browse thousands of discounted Canadian-made dress pants, sport coats, and suits, including many famous labels. Sizes run from extra short to extra tall and from regular to oversize; the quality is solid and the service is good. ✉ *100 Yonge St., at King St., Financial District* ☎ *416/363-5442* ⊕ *www.mooresclothing.com* Ⓜ *King.*

Chapter 4

OLD TOWN AND THE DISTILLERY DISTRICT

Updated by
Kimberly Lyn

● Sights ★★★★☆ 🍴 Restaurants ★★★★☆ 🛏 Hotels ★★★☆☆ 🛍 Shopping ★★★★☆ 🍸 Nightlife ★★★☆☆

NEIGHBORHOOD SNAPSHOT

TOP EXPERIENCES

■ **Buy the best local produce:** Check out more than 100 vendors at the St. Lawrence Market, one of the world's best indoor food markets.

■ **Dive into the Distillery District:** Stroll along the cobblestone streets and take in the restored Victorian industrial buildings.

■ **Go out on the town:** An after-work crowd heads to atmospheric Old Town during the week, while weekends are for laid-back dining and atmosphere.

■ **Shop 'til you drop:** The Distillery District has become one of the city's most eclectic shopping destinations.

■ **Take in a show:** Some of the city's best small theater companies make their home in these distinct districts.

GETTING HERE

Old Town is in the eastern reaches of downtown, with the borders of Yonge Street to the west, Parliament Street to the east, Queen Street to the north, and Front Street to the south. Take the subway to King or Queen subway stations and walk five minutes east. You can also take the 504 King street-car or 501 Queen streetcar. The Distillery District is just east of Old Town, south of Front Street between Parliament and Cherry Streets. The area is pedestrian-only, but parking lots and street parking are available. On the TTC, take the Parliament bus south from Castle Frank subway station, the Cherry Street bus from Union station, or the 504 King streetcar to Parliament.

PLANNING YOUR TIME

Allow yourself at least two hours to wander the cobblestone streets and artisanal shops of the Distillery District. Be sure to see the modern art statues along Gristmill Lane and have a drink at Mill Street Brewery. You'll need at least half a day to wander the streets of Old Town. There are plenty of cool shops, restaurants, and art galleries in the neighborhood.

FUN FACT

■ Old Town Toronto contains the original 10 blocks of the city, making it an essential part of Toronto's identity. Historically known as the Town of York, you'll find the largest concentration of 19th-century buildings in the province here, such as Toronto's First Post Office and St. Lawrence Hall. Since 1803, St. Lawrence Market has helped anchor the heart and identity of the city and its surrounding community; to this day, it remains one of the world's best food markets and a culinary destination with more than 100 specialty vendors.

Old Town was one of the first neighborhoods in Toronto, getting its name in the early 1800s. Today, it's a mix of historic attractions—including Toronto's First Post Office, St. James Cathedral, and the world-famous St. Lawrence Market—and glittering new developments that bring with them some of the city's hottest restaurants and shops.

Farther east, the pedestrian-only Distillery District is one of Toronto's hottest entertainment destinations. Its cobblestone streets are filled with restored Victorian-era factories that once housed a large whiskey distillery and other businesses. The historic area is now filled with contemporary galleries, bustling pubs, and funky boutiques.

Old Town

A must-visit for history buffs and food freaks alike, the St. Lawrence Market started its storied life as Toronto's first city hall, then a prison. Now, the sprawling space is jammed with vendors offering all manner of meats, cheeses, breads, produce, and artisanal foods. Be sure to pick up a peameal (aka Canadian) bacon sandwich at Carousel Bakery, and check out the farmers' market on Saturday.

 Sights

Berczy Park

CITY PARK | This small but charming public space is home to a gorgeous two-tiered water fountain surrounded by 27 whimsical dog sculptures—and one cat—making it a delightful spot for a short respite and the perfect Instagram pic. Designed by celebrated Claude Cormier + Associés, the grand cast-iron fountain is encircled by the statues, whose eyes reverently look to the golden bone positioned at the top. Ample seating and grass make Berczy Park a relaxing oasis in the heart of the city where people and their dogs love to gather. During the colder months the fountain is turned off, but it remains worth the visit to see the dog statues cutely decorated with Santa hats for the holiday season. ⊠ *35 Wellington St. E, Old Town* Ⓜ *King.*

Flatiron Building

NOTABLE BUILDING | One of several wedge-shape buildings scattered around North America, Toronto's Flatiron occupies the triangular block between Wellington, Scott, and Front Streets. It was erected in 1892 as the head office of the Gooderham and Worts distilling company. On the back of the building, a witty trompe l'oeil mural by Derek Besant is drawn around the windows, making it appear that part of the building has been tacked up on the wall and is peeling off. ⊠ *49 Wellington St. E, between Church and Scott Sts., Old Town* Ⓜ *King*.

Museum of Illusions

OTHER MUSEUM | FAMILY | While this small museum may not pack as big of a punch as the city's larger arts destinations, it's a fun spot to bring the kids on a rainy afternoon. The various illusions will mess with everyone's minds, and there's everything from holograms to an anti-gravity room and a rotating room (where it looks like you're turned upside down). It's a great spot to snap some photos. ⊠ *132 Front St. E* ☎ *416/889–2285* ⊕ *museumofillusions.ca* 🎟 *C$27.24*.

St. James Cathedral

CHURCH | Bank towers dwarf it now, but this Anglican church with noble Gothic spires has the tallest steeple in Canada. Its illuminated clock once guided ships into the harbor. This is the fourth St. James Cathedral on the site; the third burned down in the Great Fire of 1849. As part of the church's bicentennial in 1997, a peal of 12 bells was installed. Stand near the church most Sundays after the 9 am service ends (about 10:10 am) and you'll be rewarded with a glorious concert of ringing bells. ⊠ *106 King St. E, Old Town* ☎ *416/364–7865* ⊕ *stjamescathedral.ca* Ⓜ *King*.

St. Lawrence Hall

NOTABLE BUILDING | Built in 1850 on the site of the area's first public meeting space, St. Lawrence Hall is Renaissance revival architecture at its finest. The hall was intended for musical performances and balls, and famed opera soprano Jenny Lind sang here, but it's also the spot where antislavery demonstrations were held, and where P. T. Barnum first presented Tom Thumb. Take time to admire the exterior of this architectural gem, now used for everything from concerts to wedding receptions. If you take part in one of the many walking tours of the area, you'll likely see photos (in the lounge on the third floor) featuring notable figures who performed, lectured, or were entertained here. ⊠ *157 King St. E, Old Town* ☎ *416/392–7809* ⊕ *www. stlawrencemarket.com* Ⓜ *Union*.

★ St. Lawrence Market

MARKET | St. Lawrence Market is an iconic and historical city landmark, renowned as one of the world's greatest food markets. Since the market's construction in the early 19th century, it has served many functions such as a post office, Toronto's original City Hall, and a police station. The market resides over two spaces; the South Market is located on the south side of Front Street in a large brick building that is home to more than 100 vendors. Many businesses are family owned and operated, specializing in local and imported goods, fresh produce, meat, seafood, and artisanal cheese. Grab something to eat from one of the popular take-out spots such as Buster's Sea Cove, Yip's Kitchen, or Carousel Bakery, which sells the famous Canadian bacon (also known as "peameal bacon") in a bun. The North Market is located on the north side of Front Street and is undergoing redevelopment, aiming for a 2023 completion. The popular, weekly Saturday Farmers' Market is temporarily relocated to a building just south of the South Market. As of May 2022, the weekly Sunday Antiques Market has ceased operation. ⊠ *Front and Jarvis Sts., Old Town* ☎ *416/392–7219* ⊕ *www. stlawrencemarket.com* 🕙 *Closed Mon.* Ⓜ *Union*.

Toronto's First Post Office

GOVERNMENT BUILDING | FAMILY | This small working post office dates from 1833 and still functions with quill pens, ink

The outstanding St. Lawrence Market, one of the finest in the world, sells a huge variety of local and imported culinary specialties.

pots, and sealing wax—you can use the old-fashioned equipment to send a letter for C$5 plus postage stamp. Exhibits include reproductions of letters from the 1830s. Distinctive cancellation stamps are used on all outgoing letters. ⊠ 260 Adelaide St. E, Old Town ☎ 416/865–1833 ⊕ www.townofyork.com Ⓜ King.

Restaurants

Bindia Indian Bistro

$$$ | INDIAN | FAMILY | Bindia serves delicious North Indian fare that will make your taste buds sing the moment you taste juicy meat and freshly baked naan cooked in its tandoor oven. This neighborhood staple is conveniently located in the heart of the St. Lawrence Market, offering casual, warm, and friendly service. **Known for:** juicy tandoori jumbo prawns; nouveau North Indian cuisine; Friday night community jazz performances. Ⓢ Average main: C$22 ⊠ 15 Market St., Old Town ☎ 416/863-0000 ⊕ bindia. ca Ⓜ Union.

The Carbon Bar

$$$ | BARBECUE | The scent of smoky Texas-style barbecue from Carbon Bar's wood firepit immediately hits your nose and activates your salivary glands when you enter the spacious, sophisticated, yet laid-back spot. Ordering the Pitmaster barbecue platter is a must: it comes with five types of meat and is worth sharing with a group or tackling alone if you dare. **Known for:** casual and spacious venue great for groups; one of the largest bourbon listings in Toronto; Pitmaster platter with five types of meat. Ⓢ Average main: C$30 ⊠ 99 Queen St. E, Old Town ☎ 416/947-7000 ⊕ thecarbonbar.ca ♥ Closed Mon. Ⓜ Queen.

Nami Japanese Restaurant

$$$$ | JAPANESE | Established in 1984, Nami is one of the first authentic Japanese restaurants in Toronto and continues to serve fresh sushi sourced locally and from Japan to a loyal clientele. Kimono-clad servers and wood booths replicate an older version of Kyoto. **Known for:** authentic Wagyu beef; sukiyaki served in

Sights ▼

1 Berczy Park **B3**
2 Flatiron Building......... **B3**
3 Museum of Illusions.... **D3**
4 Ontario Spring Water
  Sake Company
  (IZUMI Brewery)......... **E3**
5 St. James Cathedral..... **C2**
6 St. Lawrence Hall........ **C2**
7 St. Lawrence Market.... **C3**
8 Toronto's First
  Post Office............... **D2**

Restaurants ▼

1 Bindia Indian Bistro **C3**
2 The Carbon Bar.......... **C1**
3 El Catrin.................. **E3**
4 Madrina Bar y Tapas.... **E3**
5 Nami Japanese
  Restaurant............... **B2**
6 Pearl Diver............... **C2**
7 PJ O'Brien............... **B3**
8 Restaurant 20
  Victoria.................. **B2**

Quick Bites ▼

1 Brick Street Bakery **E3**
2 NEO COFFEE BAR....... **D2**
3 Roselle Desserts......... **E2**
4 Scooped by
  Demetres **E3**

Hotels ▼

1 The Omni
  King Edward Hotel...... **B2**

a traditional Japanese hot iron pot; one of the first Japanese restaurants in Toronto. [$] *Average main: C$50* ✉ *55 Adelaide St. E* ☎ *416/362–7373* 🌐 *namirestaurant.ca* 🕒 *Closed Sun. No lunch Sat.* [M] *King.*

Pearl Diver
$$$$ | **SEAFOOD** | This neighborhood staple has been serving fresh and delicious seafood dishes for more than 15 years. Oysters make up the backbone of Pearl Diver's menu, alongside popular menu items like pan-seared steelhead trout, the PD burger, and the mouthwatering seafood tower adorned with oysters, pickled mussels, crab legs, and more. **Known for:** freshly sourced and expertly shucked oysters; delicious two-tier seafood tower; casual, homestyle vibe. [$] *Average main: C$35* ✉ *100 Adelaide St. E* ☎ *416/366–7827* 🌐 *pearldiver.to* 🕒 *Closed Mon.* [M] *King.*

PJ O'Brien
$$$ | **IRISH** | This traditional pub will make you feel like you're in Dublin the second you step inside. Tuck into an authentic meal of Irish Kilkenny Ale–battered fish-and-chips, beef-and-Guinness stew, and bread pudding steeped in whiskey and custard, just like Gran made. **Known for:** broken up into different areas for music lovers, sports fans, and other groups; dependably good pub grub; affable staff. [$] *Average main: C$22* ✉ *39 Colborne St., Old Town* ☎ *416/815–7562* 🌐 *www.pjobrien.com* 🕒 *Closed Sun. and Mon.* [M] *King.*

★ **Restaurant 20 Victoria**
$$$$ | **EUROPEAN** | This intimate establishment serves refined, European classic fare made with thought and painstaking care, beautifully presented and delicious on the palate. Warm and friendly staff greet guests inside this modern space with old-world charm; here, the pace is relaxed, and the restaurant's minimalist kitchen is on full display. **Known for:** attentive and friendly service and staff; seasonal tasting menu; small and intimate romantic setting. [$] *Average main: C$C$125* ✉ *20 Victoria St.* ☎ *416/804–6066* 🌐 *instagram.com/twentyvictoria* 🕒 *Closed Sat.–Mon.* [M] *King.*

Coffee and Quick Bites

NEO COFFEE BAR
$ | **CAFÉ** | Located on a quiet side street, NEO COFFEE BAR is a well-loved shop that serves quality coffees and teas, with a focus on creating Japanese fusion pastries. Opened in 2015, the shop's beautiful space combines the best of Japanese and Scandinavian design with its warm wood finishes, concrete surfaces, and minimalist furniture, which has won it design accolades. **Known for:** seasonal drinks and pastries; house-made roll cakes; matcha latte made from Uji Matcha from Kyoto. [$] *Average main: C$5* ✉ *161 Frederick St., Suite 100, Old Town* ☎ *647/348–8811* 🌐 *www.neocoffeebar.com* ☞ *Debit and credit cards only* [M] *King.*

★ **Roselle Desserts**
$ | **DESSERTS** | Fulfill your dessert fantasies by picking up a sweet treat from Roselle, one of the city's finest dessert shops. Stephanie Duong and Bruce Lee opened Roselle in 2015; since then, they've fed the sweet cravings of Torontonians with their playful take on classic flavors using French techniques. **Known for:** creating playful desserts using French techniques; seasonal pavlova using fresh fruit; rotating cake cup flavors. [$] *Average main: C$10* ✉ *362 King St. E, Old Town* ☎ *416/368–8188* 🌐 *www.roselleto.com* 🕒 *Closed Mon.–Thurs.* ☞ *Debit and credit cards only* [M] *King.*

Hotels

The Omni King Edward Hotel
$$$ | **HOTEL** | Toronto's landmark "King Eddy" Hotel, which has hosted the well-heeled for over a century, continues to be a favorite choice for special occasions

and a nod to grand hotels of the past. **Pros:** mix of historic charm with modern luxury; central location; friendly service. **Cons:** expensive parking is valet-only; charge for online access; lots of street traffic. Ⓢ *Rooms from: C$309* ✉ *37 King St. E, east of Yonge St., Old Town* ☎ *416/863–9700, 888/444–6664* ⊕ *www. omnihotels.com/hotels/toronto-king-edward* ⇨ *301 rooms* |❍| *No Meals* Ⓜ *King.*

🍸 Nightlife

BARS

Betty's

BARS | This laid-back dive bar has an excellent selection of draft beers and classic pub fare, from poutine to nachos and chicken wings. It's a fun spot to watch sports. ✉ *240 King St. E, Old Town* ☎ *416/368–1300* ⊕ *www.bettystoronto. com* Ⓜ *King.*

Bier Markt

BARS | With more than 150 beers from 30 countries, including 50 on tap, this enormous restaurant/bar has a corner on the international beer market, but the best thing about it is the oversize year-round sidewalk patio on the Esplanade, ideal for an afternoon brew. ∎ **TIP→ The lines are ridiculous on weekends—do as the locals do and go midweek instead.** ✉ *58 The Esplanade, just west of Church St., Old Town* ☎ *416/862–7575* ⊕ *www. thebiermarkt.com* Ⓜ *Union or King.*

C'est What

BARS | In a cozy underground setting that's part beer cellar, part library, and part pool hall, C'est What offers more than 40 taps of Canadian beer, plus a menu of globally inspired pub grub. The main room is home to a couple of pool tables and a comfy fireplace area lined with couches, while an adjoining room hosts live folk, rock, and roots acts a few times a week. ✉ *67 Front St. E, Old Town* ☎ *416/867–9499* ⊕ *www.cestwhat.com* ◷ *Closed Mon.* Ⓜ *Union.*

Pravda Vodka Bar

BARS | Once a Soviet themed-bar, Pravda now channels the opulence of a 1920s speakeasy; it offers happy hour cocktails and operates as a supper club in the early evening, which is popular with the after-work crowd. As the night wears on, it transforms into a lively nightclub with a DJ and performances by an aerialist, belly dancer, or live musicians. Take a tour of its glass-encased walk-in freezer on the second floor, where you can don a fur coat and sample more than 70 vodka brands from around the world, such as French, Latvian, and Polish vodkas, each for a fee. ✉ *44 Wellington St. E, between Church and Yonge Sts., Old Town* ☎ *416/366–0303* ⊕ *www.pravdavodkabar. com* ◷ *Closed Sun.–Wed.* Ⓜ *King.*

The Sultan's Tent and Cafe Moroc

THEMED ENTERTAINMENT | Not far from the historic St. Lawrence Market, the Sultan's Tent and its front bar, Cafe Moroc, re-create a traditional Moroccan banquet atmosphere, complete with plush divans and metal lanterns. In addition to wine and beer, they have a specialty cocktail list that puts a North African spin on classic drinks, like the Arabian Caesar or the Moroccan old-fashioned. There's live music and belly dancers every evening. ✉ *49 Front St. E, Old Town* ☎ *416/961– 0601* ⊕ *www.thesultanstent.com* Ⓜ *King.*

🎭 Performing Arts

MAJOR VENUES

Meridian Hall

ARTS CENTERS | Formerly the Sony Centre, this iconic 3,172-seat hall was deemed a heritage building by the City of Toronto in 2008 and boasts an international program of diverse yet mostly mainstream artists. Paul Simon, the Just for Laughs Comedy Festival, the Alvin Ailey American Dance Theater, and RuPaul's Drag Race Werq the World Tour are among those who have graced the hall's stage. ✉ *1 Front St. E, at Yonge St., Old Town* ☎ *416/368– 6161 box office, 800/708–6754 toll free*

⊕ *tolive.com/Meridian-Hall* Ⓜ *Union or King.*

THEATERS
Canadian Stage
THEATER | Canadian Stage is the country's leading contemporary performing arts organization, focusing on cross-disciplinary works that integrate theater, dance, film, visual arts, and more to reflect the complexity and cultural richness of Canada. It stages productions at the Bluma Appel Theatre (✉ *27 Front St. E*), which seats 867, and the more intimate Berkeley Street Theatre (✉ *26 Berkeley St.*), which has a capacity of 244 seats. ✉ *Bluma Appel Theatre, 27 Front St. E, Old Town* ☎ *416/368–3110 box office* ⊕ *www. canadianstage.com* Ⓜ *Union.*

Théâtre Français de Toronto
THEATER | High-quality French-language drama—with English subtitles—is performed at this theater, whose French and French-Canadian repertoire ranges from classical to contemporary. A children's play and a teen show are part of the season, which features about a half dozen plays. ✉ *Berkeley Street Theatre, 26 Berkeley St., Old Town* ☎ *416/534–6604* ⊕ *www.theatrefrancais.com* Ⓜ *King.*

Young People's Theatre
THEATER | FAMILY | YPT is Canada's largest and oldest professional theater for young people, which produces arts and theater education programming. Professional actors perform contemporary pieces that are relevant and kid-focused, from a heavily interactive romp like *Where the Wild Things Are* to a dramatic thought-provoker like *Hana's Suitcase*—the story of a young girl living during the Holocaust. Productions aren't condescending, nor do they compromise on dramatic integrity. They are as entertaining for adults as for kids. ✉ *165 Front St. E, between Jarvis and Sherbourne Sts., Old Town* ☎ *416/862–2222 box office* ⊕ *www.youngpeoplestheatre.org* Ⓜ *King or Union.*

👜 Shopping

ART AND CRAFTS GALLERIES
Feheley Fine Arts
ART GALLERIES | Browse traditional, as well as contemporary and even avant-garde art from the Canadian Arctic—a far cry from the traditional whale carvings and stone-cut prints you may expect—at this family-owned gallery founded in 1961. ✉ *65 George St., at King St. E, Old Town* ☎ *416/323–1373* ⊕ *www.feheleyfinearts. com* 🕙 *Closed Sun. and Mon.* Ⓜ *King.*

AUCTIONS
Waddington's
AUCTIONS | Canada's biggest auction house hosts more than 100 auctions every year, in person and online. They feature Canadian and international fine art, including many prestigious collector and catalogue auctions; in addition, special auctions include Indigenous art, jewelry, and decorative arts. ✉ *275 King St. E, 2nd fl., Old Town* ☎ *416/504–9100, 877/504–5700* ⊕ *www.waddingtons.ca* 🕙 *Closed Sat.* Ⓜ *King, then 504 streetcar east.*

BOOKS
D & E Lake Ltd.
BOOKS | One of the city's longest-running rare bookstores occupies a nondescript brick building overflowing with more than 50,000 titles dating from the Renaissance to the present day. Family owned and operated since 1978, you will be astounded by the innumerable variety of books that cover every inch of this building ranging from art to fiction, travel to politics. Knowledgeable and friendly staff are ready to recommend fascinating reads. D & E Lake also specializes in selling fine art, coins, and modern and vintage maps and posters—all as impressive as the shop's book collection. ✉ *239 King St. E, Old Town* ☎ *416/863–9930* ⊕ *delakeltd.com* Ⓜ *King.*

CLOTHING

HAVEN

MEN'S CLOTHING | For more than 10 years, HAVEN has been the go-to shop for premium and modern men's clothing, shoes, and accessories, as well as hard-to-find Japanese labels such as Junya Watanabe, NEEDLES, and KAPITAL. The store occupies an expansive, 1,500-square-foot, light-filled space with soaring ceilings and knowledgeable, friendly staff. Exclusively available in store is HAVEN's namesake brand; inspired by classic Canadian designs, it offers utilitarian clothing in cotton, wool, and Gore-Tex to complement the country's climate. ⊠ *90 Richmond St. E, 2nd fl., Old Town* ☎ *416/901-1195* ⊕ *havenshop.com* Ⓜ *Queen.*

HOME DECOR

Flatiron's Christmas Market

HOUSEWARES | Flatiron's Christmas Market is the only year-round Christmas store in Old Town Toronto and is one of the oldest gift shops in the neighborhood. The owners are proud supporters and members of the LGBTQ+ community; their small shop is packed full of imported and handmade European Christmas decorations, as well as off-season gifts such as Canadian souvenirs, home decor, and more. Its novelty and cute offerings have attracted celebrity clientele such as Liza Minnelli, Catherine Zeta-Jones, and Halle Berry—this is the perfect spot to buy small and unique gifts for your loved ones back home. ⊠ *35 Jarvis St., Old Town* ☎ *416/365-1506* ⊘ *Closed Sun. and Mon.* Ⓜ *King.*

Distillery District

This restored collection of Victorian industrial buildings, complete with cobblestone lanes, has become a hub of independent restaurants, boutiques, and art spaces, with the carefully preserved former Gooderham and Worts Distillery (founded in 1832) reborn as a cultural center. The 13-acre site includes 47 19th-century buildings and a pedestrian-only village that houses more than 100 tenants—including galleries, artist studios and workshops, shops, breweries, upscale eateries, bars, and cafés. Live music, outdoor exhibitions, fairs, and special events take place year-round, but summer months are the best time to visit. Hour-long walking tours are offered during the week.

◉ Sights

Ontario Spring Water Sake Company (IZUMI Brewery)

BREWERY | Toronto's first sake brewery uses natural Ontario spring water from Muskoka and traditional Japanese techniques to create its award-winning sake under the name IZUMI Brewery. The company has a small tasting bar and retail shop with products made with the sake *kasu* (the lees, or yeast, leftover from fermentation), such as soaps, salad dressings, and miso soup, as well as ceramics and sake glassware. You can also take a tour of the brewery on weekends to learn about Junmai (pure rice) and Namazake (unpasteurized sake), to find out how sake is made, and to enjoy a guided tasting of four sakes. ⊠ *51 Gristmill La., Bldg. 4, Distillery District* ☎ *416/365-7253* ⊕ *www.ontariosake. com* 🎫 *Tours C$19.95* ⊘ *Closed Mon. and Tues.*

🍴 Restaurants

★ El Catrin

$$$ | **MEXICAN** | With a 5,000-square-foot, year-round patio and stunning floor-to-ceiling murals, El Catrin is the hottest place in the Distillery District. Delicious eats include traditional tacos al pastor with shaved pork and pineapple salsa, ceviche, 24-hour-braised short rib in mole sauce, and guacamole prepared tableside. **Known for:** adventurous diners can

sample flash-fried crickets; more than 100 types of mescal and tequila available; huge patio open year-round. $ *Average main: C$25* ⊠ *18 Tank House La., Distillery District* ☎ *416/203–2121* ⊕ *www.elcatrin.ca* Ⓜ *Union.*

Madrina Bar y Tapas

$$$$ | TAPAS | Enjoy classic and modern Catalan tapas at this lively restaurant where guests are taken on a tasting journey by executive chef Ramon Simarro. Shareable plates allow for maximum sampling of Madrina's menu, alongside a large selection of Spanish wines and gins (more than 70) to complement your meal. **Known for:** steak tartare on roasted marrow bone, one of the best in the city; lively day and nighttime atmosphere; more than 70 types of gins. $ *Average main: C$70* ⊠ *2 Trinity St.* ☎ *416/548–8055* ⊕ *www.madrinatapas.com* Ⓜ *Union.*

🍩 Coffee and Quick Bites

Brick Street Bakery

$ | BAKERY | If the smell of fresh bread and buttery croissants doesn't draw you into this charming bakery, the decadent sweets on display—like cinnamon buns, butter tarts, or scones—certainly will. For heartier appetites there are items like pulled pork sandwiches and steak-and-stout pie. **Known for:** no indoor seating and minimal outdoor seating, most people take their meals to go; handcrafted sandwiches and soups; freshest bread in the neighborhood. $ *Average main: C$9* ⊠ *27 Trinity St., Distillery District* ☎ *416/214–4949* ⊕ *www.brickstreetbakery.com* Ⓜ *Union.*

Scooped by Demetres

$ | ICE CREAM | Try adventurous, rich ice cream and vegan sorbetto flavors such as Mango Passion Fruit, Cajeta Swirled Goat Cheese, or Roses of Paradise at Scooped by Demetres. This spot is owned and operated by beloved Toronto dessert shop Demetres, which has been creating artisanal, handcrafted ice creams for more than 30 years. **Known for:** freshly made waffle cones in-store; vegan sorbetto flavors; rotating menu of 20 memorable ice cream flavors. $ *Average main: C$6* ⊠ *46 Gristmill La., Distillery District* ☎ *416/988–2482* ⊕ *scoopedbydemetres.com* Ⓜ *Union.*

🍸 Nightlife

BARS
Mill Street Brewery

BREWPUBS | Brewing some of Toronto's most widely enjoyed craft beers, Mill Street Brewery runs a pair of adjoining brewpubs in the Distillery District. Enter off Tank House Lane to find the Mill Street Brew Pub, home of dressed-up bar eats, or veer down a side alley to feast at the modern Beer Hall. Both bars have several beer taps, with choices ranging from Mill Street staples like Organic Lager and Tankhouse Ale to seasonal and one-off beers. A bottle shop attached to the Brew Pub offers a selection of Mill Street offerings to go. ⊠ *21 Tank House La.* ☎ *416/681–0338* ⊕ *millstreetbrewery.com/en/pubs/mill-street-toronto.*

🎭 Performing Arts

THEATERS
★ Soulpepper Theatre Company

THEATER | Established in 1998 by some of Canada's leading theater artists, Soulpepper is Toronto's largest not-for-profit theater company. It produces classic and newly commissioned plays, musicals, and concerts year-round. ⊠ *Young Centre for the Performing Arts, 50 Tank House La., Distillery District* ☎ *416/866–8666 box office, 888/898–1188 toll free* ⊕ *www.soulpepper.ca* ⊙ *Closed Mon.*

🛍 Shopping

ART GALLERIES
Corkin Gallery

ART GALLERIES | Founded in 1979, Corkin Gallery is one of the most fascinating in the city with its mission to showcase art spanning the 20th and 21st centuries. The gallery's unique, industrial space complements the experience of viewing its roster of artists, such as Barbara Astman and David Urban, and spanning media from painting to photography, sculpture, and mixed media. ✉ *7 Tank House La., Distillery District* ☎ *416/979–1980* ⊕ *www.corkingallery.com* ⊗ *Closed Sun. and Mon.* Ⓜ *King.*

CLOTHING
★ Gotstyle

MIXED CLOTHING | This Torontonian start-up has hit the nail on the head, providing stylish men's clothes—Tiger of Sweden, Sand Copenhagen, and John Varvatos—to residents of the city's downtown condos. This huge airy branch carries ladies' clothing as well, including brands like Melissa Nepton, Soia & Kyo, and Hilary MacMillan. Head up to the lush purple-carpeted mezzanine level for business and evening wear and a round on the purple pool table. ✉ *21 Trinity St., Distillery District* ☎ *416/260–9696* ⊕ *www.gotstyle.com* Ⓜ *King or Castle Frank.*

JEWELRY AND ACCESSORIES
Corktown Designs

JEWELRY & WATCHES | Most of the reasonably priced jewelry at this Distillery District shop is Canadian-designed, and all of it is unique and handmade. Pieces range from inexpensive glass-and-silver pendants to Swiss-made stainless steel rings and pricier pieces set with pearls and other semiprecious stones. ✉ *5 Trinity St., Distillery District* ☎ *416/861–3020* ⊕ *www.corktowndesigns.com* Ⓜ *King.*

SHOES, HANDBAGS, AND LEATHER GOODS
John Fluevog

SHOES | Fluevog's funky shoes are perfectly displayed in this roughly converted high-ceilinged industrial space. The building was once the distillery boiler house, which explains the three-story brick oven that takes up a third of the floor-space, and the safety ladder leading to an overhead catwalk. Take a seat on the stunning embossed leather couch when trying on the fun, quirky merchandise. ✉ *4 Trinity St., Distillery District* ☎ *416/583–1970* ⊕ *www.fluevog.com* Ⓜ *King or Castle Frank.*

WINE AND SPECIALTY FOOD
★ Soma Chocolatemaker

CHOCOLATE | You can almost satisfy your sweet tooth just by inhaling the delicate wafts of chocolate, dried fruits, and roasted nuts in this gourmet chocolate shop that specializes in fair-trade ingredients. Big sellers include truffles, mango chili and raspberry fruit bars, and gelato. For something different, try the Bicerin, a thick mixture of melted chocolate, espresso, and whipped cream. ✉ *32 Tank House La., Distillery District* ☎ *416/815–7662* ⊕ *www.somachocolate.com* Ⓜ *King or Castle Frank.*

Chapter 5

YONGE-DUNDAS SQUARE AREA

Updated by
Kimberly Lyn

◉ Sights	🍴 Restaurants	🏨 Hotels	🛍 Shopping	🍸 Nightlife
★★★☆☆	★★★★☆	★★★★★	★★★★★	★★☆☆☆

NEIGHBORHOOD SNAPSHOT

TOP EXPERIENCES

■ **The lights are much brighter here:** Take in the hustle and bustle of Yonge-Dundas Square, Toronto's answer to Times Square.

■ **The best in window shopping:** Do some browsing at the Eaton Centre, the city's much-loved (and sometimes vilified) shopping center.

■ **Two theaters for the price of one:** Don't miss a chance to see the world's last stacked Victorian theaters: the Elgin and the Winter Garden.

■ **Take a trip around the world:** Enjoy international foods and lively music from street musicians at larger-than-life Yonge-Dundas Square.

■ **Learn about the fabric of Canada:** Explore fashion history at the Textile Museum of Canada, which has 15,000 artifacts from across the globe.

■ **The sound of music:** Near-perfect acoustics and excellent sight lines are the draw at Canada's best concert theater, Massey Hall.

GETTING HERE

The subway stations Dundas and Queen, conveniently at either end of the Eaton Centre, are the main transportation hubs for this part of the city. There are also streetcar lines running along Dundas and Queen Streets, linking this area to Chinatown and Kensington Market, and Queen West, respectively. This is one of the busiest intersections in the city, so parking is tougher to find the closer you get to Yonge and Dundas, though there is a garage underneath the Eaton Centre.

PLANNING YOUR TIME

Depending on your patience and the contents of your wallet, you could spend anywhere from 1 to 10 hours in the colossal Eaton Centre, shopping until you drop. The Textile Museum of Canada merits an hour, and you could easily while away an afternoon people-watching in Yonge-Dundas Square.

FUN FACT

■ Dubbed "the heart of the city," this popular area draws millions of visitors due to its central location and access to an array of dining and entertainment options and major retail shops. The Yonge and Dundas Streets intersection is the busiest in Canada; here you can walk through the city's first pedestrian scramble, installed in 2008. Adjacent is Yonge-Dundas Square, a 1 acre outdoor and public event space, which holds free events throughout the year and has seen many memorable moments; in 2006, Beyoncé performed a free concert here and in 2019 it overflowed with basketball fans celebrating the Toronto Raptors' NBA championship win. Many major TV shows and movies have filmed in the area—such as *The Shape of Water* (2017) and *Suicide Squad* (2016)—attracted to the neighborhood's history, bright lights, and vibrant nature.

Yonge Street is Toronto's main artery: it starts at Lake Ontario and slices the city in half as it travels through downtown's Yonge-Dundas Square and north to the suburbs. There's usually a crowd gathered below the enormous billboards and flashy lights in the Square, especially in the summer, when the large public area comes alive with outdoor festivals and entertainment.

All visitors tend to end up here at some point during their trip. Usually it's the enticement of nonstop shopping in the Eaton Centre, Toronto's biggest downtown shopping mall, or the shops lining Yonge Street nearby. Others see the allure of outdoor markets, ethnic food festivals, and street concerts in larger-than-life Yonge-Dundas Square.

👁 Sights

★ Textile Museum of Canada
OTHER MUSEUM | With a more than 45-year history of exploring ideas and building cultural understanding through its collection of 15,000 artifacts from across the globe, this boutique museum's exhibitions and programming connect contemporary art and design to international textile traditions. ✉ 55 Centre Ave., Dundas Square Area ☎ 416/599–5321 ⊕ www.textilemuseum.ca 🎟 C$15 🕐 Closed Sun.–Tues. Ⓜ St. Patrick.

★ Yonge-Dundas Square
PLAZA/SQUARE | A public square at a major downtown crossroads, Toronto's answer to New York's Times Square is surrounded by oversize billboards and bright light displays. Visitors and locals converge on the tables and chairs that are scattered across the square when the weather is fine, and kids (and the young at heart) frolic in the 20 water fountains that shoot out of the cement floor like miniature geysers. From May to October, there's something happening every weekend—it could be an artisan market, an open-air film viewing, a summertime festival, or a live musical performance. ✉ 1 Dundas St. E, Dundas Square Area ⊕ www.ydsquare.ca Ⓜ Dundas.

🍴 Restaurants

Dundas Square has bright neon screens beaming down the newest fashions and trends. The area is dominated by big chains and Asian franchises but also a variety of neighborhood spots.

Barberian's Steak House
$$$$ | **STEAKHOUSE** | A Toronto landmark where wheeling, dealing, and lots of eating have gone on since 1959, Barberian's also has a romantic history:

Sights ▼

1 Textile Museum
  of Canada................ **B4**
2 Yonge-Dundas
  Square **D3**

Restaurants ▼

1 Barberian's
  Steak House.............. **C3**
2 Hong Shing **B3**
3 Kinka Izakaya **E2**
4 Lai Wah Heen **B3**
5 Salad King **C3**

Quick Bites ▼

1 Egg Club **E3**
2 GB Hand-Pulled
  Noodle **C3**
3 TSURIJI Dundas **B3**
4 Uncle Tetsu's Japanese
  Cheesecake.............. **C3**
5 World Food Market..... **D3**

Hotels ▼

1 Chelsea Hotel **C2**
2 DoubleTree by Hilton
  Downtown............... **B4**
3 Marriott Eaton Centre...**C4**
4 Pantages Hotel.......... **D4**
5 Saint James Hotel **D2**

Elizabeth Taylor and Richard Burton got engaged here (for the first time). It's one of the oldest steak houses in the city, and the menu is full of classic dishes, such as Caesar salad and jumbo shrimp cocktail. **Known for:** beautifully maintained midcentury modern decor; steaks ranging from porterhouse to filet mignon; enormous underground wine cellar. [$] *Average main: C$50* ✉ *7 Elm St., Dundas Square Area* ☎ *416/597–0335* 🌐 *www.barberians.com* 🕑 *No lunch Sat.–Wed.* [M] *Dundas.*

Hong Shing

$$ | CHINESE | FAMILY | Hong Shing has deep community roots: customers swear that they make the best crispy beef and General Tso's chicken dishes in the city, and hometown celebrities Drake and Simu Liu are regulars. For two generations, this family-run Chinese restaurant has served delicious food inspired by China's many regional cuisines. **Known for:** best General Tso's chicken dish in the city; shareable family-style dishes; laid-back atmosphere good for couples and families. [$] *Average main: C$17* ✉ *195 Dundas St. W, Dundas Square Area* ☎ *416/977–3338* 🌐 *www.hongshing.com* [M] *St. Patrick.*

Kinka Izakaya

$$ | JAPANESE | When Kinka Izakaya opened in 2009, it quickly defined the Japanese izakaya-style dining experience (drinks and small plates) in the minds of Torontonians; it's lively, complete with an open kitchen and ultra-friendly staff. The Truffle Carbonara Udon with mushrooms, onions, soft-boiled egg, and truffle oil reaches new heights. **Known for:** Japanese beer and cocktails; snack-size Japanese tapas; bustling atmosphere. [$] *Average main: C$16* ✉ *398 Church St., Dundas Square Area* ☎ *416/977–0999* 🌐 *www.kinka.com* [M] *College.*

Lai Wah Heen

$$$$ | CHINESE | An elegant dining room and formal service with silver serving dishes set the scene for upscale Asian food. The 100-dish inventory features excellent dishes like wok-fried shredded beef tenderloin with sundried chili peppers alongside delicacies dotted with truffle and foie gras. **Known for:** elegant setting; tableside Peking duck service; excellent lunchtime dim sum. [$] *Average main: C$40* ✉ *DoubleTree by Hilton Hotel, 108 Chestnut St., 2nd fl., Dundas Square Area* ☎ *416/977–9899* 🌐 *www.laiwahheen.com* [M] *St. Patrick.*

Salad King

$$ | THAI | A long-running favorite for students and shoppers looking for a budget-friendly meal, Salad King occupies a second-floor dining room above Yonge Street. Mains hover at the C$15 mark, including a variety of curries and stir-fries. **Known for:** quirky spice scale peaks at "may cause stomach upset"; communal seating means getting to know the locals; colorful atmosphere. [$] *Average main: C$15* ✉ *340 Yonge St., 2nd fl., Dundas Square Area* ☎ *416/593–0333* 🌐 *www.saladking.com* [M] *Dundas.*

☕ Coffee and Quick Bites

Egg Club

$ | ASIAN | Egg Club's breakfast sandwiches are hailed as some of the best in the city because of their expertly folded eggs, which are housed in a sweet and soft Japanese milk bread called *shokupan*. Sandwiches are made in an open kitchen before your eyes and sauces are also created in-house. **Known for:** hash brown made from a secret potato mixture; sandwiches made from Japanese milk bread; one of the best breakfast sandwiches in the city. [$] *Average main: C$7* ✉ *88 Dundas St. E, Toronto* ☎ *416/551–8070* 🌐 *www.eggclub.ca* ☞ *Cash not accepted* [M] *Dundas.*

GB Hand-Pulled Noodle

$$ | CHINESE | Watch tasty, filling Chinese noodles get stretched, folded, and beaten by hand to order at this busy and tiny shop, which specializes in Lanzhou-style *lamian*. Choose from seven types of noodle thickness in a beef broth; most people choose thicker noodles, which allows you to experience their full chewy texture and the soup flavor to cling to them more. The portion size of noodle soups is generous; ordering a small will easily satisfy people with modest appetites, but if you eat a lot dare to get a large or extra-large portion. **Known for:** seven varieties of noodle thickness, from thin to extremely wide; fresh, house-made Lanzhou-style noodles; generous soup portions made from a beef broth. [$] *Average main: C$14* ✉ *Horizon on Bay, 66 Edward St., 1st fl., Dundas Square Area* ☎ *647/872–1336* [M] *Dundas.*

TSUJIRI Dundas

$ | JAPANESE | TSUJIRI is a popular Japanese dessert café that came to the city in 2016 and introduced new ways to experience authentic and high-quality Japanese matcha, in the form of innovative drinks and sweets. Popular menu items include their green-tea soft serve, matcha rare cheesecake, and o-matcha espresso. **Known for:** green-tea-flavored soft serve ice cream; innovative matcha desserts; high-quality and authentic Japanese matcha. [$] *Average main: C$5* ✉ *147 Dundas St. W, Dundas Square Area* ☎ *647/351–7899* 🌐 *www.tsujiri.ca* ☞ *Cash not accepted* [M] *Dundas.*

Uncle Tetsu's Japanese Cheesecake

$ | JAPANESE | When this Japanese franchise came to Canada in 2015, people lined up to try their take on cheesecake, which is a little eggier, firmer, and less sweet than the typical New York variety. The company was so successful, they launched several additional locations throughout the city. **Known for:** long lines at peak hours; signature boxed cheesecakes; matcha cheesecakes on Monday. [$] *Average main: C$10* ✉ *595 Bay St., Dundas Square Area* ☎ *437/266–9196* 🌐 *uncletetsu-ca.com* [M] *Dundas.*

World Food Market

$$ | INTERNATIONAL | The 17 food vendors stationed at this outdoor market provide you with the opportunity to experience the diversity that Toronto is known for at an affordable price; from Caribbean to Nepalese, Indian to Lebanese and more, you can travel the culinary globe here. Opened in 1997, World Food Market is a local landmark that operates 365 days a year; the food is made fresh, and you can eat it under a covered and heated patio. **Known for:** crispy, twister potato tower by BRUNCHIN'; affordable and freshly made food; 17 halal food vendors. [$] *Average main: C$13* ✉ *335 Yonge St., Dundas Square Area* 🌐 *worldfoodmarket.ca* [M] *Dundas.*

Hotels

Chelsea Hotel

$$$ | HOTEL | FAMILY | Canada's largest hotel has long been popular with families and tour groups, so be prepared for a flurry of activity. **Pros:** extremely family-friendly vibe; adults-only swimming pool; good service. **Cons:** long lines at check-in and check-out; fills up with tour groups; slow elevators. [$] *Rooms from: C$277* ✉ *33 Gerrard St., Dundas Square Area* ☎ *416/595–1975, 800/243–5732 toll free* 🌐 *chelseatoronto.com* 🔑 *1,590 rooms* 🍴 *No Meals* [M] *College or Dundas.*

DoubleTree by Hilton Downtown

$$$ | HOTEL | This laid-back hotel is a quick walk to the hustle and bustle of Yonge-Dundas Square and the cultural offerings of the Eaton Centre. **Pros:** a couple of excellent restaurants; reasonable rates for the location; helpful service. **Cons:** decor is a bit dated; parking fills up quickly; some rooms are small. [$] *Rooms from: C$260* ✉ *108 Chestnut St., Dundas Square Area* ☎ *416/977–5000* 🌐 *www.hilton.com/en/doubletree* 🔑 *490 rooms* 🍴 *No Meals* [M] *St. Patrick.*

Marriott Eaton Centre

$$$$ | **HOTEL** | Shoppers love the Marriott because it's right next door to the Eaton Centre and steps from Yonge-Dundas Square. **Pros:** knowledgeable employees; superconvenient location; large guest rooms. **Cons:** may be noisy; parking area fills up quickly; free Wi-Fi only for loyalty members. [$] *Rooms from: C$395* ✉ *525 Bay St., Dundas Square Area* ☎ *416/597–9200* 🌐 *www.marriotteatoncentre.com* 🛏 *451 rooms* 🍴 *No Meals* [M] *Dundas.*

Pantages Hotel

$$$ | **HOTEL** | Clean lines, gleaming hardwood flooring, and brushed-steel accents exude contemporary cool at this all-suites hotel. **Pros:** central location close to Eaton Centre and St. Lawrence Market; 24-hour restaurant on-site; great for long stays. **Cons:** some rooms in need of upgrading; lobby and lower floors can be noisy; no on-site parking. [$] *Rooms from: C$270* ✉ *200 Victoria St., Dundas Square Area* ☎ *416/362–1777* 🌐 *www.pantageshotel.com* 🛏 *95 suites* 🍴 *No Meals* [M] *Queen.*

Saint James Hotel

$$ | **HOTEL** | With a facade dotted with bay windows and topped with a wall of glass, this boutique hotel has plenty of clean-cut charm, with modern rooms with handsome hardwood floors and contemporary furniture. **Pros:** Freshii on-site offering fresh and nutritious meals; good value for the area; comfortable beds. **Cons:** some rooms can be dark; some street noise; long walk to parking. [$] *Rooms from: C$240* ✉ *26 Gerrard St. E, Dundas Square Area* ☎ *416/645–2200* 🌐 *www.thesaintjameshotel.com* 🛏 *36 rooms* 🍴 *No Meals* [M] *Dundas or College.*

🍸 Nightlife

With more neon lights than anywhere else in the city, and a big central square used for outdoor concerts and films, Yonge-Dundas Square is almost always busy. There are a number of good bars ideal for a drink before or after a show.

BARS

Jazz Bistro

LIVE MUSIC | Finding a quiet place to relax and listen to great music is not so common in Toronto but, luckily, there's the Jazz Bistro. The sound system is state-of-the-art and the beautiful Steinway piano is affectionately referred to by regulars as the Red Pops. Blues, jazz, Latin, and world music acts perform almost every night. There's food, too. ✉ *251 Victoria St., Dundas Square Area* ☎ *416/363–5299* 🌐 *www.jazzbistro.ca* ⏲ *Closed Sun. and Mon.* [M] *Dundas.*

The Queen and Beaver Public House

PUBS | Toronto's British heritage thrives at this classy bar with a full restaurant, where the black-and-white photos on the walls reveal its true passion: soccer. A Manchester United game is never missed, though NHL and other sporting events are also shown. The wine list is admirable for a pub while the beer and cider selection is focused on Ontario brews. Dressed-up British staples—available in the bar or ground-floor dining room—range from Scotch eggs to an excellent hand-chopped beef burger. ✉ *35 Elm St., Dundas Square Area* ☎ *647/347–2712* 🌐 *www.queenandbeaverpub.ca* [M] *Dundas.*

🎟 Performing Arts

The Yonge-Dundas area is home to some of the most notable historical theaters in the city, including the Elgin and Winter Garden.

MAJOR VENUES

★ Elgin and Winter Garden Theatre Centre

THEATER | This jewel in the crown of the Toronto arts scene consists of two former vaudeville halls, built in 1913, one on top of the other. It's the last operating double-decker theater complex in the world (the Elgin is downstairs and the Winter Garden upstairs) and a Canadian National Historic Site. Until 1928, the theaters hosted silent-film and vaudeville legends like George Burns, Gracie Allen,

and Edgar Bergen with Charlie McCarthy. Today's performances are still surrounded by magnificent settings: Elgin's dramatic gold-leaf-and-cherub-adorned interior and the Winter Garden's *A Midsummer Night's Dream*–inspired decor, complete with tree branches overhead. These stages host Broadway-caliber musicals, comedians, jazz concerts, operas, and Toronto International Film Festival screenings. Guided tours are offered for C$12. ⊠ *189 Yonge St., Dundas Square Area* ☎ *416/314–2901* ⊕ *www.heritagetrust.on.ca* Ⓜ *Queen*.

★ Massey Hall
CONCERTS | This historical and internationally renowned concert venue is known for near-perfect acoustics and for hosting acclaimed artists since 1894—from Dizzy Gillespie to Justin Bieber, as well as comedians, indie bands, dance performances, and theater plays. After a three-year closure, Massey Hall reopened in 2021 revealing a beautifully repaired facade; detailed hand restoration of its signature ceiling arches; and the construction of the Allied Music Centre, a seven-story glass tower, which provides additional space for events. ⊠ *178 Victoria St., at Shuter St., Dundas Square Area* ☎ *416/872–4255 box office* ⊕ *masseyhall.mhrth.com* Ⓜ *Queen*.

THEATER
Ed Mirvish Theatre
THEATER | This 1920 vaudeville theater has had numerous names over the years, including the Pantages, the Imperial, and the Canon. Now named in honor of local businessman and theater impresario Ed Mirvish, it's one of the most architecturally and acoustically exciting live theaters in Toronto. The theater itself is considered one of the most beautiful in the world and was refurbished in 1989. Designed by world-renowned theater architect Thomas Lamb, it has a grand staircase, gold-leaf detailing, and crystal chandeliers. ⊠ *244 Victoria St., Dundas Square Area* ☎ *416/872–1212, 800/461–3333 box office* ⊕ *www.mirvish.com* Ⓜ *Dundas*.

Shopping

Dundas Square is the go-to place for chain stores and cheap souvenir shops, which line Yonge Street to the north (though their numbers are beginning to dwindle). The mammoth Eaton Centre shopping mall has more than 200 stores (Coach, Banana Republic, and the Apple Store, to name a few).

SHOPPING CENTERS
★ Toronto Eaton Centre
MALL | The 2 million–square-foot Toronto Eaton Centre shopping mall has been both praised and vilified since it was built in the 1970s, but it remains incredibly popular. From the graceful glass roof, arching 127 feet above the lowest of the mall levels with artist Michael Snow's exquisite flock of fiberglass Canada geese floating poetically in open space down to all the shops, there's plenty to appreciate.

There's a huge selection of shops and eateries, but here is a simple guide: the basement level contains the massive Urban Eatery food court. From there, the prices get higher with the altitude, with the top-floor Saks Fifth Avenue being every label-conscious shopper's dream. ⊠ *220 Yonge St., Dundas Square Area* ☎ *416/598–8560 guest services* ⊕ *www.torontoeatoncentre.com* Ⓜ *Dundas or Queen*.

SPAS
Elmwood Spa
SPAS | This four-floor spa, located steps away from Yonge-Dundas Square, is a convenient spot to spend a day unwinding. A variety of facials, scrubs, and massages are available; those who spend a certain amount on services get complimentary access to the complex's swimming pool, a whirlpool, and steam rooms. The on-site restaurant serves light fare, with a prix-fixe option and a patio on-site; there's also a juice bar. ⊠ *18 Elm St., Dundas Square Area* ☎ *416/977–6751* ⊕ *elmwoodspa.com* Ⓜ *Dundas*.

CHINATOWN, KENSINGTON MARKET, AND QUEEN WEST

6

Updated by
Jesse Ship

👁 Sights	🍽 Restaurants	🛏 Hotels	⬤ Shopping	🍸 Nightlife
★★★★★	★★★★★	★★★☆☆	★★★★★	★★★★★

NEIGHBORHOOD SNAPSHOT

TOP EXPERIENCES

■ **Hit the streets:** Kensington Market is overflowing with bohemian spirit, especially on Sunday when the streets fill with buskers, food vendors, and street artists.

■ **Taste a bit of this and a bit of that:** Dim sum in Chinatown is the best way to sample a wide selection of everything that's on the menu.

■ **Spend the afternoon shopping:** It's changed a lot over the years, but Queen West is still busy, buzzy, and a great place to shop.

■ **Meet the Old Masters:** At the well-regarded Art Gallery of Ontario you can take in works by Rembrandt, Warhol, Monet, and Matisse, to name a few.

■ **Expand your palate:** If you're looking to try something new, the eateries on Queen West serve dishes that span the globe.

FUN FACT

■ Built in 1921, the northeast corner of Dundas and Spadina once housed the world-famous Standard theater, a pillar of the Yiddish-speaking community. It changed hands, and names, several times over the decades, switching functions from notorious burlesque theater to Cantonese cinema. The massive auditorium now sits preserved in brick with its presence unknown to most passersby.

GETTING HERE

The Osgoode subway station is ideal for getting to Queen West, as is the 501 streetcar. The 510 Spadina streetcar (which originates at the Spadina subway station) services Chinatown and Kensington Market.

PLANNING YOUR TIME

When on Queen West, the Campbell House merits at least a half hour; the Art Gallery of Ontario an hour or more. Chinatown is at its busiest (and most fun) on weekends, but be prepared for very crowded sidewalks and much jostling. Kensington is great anytime, although it can feel a bit sketchy at night, and it gets mobbed on weekend afternoons. Just strolling around any of these neighborhoods can gobble up an entire afternoon.

The areas along Dundas and Queen Streets typify Toronto's ethnic makeup and vibrant youthfulness. To many locals, the Dundas and Spadina intersection means Chinatown and Kensington Market. While aging hipsters bemoan the fall of Queen West, which is bit by bit becoming an extension of the Eaton Centre, it's still a go-to for stalwart live music venues.

Chinatown and Kensington Market, often explored together, are popular destinations for tourists and locals alike. On a weekend morning, the sidewalks are jam-packed with pedestrians shopping for cheap produce and Chinese trinkets, lining up for a table at one of Chinatown's many restaurants, or heading to "the Market" for a little afternoon shopping. On the last Sunday of each month (May–October), Kensington Market goes car-free for Pedestrian Sundays, as the streets explode with live entertainment, street performances, and vendors selling handicrafts and clothing.

Queen West is busy any time of the year, mostly with teenagers hanging out at the Bell Media HQ (formerly MuchMusic studios) building and young fashionistas-in-training shopping up a storm.

Chinatown

Toronto's largest Chinatown has been going strong since a wave of Chinese immigration in the 1960s, and though rents are rising and hip cafés

and streetwear boutiques have been creeping into the area, this stretch of Spadina Avenue is still home to some of the city's best Chinese eateries. Toronto's Chinatown has a population of more than 100,000 and it's packed with restaurants, bakeries, herbalists, and markets selling fresh fish and produce. It's busy all the time, especially at its epicenter, the Spadina–Dundas intersection.

◉ Sights

★ Art Gallery of Ontario
ART MUSEUM | The AGO is hard to miss: the monumental glass and titanium facade designed by Toronto native Frank Gehry hovering over the main building is a stunning beauty. Just south of the gallery in Grange Park you'll find visitors of all ages climbing in and around Henry Moore's *Large Two Forms* sculpture. Inside, the collection, which had an extremely modest beginning in 1900, is now in the big leagues, especially in terms of its exhibitions of Canadian paintings from the 19th and 20th centuries. Be sure to take a pause in the light

Did You Know?

The Art Gallery of Ontario was architect Frank Gehry's first building in Canada, and the gorgeous Galleria Italia is one of its highlights.

and airy Walker Court to admire Gehry's baroque-inspired spiral staircase.

The Canadian Collection includes major works by the members of the Group of Seven (a group of early-20th-century Canadian landscape painters, also known as the Algonquin School), as well as artists like Cornelius Krieghoff, David Milne, and Homer Watson. The AGO also has a growing collection of works by such world-famous artists as Rembrandt, Warhol, Monet, Renoir, Rothko, Picasso, Rodin, Degas, Matisse, and many others. The bustling Weston Family Learning Centre offers art courses, camps, lectures, and interactive exhibitions for adults and children alike. Free tours (daily 11 to 3 and Wednesday and Friday evening at 7) start at Walker Court. Savvy travelers can book a free visit online on Wednesday evenings, between 6 and 9. ✉ *317 Dundas St. W, at McCaul St., Chinatown* ☎ *416/979–6648, 416/979–6648* 🌐 *www.ago.net* 🎟 *C$25* 🕓 *Closed Mon.* [M] *St. Patrick.*

Spadina Avenue

NEIGHBORHOOD | The part of Spadina Avenue (pronounced spa-*dye*-nah) that runs through Chinatown, from Dundas Street to Queen Street, has never been chic. For decades it has housed a collection of inexpensive stores, import-export wholesalers, ethnic food stores, and eateries, including some first-class, plastic-tablecloth Chinese restaurants. Each new wave of immigrants—Jewish, Chinese, Portuguese, East and West Indian, South American—has added its own flavor to the mix. While changes in the neighborhood are heralded by modern bubble-tea shops and traditional northern and southern Chinese cuisine expanding past Cantonese mainstays, the basic bill of fare is still bargains galore: yards of remnants piled high in bins, designer clothes minus the labels, and the occasional rock-and-roll nightspot or late-night greasy spoon. A streetcar line runs down the wide avenue to Front Street. ✉ *Spadina St. between Dundas and College Sts., Chinatown* [M] *St. Patrick.*

🍴 Restaurants

While urban sprawl has led to the creation of many mini-Chinatowns in the city, this is the original. University students and chefs from all over the city gather here for bubble tea, cheap eats, and late-night bites. There are various regional Chinese cuisines from spicy Szechuan to exotic Cantonese. Weekend mornings are perfect for dim sum—it's a great way to sample Chinese staples.

AGO Bistro

$$$ | **BISTRO** | Like the art gallery in which it's located, this bistro was designed by starchitect Frank Gehry, whose touches are seen in the minimalist decor and geometric ceilings. The dishes themselves, like the Basque-style eggs with chorizo, or grilled cornish hen with dandelion greens on coconut curry, are plated as works of art. **Known for:** prix-fixe meals inspired by gallery exhibits; French meets western Canadian dishes; handcrafted cocktails. [$] *Average main: C$24* ✉ *317 Dundas St. W, at Beverley St.* ☎ *416/979–6688* 🌐 *ago.ca/dine/ago-bistro* 🕓 *Closed Mon.* [M] *St. Patrick.*

Banh Haus

$ | **VIETNAMESE** | Imagine yourself lost at a Saigon night market at this trendy sandwich and snack bar that specializes in banh mi (Vietnamese sandwiches). Not satisfied with the traditional crusty white bread, Banh Haus offers whole-wheat and fried *banh tieu* (Vietnamese donut) buns as a vessel for fillings like grilled lemongrass chicken, five-spice sweet pork sausage, or deep-fried tiger shrimp. **Known for:** Vietnamese-style patio with micro-stool seating; Vietnamese coffee drinks; exotic fruit smoothies. [$] *Average main: C$11* ✉ *81 Huron St., lower level, Chinatown* 🌐 *banhhaus.life* [M] *St. Patrick.*

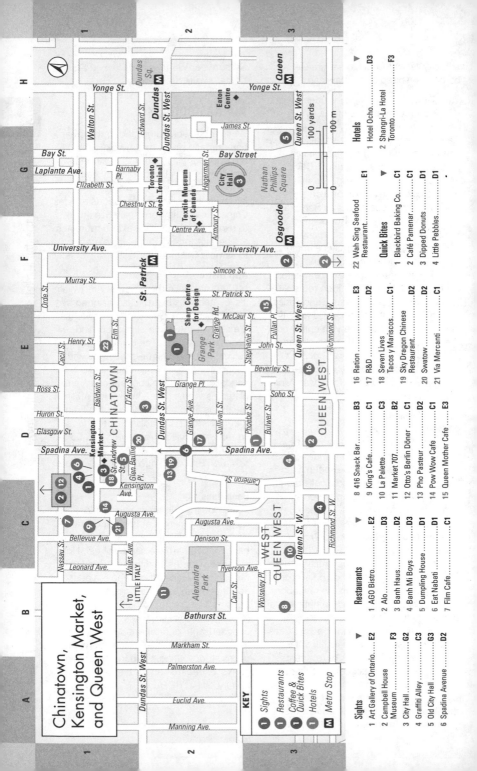

Chinatown, Kensington Market, and Queen West

KEY
- **1** Sights
- **1** Restaurants
- **1** Coffee & Quick Bites
- **1** Hotels
- **M** Metro Stop

Sights ▶
1 Art Gallery of Ontario.....E2
2 Campbell House Museum.....F3
3 City Hall.....G2
4 Graffiti Alley.....C3
5 Old City Hall.....G3
6 Spadina Avenue.....D2

Restaurants ▶
1 AGO Bistro.....E2
2 Alo.....D3
3 Banh Haus.....D2
4 Banh Mi Boys.....D3
5 Dumpling House.....D1
6 Eat Nabati.....D1
7 Film Cafe.....C1
8 416 Snack Bar.....B3
9 King's Cafe.....C1
10 La Palette.....C3
11 Market 707.....B2
12 Otto's Berlin Döner.....C1
13 Pho Pasteur.....D2
14 Pow Wow Cafe.....C1
15 Queen Mother Cafe.....E3
16 Ration.....E3
17 R&D.....D2
18 Seven Lives Tacos y Mariscos.....C1
19 Sky Dragon Chinese Restaurant.....D2
20 Swatow.....D2
21 Via Mercanti.....C1
22 Wah Sing Seafood Restaurant.....E1

Quick Bites ▶
1 Blackbird Baking Co.....C1
2 Café Pamenar.....C1
3 Dipped Donuts.....D1
4 Little Pebbles.....D1

Hotels ▶
1 Hotel Ocho.....D3
2 Shangri-La Hotel Toronto.....F3

Dumpling House

$$ | CHINESE | Fried dumplings stuffed with juicy shrimp and pork or the health-conscious steamed spinach and black mushroom wrappers are the stars of the show but ordering from the selection of northern Chinese staples is highly recommended too. Top crowd-pleasing picks are the ultra-thinly sliced semi-cooked potato threads cooked in a jolting spicy vinegar, and noodley tofu strips boiled and lightly stir-fried with pork and veggies. **Known for:** homey atmosphere; dumplings wrapped fresh by staff in the window; fast service. [$] *Average main: C$14* ⊠ *328 Spadina Ave., Chinatown* ☎ *416/596-8898* ⊕ *restaurantwebexpert.com/DumplingHouse* ▭ *No credit cards* Ⓜ *St. Patrick.*

Pho Pasteur

$$ | VIETNAMESE | When you're having a late-night craving for Vietnamese food, this is the place for authentic bowls of pho or hearty curries with a crusty baguette to sop up the sauces. To drink, savor a slow-drip coffee with sweetened condensed milk or an exotic fruit milkshake in flavors like soursop or avocado. **Known for:** South Vietnamese–style goat curry; open around the clock; no-frills decor. [$] *Average main: C$15* ⊠ *525 Dundas St. W, Chinatown* ☎ *416/351-7188* ⊕ *phopasteur.ca* ▭ *No credit cards* Ⓜ *St. Patrick.*

R&D

$$$ | ASIAN FUSION | The idea here is that traditional Asian street food can exist side by side with modern haute cuisine, against a backdrop of fiery open kitchens and cavernous dining rooms. Experimental entrées borrow European ingredients like cauliflower couscous, maple syrup, and pan-seared foie gras on brioche. **Known for:** nightly "Lucky 7" cocktail hour; tasty beef cheek banh mi; dim sum–style appetizers. [$] *Average main: C$23* ⊠ *241 Spadina Ave., Chinatown* ✛ *1 block south of Dundas*

☎ *416/586–1241* ⊕ *www.rdspadina.com* ◷ *Closed Mon. and Tues.* Ⓜ *Osgoode.*

★ Sky Dragon Chinese Restaurant

$ | CANTONESE | Downtown Toronto's quintessential dim sum eatery overlooks all of Chinatown from its secret rooftop perch at the Dragon City Mall. Carts with towers of bamboo steamed baskets containing shrimp dumplings or black-bean-sauce chicken feet ("phoenix claws" in Chinese), banquet-size platters of noodles, and traditional delicacies like black or yellow curried cuttlefish are pushed around the hall by gregarious servers who tick off boxes from your order list as they are served. **Known for:** surprisingly expansive views through the huge windows; traditional Cantonese dim sum service; savory chive-and-shrimp dumplings. [$] *Average main: C$8* ⊠ *Dragon City Mall, 280 Spadina Ave., top fl., Chinatown* ☎ *416/408–4999* Ⓜ *Spadina.*

Swatow

$$ | CHINESE | If there is an equivalent to a fast-paced, casual Hong Kong–style diner in Chinatown, this would be it: the food is inexpensive and honest, and the setting is bright and spare. Diners enjoy heaping bowls of congee and customized noodle soups, including the best fish ball and shrimp dumpling bowls in town. **Known for:** excellent fried rice; open on holidays; communal tables. [$] *Average main: C$15* ⊠ *309 Spadina Ave., Chinatown* ☎ *416/977–0601* ⊕ *www.swatowrestauranttoronto.com* ▭ *No credit cards* Ⓜ *St. Patrick.*

Wah Sing Seafood Restaurant

$$ | CHINESE | One of a jumble of Asian eateries clustered on a tiny street opposite Kensington Market, this spacious restaurant is beloved for its two-for-one lobster deals. The crustaceans are delicious and tender, served either with black-bean sauce or a ginger-and-green-onion sauce. **Known for:** aquarium filled with a selection of fresh fish; whole

Toronto's network of streetcars provides an excellent method of transportation for getting around downtown.

braised duck; simple and delicious dishes. $ *Average main: C$17* ✉ *47 Baldwin St., Chinatown* ☎ *416/599–8822* ⊕ *www. wahsing.ca* Ⓜ *St. Patrick.*

Shopping

Spadina's collection of inexpensive clothing stores and exotic food shops (not only Chinese, but also Vietnamese, Japanese, and Thai) give you your money's worth. A cluster of galleries surrounds the Art Gallery of Ontario just east of the area. Take the north–south Spadina streetcar or the east–west College or Dundas streetcar to Spadina Avenue, or walk from St. Patrick.

ART GALLERIES
Bau-Xi Gallery

ART GALLERIES | Paul Wong, an artist and dealer from Vancouver, started this gallery, which is directly across the street from the Art Gallery of Ontario. The paintings and sculpture are a window

into contemporary Canadian art, featuring both emerging and established artists. Just a few steps down at 324 Dundas Street West is Bau-Xi Photo, which shows Canadian and international fine art photography. ✉ *340 Dundas St. W, at McCaul St., Chinatown* ☎ *416/977–0600* ⊕ *www.bau-xi.com* Ⓜ *St. Patrick.*

GIFTS AND SOUVENIRS
shopAGO

SOUVENIRS | Exiting through this gift shop is not mandatory, but you'll want to check out the overwhelming selection of curiosities, from touring exhibit memorabilia and books on maximal architecture to pop-art–inspired toys and prints of celebrated paintings. Adults and kids can shop side by side among the books and fun educational items. ✉ *Art Gallery of Ontario, 317 Dundas St. W, at McCaul St., Chinatown* ☎ *416/979–6610* ⊕ *www. ago.net/shop* Ⓜ *St. Patrick.*

Textile Museum Shop

CRAFTS | Tucked away on the second floor of the already hidden Textile Museum, this shop is one of the city's best-kept secrets and an absolute treasure trove. It overflows with textile-based art from Canadian artisans, as well as works by craftspeople from around the world keeping traditional, and often disappearing, skills alive. There are loads of books, scarves galore, unusual bags and hats, and crafty stuff for kids, too; many items are accessibly priced. ■ TIP→ Check out the changing exhibition on the second and third floors while you're here (admission charge) to develop a taste for the shop's featured items; past exhibits have included Finnish designer Marimekko and Afghan war rugs. ⊠ 55 Centre Ave., at Dundas St. W and University Ave., Chinatown 🕾 416/599–5321 ⊕ www.textilemuseum. ca Ⓜ St. Patrick.

HOME DECOR

Tap Phong Trading Co. Inc.

OTHER SPECIALTY STORE | The mops, brooms, and multicolor bins and buckets stacked outside make this kitchenware and restaurant equipment store appear much like all the other Chinese knick-knack shops along Spadina. However, once you're inside you'll find endless aisles stacked to the rafters with rice bowls and bamboo steamers, and restaurateurs piling up their shopping trollies with glasses and servingware to feed the masses. ■ TIP→ A gap halfway along the north wall leads to the industrial-scale equipment. ⊠ 360 Spadina Ave., south of Baldwin St., Chinatown 🕾 416/977–6364 ⊕ www.tapphong.com Ⓜ Spadina.

🎭 Performing Arts

El Mocambo

MUSIC | This historic music venue is famous for legendary '70s concerts by the Rolling Stones and Elvis Costello, but after local celebrity investor Michael Wekerle bought it and gave it an expensive renovation, it's active again in the 2020s. Still an intimate space with two different stages, the Elmo (as it's affectionately known) is now a very shiny, neon-lit tribute to classic rock with some of the crispest sound and lighting in town. Tickets can be costly. ⊠ 464 Spadina Ave., Chinatown ⊕ elmocambo. com Ⓜ 510 Spadina streetcar.

Kensington Market

This collection of colorful storefronts, crumbling brick houses, delightful green spaces, and funky street stalls titillates all the senses. On any given day you can find Russian rye breads, Mexican paletas stands, fresh fish, imported cheese, and ripe fruit. And Kensington's collection of vintage-clothing stores is the best in the city.

The neighborhood took root in the early 1900s, when Russian, Polish, and Jewish inhabitants set up stalls in front of their houses. Since then, the area has become a sort of United Nations of stores. Jewish and Eastern European shops sit side by side with Portuguese and Caribbean ones, as well as with a sprinkling of Vietnamese and Chinese establishments.

■ TIP→ Weekends are the best days to visit, preferably by public transit; parking is difficult. Also note that the neighborhood is pedestrianized from dawn to dusk on the last Sunday of every month.

🍽 Restaurants

In true Toronto fashion, Kensington Market's restaurants are a blend of cuisines from Caribbean to Italian. There are plenty of spots to grab a quick bite, but there are also some standout places for a leisurely meal.

Eat Nabati

$$ | MIDDLE EASTERN | Enter a Middle Eastern paradise where vegans and the health conscious can feast on delicious mock-meat renditions of classics like chicken shawarma and beef kebabs doused in a variety of flavored tahinis, like beet and lemon. Chef Isra recreated her grandmother's Egyptian recipes so faithfully that not even she can tell them apart. **Known for:** the rice and lentils are comfort in a bowl; everything is made fresh and worth the wait; rotating desserts. $ *Average main: C$12* ✉ *160 Baldwin St., Kensington Market* ☎ *289/277–0008* ⊕ *www.eatnabati.com.*

Film Cafe

$$ | ECLECTIC | Located smack in the middle of Kensington Market, locals flock to this highly versatile cultural hub that effortlessly merges brunch restaurant, gelateria, and evening cabaret. The sprawling front and back patio make it an ideal location for soaking in local culture over an umami-rich Japanese omelet and pink sakura latte, or cocktails paired with late-night Latin-themed bites. **Known for:** eclectic menu; film screenings; creative coffees, smoothies, and cocktails. $ *Average main: C$15* ✉ *230 Augusta Ave., Kensington Market* ☎ *647/347–1913* ⊕ *www.filmcafetoronto.com.*

King's Café

$ | ASIAN FUSION | In a neighborhood where the bohemian vegetarian lifestyle is the norm, King's Café has become a mainstay for artists, students, and young professionals seeking vegan grub with an Asian accent. The setting is a serene and airy eatery with wide windows looking out onto bustling Augusta Avenue. **Known for:** vegan takes on dim sum classics; purple rice in lovely bento boxes; tea and spices for sale. $ *Average main: C$11* ✉ *192 Augusta Ave., Kensington Market* ☎ *416/591–1340* ⊕ *kingsvegetarianfood.ca* Ⓜ *St. Patrick.*

Market 707

$ | INTERNATIONAL | For a unique take on cheap eats, head east of Bathurst to Market 707, a strip of food stalls built out of repurposed shipping containers. Highlights include poutine at Nom Nom Nom; authentic lamb-fat–infused Damascus-style shawarmas and burgers from Chef Harwash; soul-warming Filipino at Kanto by Tita Flips; and authentic Japanese rice balls stuffed with burdock and red miso pork, along with other hearty staples from Omosubi Bar Suzume. **Known for:** huge variety of cuisines available; streetside eating; innovative urban design. $ *Average main: C$9* ✉ *707 Dundas St. W, east of Bathurst St., Kensington Market* ☎ *416/392–0335* ⊕ *scaddingcourt.org/market-707* ⊟ *No credit cards* ⊙ *Closed Mon.* Ⓜ *St. Patrick.*

Otto's Berlin Döner

$$ | GERMAN | Otto's brings a nightlife-worthy spin to street snacks. The owners are former club promoters who fell in love with Berlin's most popular street eats and set about bringing them to Toronto. **Known for:** wide selection of beers on tap; Berlin-style street food; lightning-fast service. $ *Average main: C$12* ✉ *256 Augusta Ave., Kensington Market* ☎ *647/347–7713* ⊕ *www.ottosdoner.com* Ⓜ *Queen's Park.*

Pow Wow Cafe

$$ | CANADIAN | Chef Shawn Adler prepares dinner-plate-covering native "tacos" at his rustic 12-seater café and similarly sized front patio. Mains include piles of toppings for fusion brunch–focused dishes that incorporate everything from Indian curries, poached duck eggs, and edible flowers. **Known for:** smoked salmon croquettes are the perfect appetizer; the beef taco with cumin sour cream; guaranteed large portions. $ *Average main: C$18* ✉ *213 Augusta Ave., at Baldwin St., Kensington Market* ☎ *416/551–7717.*

★ Seven Lives Tacos y Mariscos

$ | MEXICAN | With only 10 seats, this taco joint almost always has long lines, but it's worth the wait. The menu brings the best of SoCal and Tijuana seafood together, featuring taco options like the *gobernador* (smoked marlin and shrimp), and a vegetarian option with corn fungus (trust us, it tastes better than it sounds). **Known for:** delicious shrimp-and-cheese tacos; range of fiery hot sauces; gluten-free tortillas available. $ *Average main: C$6.50* ✉ *69 Kensington Ave., Kensington Market* ☎ *416/803–1086* ⊕ *sevenlivesto.ca* Ⓜ *St. Patrick.*

★ Via Mercanti

$$$ | ITALIAN | The thin-crust pies at this airy family-run pizzeria are authentically Neapolitan and consistently earn top marks on local (and even global) critics' lists thanks to their fresh ingredients and use of traditional methods. Pasta mains (with gluten-free options) like a fiery Naples-style rigatoni and seafood linguini may take second place but are certainly worth a look. **Known for:** the ciambella ripiena, a ricotta and hot soppressata–stuffed crust pie; sidewalk patio; extensive antipasti (traditional Italian appetizer) list. $ *Average main: C$22* ✉ *188 Augusta Ave., Kensington Market* ☎ *647/343-6647* ⊕ *www.pizzeriaviamercanti.ca.*

☕ Coffee and Quick Bites

Blackbird Baking Co.

$ | BAKERY | Hearty sandwiches stuffed with toppings like mortadella, grilled veggies, and spreads made in-house are accompanied by selections of traditional brioche buns, and creative palm-size Viennoiseries at the local legendary boulangerie. It helps to get there earlier in the day to take score of other baked delights like tomato danishes and quirky chocolate corks. **Known for:** providing baked goods for restaurants around the city; crusty sourdough loaves; organic grains. $ *Average main: C$8* ✉ *172 Baldwin St., Kensington Market* ☎ *416/546–2280* ⊕ *blackbirdbakingco.com.*

Café Pamenar

$ | CAFÉ | There's no better place for a quick espresso or another pick-me-up than at the poured-concrete walls of this uber-hip meeting spot, complete with front and back patios. Show up by night for a full-length bar menu of local and imported craft beers and an apothecary of spirits. **Known for:** extensive gin list; Persian-influenced drinks; frequent evening musical programming. $ *Average main: C$7* ✉ *307 Augusta St., Kensington Market* ☎ *647/352–3627* ⊕ *cafepamenar.com.*

★ Dipped Donuts

$ | BAKERY | These award-winning cakey brioche donuts are fried fresh in the wee hours of the morning, dipped, and then ready to fly off the shelves by the time the converted storefront opens at 8:30 am. From the milky London Fog with an Earl Grey glaze to mini salted caramel Boston Creme bombs, you just can't go wrong. **Known for:** strong coffee from local Propeller Specialty Roasters; vegan options; organic ingredients sourced from Kensington Market shops. $ *Average main: C$4* ✉ *161 Baldwin St., Kensington Market* ☎ *647/906–3668* ⊕ *www.dippeddonuts.ca* ⊘ *Closed Mon.*

★ Little Pebbles

$ | BAKERY | Japanese perfectionism merges with French tradition at this minimalist coffee and pastry shop. The owners are always dreaming up new croissant creations like a flaky croissant cube (that needs to be seen to be believed), and the croffle, a—you guessed it—croissant/waffle hybrid prepared in a half-dozen ways, from churro-caramel sweet to ham-and-pesto savory. **Known for:** gooey mochi (sticky rice dough) stuffed with chocolate and strawberries; ceremonial-grade matcha imported from Japan; "happy hour" coffee specials from local De Mello Roastery. [$] *Average main: C$7* ✉ *160 Baldwin St., Store 8, Kensington Market* ☎ *416/792–0404* 🌐 *little-pebbles.com.*

Shopping

Tucked behind Spadina West to Bathurst Street, between Dundas and College Streets to the south and north, is this hippie-meets-hipster collection of inexpensive vintage-clothing stores, cheap ethnic eateries, coffee shops, head shops, and specialty food shops specializing in cheeses, baked goods, fish, dry goods, health food, and more.

■ TIP→ Be warned—this area can be extraordinarily crowded on weekends; do not drive. Take the College streetcar to Spadina or Augusta, or the Spadina streetcar to College or Nassau.

CLOTHING

Bungalow

ANTIQUES & COLLECTIBLES | Teak tables, chairs, and cabinets give this vintage shop the feel of a strangely cavernous 1970s bungalow. Organized racks are filled with Hawaiian and secondhand T-shirts, vintage 1970s dresses, and comfortably worn jeans, but you'll also find new styles, too. ✉ *273 Augusta Ave., Kensington Market* ☎ *416/598–0204* 🌐 *www.bungalow.to* [M] *Spadina.*

Courage My Love

SECOND-HAND | The best and longest-running vintage store in Kensington Market is crammed with the coolest retro stuff, from sunglasses to sundresses, plus an ample supply of cowboy boots and gently used Birkenstock sandals for guys and gals, all at low prices. Not everything is secondhand here: there's a wall of sparkly Indian-inspired clothing, lots of costume jewelry, Mexican *luchador* masks, and a selection of unique buttons. ✉ *14 Kensington Ave., Kensington Market* ☎ *416/979–1992* [M] *St. Patrick.*

Shoney's Clothing

SECOND-HAND | It might take some digging but Shoney's no nonsense, uncurated collection of vintage wares is replete with diamonds in the rough. The stock is frequently replenished so you never know what you'll find among the obscure band tees, gently used Roots hoodies, and glamorous silk bathrobes that share the racks with Italian military surplus, flashy '70s furs, international soccer kits, and cycling jerseys. Their outside $5 rack is often bursting with snaggable deals. ✉ *222 Augusta Ave., Kensington Market* ☎ *416/979–0700* 🌐 *kensingtonmarket.to/places/shoneys-clothing.*

Tom's Place

MIXED CLOTHING | Find bargains aplenty on brand-name suits and shirts from brands like Calvin Klein, Armani, and DKNY at this remnant from the market's old-world textile industry days. The larger-than-life Tom Mihalik, the store's owner, keeps his prices low (and will often go lower, if you ask politely). The sales staff can quickly navigate the selection and help you put together a complete and well-accessorized look. ✉ *190 Baldwin St., at Augusta St., Kensington Market* ☎ *416/596–0297* 🌐 *www.toms-place.com* [M] *St. Patrick.*

FOOD

Super Natural Market

SUPERMARKET | Organic, natural, and hormone-free products are the core offerings here. Build yourself a healthy picnic basket for a lunch in nearby Trinity-Bellwoods park with Ontario farm-raised deli meats; organic, grass-fed, fermented European cheeses; locally grown sprouts; and enticing bulk treats sweetened with raw cane sugar whenever possible. ✉ *210 Augusta Ave., Kensington Market* ☎ *416/591–6844* 🌐 *supernaturalmarket.ca.*

GIFTS AND SOUVENIRS
Good Egg
BOOKS | Dubbed "a book shop for people who like to eat," you'll find a smattering of everything needed to elevate your culinary experiences here, from the latest trendy cookbooks to tasteful accents like hand-crafted chambray napkins and whimsical illustrated coffee mugs. A true community hub, the shop also publishes cookbooks focused on singular ingredients written by celebrated local food writers, and its upcycled thrifting section is not to be overlooked for rare vintage finds. ⊠ *156 Augusta Ave.* ☎ *416/596–1171* ⊕ *goodegg.ca.*

Kid Icarus
OTHER SPECIALTY STORE | At this old-school printing company, you'll find a range of whimsical illustrations including band posters, mock-retro tourism posters, and other one-of-a-kind creations. You'll also find screen-printed "Greetings from Toronto" postcards, art supplies, and contemporary indie crafts in the gift shop. ⊠ *205 Augusta Ave., Kensington Market* ☎ *416/977-7236* ⊕ *www.kidicarus.ca* Ⓜ *Spadina.*

Queen West

Queen West has become increasingly corporate as the years pass and rents rise, but this mazelike array of back alleys is a homegrown outdoor shrine to street art. The result of a city revitalization project, Graffiti Alley (sometimes referred to as Rush Lane) serves as an ever-changing museum of work by some of the city's foremost street artists, and is a perennially popular setting for music videos and photo shoots.

Sights

Campbell House Museum
HISTORIC HOME | The Georgian mansion of Sir William Campbell, the sixth chief justice of Upper Canada, is now one of Toronto's best house museums. Built in 1822 in another part of town, the Campbell House was moved to this site in 1972. It has been restored with elegant early-19th-century furniture, and knowledgeable guides detail the social life of the upper class. Don't overlook the *Lost & Found* garden exhibit, salvaged from heritage buildings. ⊠ *160 Queen St. W, Queen West* ☎ *416/597–0227* ⊕ *www. campbellhousemuseum.ca* ⊠ *C$10* ⓧ *Closed Jan. and Mon.* Ⓜ *Osgoode.*

City Hall
GOVERNMENT BUILDING | The design for Toronto's modern city hall, just across the way from the Old City Hall building, resulted from a 1956 international competition that received 520 submissions from architects from 42 countries. The winning presentation by Finnish architect Viljo Revell was controversial—two curved towers of differing height—but logical: an aerial view of City Hall shows a circular council chamber sitting like an eye between the two towers that contain office space. Revell died before his masterwork was opened in 1965, but the building has become a symbol of the thriving metropolis. A remarkable mural within the main entrance, *Metropolis,* was constructed by sculptor David Partridge from 100,000 nails.

Annual events at City Hall include November's Cavalcade of Lights celebration, featuring fireworks and live music amid the glow of more than 525,000 lights illuminated across both the new and old city halls.

Did You Know?

In 1973, an album of photographs found in a trash bin was donated to the Campbell House Museum. It included almost 60 interior images of the house from 1885 and formed the basis of the home's renovation that began in the late 1990s.

In front of City Hall, the 9-acre Nathan Phillips Square (named after the mayor who initiated the City Hall project) has become a gathering place for everything from royal visits to protest rallies, picnic lunches, and concerts. The reflecting pool is a delight in summer, and even more so in winter, when it becomes a skating rink. The park is also home to a Peace Garden for quiet meditation and Henry Moore's striking bronze sculpture The Archer. ⊠ 100 Queen St. W, at Bay St., Queen West ☎ 416/338–0338 ⊕ www. toronto.ca Ⓜ Queen.

Graffiti Alley

STREET | Toronto is filled with back alleys and laneways, most of which are not very nice to look at, but Graffiti Alley is a vibrant amateur spray paint gallery. Running behind Queen West from Spadina to Portland Street, the alleyway is filled with colorful work from local graffiti writers and gets a constant stream of gawkers and photographers dodging garbage and recycling bins to see the art. It's become such an institution that its former nickname is now its official street name, with a street sign and everything. ⊠ Graffiti Alley, Queen West Ⓜ 510 Spadina or 501 Queen streetcar.

Old City Hall

GOVERNMENT BUILDING | Opened in 1899, and used until 1965 when the new City Hall was built across the street, the old municipal building now operates solely as a courthouse. This imposing building was designed by E. J. Lennox, who was also the architect for Casa Loma and the King Edward Hotel. Note the huge stained-glass window as you enter. The fabulous gargoyles above the front steps were apparently the architect's witty way of mocking certain turn-of-the-20th-century politicians; he also carved his name under the eaves on all four faces of the building. The building has appeared in countless domestic and international TV shows and feature films. ⊠ 60 Queen St. W, Queen West ⊗ Closed weekends Ⓜ Queen.

🍴 Restaurants

Queen West is a boisterous mix of galleries, hip clothing stores, and lots of good, reasonably priced restaurants.

★ Alo

$$$$ | FRENCH FUSION | The 10- to 16-course dinners here breathed new life into the concept of the tasting menu for many Torontonians, thanks to a chef who channels refined French cooking techniques into beautifully composed plates. Courses from the ever-changing offerings have included striped bass with chanterelles and baby artichokes, Nova Scotia lobster tail paired with romesco and shishito peppers, and rack of pork offset with bing cherries, Swiss chard, and a dusting of pistachios. **Known for:** need to reserve weeks in advance; multicourse tasting menus; stunning presentation. $ Average main: C$135 ⊠ 163 Spadina Ave., 3rd fl., Queen West ☎ 416/260–2222 ⊕ www.alorestaurant.com ⊗ Closed Sun. and Mon. Ⓜ Osgoode.

Banh Mi Boys

$ | ASIAN | Brothers David, Philip, and Peter Chau have banh mi in their blood—their parents opened one of the original Vietnamese sandwich shops in Chinatown—but they've taken the classic and dockod it out with top notch ingredients such as melt-in-your-mouth pork belly, duck confit, and kalbi beef. Other offerings include Asian-inspired tacos and steamed bao. **Known for:** a modern take on a classic eatery; crunchy kimchi fries; five-spice pork belly. $ Average main: C$9 ⊠ 392 Queen St. W, Queen West ☎ 416/363–0588 ⊕ www.banhmiboys. com Ⓜ Osgoode.

416 Snack Bar

$ | **ECLECTIC** | It takes its name from the city's most popular area code, so it's no surprise that 416—a dim, boisterous bar that echoes the general vibe of West Queen West—draws inspiration from the city around it. The menu of inexpensive small plates, best enjoyed with a cocktail or two, is a fun mishmash of cultures, from Jamaican to Chinese to Peruvian, that serves as a one-stop culinary crash course to this city of immigrants. **Known for:** sometimes controversial no-cutlery policy; fun spot for a first date; buzzy atmosphere. $ *Average main: C$8* ⊠ *181 Bathurst St., Queen West* ☎ *416/364–9320* ⊕ *416snackbar.com* ⊗ *No lunch Mon.–Thurs.*

★ La Palette

$$$ | **FRENCH** | Known as one of the city's tried-and-true French bistros, this brightly decorated spot lives up to expectations with a menu full of excellent standards, including steak frites, rare venison chop, and mussels in white wine. The long bar at the front of the restaurant is a great spot for drinks or solo dining. **Known for:** short but well-curated wine list; three-course prix-fixe dinner; great brunch. $ *Average main: C$28* ⊠ *492 Queen St. W* ☎ *416/929–4900* ⊕ *www.lapalette. ca* ⊗ *No dinner weekends. Closed Tues.* Ⓜ *Osgoode.*

Queen Mother Cafe

$$ | **ASIAN FUSION** | A laid-back neighborhood institution, the Queen Mother has been popular with art students and broadcast-media types since the 1980s. The food is international, leaning toward Southeast Asian with European accents. **Known for:** atmosphere is somewhere between a pub and a pastry shop; try the chicken with a zesty lime coriander sauce; gluten-free salad bowls. $ *Average main: C$16* ⊠ *208 Queen St. W, at St. Patrick St., Queen West*

☎ *416/598–4719* ⊕ *www.queenmothercafe.ca* Ⓜ *Osgoode.*

Ration

$$ | **CANADIAN** | Dishes at this zero-waste, locally foraged, alchemical eatery are on the smaller side but pack the complexity of lead freshly turned to gold. Mainstays on the often-changing menu include a risotto accented with wild Ontario ramps, al dente sweet peas, and pureed asparagus stems (that would otherwise end up in the bin), adding an extra dimension of vegetalia. **Known for:** dedication to sustainable cooking methods and natural aging processes; exquisite cocktails like the floral Summertime Wine: sake, Prosecco, jasmine milk tea, and a pear-and-white-wine reduction; two-and-a-half-hour tasting menu experience. $ *Average main: C$17* ⊠ *335 Queen St. W., Queen West* ☎ *647/366–9206* ⊕ *www. rationbeverley.com.*

Hotels

In this trendsetting neighborhood, along Queen Street West beyond Bathurst Street, the hotels get more experimental and cutting-edge the farther west you go. Many highlight local art and music, and have noteworthy restaurants that practice sustainability.

Hotel Ocho

$$ | **HOTEL** | In a turn-of-the-century warehouse building, this boutique hotel's exposed brick-and-beam look typifies the Queen West "cool" factor. **Pros:** close to dozens of bars and restaurants; full-service international restaurant; beautiful renovation. **Cons:** restaurant often closed for events; minimal breakfast offerings; loud air-conditioners. $ *Rooms from: C$199* ⊠ *195 Spadina Ave., Queen West* ✛ *1 block north of Queen and Spadina* ☎ *416/593–0885* ⊕ *www.hotelocho. com* ➡ *12 rooms* ⦿ *Free Breakfast* Ⓜ *Osgoode.*

Shangri-La Hotel Toronto

$$$$ | **HOTEL** | It's hard to miss the distinctive giant windows of the luxury chain's Toronto location, where the level of chicness meets the high standard of service. **Pros:** luxury pool with private cabanas and built-in TVs; big-name restaurants on-site; 42-seat screening room. **Cons:** pricey dim sum and lobby tea service; check-in can be slow; lobby can get very busy. [$] *Rooms from: C$550* ✉ *188 University Ave., at Richmond St., Queen West* ☎ *647/788–8888* 🌐 *www.shangri-la.com/toronto* 🛏 *202 rooms* 🍴 *No Meals* [M] *Osgoode.*

Nightlife

BARS

BarChef

COCKTAIL LOUNGES | The dark apothecarian interior at BarChef features dimly lit chandeliers and tabletop candles, which set the stage for wild and wonderful concoctions that force patrons to reimagine classic cocktails. The bartender's bag of tricks includes liquid nitrogen, so cocktails foam over like a foggy mist onto the table or turn into ice shards for a sensory experience that looks as good as it tastes. Purists can order a classic French absinthe fountain while fans of whiskey should order the signature Vanilla and Hickory Smoked Manhattan, served in a smoke-filled jar (but be warned, it clocks in at a hefty C$50). While not highlighted, a full page of the menu is devoted to meats, cheeses, and elevated bar snacks. ✉ *472 Queen St. W* ☎ *416/868–4800* 🌐 *www.barcheftoronto.com.*

Bar Hop Brewco

BARS | One of the city's most interesting destinations for beer, Bar Hop Brewco features an ever-changing lineup of 40 rare and one-off beers on tap. The location just off Queen West features an aging room for beers, a large and sunlit rooftop patio overlooking the main drag, and a menu of refined beer-laced eats like Porter-glazed garlicky mushrooms, bacon-and-blue-cheese mussels with baguette, and bone marrow poutine. ✉ *137 Peter St., Queen West* ☎ *647/348–1137* 🌐 *www.barhopbar.com* [M] *Osgoode.*

★ Drom Taberna

CABARET | Part rustic Balkan eatery, part cabaret, Drom Taberna is alive with the spirit of the Romani people. Every night of the week you'll be able to experience a wide range of global sounds from Middle Eastern–influenced flamenco to interactive Balfolk dancing. Menu must-tries include *čevapi* (a Bosnian grilled meat staple) and goulash, and no meal would be complete without a bowl of Ukrainian-style borscht. Armenian, Croatian, and Georgian wines dominate the drinks list, along with a dozen different herbal digestifs, rakijas, and *palinkas* (fruit brandies). ✉ *458 Queen St. W, Queen West* ☎ *647/748–2099* 🌐 *www.dromtaberna.com* 🕒 *Closed Tues.* [M] *Osgoode.*

MUSIC VENUES

★ Horseshoe Tavern

LIVE MUSIC | This legendary, low-ceilinged rock bar on Queen West has earned a reputation as the place to play for local acts and touring bands alike. Opened in 1947 as a country music venue, the Shoe (as it's often called) hosted greats like Loretta Lynn, Willie Nelson, Hank Williams, and the Carter Family. The venue's scope widened to include the emerging folk, rock, and punk scenes in the 1960s and '70s, giving way to early appearances by the Police, Tom Waits, and Talking Heads. The Rolling Stones even played a now-legendary surprise set here in 1997. Today, the venue books rock, indie, and punk acts from home and abroad. ✉ *370 Queen St. W, at Spadina Ave., Queen West* ☎ *416/598–4226* 🌐 *www.horseshoetavern.com* [M] *Osgoode.*

The Rex Hotel Jazz and Blues Bar

LIVE MUSIC | Legendary on the Toronto jazz circuit since it opened in the 1980s, the Rex has two live shows every night, and multiple acts on weekend afternoons and evenings. Shows range from free (bring some cash for when the band passes the tip jar) to C$10. The kitchen serves diner fare, and there are even affordable hotel rooms available on-site. ⊠ *194 Queen St. W, at St. Patrick St.* ☎ *416/598–2475* ⊕ *www.therex.ca* Ⓜ *Osgoode.*

Rivoli

LIVE MUSIC | One of Queen West's oldest venues, the Rivoli showcases indie music, theater, and comedy. Arcade Fire, Adele, and Tori Amos all graced the intimate back room's stage early in their careers, and for a cover charge (usually under C$12), you can catch what might be Toronto's next big thing. The low-lit front dining room offers a cozy atmosphere for snacking on their famous "wookie" balls or pad Thai, while the front patio is prime real estate for watching eclectic Torontonians go about their days. Head upstairs to shoot some pool at one of 11 pay-by-the-hour tables. ⊠ *332 Queen St. W, at Spadina Ave., Queen West* ☎ *416/596–1501* ⊕ *www. rivoli.ca* Ⓜ *Osgoode.*

Performing Arts

DANCE
The National Ballet of Canada

BALLET | Canada's internationally recognized classical-ballet company was founded in 1951 and is made up of more than 70 dancers and its own orchestra boasting alumnus Karen Kain as artistic director. It's the only company in Canada to perform a full range of traditional full-length ballet classics, including frequent stagings of *Swan Lake* and *The Nutcracker*. The company also performs contemporary works and is dedicated to the development of Canadian choreography.

The season runs late fall through spring at the Four Seasons Centre for the Performing Arts, Canada's first purpose-built ballet opera house. ⊠ *Four Seasons Centre for the Performing Arts, 145 Queen St. W* ☎ *416/345–9595, 866/345–9595 outside Toronto* ⊕ *national.ballet.ca* Ⓜ *Osgoode.*

THEATER
Theatre Passe Muraille

THEATER | Toronto's oldest alternative theater company, established in 1968, focuses on presenting themes of the unique Canadian cultural mosaic through collaborative productions and has launched the careers of many actors and playwrights. ⊠ *16 Ryerson Ave., near Queen and Bathurst Sts., Queen West* ☎ *416/504–7529* ⊕ *www.passemuraille. ca* Ⓜ *Osgoode or Bathurst.*

Shopping

ANTIQUES
Abraham's Trading Inc.

ANTIQUES & COLLECTIBLES | Indicative of a Queen West long gone, the most remarkable thing about Abraham's is that somehow it survives. Handwritten signs snarl "don't even think about it" amid a jumble of haphazardly piled rusty props and dusty "antiques" from doctor's bags and deer trophies to worn church doors, creepy clown shoes, and a sparkling collection of 1950s microphones. Purchasing anything will take some guts—few prices are marked, although everything, they say, is for sale. ⊠ *635 Queen St. W, Queen West* ☎ *416/504–6210* Ⓜ *Osgoode or Bathurst.*

ART GALLERIES
401 Richmond

ART GALLERIES | Packed with galleries, interesting shops, and two cafés, this beautifully refurbished industrial building is an essential component of Toronto's contemporary art scene. Check out YYZ

Artists' Outlet, which holds consistently engaging shows, or Gallery 44 for contemporary photography. There's also the respected artist collective Red Head Gallery. Don't miss well-stocked Swipe for books on all things design and Spacing for stylish Toronto-themed T-shirts, prints, and knickknacks. ✉ *401 Richmond St. W* ☎ *416/595–5900* ⊕ *www.401richmond. com* ⊘ *Closed Sun. and Mon.* Ⓜ *Spadina or Osgoode.*

BOOKS

Swipe Design | Books + Objects

BOOKS | Books on advertising, art, architecture, and urban planning pack the shelves of this aesthetically pleasing store, fittingly located in the arty 401 Richmond heritage building. Part of the store is devoted to modern gifts, including elegant writing tools, modern jewelry, and Pantone-theme everything. ✉ *401 Richmond St. W, Suite B-04, at Spadina Ave.* ☎ *416/363–1332, 800/567–9473* ⊕ *www.swipe.com* ⊘ *Closed Sun. and Mon.* Ⓜ *Osgoode or Spadina.*

CLOTHING

Black Market

SECOND-HAND | Determined vintage buffs hunt through the racks of band T-shirts, faded jeans, worn shoes, and biker jackets in this unfinished upstairs warehouse-style location. It's also famous for its signature in-house screen-print tee designs. ✉ *347 Queen St. W* ☎ *416/599–5858* ⊕ *www.blackmarkettoronto.com* Ⓜ *Osgoode.*

Durumi

JEWELRY & WATCHES | Feminine, Korean-inspired styles such as slip dresses, wide-leg trousers, blouse-y tops, and delicate jewelry are sold at Durumi. ✉ *416 Queen St. W, west of Spadina, Queen West* ☎ *647/727–2591* ⊕ *www.thedurumi.com* Ⓜ *Osgoode or Spadina.*

Lululemon Athletica

SPORTING GOODS | The Canadian yoga brand's massive concept store on Queen West is a must-visit for runners and yogis alike. Along with plenty of athletic and loungewear for men and women, there is a 1,000-square-foot yoga and dance community studio. ✉ *318 Queen St. W, at Spadina Ave.* ☎ *226/779–7415* ⊕ *www. lululemon.com* Ⓜ *Osgoode.*

Original

WOMEN'S CLOTHING | A blaze of rainbow colors, Original is glamorous, life-affirming, and a little outrageous. If you're heading to a gala or you're after a crinoline dress (in fuchsia), you *need* to come here. The endless selection of platforms, pumps, and wedges is outdone only by the dress section, up a multicolor flight of stairs. ✉ *515 Queen St. W, at Augusta Ave., Queen West* ☎ *416/603–9400* ⊕ *www.originaltoronto.com* Ⓜ *Osgoode.*

Tribal Rhythm

CRAFTS | A few vintage gems and pretty silk scarves may be found among the army jackets, cub scout uniforms, and 1970s polyester shirts and cowgirl attire, but most of the inventory is simply fun and kitschy. Imported Thai and Indian trinkets, body jewelry, tiaras, and wigs are part of the charming and eclectic mix. ✉ *248 Queen St. W, below street level, at John St., Queen West* ☎ *416/595–5817* Ⓜ *Osgoode.*

MUSIC

Sonic Boom

MUSIC | More than 1,500 daily arrivals fill the rows of this bright and cavernous mostly secondhand shop famous for its Broadway-caliber window installations. They carry many albums of local indie musicians, and you might even catch a live in-store performance. ✉ *215 Spadina Ave., at Sullivan St.* ☎ *416/532–0334* ⊕ *www.sonicboommusic.com* Ⓜ *Spadina or Osgoode.*

SHOES, HANDBAGS, AND LEATHER GOODS

Getoutside

SHOES | This buzzy Queen West main-stay stocks style for men and women including Hunter wellies, Frye boots, Birkenstock sandals, Sperry Top-Siders, Converse and Vans sneakers, and a great selection of Laurentian Chief and Minnetonka street moccasins and mukluks. ⊠ *437 Queen St. W, at Spadina Ave.* ☎ *416/593–5598* ⊕ *www.getoutsideshoes.com* Ⓜ *Osgoode or Spadina.*

SPAS

The Ten Spot

SPAS | With 16 locations around Toronto, this chain of beauty bars specializes in waxing, manicures, and facials and carries a selection of beauty products from independent and luxury brands. ⊠ *749 Queen St. W* ☎ *416/915–1010* ⊕ *www.the10spot.com.*

SPORTING GOODS

Duer

SPORTING GOODS | Designed in British Columbia, these jeans and chinos are made for biking, climbing, or even the boardroom. The secret is their breathable, stretchy fabrics with reinforced stitching in the necessary "pain" points along with trendy cuts and colors. ⊠ *491 Queen St. W, Queen West* ☎ *647/794–1341* ⊕ *www.duer.ca* Ⓜ *Osgoode.*

MEC

SPORTING GOODS | Mountain Equipment Co-op's flagship store is as busy as basecamp at Mt. Kilimanjaro. It's an excellent spot to pick up emergency winter gear, water purification tablets, or a camping coffee kit. The merino undershirts are highly coveted as they'll keep you toasty on winter nights. ⊠ *300 Queen St. W, at Beverly St., Queen West* ☎ *416/340–2667* ⊕ *www.mec.ca/en/stores/toronto* Ⓜ *Osgoode.*

Chapter 7

WEST QUEEN WEST, OSSINGTON, AND PARKDALE

Updated by
Richard Trapunski

● Sights	🍴 Restaurants	🛏 Hotels	🛍 Shopping	🍸 Nightlife
★★☆☆☆	★★★★★	★★★★☆	★★★★★	★★★★★

NEIGHBORHOOD SNAPSHOT

TOP EXPERIENCES

■ **Discover up-and-coming designers:** Browse West Queen West's indie boutiques to find the city's coolest clothes.

■ **Take a walk in the park:** Head to leafy Trinity Bellwoods Park for some people-watching in the shade.

■ **Grab a brew:** Go for a bar crawl along Ossington and West Queen West, stopping at the Bellwoods Brewery patio.

■ **Hang with the hipsters:** Take in a live performance or an art exhibit at the Gladstone House or the Drake Hotel.

■ **Expand your culinary horizons:** Eat delicious Tibetan food in Parkdale, or a mix of everything in West Queen West.

GETTING HERE

To get to West Queen West, take the 501 Queen streetcar and get off at Ossington. For Parkdale, take the same streetcar to Dufferin or Lansdowne Avenue.

To explore Ossington, take the 510 Queen streetcar to Ossington, the 505 Dundas streetcar to Ossington, or take the Line 2 subway to Ossington station and then take the 63 Ossington bus south.

PLANNING YOUR TIME

Afternoons (particularly weekends) are great for strolling and shopping along Queen. West Queen West and Ossington's nightlife scene tends to pull in people throughout the week, but things really get hopping on Friday and Saturday night.

FUN FACTS

■ Ossington and Parkdale saw such explosions in dining and nightlife that both were subject to moratoriums on new bars and restaurants in the early 2010s.

■ Trinity Bellwoods Park was once the home of Trinity College before it was rebuilt and incorporated into the University of Toronto.

■ The West Queen West neighborhood is known for its famous, and somewhat mythical, albino squirrel. There's even a coffee shop—the White Squirrel—named after it.

Originally a residential area for Portuguese immigrants and a home to Vietnamese karaoke bars and restaurants, Ossington and West Queen West are now *the* place for bohemian artists to set up shop, young chefs to take risks, and hipsters to party until the sun comes up. Neighboring Parkdale is also getting in on the scene, too.

Toronto is sprawling, but the city's excellent public transportation system makes it a cinch to get outside the city center to explore these hipper regions of the city's west end. Head out along Queen Street west of Bathurst, dubbed "West Queen West" by locals, and you'll start to see the neighborhood change. While it's still possible to find a run-down hardware store shouldering a high-end hipster bar, more of the latter are moving in these days. Many of the familiar chains that populate Queen West are spreading into the area as the neighborhood gentrifies, but there's still plenty of indie boutiques, local restaurants, and hip watering holes that capitalize on the area's cool cred.

West Queen West

West Queen West's major landmarks, the Drake Hotel and the Gladstone House, enjoy much success for their creative, eclectic decor and happening nightlife. Businesses like these, once the new cool kids on the block, are now cultural institutions in an area that has seen waves of gentrification. An eclectic smattering of restaurants and art galleries vie for real estate with fair-trade coffee shops and boutiques featuring Canada's hottest new designers—not to mention actual real estate developers, who are building up the area with condos. Trinity Bellwoods Park punctuates the neighborhood at the center and provides a beautiful setting for a picnic or a bench break. The area is served by the 301 and 501 streetcars, but the subway does not go out here.

◉ Sights

Trinity Bellwoods Park
CITY PARK | FAMILY | Bellwoods is the top destination for west-enders to kick back on a sunny day. The tree-lined park runs between Dundas West and Queen West, which makes for a scenic stroll if you're heading between neighborhoods. It's a great spot for picnicking and people-watching—or dog-watching, if you take a bench next to the dog bowl. It's especially attractive in mid-May, when the cherry trees bloom pink, or when the leaves turn in the fall. ⊠ *790 Queen St. W, West Queen West* Ⓜ *501 Queen or 505 Dundas West streetcar.*

Trinity Bellwoods Park is a great place to soak in the changing fall colors.

🍴 Restaurants

West Queen West is home to some of the city's best restaurants in a range of cuisines from sustainable seafood to fondue, and everything in between.

Le Swan

$$$ | FRENCH | Once a classic Toronto diner, this intimate spot from local restaurateur Jen Agg pays homage to its greasy-spoon roots but with a French twist. The frequently evolving menu balances steak frites and Nicoise salads with tuna melts, onion rings, and grilled cheeses. **Known for:** vintage diner setting; excellent wine list; late-night fondue. [$] *Average main: C$22* ✉ *892 Queen St. W, West Queen West* ☎ *416/536–4440* 🌐 *leswan.ca* 🕓 *No lunch* [M] *501 Queen streetcar, Shaw St. stop.*

Oyster Boy

$$$ | SEAFOOD | Whether you order them baked, fried, or raw, oysters are the thing at this casual neighborhood spot. A chalkboard spells out what's fresh, along with sizing and prices for each, and there is an excellent selection of house-made condiments. **Known for:** extensive selection of oysters from Canada's east and west coasts; oyster shucking class on Sunday; sustainably sourced seafood. [$] *Average main: C$28* ✉ *872 Queen St. W, West Queen West* ☎ *416/534–3432* 🌐 *oysterboy.ca* 🕓 *No lunch weekdays* [M] *501 Queen streetcar, Strachan stop.*

☕ Coffee and Quick Bites

Cafe Neon

$$ | CAFÉ | Head to this colorful café for locally roasted espresso and reasonably priced Mediterranean brunch. Inspired by Greek *kafeneio* meeting places, it's a great spot to while away a few hours. **Known for:** full brunch menu with Greek touches; fresh bread on weekends; locally roasted coffee. [$] *Average main: C$17* ✉ *1024 Queen St. W, West Queen West* ☎ *647/351–6366* 🌐 *cafeneon.ca* [M] *501 Queen streetcar, Ossington stop.*

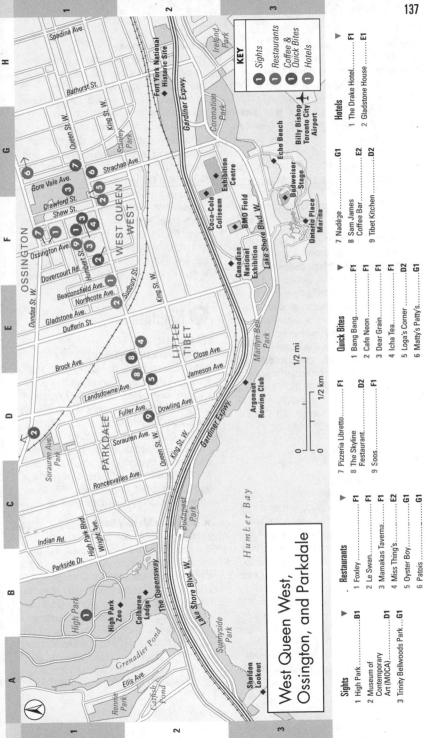

West Queen West, Ossington, and Parkdale

Sights ▶
1 High Park B1
2 Museum of Contemporary Art (MOCA) D1
3 Trinity Bellwoods Park ... G1

Restaurants ▶
1 Foxley F1
2 Le Swan F1
3 Mamakas Taverna F1
4 Miss Thing's E2
5 Oyster Boy G1
6 Patois G1
7 Pizzeria Libretto F1
8 The Skyline Restaurant D2
9 Soos F1

Quick Bites ▶
1 Bang Bang F1
2 Cafe Neon F1
3 Dear Grain F1
4 Icha Tea F1
5 Loga's Corner D2
6 Matty's Patty's G1
7 Nadège G1
8 Sam James Coffee Bar .. E2
9 Tibet Kitchen D2

Hotels ▶
1 The Drake Hotel F1
2 Gladstone House E1

KEY
1 Sights
1 Restaurants
1 Coffee & Quick Bites
1 Hotels

Icha Tea

$ | CAFÉ | Toronto is filled with quick bubble tea—including many chains from Taiwan and other parts of Asia—but Icha Tea is a slower, homegrown shop that brews high-quality loose-leaf teas. **Known for:** for-sale plants from Springer Garden and fashion accessories by June Studio; loose-leaf teas sourced from China; educational tea tastings. $ *Average main: C$7* ⊠ *996 Queen St. W, West Queen West* ☎ *416/546–6292* ⊕ *ichatea.ca* Ⓜ *501 Queen streetcar, Ossington stop.*

Nadège

$ | BAKERY | This hot-pink patisserie is a top destination for Torontonians with a sweet tooth. Long glass cases are filled with French macarons, cakes, and fanciful pastries, as well as savory options like croissant sandwiches and salads, while the walls are lined with a candy shop's worth of sweets (all made in-house). **Known for:** location on the corner of Trinity Bellwoods Park; chocolates in cute packaging; rainbow-color macarons. $ *Average main: C$12* ⊠ *780 Queen St. W, West Queen West* ☎ *416/203–2009* ⊕ *nadege-patisserie.com* Ⓜ *501 Queen streetcar, Claremont St. stop.*

Hotels

★ The Drake Hotel

$$$ | HOTEL | More than just a hotel, the Drake is also a bar, a club, and an art gallery that has been a focal point for local media for two decades. **Pros:** locally made snacks and drinks; stylish rooms packed with quirky touches; access to scenester art, culture, and dining. **Cons:** no on-site gym or fitness center; party crowd takes over on weekends; smallish rooms in the classic wing. $ *Rooms from: C$332* ⊠ *1150 Queen St. W, West Queen West* ☎ *416/531–5042* ⊕ *www. thedrake.ca* ⤶ *51 rooms* ⦿| *No Meals* Ⓜ *501 Queen streetcar, Abell St. stop.*

★ Gladstone House

$$$$ | HOTEL | Some boutique hotels pop art on their walls and call it a day, but this Victorian-era beauty (complete with an antique hand-operated elevator) uses guest rooms as a canvas for a rotating cast of local artists. **Pros:** on-site art installations; licensed lounges throughout the building; new fitness, yoga, and Pilates spaces. **Cons:** some noise from busy West Queen West neighborhood; condo construction across the street hinders some room views; inconsistent room sizes, some very small. $ *Rooms from: C$379* ⊠ *1214 Queen St. W* ☎ *416/531–4635* ⊕ *www.gladstone-house.ca* ⤶ *55 rooms* ⦿| *No Meals* Ⓜ *501 Queen streetcar, Gladstone Ave. stop.*

Nightlife

BARS

★ The Drake Underground

BARS | Locals know the Drake as a hub for art, culture, food, and nightlife, with multiple spaces hosting events on any given night. The basement is home to the Drake Underground, a venue that hosts live music and DJ nights, while the rooftop Sky Yard patio serves drinks surrounded by eye-popping art installations. ⊠ *1150 Queen St. W, West Queen West* ☎ *416/531–5042* ⊕ *www.thedrakehotel. ca* Ⓜ *501 Queen streetcar, Abell St. stop.*

★ Gladstone Melody Bar

BARS | The Gladstone draws an artsy Toronto crowd that appreciates creative endeavors like music performances, cabaret and burlesque, and trivia nights. A 2022 relaunch gives the trusted community and LGBTQ+-friendly programming a bright neon pop art backdrop, with a light-up dance floor, '70s and '80s art-pop records on the wall, and TVs broadcasting what's on stage during busy events. Regulars flock to popular karaoke nights—both recorded and with a live band—and drag brunches. The Bar + Bistro has an accessible comfort food menu with Mediterranean and North African twists, plus plenty of themed cocktails that play off the Gladstone House's long history. The Gladstone Ballroom, once the centerpiece, now hosts mostly private events and weddings, but does sometimes host big party spillover. Original pieces from local artists are on nearly every wall. ✉ 1214 Queen St. W, West Queen West ☎ 416/531–4635 ⊕ gladstonehouse.ca Ⓜ 501 Queen streetcar, Gladstone Ave. stop.

🎭 Performing Arts

THEATERS
The Great Hall
MUSIC | This sweeping Queen Anne revival–style building, built in 1889, is one of the city's grandest concert venues, with four event spaces packed over three stories. The Main Hall is a cavernous auditorium with a second-floor gallery overlooking the main floor below, though events are also often held in the basement-level Longboat Hall, which was once a gymnasium in the building's former life as a YMCA. The space hosts everything from touring bands to theater events to craft shows. Stop in to Otto's Bierhalle, which occupies the ground floor, for craft beer and great German-style snacks. ✉ 1087 Queen St. W, West Queen West ☎ 416/792–1268 ⊕ thegreathall.ca Ⓜ 501 Queen streetcar, Dovercourt stop.

The Theatre Centre
THEATER | Built in 1909 as a library funded by industrialist Andrew Carnegie, this heritage property underwent extensive renovations and reopened as a theater space in 2016. There's a café and bar as well. ✉ 1115 Queen St. W, West Queen West ☎ 416/538–0988 ⊕ theatrecentre.org Ⓜ 501 Queen streetcar, Dovercourt stop.

🛍 Shopping

West of Bathurst, Queen Street is the place to go for cool shops and slick home goods stores. The cool quotient steps up a notch as the street extends farther west, beyond Trinity Bellwoods Park, with mid-century modern antique shops, cutting-edge galleries, and a flurry of big-name designers.

ART GALLERIES
★ Craft Ontario Shop
CRAFTS | This shop, run by the Ontario Crafts Council, stocks an excellent selection of Canadian crafts, including blown glass, fine woodwork, textiles, jewelry, and pottery—from earthy stoneware to contemporary ceramics. There's also a gallery featuring work by artists and craftspeople from around Ontario. Upstairs is the Devil's Workshop, which sells jewelry by local makers and hosts a popular DIY wedding band workshop. ✉ 1106 Queen St. W, West Queen West ☎ 416/921–1721 ⊕ www.craftontario.com Ⓜ 501 Queen streetcar, Dovercourt stop.

BOOKS
Silver Snail
BOOKS | While it's moved its location over the years like a traveling hobbit, this shop is one of Toronto's most beloved comic book providers. Along with thousands of illustrated paperback and hardcover tomes, the Snail has been stocking shelves over the last 45 years with hard-to-find collectibles such as Studio Ghibli figurines, fearsome futuristic model kits of the Gundam and Evangelion variety, and other covetable fandom favorites. ✉ 809 Queen St. W, West Queen West ☎ 647/646–0889 ⊕ silversnail.com Ⓜ 501 Queen streetcar, Claremont St. stop.

★ Type Books
BOOKS | The carefully selected fiction and nonfiction at Type Books includes local authors, as well as fun cards and gifts. The art and architecture section has

West Queen West is home to an increasing number of trendy boutiques and cutting-edge galleries.

pride of place at the front of the shop, and the extensive children's area is in a bright spot up a few steps at the back. ✉ *883 Queen St. W, West Queen West* ☎ *416/366–8973* ⊕ *www.typebooks.ca* Ⓜ *501 Queen streetcar, Claremont St. stop.*

CANNABIS
Dynasty Pot Shop
OTHER SPECIALTY STORE | Retail cannabis shops have taken over Toronto, and Dynasty is a rare one that stands out—not just for its sleek and quirky design, but also its focus on the harvest quality of its plants. That's because it grew out of the next-door sister store Dynasty Plant Shop, which carries a similarly well-curated set of products. Expect good vibes, approachable staff, and clothing and accessories. ✉ *1086 Queen St. W, West Queen West* ☎ *416/516–0668* ⊕ *dynastypotshop.com* Ⓜ *501 Queen streetcar, Dovercourt stop.*

CLOTHING
★ Gravitypope
MIXED CLOTHING | This Canadian chain, frequented by fashionistas in the know, has an impressive selection that includes Paul Smith, Comme des Garçons, and Ami. The collections include menswear and womenswear, but shoes are the specialty, with designers including Church's, Camper, Hunter, rag & bone, Doc Martens, and many more. ✉ *1010 Queen St. W, West Queen West* ☎ *647/748–5155* ⊕ *www.gravitypope.com* Ⓜ *501 Queen streetcar, Ossington stop.*

Horses Atelier
WOMEN'S CLOTHING | This homegrown womenswear label counts some of Toronto's coolest artists, musicians, and actors among its fans. The tiny flagship shop stocks the latest in Horses' limited-run pieces, all hand-sewn in Toronto. The chic, albeit pricey, modern staples include smoking dresses, stylish jumpsuits, and patterned jackets.

✉ *198 Walnut Ave., West Queen West* ☎ *416/504–9555* ⊕ *horsesatelier.com* ⊘ *Closed Mon. and Tues.* Ⓜ *501 Queen streetcar, Claremont St. stop.*

HOME DECOR

Quasi Modo

FURNITURE | Tasteful modern design pieces such as Herman Miller lounge chairs, Vipp coffee tables, and Foscarini lamps are just a sampling of the high-end design you'll find here—there's not a knockoff in sight. There are also sleek modern homewares for the kitchen and bathroom as well. ✉ *1079 Queen St. W, West Queen West* ☎ *416/703–8300* ⊕ *www.quasimodomodern.com* ⊘ *Closed Sun.* Ⓜ *501 Queen streetcar, Dovercourt stop.*

Urban Mode

FURNITURE | Modern and trend-oriented furniture and home decor at this West Queen West spot include the playful furniture designs of Blu Dot, along with space-age sofas from Softline and bold Scandinavian creations from Muuto. ✉ *145 Tecumseth St., West Queen West* ☎ *416/591–8834* ⊕ *www.urbanmode. com* ⊘ *Closed Sun.* Ⓜ *501 Queen streetcar, Palmerston stop.*

SHOES, HANDBAGS, AND LEATHER GOODS

Heel Boy

SHOES | A tried-and-true spot for cool and cute footwear for any gender, Heel Boy stocks unique styles by well-known brands like Hunter, Ted Baker, Sam Edelman, and Superga, as well as on-trend bags and accessories. ✉ *773 Queen St. W, West Queen West* ☎ *416/362–4335* ⊕ *www.heelboy.com* Ⓜ *501 Queen streetcar, Palmerston stop.*

Zane

JEWELRY & WATCHES | This sleek accessory boutique is the place for trendy offbeat pieces like handbags by local designers Spicy Princess and Opelle, Le Specs

sunglasses, stunning handmade jewelry from Canadian indie designers like Jenny Bird and Biko, and Larson & Jennings watches. ✉ *753 Queen St. W, West Queen West* ☎ *647/352–9263* ⊕ *www. visitzane.com* Ⓜ *501 Queen streetcar, Palmerston stop.*

Ossington

If your Toronto travel plans include a bar crawl or trendy bite to eat, odds are you'll end up on the Ossington strip, which has become one of the city's hottest nightlife destinations in recent years.

🍴 Restaurants

★ Foxley

$$ | ASIAN | Like the appealingly bare-bones aesthetic of its space (exposed brick, hardwoods, and candlelight), this creative contemporary Pan-Asian bistro offers unadorned dishes that are jammed with flavor. After traveling for a year, chef-owner Tom Thai returned to Toronto with inspiration from Asia, Latin America, and the Mediterranean to produce a menu featuring tapas-style offerings like arctic char ceviche, lamb and duck prosciutto dumplings, and grilled side ribs with a sticky shallot glaze. ■**TIP→ The restaurant doesn't take reservations, so get here early or late to avoid the rush. Known for:** well-priced wine list; sharing plates; seasonal back patio. Ⓢ *Average main: C$20* ✉ *207 Ossington St., Ossington* ☎ *416/534–8520* ⊘ *No lunch. Closed Sun.* Ⓜ *63 Ossington bus, Dundas West stop.*

★ Mamakas Taverna

$$$$ | GREEK | The Danforth might be the epicenter of Greek food in Toronto, but across town on trendy Ossington, Mamakas is doing some of the city's best Greek cooking—Aegean to be exact. Diners snack on classic mezes like rich, creamy tzatziki and roasted eggplant before diving into more unusual dishes like lamb tartare or tea-brined chicken. **Known for:** Athenian market-inspired decor; Summer Sea Market seafood specials; delicious desserts. $ *Average main: C$40* ✉ *80 Ossington Ave., Ossington* ☎ *416/519–5996* ⊕ *mamakas.ca* ⊘ *No lunch* Ⓜ *63 Ossington bus, Argyle St. stop.*

★ Patois

$$$ | JAMAICAN | The Asian-Jamaican mishmash you see at hip Dundas West joint Patois is unlike any other in town. The spot is fueled by dishes from chef Craig Wong's Jamaican-Chinese upbringing, with plenty of tropical cocktails to wash it all down. **Known for:** colorful cocktails like rum punch; family-style "feasts" that let you try the whole menu; Tuesday and Wednesday "patty hours" with free Jamaican patties. $ *Average main: C$22* ✉ *794 Dundas St. W, Ossington* ☎ *647/350–8999* ⊕ *patoistoronto.com* ⊘ *Closed Mon.* Ⓜ *505 Dundas streetcar, Bathurst stop.*

Pizzeria Libretto

$$$ | PIZZA | Authentic thin-crust pizzas are fired in an imported wood-burning oven at this pizza joint that adheres to the rules set by Naples's pizza authority. Go classic with the Margherita D.O.P.—with San Marzano tomatoes, fresh basil, and *fior di latte* mozzarella—or branch out with *nduja* (spicy salami) or duck confit pies. **Known for:** casual atmosphere; vegan and gluten-free options; New York and Neopolitan pizza styles. $ *Average main: C$21* ✉ *221 Ossington Ave.* ☎ *416/532–8000* ⊕ *www.pizzerialibretto.com* ⊘ *Closed Mon. and Tues. No lunch.*

Soos

$$ | MALAYSIAN | This Malaysian street food spot is a hidden gem on the busy Ossington strip. There are a variety of sharing-style plates like *kapitan* chicken tacos, *rendang* beef, and delicious stuffed roti—but a popular option is the C$55 "feed me" tasting menu. **Known for:** excellent vegan options; affordable and inventive tasting menu; modern takes on Malaysian street food. $ *Average main: C$20* ✉ *94 Ossington Ave., Ossington* ☎ *416/901–7667* ⊕ *soostoronto.com* ⊘ *Closed Mon. and Tues.* Ⓜ *63 Ossington bus, Argyle St. stop.*

☕ Coffee and Quick Bites

Bang Bang

$ | ICE CREAM | The lines might be long at this ice cream shop specializing in artisanal options like Cinnamon Toast and London Fog—but oh is it worth the wait. The flavors are good on their own, but the queues form for their incredible ice cream sandwiches made with freshly baked cookies, Hong Kong waffles, carrot cake, and cinnamon buns. **Known for:** quirky ice cream flavors that change daily; ice cream sandwiches with freshly baked cookies; homemade cinnamon buns and waffles. $ *Average main: C$9* ✉ *93A Ossington Ave., Ossington* ☎ *416/531–1900* ⊕ *bangbangicecream.ca* ⊘ *Closed Mon.* Ⓜ *63 Ossington bus, Argyle St. stop.*

Dear Grain

$ | BAKERY | On an Ossington strip with plenty of restaurants but not many bakeries, Dear Grain is a veritable mecca of sourdough. The first standalone shop (or "Sourdough Studio") for the bread brand that built a cult following during the pandemic, this shop has a big wall of fresh daily loaves plus pastries, wines, tinned fish, local condiments and spreads, and even picnic boxes with meats and cheeses you can take over to nearby Trinity Bellwoods. **Known for:** local gourmet wines, spreads, condiments, and snacks; full coffee bar; fresh sourdough breads. $ *Average main: C$8* ✉ *48 Ossington Ave., Ossington* ☎ *416/532–7243* ⊕ *deargrain.com* ⊘ *Closed Mon.* Ⓜ *63 Ossington bus, Argyle St. stop.*

Matty's Pattys

$$ | **BURGER** | Local celebrity chef/often-shouting TV personality Matty Matheson always has a number of spots opening and closing in Toronto, but if you want to try the delectable smash burgers that made him famous, Matty's Pattys is the place. Called a "burger club," it's a no-frills mostly-takeout spot with single, double, and triple cheeseburgers (or plant-based burgers), milkshakes, and chili cheese fries. **Known for:** popular takeout spot for nearby Trinity Bellwoods Park; local craft beer and chocolate milkshakes; smash burgers made from triple AAA beef brisket and chuck. [$] *Average main: C$12* ✉ *923A Queen St. W, Ossington* ☎ *416/546–8091* 🌐 *mattyspattys-burgerclub.com* [M] *501 Queen streetcar, Strachan Ave. stop.*

Nightlife

BARS

★ Bellwoods Brewery

BREWPUBS | This restaurant, bar, and on-site brewery has been a smash hit since it opened in 2012. If the sun is shining, expect a line for the spacious patio, a great spot to sample the always evolving craft beer selection. Sour-beer fans should try the seasonal fruit-infused Jelly King, which has beer drinkers queueing up at the bottle shop on release day. The hearty snacks run the gamut from Canadian cheeses and terrine to a crispy Newfoundland cod sandwich. ✉ *124 Ossington Ave.* 🌐 *bellwoodsbrewery.com* [M] *63 Ossington bus, Argyle St. stop.*

Cocktail Bar

BARS | Restaurateur Jen Agg is a household name in Toronto, and the drinks are never an afterthought at her restaurants or at Cocktail Bar, where the ceiling is covered in pressed tin tiles and bottles gleam behind glass-paned cabinet doors. Across the street from Agg's other flagship spots Rhum Corner and Bar Vendetta, this boozy spot respects classic cocktail tradition—think Manhattans and absinthe concoctions, but rarely any vodka—but isn't afraid to take a few left turns either. ✉ *923 Dundas St. W, Ossington* ☎ *416/792–7511* 🌐 *hoof-cocktailbar.com* [M] *505 Dundas streetcar, Grace St. stop.*

Communist's Daughter

BARS | This dark but friendly little bar opened at the corner of Dundas and Ossington in the early 2000s, long before the neighborhood became trendy. Now, with its snack bar sign from its earlier incarnation and old-fashioned vinyl jukebox filled with punk and indie rock classics, the Commie (as the regulars sometimes call it) is an institution. Not much more than a bar and a few tables, it's the kind of spot you can go to, have a couple of pints, and find yourself in a deep conversation with someone you just met. ✉ *1149 Dundas St. W, Ossington* [M] *505 Dundas streetcar.*

Dakota Tavern

LIVE MUSIC | Sitting just north of the booming Ossington strip, this cozy basement bar and music venue has been a neighborhood favorite for over a decade and a half. The wood-paneled, whiskey-soaked vibe might remind you more of Nashville than Toronto, but this concrete city has always had an urban cowboy streak, especially in the music scene. The Dakota is a great spot to catch a high-energy bluegrass hoedown or an intimate singer-songwriter or indie rock showcase. ✉ *249 Ossington Ave., Ossington* ☎ *416/850–4579* 🌐 *dakotatavern.ca.*

The Garrison

LIVE MUSIC | Once a Portuguese sports bar, after over a decade on Dundas West, this spot has become a key local live music venue. The back room isn't huge, but it's a popular spot for up-and-coming touring musicians as well as locals looking to make a mark, not to mention many hopping DJ nights. It also hosts occasional live music and events like the quirky non-expert lecture series Trampoline Hall. A front room bar/cantina is a neighborhood hangout spot. ✉ *1197 Dundas St. W, Ossington* ☎ *416/519–9439* ⊕ *garrisontoronto.com* Ⓜ *505 Dundas streetcar, Ossington Ave. stop.*

Reposado
BARS | This classy tequila bar was ahead of the bar buzz on Ossington (it opened in 2007) and is still going strong. The dark wood, large windows, big back patio, and mix of DJs and live jazz set the tone for a serious list of tequilas meant to be sipped, not slammed. There are also enjoyable Mexican nibbles like ceviche and tacos. Reposado has also expanded into a bodega next door with enviable bottles available for takeout. ✉ *136 Ossington Ave., Ossington* ☎ *416/532–6474* Ⓜ *63 Ossington bus, Argyle St. stop.*

DANCE CLUBS
★ Lula Lounge
LIVE MUSIC | Latin-music lovers of all ages dress up to get down to live Afro-Cuban, Brazilian, and salsa music at this old-school hot spot. Now over two decades old, Lula has become a global music institution, going beyond those genres into samba, cumbia, reggae, Indigenous throat singing, and anything else you can think of. Weekend salsa nights include dance lessons, live band performances, and a prix-fixe menu (C$64). Lula is also an arts center, with dance and drumming lessons and a multitude of festivals and cultural events. ✉ *1585 Dundas St. W* ☎ *416/588–0307* ⊕ *www.lula.ca* Ⓜ *505 Dundas streetcar, Sheridan Ave. stop.*

🛍 Shopping

ART GALLERIES
Stephen Bulger Gallery
ART GALLERIES | The collection of roughly 30,000 photos focuses on historical and contemporary Canadian photography, with ongoing exhibitions. ✉ *1356 Dundas St. W, Ossington* ☎ *416/504–0575*

⊕ *www.bulgergallery.com* ◷ *Closed Sun. and Mon.* Ⓜ *505 Dundas streetcar, Rusholme stop.*

CLOTHING
Annie Aime
MIXED CLOTHING | Bright comfy threads with a European aesthetic and a focus on sustainable production are the focus here. Expect items from French designers Cotelac and Elsa Esturgie, and Turkish-made deconstructed sweaters from Crea Concept. The eye-catching graffiti painting inside makes for a perfect fashion backdrop. ✉ *42 Ossington Ave., Ossington* ☎ *416/840–5227* ⊕ *www.annieaime.com* Ⓜ *501 Queen streetcar, Ossington Ave. stop.*

I Miss You Vintage
MIXED CLOTHING | The immaculately restored picks in this upscale consignment shop include familiar names such as Pucci, Hermès, Dior, and Yves Saint Laurent. Gentlemen can head next door to I Miss You Man for vintage Versace button-downs, gently used Acne jackets, and Dior jeans—all in near-mint condition. ✉ *63 Ossington Ave., Ossington* ☎ *416/916–7021* ⊕ *imissyouvintage.com* Ⓜ *501 Queen streetcar, Ossington stop.*

Town Moto
OTHER SPECIALTY STORE | Hardcore bikers, Sunday riders, and fans of leather jackets will love this shop that's jam-packed with motorcycle gear. On top of those stylish biker jackets, there's an impressive selection of helmets, goggles, gloves, and boots, as well as motorcycle-themed posters by local artists and a slew of T-shirts. ✉ *132 Ossington Ave., Ossington* ☎ *416/856–8011* ⊕ *www.townmoto.com* Ⓜ *63 Ossington bus, south from Ossington subway station.*

VSP Consignment
MIXED CLOTHING | Want to score a designer label on a dime? Head to this beautifully laid out consignment store. A cult following of style-seekers flock to VSP, where the staff curate a selection of gently

worn pieces from Prada, Marni, Victoria Beckham, Gucci, Celine, and other top-shelf brands. ✉ *1410 Dundas St. W, Little Portugal* ☎ *416/588–9821* ⊕ *www.vspconsignment.com* Ⓜ *505 Dundas streetcar, Gladstone Ave. stop.*

MUSIC
★ Rotate This
MUSIC | Music lovers in the know come here for underground and independent music from Canada, the United States, and beyond. Whether you're a hardcore collector who wants to flip through the new secondhand record arrivals or just a casual fan with a record player, it's a long-running paradise of vinyl. ✉ *186 Ossington Ave., Ossington* ☎ *416/504–8447* ⊕ *www.rotate.com* Ⓜ *63 Ossington streetcar, Dundas West stop.*

Parkdale

Farther west than even West Queen West is Parkdale, a fairly gritty neighborhood that's become home to North America's largest Tibetan community. Shops offering everything from beef *momos* (dumplings) to singing bowls infuse the area with a unique local character. The area's authenticity has brought in waves of hip restaurants, bars, and coffee shops, which are sometimes at odds with longtime residents (a late 2010s attempt by a restaurant group to rebrand as Veqandale failed spectacularly). Even farther west is High Park, a sprawling green space with a beautiful pond.

◉ Sights

★ High Park
CITY PARK | **FAMILY** | One of North America's loveliest parks, High Park is especially worth visiting in summer—when special events include professionally staged Shakespeare productions—and in spring when thousands of visitors flock to see the cherry blossoms flower on High Park's sakura trees. Popular fishing spot Grenadier Pond is named after the British soldiers who crashed through the soft ice while rushing to defend the town against invading American forces in 1813. The High Park Zoo, open daily from dawn to dusk, is more modest than the Toronto Zoo but a lot closer to downtown and free. Kids love walking among the deer, Barbary sheep, emus, yaks, llamas, peacocks, and bison.

The park was once privately owned by John George Howard, Toronto's first city architect. Colborne Lodge, his country home built in 1837 on a hill overlooking Lake Ontario, contains its original fireplace, bake oven, and kitchen, as well as many of Howard's drawings and paintings. Other highlights of the 399-acre park are a large swimming pool, tennis courts, fitness trails, and hillside gardens with roses and sculpted hedges. There's limited parking along Bloor Street north of the park, and along the side streets on the eastern side. ✉ *Bordered by Bloor St. W, Gardiner Expressway, Parkside Dr., and Ellis Park Rd. Main entrance off Bloor St. W at High Park Ave., High Park* ⊕ *www.toronto.ca/explore-enjoy/parks-gardens-beaches/high-park* Ⓜ *High Park.*

Museum of Contemporary Art (MOCA)
ART MUSEUM | Located in a former industrial building across the street from a working chocolate factory, the MOCA regularly hosts exhibitions from cutting-edge contemporary art stars from Canada and all over the world. The museum still retains some of its ramshackle concrete past, which makes it feel anything but sterile, and the C$10 price makes it one of the more affordable cultural spots in the city. If you get hungry or thirsty, grab a coffee or pastry from local café Forno Cultura in the lobby. ✉ *158 Sterling Rd., Parkdale* ☎ *416/530–2500* ⊕ *moca.ca* ✦ *C$10* Ⓜ *505 Dundas streetcar, Sterling Rd. stop.*

Did You Know?

High Park, Toronto's largest public park, is popular with hikers, who enjoy its many trails. There's also a modest zoo and Colborne Lodge, the home of John Howard, who once owned this land and gave it to the city under the condition that it remain a park. In the yard of Colborne House you can find a cannon that once stood on the lakefront as a deterrent to U.S. forces, who considered invading Toronto during the War of 1812.

🍴 Restaurants

Miss Thing's

$$$ | **HAWAIIAN** | This Hawaiian-inspired restaurant and tiki bar is a hip hangout, delicious eatery, and occasional nighttime hot spot. The menu includes pineapple fried rice served in an actual pineapple, poke bowls, and plenty of vegan options (fried "chicken" from its sister takeout spot Lovebird is available). **Known for:** lively nightlife crowd; colorful cocktails served in watermelons and coconuts; Hawaiian-inspired share plates. [$] *Average main: C$22* ✉ *1279 Queen St. W, Parkdale* ☎ *416/516–8677* 🌐 *missthings.com* 🕓 *Closed Mon. and Tues.* [M] *501 Queen streetcar, Brock Ave. stop.*

The Skyline Restaurant

$$ | **DINER** | Time seems to slow down at the Skyline, a classic old-school diner that's become a neighborhood hangout for tattooed youngsters and longtime Parkdale characters alike. Club sandwiches, patty melt burgers, and homemade pies make you feel like you're in a 1960s time machine, but long lines for brunch re-root you in present-day Toronto. **Known for:** beer and cocktails at night; relaxed and friendly neighborhood vibe; popular brunch on weekends. [$] *Average main: C$16* ✉ *1426 Queen St. West, Parkdale* 🌐 *www.theskylinetoronto.com* [M] *501 Queen streetcar, Ohara Ave. stop.*

☕ Coffee and Quick Bites

Loga's Corner

$ | **TIBETAN** | The Tibetan dumplings are super-tasty at this no-frills family-run counter-serve spot. **Known for:** friendly family staff; cheap but delicious eats; daily menu written on chalkboard. [$] *Average main: C$7* ✉ *216 Close Ave., Parkdale* ☎ *647/761–0965* [M] *501 Queen streetcar, Lansdowne Ave. stop.*

Sam James Coffee Bar

$ | **CAFÉ** | In a city filled with independent "third wave" coffee bars, competition-trained espresso guru Sam James is a pioneer of lovingly made cappuccinos and lattes. The big, open, black-and-white styled Parkdale shop is filled with friendly local characters, a laid-back vibe, and an on-site bakery. **Known for:** friendly neighborhood vibe; freshly made sourdough from baker Patti Robinson; skilled baristas and flavorful coffee. [$] *Average main: C$5* ✉ *6 Brock Ave., Parkdale* 🌐 *samjamescoffeebar.com* [M] *501 Queen streetcar, Brock Ave. stop.*

Tibet Kitchen

$ | **TIBETAN** | Parkdale has a number of great momo places, but Tibet Kitchen stands out with a cozy sit-down atmosphere and a menu that takes just enough liberties with classic recipes. Chicken, beef, and veggie dumplings are all great, but you can also get them doused in mild curry broth or a sweet, tangy tamarind sauce. **Known for:** chili chicken with rave reviews; good portion sizes; spacious back patio. [$] *Average main: C$13* ✉ *1544 Queen St. W, Parkdale* ☎ *416/913–8726* 🌐 *tibetkitchen.ca* 🕓 *Closed Tues.* [M] *501 Queen streetcar, Sorauren Ave. stop.*

🛍 Shopping

CLOTHING

In Vintage We Trust

MIXED CLOTHING | Looking for a vintage jacket bearing the logo of your favorite sports team? You'll probably find it at this Parkdale boutique, which stocks retro clothing at reasonable prices. Vintage denim, broken-in concert tees, and even vinyl records are on the shelves. It's a good place to find clothes you won't find anywhere else, with ultra-knowledgeable owners willing to tell you the whole history of the items in great detail. ✉ *1580 Queen St. W, Parkdale* ☎ *416/781–0395* 🌐 *invintagewetrust.com* [M] *501 Queen streetcar, Sorauren Ave. stop.*

JEWELRY AND ACCESSORIES
Studio Brillantine

SOUVENIRS | For more than 25 years,
design gift shop Studio Brillantine has
been one of the quirkiest stores in Parkdale. There's a mix of high-end brands
and fun collectibles in a wide variety of
price points. Highlights include Comme
des Garçons wallets, Vivienne Westwood
jewelry, Issey Miyake Bao Bao foldable
bags, Alessi houseware, and sought-after
(and very cute) blind boxes with brands
like Japan's Smiskis. ✉ *1518 Queen St.
W, Parkdale* ☎ *416/536–6521* ⊕ *studio-
brillantine.com* ☞ *Open by appointment
only.* Ⓜ *501 Queen streetcar, Lansdowne
Ave. stop.*

Chapter 8

LESLIEVILLE, GREEKTOWN, LITTLE INDIA, AND THE BEACH

8

Updated by
Natalia Manzocco

 Sights   Restaurants   Hotels   Shopping   Nightlife

★★☆☆☆   ★★★★☆   ★★☆☆☆   ★★★★☆   ★★★☆☆

NEIGHBORHOOD SNAPSHOT

TOP EXPERIENCES

■ **Discover interesting eateries:** Dig into a gyro in Greektown, or eat a dosa that's larger than your head in Little India.

■ **Head back to the beach:** Toronto has some pretty stretches of sand, many of them in a neighborhood helpfully called The Beach.

■ **Music all night long:** Take in big-name bands at the Danforth Music Hall or the Opera House.

■ **Find a bargain:** Browse the hip boutiques along the main drag in Leslieville.

■ **Look for the lighthouse:** Tommy Thompson Park is the place for strolling, biking, or bird-watching.

GETTING HERE

To explore Leslieville, take the 501 Queen streetcar east from downtown to Coxwell Avenue and walk west along Queen Street East. (To reach The Beach, continue riding the 501 Queen streetcar until you get to Beech Avenue.)

To explore Little India, take the 506 Carlton streetcar from downtown, get off at Coxwell Avenue and head west.

To get to Greektown, take the Line 2 Bloor–Danforth subway to Pape station and walk west along Danforth Avenue.

PLANNING YOUR TIME

With its array of small boutiques, Leslieville is a good place to stroll around in during the day. Stick around for dinner or grab a nightcap—the low-key bar scene tends to attract locals throughout the week. By contrast, The Beach is great to explore on a sunny day, though the area tends to be pretty dead after dark. Little India and Greektown both come alive during the day on weekends, when locals and families are out in full force, and both are busy destinations for dinner on Friday and weekends.

FUN FACTS

■ Toronto's Greektown was featured in a number of scenes from the hit comedy *My Big Fat Greek Wedding*, while Leslieville's residential alleys feature prominently in *A Christmas Story*, and the R. C. Harris Water Treatment Plant in The Beach's eastern reaches has popped up in *RoboCop*, *Half Baked*, and other flicks. Little India, meanwhile, owes its existence in small part to the world of cinema: When the Naaz Theatre, reportedly the first place in North America to exclusively show Bollywood movies, opened in the early '70s, more South Asian businesses soon followed.

Toronto's East End may be removed from the big tourist draws, but the area is home to charming neighborhoods, beaches, and some of the city's best international restaurants.

Along Queen Street East, the thoroughfare that passes through many of the city's most interesting neighborhoods, Leslieville is home to an increasingly hip mix of bars, shops, and restaurants. The offerings here lean toward local designer boutiques, cozy eateries, and a number of indie coffee shops. To the north is the Danforth, better known to locals as Greektown. Late-night tavernas and authentic restaurants keep this neighborhood busy at all hours.

Running along Gerrard Street north of Leslieville is the area known as Little India. The neighborhood hosts the largest collection of South Asian businesses in North America, and includes everything from crystal sellers to sari shops. The area comes alive in the evening and on weekends, when families head out for a meal or street snacks.

Pass through Leslieville along Queen East and you'll get to The Beach, a laid-back area lined with heritage homes. The beaches that give the area its name are a popular destination for swimmers and sunbathers in the summertime. Businesses here cater to well-to-do local families, with funky womenswear, relaxed dining, and cute housewares shops. An annual jazz festival in July (⊕ beachesjazz. com) attracts thousands of listeners.

Leslieville

This low-key, walkable neighborhood is home to tons of hidden-gem restaurants, stores, and cafés.

Sights

Tommy Thompson Park

CITY PARK | This park comprises a peninsula that juts 5 km (3 miles) into Lake Ontario. Created from rubble from construction sites around the city and sand dredged for a new port, the peninsula has quickly become one of the best areas in the city for cycling (quad-cycles are available for rent), jogging, walking, photography, and bird-watching. The peninsula is home to the largest breeding colony of double-crested cormorants in North America, as well as dozens of species of terns, ducks, geese, and great egrets. At the end of the spit of land, you'll find a red-and-white lighthouse, in addition to amazing views of downtown and an awesome sense of isolation in nature. Bird-watching is best from May to mid-October. To get here, head east along Queen Street to Leslie Street, then south to the lake. Dogs and private vehicles are not permitted. ⊠ 1 Leslie St. ☎ 416/661–6600 ext. 5770 ⊕ trca.ca Ⓜ Pape.

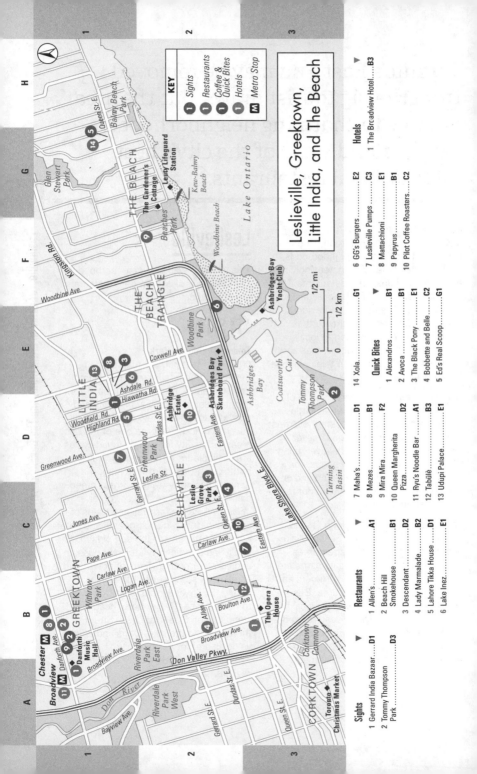

Leslieville, Greektown, Little India, and The Beach

KEY

- **1** Sights
- **1** Restaurants
- **1** Coffee & Quick Bites
- **1** Hotels
- **M** Metro Stop

Sights ▶
1 Gerrard India Bazaar.....**D1**
2 Tommy Thompson Park.....**D3**

Restaurants ▶
1 Allen's.....**A1**
2 Beach Hill Smokehouse.....**B1**
3 Descendant.....**D2**
4 Lady Marmalade.....**B2**
5 Lahore Tikka House.....**D1**
6 Lake Inez.....**E1**
7 Maha's.....**D1**
8 Mezes.....**B1**
9 Mira Mira.....**F2**
10 Queen Margherita Pizza.....**D2**
11 Ryu's Noodle Bar.....**A1**
12 Tabülè.....**B3**
13 Udupi Palace.....**E1**
14 Xola.....**G1**

Quick Bites ▶
1 Alexandros.....**B1**
2 Avoca.....**B1**
3 The Black Pony.....**E1**
4 Bobbette and Belle.....**C2**
5 Ed's Real Scoop.....**G1**
6 GG's Burgers.....**E2**
7 Leslieville Pumps.....**C3**
8 Mattachioni.....**E1**
9 Papyrus.....**B1**
10 Pilot Coffee Roasters.....**C2**

Hotels ▶
1 The Broadview Hotel.....**B3**

🍴 Restaurants

Descendant

$$$ | **ITALIAN** | Toronto has its fair share of delicate, thin-crust Neapolitan pizzas, but this is where the locals go to indulge their carb cravings with thick Detroit-style pies cooked in rectangular pans. Go simple with the classic pepperoni, or try an international twist with the Jaffna (a twist on Sri Lankan *kothu* roti) or a jerk chicken version with pineapple. **Known for:** hip industrial setting; unusual local beers; long waits at peak times. [$] *Average main: C$22* ✉ *1168 Queen St. E* ☎ *647/347–1168* 🌐 *descendantdsp.com* 🕒 *Closed Mon.*

★ Lady Marmalade

$$ | **ECLECTIC** | A Leslieville staple, this brunch spot occupies an airy two-floor space with huge windows in a converted old home just north of the main Queen East drag. It's a lovely spot for hearty, homey dishes like cheddar jalapeño waffles, washed down with coffee in vintage Corningware mugs. **Known for:** gorgeous modern dining room; great variations on eggs Benedict; long waits at peak times. [$] *Average main: C$18* ✉ *265 Broadview Ave., Leslieville* ☎ *647/351–7645* 🌐 *ladymarmalade.ca* [M] *Broadview.*

Queen Margherita Pizza

$$ | **PIZZA** | This industrial-chic space with dark wooden floors and tables is all about authenticity when it comes to Neapolitan-style pizza. Perennial favorites include the classic Margherita, topped with tomato sauce, mozzarella, and basil, as well as the Dominator, with rapini, fennel sausage, and smoked mozzarella. **Known for:** thin-crust pies with gently charred crusts; solid apps like arancini and calamari; popular prix-fixe deal. [$] *Average main: C$18* ✉ *1402 Queen St. E, Suite 8* ☎ *416/466–6555* 🌐 *www.qmpizza.com* 🕒 *Closed Mon. and Tues.* [M] *Pape.*

★ Tabülè

$$ | **MIDDLE EASTERN** | Bold Middle Eastern flavors and spices are showcased at Tabülè, where traditional appetizers include baba ghanoush and hummus served with warm flatbread, and standout falafel fried to a deep golden brown and served with thick, rich tahini sauce. Grilled meats and seafood are also excellent. **Known for:** Moroccan-chic decor; varied drinks list; colorful back patio. [$] *Average main: C$20* ✉ *810 Queen St. E, Leslieville* ☎ *416/465–2500* 🌐 *tabulequeen.com* [M] *Broadview or Queen.*

☕ Coffee and Quick Bites

Bobbette and Belle

$ | **BAKERY** | Known for making Pinterest-perfect cakes for some of the city's splashiest fetes, this charming bakery also offers bite-sized baked goods for a spot of on-the-go luxury. **Known for:** extravagantly decorated cupcakes; macarons in a rainbow of flavors; locally roasted espresso. [$] *Average main: C$10* ✉ *1121 Queen St. E, Leslieville* ☎ *416/466–8800* 🌐 *bobbetteandbelle.com* 🕒 *Closed Mon.* [M] *Queen.*

Leslieville Pumps

$$ | **SOUTHERN** | This combination general store and barbecue joint has long been a refuge for locals in need of a poutine, breakfast sandwich, or butter chicken at odd hours. **Known for:** barbecue sandwiches; late-night service; wide selection of candy and snacks. [$] *Average main: C$15* ✉ *913 Queen St. E, Leslieville* ☎ *416/465–1313* 🌐 *leslievillepumps.com.*

Pilot Coffee Roasters

$ | **CAFÉ** | Pilot is known for roasting some of the city's finest beans and running a growing mini-empire of cafés; this spacious, laid-back location was their first. (Be sure to peruse the bags of beans on display and grab a couple for your suitcase.) **Known for:** chill front patio; top-notch espresso; variety of coffee gear for sale. [$] *Average main: C$5* ✉ *983*

Queen St. E, Leslieville ☎ *416/465–2006* ⊕ *pilotcoffeeroasters.com* Ⓜ *Queen.*

Hotels

The Broadview Hotel

$$$$ | HOTEL | This dramatic historic building is the setting for one of the hippest hotels in town, with quirky rooms, stylish restaurants, and a sprawling rooftop deck. **Pros:** modern decor is a hipster's paradise; also a hopping nightlife destination; best bet in this part of town. **Cons:** party vibe not everyone's cup of tea; some rooms get street noise; no spa or workout area. ⓢ *Rooms from: C$399* ⊠ *106 Broadview Ave., Leslieville* ☎ *416/362–8439* ⊕ *thebroadviewhotel.ca* ⮑ *58 rooms* ꛯ *No Meals.*

Nightlife

BARS
Avling

BREWPUBS | Known as much for its industrial-chic pastel interior as it is for its reliable selection of small-batch beers, this modern brewery is proudly local-first. Many of its brews are made from 99% Ontario ingredients, and the staff grow produce and herbs for stellar seasonal small plates in a rooftop garden. ⊠ *1042 Queen St. E, Leslieville* ☎ *416/469–1010* ⊕ *avling.ca* ⊙ *Closed Mon.*

The Rooftop at the Broadview Hotel

BARS | This hotel's sceney rooftop bar has become a bona fide party destination. The lounge space is encased in a glass pyramid that allows for stunning views of the surrounding city, with a wraparound open-air deck. While you're feasting your eyes on that panorama, enjoy a house cocktail, local beer, or some of the kitchen's globe-spanning small plates. ⊠ *Broadview Hotel, 106 Broadview Ave., Leslieville* ☎ *416/362–8439* ⊕ *thebroad-viewhotel.ca* Ⓜ *Broadview.*

MUSIC VENUES
Opera House

LIVE MUSIC | This late-19th-century vaudeville theater retains some of its original charm, most notably in its proscenium arch over the stage. The 900-capacity venue hosts internationally touring acts of all genres. Locals like to reminisce about seeing such diverse acts as Nirvana, Lucinda Williams, Kings of Leon, LCD Soundsystem, M.I.A., and the Black Keys here. ⊠ *735 Queen St. E* ☎ *416/466–0313* ⊕ *theoperahousetoronto.com.*

Performing Arts

Streetcar Crowsnest

THEATER | This modern, intimate theater is home to long-running local company Crow's Theatre, which is devoted to thought-provoking contemporary theater from Canadian and international playwrights. French brasserie Gare de l'Est is on-site for pre- or post-show eats and cocktails. ⊠ *345 Carlaw Ave., Leslieville* ☎ *647/341–7390* ⊕ *crowstheatre.com.*

 Shopping

Leslieville's shopping scene maintains its artistic cred with a mix of junk shops, handcrafted goods, and slightly off-the-wall boutiques.

ANTIQUES
★ Gadabout

ANTIQUES & COLLECTIBLES | This two-floor antique shop is a rummager's paradise, and a favorite of local set designers looking for period-authentic items. The shelves groan with everything from '50s salt-and-pepper shakers to Hudson's Bay blankets, and there are racks of vintage clothing (for both women and men) with pieces that date as far back as the 19th century. You can rifle through the scores of carefully labeled apothecary drawers to trawl through opera glasses, costume jewelry, and military patches, or peer into display cases at the vintage lunchboxes and handbags. ⊠ *1300 Queen St. E, Leslieville* ☎ *416/463–1254* ⊕ *gadabout. ca* Ⓜ *Greenwood.*

ART GALLERIES
Arts Market
ANTIQUES & COLLECTIBLES | More than 50 artisans and purveyors display their wares in tiny spaces where vintage collections rub shoulders with mixed-media paintings, artisanal soaps, and jewelry. ⊠ *790 Queen St. E* ☎ *647/657–2787* ⊕ *www.artsmarket.ca.*

CLOTHING
Doll Factory by Damzels
WOMEN'S CLOTHING | The Doll Factory carries 1950s rockabilly-style pinup looks from Toronto designers Damzels in this Dress, and other retro-inspired designers from across the continent. Chunky heels, heart-shaped sunglasses and printed sundresses are on the shelves, as well as high-waisted bikinis perfect for flattering those curves. ⊠ *1122 Queen St. E, Leslieville* ☎ *416/598–0509* ⊕ *damzels. com* Ⓜ *Greenwood.*

Good Neighbour
MIXED CLOTHING | This hip boutique, which occupies two floors of a Victorian home, is a one-stop shop for the whole fashion-forward family. The ground floor is devoted to colorful women's and kid's threads, designer denim, and local selections like Bluboho jewelry and Mary Young lingerie. Head upstairs for menswear and home goods, including gorgeous glassware and candles. ⊠ *935 Queen St. E, Leslieville* ☎ *647/350–0663* ⊕ *goodnbr.com.*

Province of Canada
MIXED CLOTHING | Those in need of a souvenir tee should skip the tourist-trap shops and make a beeline for this local brand's soothing all-white boutique, where you can pick up stylish T-shirts, tanks, joggers, and sweaters—all manufactured in Canada. ⊠ *1004 Queen St. E, Leslieville* ☎ *416/551–1229* ⊕ *provinceof-canada.com* Ⓜ *Pape.*

MUSIC
Tiny Record Shop
RECORDS | Tucked in the back of colorful gift shop Token (itself a worthy stop for colorful gifts, kitchenware, and greeting cards) is the aptly named Tiny Record Shop, which offers an all-killer-no-filler selection of vinyl. If you're still missing that one rare Bowie or Stereolab LP to complete your collection, this is the place to check. ⊠ *777 Queen St. E, Leslieville* ☎ *416/479–4363* ⊕ *tinyrecordshop.com* Ⓜ *Broadview.*

Greektown

This area along Danforth Avenue named after Asa Danforth, an American contractor who cut a road into the area in 1799, has a dynamic ethnic mix, although it's primarily a Greek community. In the heart of the neighborhood, east of Chester subway station, is the area referred to as "Greektown," with a row of time-tested sports for *souvlaki* and *saganaki*—plus a handful of bakeries and cafes—interspersed among the boutiques and pubs. Summer is the best season to visit, as most eateries have patios open and are busy until the wee hours of morning.

🍴 Restaurants

Historically known as Greektown, the Danforth has gotten an infusion of international restaurants, which makes for more varied dining options.

Allen's
$$$ | IRISH | Slide into a well-worn wood booth or sit at a checkered table at this low-key steak house, complete with oak bar and pressed-tin ceiling. The steaks and Guinness-braised lamb shanks get rave reviews, but the hamburgers, ground in-house, might be Allen's secret weapon. **Known for:** willow-shaded patio in summer; 300-plus types of whiskey; decadent desserts. Ⓢ *Average main:*

Historically known as Greektown, Danforth serves some of the best Greek food in North America.

C$25 ✉ 143 Danforth Ave. ☎ 416/463–3086 🌐 www.allens.to [M] Broadview.

Beach Hill Smokehouse

$$$ | BARBECUE | This local mini-chain is faithful to the central Texas style of barbecue, producing all manner of meats—brisket, sausages, turkey, and even halal chickens—from a 7,000-pound smoker. The protein is obviously the main attraction, but sides like mac and cheese and sweets like banana pudding have their share of fans. **Known for:** burnt ends (that always sell out early); tender brisket; no-frills dining room. [$] *Average main: C$25 ✉ 429 Danforth Ave., Danforth ☎ 416/546–7633 🌐 beachhillsmokehouse.com ⏲ Closed Mon. and Tues. [M] Chester.*

Mezes

$$$ | GREEK | This long-running Greek spot has a loyal local following, thanks to consistently good food, a sizable menu, and friendly service. Classics like fried calamari and *horiatiki* salads crowned with flavorful feta are here, along with some unusual options like whole quail and fried smelts flown in from Greece. **Known for:** funky decor with wrought iron and mosaics; long Greek wine list; tasty souvlaki and dips. [$] *Average main: C$25 ✉ 456 Danforth Ave. ☎ 416/778–5150 🌐 mezes.com [M] Chester.*

Ryu's Noodle Bar

$$ | RAMEN | One of the city's fave ramen joints, Ryu's has the distinction of being one of a select few eateries invited to serve their wares at Yokohama, Japan's prestigious ramen museum. The "pork blaster" ramen with eight slices of *chashu* is the crowd favorite—but if you're feeling particularly extravagant, there's also a version topped with Angus roast beef. **Known for:** tasty seasonal specials; great pork, chicken, and veggie options; long list of toppings. [$] *Average main: C$17 ✉ 786 Broadview Ave., Danforth ☎ 647/344–9306 🌐 ryusnoodlebar.com ⏲ Closed Mon. [M] Broadview.*

☕ Coffee and Quick Bites

Alexandros

$ | GREEK | On the edge of a small plaza—a gathering spot for Danforth locals—sits this venerable hole-in-the-wall spot, known for serving hot, fresh gyros and souvlaki into the wee hours. **Known for:** late-night service; quick, tasty takeout gyros; retro interior. $ *Average main: C$10* ⊠ *484 Danforth Ave., Danforth* ☎ *416/461–3073* ⊕ *alexandros.ca* Ⓜ *Chester.*

Avoca

$ | DESSERTS | Pick up a frosty treat—and some truffles or chocolate bars to take home—at this ice cream shop and chocolatier just off the main Danforth drag. **Known for:** vegan gelato options; ice cream made in-house; wide array of beautiful truffles. $ *Average main: C$6* ⊠ *176 Hampton Ave., Danforth* ☎ *647/352–4666* ⊕ *instagram.com/avoca-chocolates* Ⓜ *Chester.*

Papyrus

$$ | MIDDLE EASTERN | This Egyptian take-out spot is a welcome herbivore-friendly destination on this souvlaki-heavy strip. Most of the satisfying, delicious dishes here are vegan, with *koshari* (a savory lentil, pasta, and tomato dish), *ful* (spiced, slow-simmered fava beans) and *tameya* (crisp, herbaceous Egyptian falafel) the biggest draws. **Known for:** konafa and saffron rosewater ice cream for dessert; hard-to-find Egyptian street food dishes; friendly, knowledgeable service. $ *Average main: C$12* ⊠ *337 Danforth Ave., Danforth* ☎ *647/352–3878* ⊕ *papyrusfood.ca* Ⓜ *Chester.*

🍸 Nightlife

BARS

Noonan's

PUBS | Crossing the threshold into this Danforth pub, decked out with cozy wooden booths (or "snugs"), is like time-warping to the Emerald Isle. Musicians playing folk and traditional Irish tunes perform here regularly, and the Guinness is always flowing. ⊠ *141 Danforth Ave., Danforth* ☎ *416/778–1804* ⊕ *noonanspub.w3spaces.com* Ⓜ *Broadview.*

The Only Cafe

BARS | The delightfully divey Only, on a relatively quiet stretch of the Danforth, is known as one of the city's best beer bars, with 25 taps plus more than 200 bottles and cans. The atmosphere is dim and raucous, with 1990s alt-rock blasting on the stereo. The bar doubles as a café during the day, and hearty vegetarian pub grub is also on offer. ⊠ *966 Danforth Ave., Danforth* ☎ *416/463–7843* ⊕ *theonlycafe.com* Ⓜ *Donlands.*

MUSIC VENUES

★ Danforth Music Hall

LIVE MUSIC | Built as a cinema in 1919, this stately theater is now a live music venue that attracts popular touring acts that run the gamut of punk, rock, rap, folk, electronic music, and even stand-up comedy. Notable performers have included Rihanna, Blue Rodeo, Lizzo, and Echo and the Bunnymen. ⊠ *147 Danforth Ave., Danforth* ☎ *416/778–8163* ⊕ *thedanforth.com* Ⓜ *Broadview.*

🛍 Shopping

BOOKS

The Scribe

BOOKS | Looking for that first-edition Bukowski, Atwood, or Murakami to complete your collection? This intimate shop specializes in rare editions of popular authors across a range of genres; head up the back stairs for the "Rare Room," where glass cases hold the biggest treasures. There's also a selection of inexpensive used books, vintage art prints, and even tarot cards. ⊠ *375 Danforth Ave., Danforth* ☎ *416/901–8835* ⊕ *thescribebookstore.com* Ⓜ *Chester.*

8

Leslieville, Greektown, Little India, and The Beach GREEKTOWN

FOOD

The Big Carrot

SUPERMARKET | This popular health-food supermarket focuses on organic produce and a wide variety of grab-and-go foods. The surrounding mini-complex contains a juice bar; an outpost of local plant-based restaurant Fresh; a zero-waste store with a variety of eco-friendly home goods, personal care items, and gifts; and a storefront devoted to vitamins and supplements. ⊠ *348 Danforth Ave., Danforth* ☎ *416/466–2129* ⊕ *thebigcarrot. ca* Ⓜ *Chester.*

HOME DECOR

IQ Living

HOUSEWARES | If you like kitchen gadgets, you might lose a couple of hours here. Check out the rainbow array of Le Creuset enamelware and design-forward kitchen tools. There's also a vast selection of insulated lunch boxes, funky Popsicle molds, barware, and any other obscure item your kitchen may be lacking. ⊠ *542 Danforth Ave., Danforth* ☎ *416/466–2727* ⊕ *iqliving.com* Ⓜ *Pape.*

Little India

Follow your nose through the sweets shops, food stalls, and curry restaurants, and allow your eyes to be dazzled by storefront displays of jewelry, Hindu deities, and swaths of sensuous fabrics ablaze with sequins. The area really comes alive in the evening, when those with hungry bellies stroll in search of a curry or biryani; many of the restaurants get especially busy on weekends. The area is home to a diverse group of people, with a number of newer non-Indian businesses reflecting the changing face of the neighborhood.

The area plays host to a few festivals throughout the year. During the biggest event, the Festival of South Asia in July (⊕ *festivalofsouthasia.com*), stages are set for colorful music and dance performances, and the streets fill with the tantalizing scents of snack stalls and the calls of vendors peddling everything from henna tattoos to spicy corn on the cob. In late autumn, the Hindu Festival of Lights (Diwali) is celebrated with a fun and fiery street fete.

Sights

Gerrard India Bazaar

MARKET | The Gerrard India Bazaar isn't a place, exactly. It's a strip of Gerrard Street that's home to dozens of shops and restaurants with a South Asian flair. One of the city's top cultural landmarks, it's the place to find colorful saris, ceramic incense burners, Indian sweets, and fresh grilled corn and cane juice from streetside vendors. It's also home of the Festival of South Asia every summer. ⊠ *Gerrard St., between Greenwood Ave. and Coxwell Ave., Little India* ⊕ *gerrardindiabazaar.com.*

 Restaurants

Lahore Tikka House

$$ | NORTH INDIAN | A trip to Little India isn't complete without hitting up this raucous Pakistani/North Indian spot, popular with locals and families. You might have a long wait at peak times (generally Friday and weekend nights), but standout biryani, kebabs, tandoori chicken, and sizzling plates of tikka will be your reward. **Known for:** colorful tuk-tuks and rickshaws as decor; huge covered side patio; house-made kulfi for dessert. $ *Average main: C$18* ⊠ *1365 Gerrard St. E, Little India* ☎ *416/406–1668* ⊕ *lahoretikkahouse.com* Ⓜ *Greenwood.*

Lake Inez

$$$$ | CONTEMPORARY | This low-lit dining room—presided over by murals of Kate Bush and Virginia Woolf—is an east-end cult fave, thanks to its warm service and nostalgic-yet-inventive small plates.

Known for: long wine list with unusual selections; delicious seafood-forward options; constantly changing seasonal menu. $ Average main: C$45 ✉ 1471 Gerrard St. E, Little India ☾ Closed Sun.–Tues.

★ Maha's

$$ | **MIDDLE EASTERN** | From the "mind-blowing chicken sandwich" to the Pharaoh's po' boy with fried shrimp, it's hard to go wrong at this cheerful, intimate family-run Egyptian brunch joint, located at Little India's eastern edge. **Known for:** long waits on sunny days and weekends; cardamom lattes; award-winning lentil soup. $ Average main: C$20 ✉ 226 Greenwood Ave., Little India ☎ 416/462–2703 ⊕ mahasbrunch.com ☾ Closed Wed.

Udupi Palace

$$ | **INDIAN** | This meat-free Indian restaurant, tucked into a large basement just below street level, is beloved by herbivores and omnivores alike. The dosas are the thing to get here, but they also do excellent renditions of classic snacks like *pakoras* and *bhaji*, as well as curries like *aloo gobi* or *saag* paneer. **Known for:** broad range of vegetarian and vegan eats; enormous rolled dosas; utilitarian decor. $ Average main: C$15 ✉ 1460 Gerrard St. E ☎ 416/405–8189 ⊕ udupipalace.ca.

🍵 Coffee and Quick Bites

The Black Pony

$$ | **CAFÉ** | With espresso, baked goods, bar snacks, beers, and cocktails on offer, this colorful café/bar (look for the neon pegasus sign) serves as a reliable local hangout from morning 'til night. **Known for:** hearty sandwiches; freshly baked sweet treats; side patio ideal for people-watching. $ Average main: C$14 ✉ 1481 Gerrard St. E, Little India ☎ 416/466–7669 ⊕ blackponybar.ca Ⓜ Coxwell.

Mattachioni

$$ | **ITALIAN** | Whether you're looking for imported pesto potato chips, a bottle of wine, a fresh cappuccino, or a hearty salad, this Italian bodega has you covered. **Known for:** great thin-crust pizzas; flavorful panini on house-baked bread; Italian groceries. $ Average main: C$15 ✉ 1501 Gerrard St. E, Little India ☎ 416/466–1111 ⊕ mattachioni.com ☾ Closed Sun. and Mon. Ⓜ Coxwell.

The Beach

This neighborhood's official name has been a source of controversy since the 1980s: The Beach versus The Beaches. It boils down to whether you view the four separate beaches—Woodbine, Balmy, Kew, and Scarboro—as one collective entity. When the area decided to welcome tourists with fancy, emblematic street signs, the long-running debate resurfaced. While officially "The Beach" won, most Torontonians still call the neighborhood The Beaches.

Beaches

Kew-Balmy Beach

BEACH | Just a 10-minute walk east on the boardwalk from Woodbine Beach, the officially merged stretch of Kew Beach, Scarboro Beach, and Balmy Beach is a bit pebbly and slightly more secluded, making it ideal for those seeking a quiet stroll or a dip in the lake. Look for the historic Leuty Lifeguard Station, which was built in the 1920s. Kayak and stand-up paddleboard rental shops sit along the shore. **Amenities:** food and drink; lifeguards; parking (fee); toilets. **Best for:** walking; sunrise; swimming. ✉ 1 Beech Ave., The Beach ⊕ toronto.ca/parks Ⓜ Woodbine.

Woodbine Beach

BEACH | The largest, and probably best-known, of all the area beaches spans 37½ acres along the coast of Lake

Ontario. You'll find beachgoers of all ages swimming, sunbathing, picnicking, strolling the boardwalk, and playing volleyball on one of the numerous outdoor courts. **Amenities:** food and drink; lifeguards; parking (fee); showers; toilets. **Best for:** partiers; sunrise; swimming; walking. ✉ *1675 Lake Shore Blvd. E, The Beach* 🌐 *toronto.ca/parks* [M] *Woodbine.*

🍴 Restaurants

Mira Mira

$$$ | **DINER** | **FAMILY** | Luxurious takes on diner and brunch classics—think Benedicts and open-faced turkey sandwiches—dominate the ever-evolving menu at this cute corner eatery. There's something for everyone, including a menu for the under-10 set, but dishes like fried truffled mushrooms and smoked pork loin are decidedly refined. **Known for:** sunny front patio; interesting cocktails and microbrews; signature steak and eggs. [$] *Average main: C$25* ✉ *1963 Queen St. E, The Beach* ☎ *416/792–6472* 🌐 *eatmiramira.com* 🕒 *Closed Mon. and Tues.* [M] *Woodbine.*

Xola

$$$ | **MEXICAN** | Clocking in at around just 20 seats, this colorful family-run neighborhood spot showcases the delicious nuances of classic Mexican cuisine. Dishes here are rich in flavor and composed with care, from duck confit tacos and grilled octopus to a mole dish that's been slow-cooked over eight hours. **Known for:** slow-cooked meats; variety of guacamoles and ceviches; sizeable selection of tequila and mescal. [$] *Average main: C$28* ✉ *2222A Queen St. E, The Beach* ☎ *647/827–9070* 🌐 *xolarestaurant.com* 🕒 *Closed Tues.* [M] *Woodbine.*

☕ Coffee and Quick Bites

Ed's Real Scoop

$ | **ICE CREAM** | This neighborhood scoop joint, featuring a long list of house-made flavors, is a hot spot for locals and families in the summer months. A second location serves Leslieville at 920 Queen Street East. **Known for:** mix of ice cream, gelato, and sorbet options; signature flavors like burnt marshmallow; house-made waffle cones. [$] *Average main: C$5* ✉ *2224 Queen St. E, The Beach* ☎ *416/699–6100* 🌐 *edsrealscoop.com.*

GG's Burgers

$ | **BURGER** | Every boardwalk needs a solid burger place—and this cute takeout counter ably covers all bases, from burger and hot dog combos to soft serve and house-made canned cocktails. **Known for:** psychedelic retro decor; cult-fave spicy chicken sandwich; crispy-edged smash burgers. [$] *Average main: C$10* ✉ *1681 Lake Shore Blvd. E, The Beach* ☎ *416/694–8811* 🌐 *ggsburgers.com* [M] *Woodbine.*

🎟 Performing Arts

History

CONCERTS | Created in concert with homegrown megastar Drake, this spacious 2,553-seat venue is a bona fide performing arts destination in the otherwise sleepy Beach, drawing boldface names across a variety of genres—Stereolab, the Psychedelic Furs, Lil Nas X, Muse, and Demi Lovato, to name just a few. ✉ *1663 Queen St. E, The Beach* ☎ *416/260–5566* 🌐 *historytoronto.com.*

Shopping

The Beach is known for casual-clothing stores, gift and antiques shops, and bars and restaurants.

FOOD

Nutty Chocolatier

CHOCOLATE | A Beach institution, the Nutty Chocolatier serves ice cream on waffle cones (made in-house daily), as well as handmade molded chocolates and truffles. Even though their house-made sweets are delicious, the sizable selection of imported candy and treats from the United Kingdom and other parts of the globe have an equally devoted following. ⊠ *2179 Queen St. E, The Beach* ☎ *416/698–5548* ⊕ *thenuttychocolatier. com* Ⓜ *Woodbine.*

HOME DECOR

Seagull Classics Ltd.

HOUSEWARES | Cottage-chic is the name of the game at this home decor shop that's all about cute, woodsy items like rugs, retro deck chairs, quirky signage, and Tiffany-style lamps. There's a nice selection of furniture, and they also do custom orders for pine shelving and cabinets. ⊠ *1974 Queen St. E, The Beach* ☎ *416/690–5224* ⊕ *seagullclassics.com* Ⓜ *Woodbine.*

Activities

WATER SPORTS

Kayak and canoe rentals are fairly easy to come by at The Beach, but stand-up paddleboarding has become an increasingly popular activity on the Lake Ontario shores.

iPaddle Adventures

KAYAKING | Single kayaks, tandem kayaks, and stand-up paddleboards can be booked (with 24-hour advance notice) at this rental spot. You can also book a single, double, or group kayak or SUP lesson, or arrange for an "illuminated" SUP session on under-lit paddleboards that goes from sunset into the evening. ⊠ *Ashbridge's Bay Park, The Beach* ⊹ *Northwest end of the boardwalk* ☎ *416/553–4067* ⊕ *ipaddleadventures. com* Ⓜ *Woodbine.*

WSUP Toronto

STAND UP PADDLEBOARDING | Located steps from the shoreline between Woodbine and Kew-Balmy Beach, WSUP offers private, semi-private, and group lessons in stand-up paddleboarding, as well as gear rentals. On top of introductory classes, their programming includes sunrise sessions and "fluid yoga" classes held on paddleboards. ⊠ *77 Kewbeach Ave., The Beach* ⊕ *wsuptoronto.ca* Ⓜ *Woodbine.*

Chapter 9

QUEEN'S PARK, THE ANNEX, AND LITTLE ITALY

Updated by
Natalia Manzocco

👁 Sights	🍽 Restaurants	🛏 Hotels	🛍 Shopping	🍸 Nightlife
★★★★☆	★★★★☆	★★☆☆☆	★★★☆☆	★★★☆☆

NEIGHBORHOOD SNAPSHOT

TOP EXPERIENCES

■ **Feel like royalty at Casa Loma:** This grand display of extravagance has 98 rooms, two towers, creepy passageways, and lots of secret panels.

■ **Take a culinary trip:** Grab some great food—Italian or otherwise—in Little Italy, a perennial dining destination.

■ **Marvel at Queen's Park:** Visit the handsome parliamentary buildings around the perimeter of one of the city's prettiest parks.

■ **Show your school spirit:** Explore the University of Toronto's historic campus, starting with the splendor of Hart House.

■ **Grab a drink in the Annex:** Linger over a coffee or a pint in this charming historical neighborhood.

GETTING HERE

Use the subway to reach the University of Toronto (St. George and Queen's Park stations), Casa Loma (Dupont station), the Annex (Spadina and Bathurst stations), and Queen's Park (Queen's Park station). Little Italy can be reached by Streetcar 506 along College Street (since College Street turns into Carlton Street at Yonge, this streetcar is often also referred to as the "Carlton Car").

PLANNING YOUR TIME

The Queen's Park and Annex areas are nice places to take a stroll any time of year, because many of the attractions bring you indoors. A visit to the legislature and one or two of the museums or libraries would make a nice half-day (or more) program. Give yourself at least a few hours for a full tour of Casa Loma and about an hour for the Bata Shoe Museum. Make an evening of dinner and drinks in Little Italy.

FUN FACTS

■ The University of Toronto, which sits sandwiched between Queen's Park and the Annex, has been the site of numerous scientific breakthroughs, including the discovery of insulin by Frederick Banting and Charles Best in 1921, and the construction of North America's first electron microscope in 1938.

■ The surrounding area's intellectual bent (and rows of lovely old homes) have attracted numerous artists and academics, with Margaret Atwood, David Suzuki, Catherine O'Hara, and Meghan Markle all calling the area home over the years.

This vast area that encompasses a huge chunk of Toronto's downtown core holds several important attractions, but it couldn't feel further from a tourist trap if it tried, bringing together Toronto's upper crust, Ontario's provincial politicians, Canada's intellectual set, and a rapidly evolving former Italian neighborhood.

Take a break in one of the Annex's many casual spots and you could be rubbing shoulders with a student cramming for an exam, a blocked author looking for inspiration, or a busy civil servant picking up a jolt of caffeine to go.

The large, oval Queen's Park circles the Ontario Provincial Legislature and is straddled by the sprawling, 160-acre downtown campus of the University of Toronto. Wandering this neighborhood will take you past century-old colleges, Gothic cathedrals, and plenty of quiet benches overlooking leafy courtyards and student-filled parks.

The University of Toronto's campus overflows west into the Annex, where students and scholarly types while away the hours after class. This frantic section of Bloor Street West abounds with ethnic restaurants and plenty of student-friendly cafés and bars, plus two of the city's must-see attractions: the Bata Shoe Museum and Casa Loma.

Similarly energetic is Little Italy, where music spills out of lively eateries and patios are packed in the summertime. The myriad wine bars and restaurants attract a mix of locals out for a leisurely dinner and special-occasion diners looking to splash out on a night to remember.

Queen's Park

To locals, Queen's Park refers to not only the neighborhood, but also the historic Ontario Legislative Building that serves as the seat of the provincial government. Built in 1893, the pink sandstone building takes its cues from British architecture, with a hefty collection of artwork from Canada and abroad. Just a few blocks west, you'll hit the edge of the University of Toronto's sprawling campus, which is packed with stately buildings, including the neo-Gothic Hart House, home to a theater, café, and gallery.

Sights

Hart House
COLLEGE | Looking for all the world like a setting from one of the Harry Potter novels, this neo-Gothic student center opened its doors in 1919. Originally restricted to male students, Hart House

KEY

- **1** Sights
- **1** Restaurants
- **1** Coffee & Quick Bites
- **1** Hotels
- **M** Metro Stop

Queen's Park, the Annex, and Little Italy

Sights ▼

1 Bata Shoe Museum **D3**
2 Casa Loma **C1**
3 Hart House **D3**
4 Lillian H. Smith Branch of the Toronto Public Library **D4**
5 Ontario Legislative Building **E3**
6 University of Toronto ... **D3**

Restaurants ▼

1 Bar Raval **C4**
2 Café Diplomatico **B4**
3 Chiado **A5**
4 Duff's Famous Wings **B4**
5 Fat Pasha **B1**
6 Fran's **E3**
7 Future Bistro **C3**
8 Giulietta **A5**
9 Le Paradis **D1**
10 Mercatto **E4**
11 Piano Piano **C3**

Quick Bites ▼

1 The Big Chill **B4**
2 Flock **E4**
3 NEO Coffee Bar **E4**
4 The Night Baker **A5**
5 PG Cluck's **B4**
6 Rustle and Still **B3**
7 Schmaltz Appetizing **B1**

Hotels ▼

1 The Annex Hotel **C3**
2 Kimpton Saint George .. **D2**

has been open to women since 1972. Keep your eyes peeled for the nearly 200 pieces of artwork scattered throughout the building, including a revolving collection of works by famed Canadian artists like the Group of Seven and Emily Carr. Each year, new pieces are carefully curated by committee, with a focus on living Canadian artists, particularly those of First Nations and culturally diverse backgrounds. The Justina M. Barnicke Gallery comprises two rooms of mixed-media art showcasing both student talent and traveling exhibitions. The stained-glass windows and vaulted ceiling in the Great Hall are impressive, but so is the cuisine at the on-site Gallery Grill, which offers a menu of grilled seafood, house-made pastas, and creative veggie options from September through June. ✉ *University of Toronto, 7 Hart House Circle, Queen's Park* ☎ *416/978–2452* ⊕ *www.harthouse.ca* Ⓜ *Museum.*

Lillian H. Smith Branch of the Toronto Public Library
LIBRARY | FAMILY | Honoring the memory of the city's first children's librarian, this branch houses the Osborne Collection of Early Children's Books, which contains over 80,000 items ranging from the 14th century to the present. In addition, the Merril Collection of Science Fiction, Speculation, and Fantasy includes another 80,000-plus items covering everything from parapsychology to UFOs. ✉ *239 College St., Queen's Park* ☎ *416/393–7746* ⊕ *torontopubliclibrary.ca* 🍽 *Free* Ⓜ *Queen's Park.*

Ontario Legislative Building
GOVERNMENT BUILDING | This 1893 Romanesque revival building is often referred to simply as "Queen's Park," after the surrounding grounds. The detail-rich exterior is made of pink Ontario sandstone; inside, the huge, lovely halls echo half a millennium of English architecture. The long hallways are hung with hundreds of oils by Canadian artists, and a permanent space is devoted to rotating works by

Indigenous artists. Take a 30-minute-long tour from the lobby (advance registration required) to see the chamber where the 124 MPPs, or members of provincial parliament, meet. It is also possible to watch parliament in session from the public gallery. Statues dot the lawn in front of the building, including one of Queen Victoria and one of Canada's first prime ministers, Sir John A. Macdonald. ✉ *1 Queen's Park* ☎ *416/325–0061* ⊕ *ola.org* 🍽 *Free* Ⓜ *Queen's Park.*

University of Toronto
COLLEGE | Almost a city unto itself, the University of Toronto's student and staff population numbers well over 100,000. The institution dates to 1827, when King George IV signed a charter for a "King's College in the Town of York, Capital of Upper Canada." The Church of England had control then, but by 1850 the college was proclaimed nondenominational, renamed the University of Toronto, and put under the control of the province. Then, in a spirit of Christian competition, the Anglicans started Trinity College, the Methodists began Victoria, and the Roman Catholics began St. Michael's; by the time the Presbyterians founded Knox College, the University was changing at a great rate. Now the 12 schools and faculties are united and accept students from all over the world. The architecture is interesting, if uneven, as one might expect on a campus that's been built in bits and pieces over 150 years. ✉ *Visitors Centre, 25 King's College Circle* ☎ *416/978–5000* ⊕ *utoronto.ca* Ⓜ *St. George or Queen's Park.*

🍴 Restaurants

Between civil servants at Queen's Park, students at University of Toronto, and office workers south along University, the dining crowds are decidedly Monday-to-Friday in this area—and many restaurants follow suit. However, there are a few solid options, especially on the fringes of the area.

Fran's

$$ | **DINER** | For generations, hungry Torontonians have ended up at this reliable round-the-clock diner for classic breakfasts and greasy-spoon dishes. Burgers and Benedicts are staples, but the menu makes room for a variety of comfort food crowd-pleasers like lasagnas, meat loaf, and steak. **Known for:** retro diner atmosphere; 24-hour service; upstairs patio. [$] *Average main: C$16* ✉ *20 College St., Queen's Park* ☎ *416/923–9867* 🌐 *fransrestaurant.com* [M] *College.*

Mercatto

$$$ | **ITALIAN** | Crowd-pleasing, reliable Italian fare—pizzas, pastas, and a few meaty mains—is the name of the game at this spacious Italian trattoria, part of a small local family of restaurants. **Known for:** warm, modern decor; good thin-crust pizzas; tasty Italian sweets. [$] *Average main: 24* ✉ *101 College St., Queen's Park* ✣ *Northeast corner of building* ☎ *416/595–5625* 🌐 *college.mercatto.ca* 🕒 *Closed weekends* [M] *Queen's Park.*

Coffee and Quick Bites

Flock

$$ | **CANADIAN** | This local mini-chain does a brisk business in fresh, slow-cooked rotisserie chicken, either sold as combo meals or atop customizable salads. **Known for:** grab-and-go service; tasty side soups; hearty, well-rounded salads. [$] *Average main: C$15* ✉ *661 University Ave., Queen's Park* 🌐 *eatflock.com* 🕒 *Closed weekends* [M] *Queen's Park.*

NEO COFFEE BAR

$ | **JAPANESE FUSION** | Whether you're in need of an espresso, a pour-over, a *hojicha* tea latte, a sandwich, or a gorgeous slice of cake, this modern Japanese café has you covered. **Known for:** industrial-chic interior; house-made baked goods; top-quality local espresso. [$] *Average main: C$9* ✉ *770 Bay St., Unit 3, Queen's Park* 🌐 *neocoffeebar.com* [M] *College or Queen's Park.*

Performing Arts

CLASSICAL MUSIC

MacMillan Theatre

MUSIC | Performances by students and faculty at the University of Toronto Faculty of Music, ranging from symphony to jazz to full-scale operas, take place September through June at the 815-seat MacMillan Theatre. Smaller-scale performances fill the 490-seat Walter Hall. As a bonus, many performances are free to attend. During the summer, you may be able to catch a performance by a visiting musician. ✉ *University of Toronto Faculty of Music, Edward Johnson Bldg., 80 Queen's Park Crescent* ☎ *416/408–0208* 🌐 *music.utoronto.ca* 🕒 *Closed July and Aug.* [M] *Museum.*

THEATER

Hart House Theatre

THEATER | The main theater space of the University of Toronto since 1919, Hart House mounts emerging-artist and student productions from September to March, with musicals, Shakespeare, contemporary plays, and classics all represented. ✉ *7 Hart House Circle* ☎ *416/978–2452* 🌐 *www.harthousetheatre.ca* [M] *Museum, St. George, or Queen's Park.*

The Annex

Born in 1887, when the burgeoning town of Toronto engulfed the area between Bathurst Street and Avenue Road north from Bloor Street to the Canadian Pacific Railway tracks at what is now Dupont Street, the countrified Annex soon became an enclave for the well-to-do; today it attracts an intellectual set. The prominent Gooderham family, owners of a distillery, erected a lovely red castle at the corner of St. George Street and Bloor Street, now the home of the exclusive York Club.

As Queen Victoria gave way to King Edward, old money gave way to new money and ethnic groups came and went. Upon the arrival of developers, many Edwardian mansions were demolished to make room for bland 1960s-era apartment buildings.

Still, the Annex, with its hundreds of attractive old homes, can be cited as a prime example of Toronto's success in preserving lovely, safe streets within the downtown area. Examples of late-19th-century architecture can be spotted on Admiral Road, Lowther Avenue, and Bloor Street, west of Spadina Avenue. Round turrets, pyramid-shaped roofs, and conical spires are among the pleasures shared by some 15,000 Torontonians who live in this vibrant community, including professors, students, writers, lawyers, and other professional and artsy types. Bloor Street between Spadina and Palmerston keeps them fed and entertained with its bohemian collection of bookstores, whole-foods shops, bars, and laid-back restaurants.

Sights

Bata Shoe Museum

OTHER MUSEUM | Created by Sonja Bata, wife of the founder of the Bata Shoe Company, this museum holds a permanent collection of more than 14,000 foot coverings and, through the changing fashions, highlights the craft and sociology of making shoes. Some items date back more than 4,000 years. Among the items that may pop up in the rotating exhibits are delicate 16th-century velvet platforms, iron-spiked shoes used for crushing chestnuts, 8-inch lime green Vivienne Westwood heels, Elton John's boots, and Elvis Presley's blue (patent leather, not suede) shoes. ✉ *327 Bloor St. W, The Annex* ☎ *416/979–7799* 🌐 *batashoemuseum.ca* 🎟 *C$14* [M] *St. George.*

Casa Loma

HISTORIC HOME | **FAMILY** | A European-style castle, Casa Loma was commissioned by financier Sir Henry Pellatt, who spent the equivalent of C$20 million building his dream home—only to lose it to the taxman a decade later. Some impressive details are the giant pipe organ, the 60-foot-high ceilings in the Great Hall, and the 5-acre estate gardens. The rooms are copies of those in English, Spanish, Scottish, and Austrian castles, including Windsor Castle's Peacock Alley. This has been the location for many a horror movie and period drama, plus Hollywood blockbusters like *Chicago* and *X-Men*. Included in the admission price is a self-guided multimedia tour (available in nine languages). **■TIP→ A tour of Casa Loma is a good 1½-km (1-mile) walk, so wear sensible shoes.** ✉ *1 Austin Terr., The Annex* ☎ *416/923–1171* 🌐 *casaloma.org* 🎟 *C$40* [M] *Dupont.*

Restaurants

Fat Pasha

$$$$ | **MIDDLE EASTERN** | A hit with locals, this cozy, low-lit spot is Middle Eastern food at its finest. The menu is a love letter to classics like hummus, shawarma, and falafel, with a few novel creations thrown in for good measure. **Known for:** showstopping halloumi-stuffed cauliflower; salatim platters of dips and apps; hidden back patio. [$] *Average main: C$32* ✉ *414 Dupont St., The Annex* ☎ *647/646–1698* 🌐 *fatpasha.com* 🕒 *Closed Mon. and Tues.* [M] *Dupont.*

Future Bistro

$$ | **CAFÉ** | Aside from European-style baked goods and all-day breakfasts, this spot also serves Old World recipes like cabbage rolls, schnitzel, and potato-cheese pierogi slathered with sour cream. It's beloved by the pastry-and-coffee crowd and by students wanting generous portions from early morning until late at night. **Known for:** sunny patio;

The European-style castle of Casa Loma looks out over Toronto's modern skyline.

huge selection of house-made desserts; all you can eat pierogi on Wednesday. $ *Average main: C$15* ✉ *483 Bloor St. W, The Annex* ☎ *416/922–5875* ⊕ *futurebistro.ca* Ⓜ *Spadina.*

Le Paradis

$$$ | FRENCH | This low-lit, warrenlike bistro has hardly changed at all since the '90s—and the regulars like it that way. The open kitchen turns out reliable French fare like steak tartare, seared scallops, and duck confit; desserts include flourless chocolate cake and house-made ice cream. **Known for:** bustling atmosphere; inexpensive wine and cocktails; helpful, unpretentious service. $ *Average main: C$30* ✉ *166 Bedford Rd., The Annex* ☎ *416/921–0995* ⊕ *www.leparadis.com* Ⓜ *Dupont.*

★ Piano Piano

$$$ | ITALIAN | On a quiet stretch of Harbord lies this low-lit modern trattoria, popular with couples and families alike. The menu spans from antipasti and fresh pastas (the mushroom cavatelli and giant ravioli are crowd-pleasers) to excellent blistered-crust pizzas and picturesque desserts—but whatever you order is bound to be great. **Known for:** delicious updated Italian classics; striking rose-patterned wallpaper and front mural; sister snack bar (Piccolo Piano) located across the street. $ *Average main: C$25* ✉ *88 Harbord St., The Annex* ☎ *416/929–7788* ⊕ *pianopianotherestaurant.com.*

☕ Coffee and Quick Bites

Rustle and Still

$$ | VIETNAMESE | Located where the Annex's western edge blends into Koreatown, this quirky café offers spins on Vietnamese sandwiches and mains, plus coffee and baked treats. **Known for:** hearty banh mi sandwiches (including vegan options); lattes made with matcha, pandan, and hojicha; plant-laden decor. $ *Average main: C$14* ✉ *605 Bloor St. W, The Annex* ☎ *647/350–8893* ⊕ *rustleandstill.com* Ⓜ *Bathurst.*

Schmaltz Appetizing

$$ | JEWISH DELI | Tucked just behind its big-brother restaurant Fat Pasha, Schmaltz is a love letter to the Jewish appetizing shops of yore, turning out fresh bagel sandwiches with traditional toppings like smoked lox and whitefish salad. **Known for:** bagels from beloved uptown bakery Gryfe's; takeout-only setting; selection of Canadian Covered Bridge chips. $ *Average main: C$16* ⊠ *414 Dupont St., The Annex* ☎ *647/350–4261* ⊕ *schmaltzappetizing. com* ☾ *Closed Mon. and Tues.* Ⓜ *Dupont.*

Hotels

While most of the hotel action happens to the east in Yorkville, a few boutique hotel properties are making inroads into the Annex.

The Annex Hotel

$$$ | HOTEL | This trendy, no-frills boutique hotel features industrial-chic, loft-inspired rooms and boasts an on-site café and wine bar, burger joint, and nightclub. **Pros:** comfy mattresses from the Ritz-Carlton's supplier; SMS-based check-in and concierge service available 24/7; rooms feature local art and views of colorful murals. **Cons:** no TVs (but fully loaded iPads are provided); little separation between toilets and showers; second-floor rooms get loud on weekends. $ *Rooms from: C$275* ⊠ *296 Brunswick Ave., The Annex* ☎ *647/694–9868* ⊕ *theannexhotels.com* ⌑ *24 rooms* ⦾| *Free Breakfast* Ⓜ *Spadina.*

★ Kimpton Saint George

$$$$ | HOTEL | FAMILY | A splashy C$40 million renovation gave this historic hotel the full boutique treatment while emphasizing its eye-grabbing architectural details. **Pros:** cloud-soft custom mattresses; complimentary happy hour; sizable gym for a boutique hotel. **Cons:** few bathrooms have tubs; service at lobby gastropub can be uneven; some street noise. $ *Rooms*

from: C$375 ⊠ *280 Bloor St. W, The Annex* ☎ *416/968–0010* ⊕ *kimptonsaint-george.com* ⌑ *188 rooms* ⦾| *No Meals* Ⓜ *Spadina.*

Nightlife

Long-running pubs dominate the nightlife scene in this neighborhood, with a few new spaces attracting a younger, hipper crowd.

BARS

Insomnia

BARS | An Annex fave since the '90s, this brick-walled spot offers a variety of drink specials throughout the week, plus bar bites and the odd live DJ set. Head right back the next morning for a tasty brunch. ⊠ *563 Bloor St. W, The Annex* ☎ *416/588–3907* ⊕ *insomniarestaurant. com* Ⓜ *Bathurst.*

Kinka Izakaya Bloor

BARS | The rowdy atmosphere—every guest is greeted with a cheerful hello in Japanese by kitchen and serving staff when you walk through the door—is just part of what makes this izakaya so charming. Grab a Sapporo, sake, or cocktail splashed with Suntory or vodka, but don't sleep on the delicious small plates. ⊠ *559 Bloor St. W, The Annex* ☎ *647/343–1101* ⊕ *kinkaizakaya.com* Ⓜ *Bathurst.*

MUSIC VENUES

Lee's Palace

LIVE MUSIC | Some of the most exciting bands in rock, indie, and punk play at this grungy-yet-venerable club with a psychedelic graffiti facade on the edge of the University of Toronto campus. Grab a Toronto-style roti (Indian curry wrapped Caribbean-style in flatbread) from the service window between sets. Upstairs is the Dance Cave, a no-frills dance club popular with students. ⊠ *529 Bloor St. W, The Annex* ☎ *416/532–1598* ⊕ *leespalace.com* Ⓜ *Bathurst.*

COMEDY CLUBS
Comedy Bar
COMEDY CLUBS | Located a short jaunt west of the Annex is this basement club, a hotbed of activity for home-grown and touring comics alike. There are sketch and stand-up shows from locals most nights of the week, but the room has also hosted boldface names like Janeane Garofalo, Marc Maron, and Mae Martin. ⊠ *945 Bloor St. W, The Annex* ☎ *416/551–6540* ⊕ *comedybar.ca* Ⓜ *Ossington.*

Performing Arts

CLASSICAL MUSIC
Tafelmusik
MUSIC | Internationally renowned as one of the world's finest period ensembles, Tafelmusik presents baroque and classical music on original instruments. Most performances are held in Trinity–St. Paul's Centre, a stunningly revitalized church hall. Tafelmusik's Sing-Along *Messiah* performance is a rollicking Christmas season highlight where the audience is invited to join in. ⊠ *Trinity–St. Paul's Centre, Jeanne Lamon Hall, 427 Bloor St. W, The Annex* ☎ *833/964–6337* ⊕ *tafelmusik.org* Ⓜ *Spadina.*

FILM
Hot Docs Ted Rogers Cinema
FILM | If you like your films factual, informative, and inspiring, then the Hot Docs Cinema is for you. The permanent home of the Hot Docs festival each spring, this century-old cinema also has an ongoing calendar of documentaries—on everything from art to politics—and crowd-pleasing classics. ⊠ *506 Bloor St. W, The Annex* ☎ *416/637–3123* ⊕ *hotdocs.ca* Ⓜ *Bathurst.*

Paradise Theatre
FILM | This art deco–era cinema located a few minutes west of the Annex underwent a splashy restoration in 2019. Classic and second-run movies are screened here, but the theater also plays host to live music—from touring acts to cover bands and string quartets—and stand-up comics. Wine, cocktails, and Italian food are served next door at Osteria Rialto. ⊠ *1006 Bloor St. W, The Annex* ☎ *416/306–8134* ⊕ *paradiseonbloor.com* Ⓜ *Ossington.*

THEATER
Tarragon Theatre
THEATER | This converted warehouse presents plays by new and established Canadian playwrights, with special focus on nurturing emerging voices in Canadian theater. The complex features multiple theater spaces and studios, and maverick companies will occasionally mount interesting experimental productions in some of the smaller rooms. ⊠ *30 Bridgman Ave., The Annex* ☎ *416/531–1827* ⊕ *tarragontheatre.com* Ⓜ *Dupont.*

Shopping

In a neighborhood near the University of Toronto campus populated largely by academics and students, a mix of restored Victorians and brick low-rises house cafés and bistros, used-book and gift stores, and the occasional fashion boutique.

BOOKS
Bakka Phoenix
BOOKS | Established in 1972, Bakka Phoenix has the distinction of being the world's oldest science fiction and fantasy bookstore. The shop is home to several thousand new and used titles, with the selection catering to readers of all ages. Knowledgeable staff members are always on hand to help find what you're looking for (or suggest something new). ⊠ *84 Harbord St., The Annex* ☎ *416/963–9993* ⊕ *bakkaphoenixbooks.com* Ⓜ *Spadina.*

BMV

BOOKS | Snag deals on classic books and new releases alike at this multilevel used bookstore (short for "Books Magazines Video"). Comics fans will also be happy with the selection of single issues and graphic novels. ✉ *471 Bloor St. W, The Annex* ☎ *416/967–5757* ⊕ *bmvbooks. com* Ⓜ *Spadina.*

CLOTHING
Common Sort

SECOND-HAND | The best-dressed Torontonians clear out their closets at this consignment store, which always has something cheap and cheerful on the racks. Brands range from fast-fashion to vintage to designer; the eagle-eyed might even spot some Marni or Max Mara. ✉ *444 Bloor St. W, The Annex* ☎ *416/532–5990* ⊕ *commonsort.com* Ⓜ *Bathurst.*

Risqué

WOMEN'S CLOTHING | Breezy, colorful, and wearable styles—from dresses and blouses to trendy accessories—fill this boutique, owned and operated by two sisters. You may spot brands like Levi's interspersed among pieces from their house line. ✉ *660 Bloor St. W, The Annex* ☎ *647/350–3633* ⊕ *risqueclothing.ca* ⊘ *Closed Mon. and Tues.* Ⓜ *Bathurst.*

Secrets from Your Sister

LINGERIE | The art of the brassiere is taken seriously at this appointment-only bra-fitting boutique. Knowledgeable (but pretension-free) staffers host fitting sessions that typically last around 30 minutes. The massive selection includes sports, fashion, strapless, seamless, and nursing bras, plus sleepwear and experimental lingerie, in wide-ranging sizes and fits. ✉ *560 Bloor St. W, The Annex* ☎ *416/538–1234* ⊕ *secretsfromyoursister.com* ⊘ *Closed Sun. and Mon.* ☞ *Open by appointment only* Ⓜ *Bathurst.*

HOME DECOR
Nella Cucina

HOUSEWARES | Shop alongside Toronto chefs for quality kitchen supplies—cheese knives, seafood shears, or unique showpieces like locally made wood cutting boards—at this multifloor shop that also hosts cooking classes. ✉ *876 Bathurst St., The Annex* ☎ *416/922–9055* ⊕ *nellacucina.ca* ⊘ *Closed Sun.* Ⓜ *Bathurst.*

Socco Annex

HOUSEWARES | Decor enthusiasts should make a pit stop at this airy boutique in the heart of the Annex. Expect to find modern glassware, handmade ceramics, and charming art prints, plus taper candles and folding plastic storage crates in every conceivable color. ✉ *474 Bloor St. W, The Annex* ☎ *416/672–0570* ⊕ *soccoannex.ca* Ⓜ *Bathurst.*

Little Italy

Little Italy has had its share of identities: it was first a stronghold for Portuguese and Italian families, then a burgeoning nightclub district, and now, finally, it seems to have found a way to balance the two. Unsurprisingly, a good meal is rarely far away. There are plenty of classic dining destinations like Café Diplomatico, a low-key Italian spot known for its popular side patio. But a new guard of modern Italian restaurants and unfussy snack joints have also settled in. The area is also home to a buzzy bar scene that comes alive on weekends.

🍴 Restaurants

Some of the city's finest pastas and pizzas are served up in Little Italy, but in true multicultural Toronto fashion, the area's best restaurants hail from several corners of the globe.

★ Bar Raval

$$$ | **SPANISH** | Inside a breathtaking room swathed in undulating waves of wood, you'll find Bar Raval, a tapas restaurant known for some marvelous food and drink. Stop by during the day and order a couple *pintxos* (a single-serving snack served on a skewer), feast on tins of smoked seafood and heartier tapas for a full meal, or stop in late for a nightcap. **Known for:** popular covered patio; standing-only tables (plus a couple stools); varied drinks list with sherry, vermouth, cocktails, and "weird wine." [$] *Average main: C$25* ✉ *505 College St., Little Italy* ☎ *647/344–8001* 🌐 *thisisbarraval.com* [M] *Bathurst.*

Café Diplomatico

$$ | **ITALIAN** | Holding court over a central Little Italy corner since 1968, Diplomatico is popular for its big sidewalk patio with umbrella-shaded tables, one of the best places in the city for people-watching. "The Dip," as it's locally known, serves reliable red-sauce Italian fare until late into the night. **Known for:** classic Italian dishes; large portions at reasonable prices; great people-watching. [$] *Average main: C$20* ✉ *594 College St., Little Italy* ☎ *416/534–4637* 🌐 *cafediplomatico.ca* [M] *Christie.*

Chiado

$$$$ | **PORTUGUESE** | It's all about elegance at this long-standing Portuguese spot, where waiters bustle past white tablecloths and polished wood armchairs. The exquisite fish, which form the menu's base, are flown in from the Azores and Madeira. **Known for:** excellent grilled seafood; classic Portuguese dishes; top-notch service. [$] *Average main: C$50* ✉ *864 College St. W* ☎ *416/538–1910* 🌐 *chiadorestaurant.com* 🕒 *Closed Sun.* [M] *Ossington.*

Duff's Famous Wings

$$ | **AMERICAN** | **FAMILY** | At this classic Toronto wing joint, crispy flats and drumettes are served with pristine celery sticks and creamy dill or blue-cheese dressing. The "medium" sauce is still fairly hot—but for those truly willing to tempt fate, the options go all the way up to "armageddon." **Known for:** pub grub–focused menu; loud, lively atmosphere; great for families. [$] *Average main: C$15* ✉ *558 College St. W, Little Italy* ☎ *416/963–4446* 🌐 *duffsfamouswings.ca* [M] *Bathurst.*

Giulietta

$$$$ | **ITALIAN** | Traditional Italian food gets a modern twist at this intimate eatery offering a wide, delicious variety of updated Italian dishes. Pastas and pizzas are both excellent, but there's standout seafoods and meats—like a showstopping strip loin for two—mixed in among the numerous veg-forward options. **Known for:** ultramodern interior design; signature grilled octopus; sizeable list of Italian wines and aperitivi. [$] *Average main: C$35* ✉ *972 College St., Little Italy* ☎ *416/964–0606* 🌐 *giu.ca* 🕒 *Closed Sun.*

☕ Coffee and Quick Bites

The Big Chill

$ | **ICE CREAM** | **FAMILY** | If you're craving a specific ice cream flavor or topping, chances are this long-standing ice cream parlor will have it ready to go. **Known for:** throwback treats like banana splits; 30-plus flavors of ice cream and frozen yogurt; colorful retro interior. [$] *Average main: C$5* ✉ *566 College St., Little Italy* ☎ *416/960–2455* 🌐 *thebigchill.ca* 💳 *No credit cards* [M] *Bathurst.*

The Night Baker

$ | **BAKERY** | Known for hefty, soft-centered cookies, from Oreo and s'more to Filipino-inspired delicacies, this bakery also ships its wares across Canada and the United States (in case you get a craving once you're back at home). **Known for:** gelato options in summertime; coffee and glasses of milk to drink; rotating cookie flavors like ube and pandan. [$] *Average main: C$5* ✉ *825 College St., Little*

Italy ☎ *416/901–5590* 🌐 *thenightbaker.com* 🕒 *Closed Mon.* [M] *Ossington.*

PG Cluck's

$$ | SANDWICHES | Folks flock from all over town for this takeout counter's fried chicken sandwiches—one of the first spots to capitalize on what has become a citywide trend. **Known for:** spicy and jalapeño-honey options; massive, juicy chicken sandwiches; tiny storefront with no seating. [$] *Average main: C$12* ✉ *610 College St., Little Italy* ☎ *416/539–8224* 🌐 *pgclucks.com* [M] *Ossington.*

🍸 Nightlife

College Street between Bathurst and Ossington isn't so much an old-school Italian neighborhood these days as it is a prime destination for bars and restaurants of all cuisines. Pubs and rowdy clubs mix with candlelit bars. The party often spills out onto the streets on weekends.

BARS

Birreria Volo

BARS | The family that runs this narrow beer bar has a side business importing rare brews from all over the world, so you know whatever's on tap—whether it's brewed in Ontario or Belgium—is going to be stellar. The setting feels decidedly Old World, complete with weathered brick walls and a hidden patio space that feels like a walled-off courtyard. A specialty grocer and bottle shop, Bottega Volo, is two doors down. ✉ *612 College St., Little Italy* ☎ *416/531–7373* 🌐 *birreria-volo.com* 🕒 *Closed Mon.* [M] *Ossington.*

The Caledonian

PUBS | This pub is dedicated to all things Scottish. If the massive mural of the St. Andrew's Cross decorating the cozy back patio doesn't give it away, the enormous whiskey selection certainly will. There are more than 500 single malts, with selections dating as far back as the '60s. The pub also hosts frequent tasting events featuring various distillers, and serves hearty Highland eats (haggis—real and vegan—included). ✉ *856 College St., Little Italy* ☎ *416/577–7472* 🌐 *thecaledonian.ca* 🕒 *Closed Mon.* [M] *Ossington.*

La Carnita

BARS | Originally launched as a pop-up taco stand, La Carnita expanded to this space on College and eventually spawned a number of sibling restaurants across the city. The tacos, hand-crafted cocktails, churros, and house-made paletas still reel diners in week after week. The space is filled with funky graffiti and the sounds of loud hip-hop beats. ✉ *501 College St., Little Italy* ☎ *416/964–1555* 🌐 *lacarnita.com* [M] *Bathurst.*

MUSIC VENUES

Axis Club

DANCE CLUBS | Renovated in 2021, this mid-size club and concert venue boasts impressive lighting and sound systems. The roster includes a mix of live acts (from pop and rap to jazz and indie), touring DJs, and dance parties. Get down on the main dance floor, or head to the upper deck for seating and a killer view of the stage. ✉ *722 College St., Little Italy* 🌐 *theaxisclub.com* [M] *Ossington.*

Free Times Cafe

LIVE MUSIC | From open mics to folk music and stand-up comedy, there's something happening almost every night of the week on this casual eatery's backroom stage. The biggest draw is a traditional Jewish brunch series called "Bella! Did Ya Eat?," complete with live klezmer music, that's held every Sunday. ✉ *320 College St., Little Italy* ☎ *416/967–1078* 🌐 *freetimescafe.com* [M] *Spadina.*

🎭 Performing Arts

FILM

The Royal Cinema

FILM | This fully restored 1939 single-screen theater hosts film fest screenings and special engagements, as well as live comedy and music. On top of the usual concessions, next-door bar Birreria Volo has opened a specialty grocer and bottle shop in the lobby, so you can grab snacks even on the days you can't catch a flick. ⊠ *608 College St., Little Italy* ☎ *416/466–4400* ⊕ *theroyal.to* Ⓜ *Christie.*

🛍 Shopping

BOOKS
Balfour Books

BOOKS | This hushed secondhand bookshop has a tempting selection of coffee table–sized art and photography books, along with more luggage-friendly novels and plays—all denoted with Scrabble-tile signs. You may even spot some rare out-of-print treasures. ⊠ *468 College St., Little Italy* ☎ *416/531–9911* ⊕ *balfourbooks.squarespace.com* Ⓜ *Bathurst.*

JEWELRY AND ACCESSORIES
Lilliput Hats

HATS & GLOVES | Dramatic wide-brimmed hats, extravagant fascinators, and practical straw hats that pack flat in your carry-on—all these can be found at Lilliput Hats. For men there are trilbies, wide-brimmed fedoras, and pork pies. Owner and milliner Karyn Ruiz has a devoted local following; notably, Ruiz made the hats Canadian rock star Gord Downie wore during his final Canadian tour. ⊠ *462 College St., Little Italy* ☎ *416/536–5933* ⊕ *lilliputhats.com* ⊙ *Closed Sun.* Ⓜ *Bathurst.*

Red Pegasus

OTHER ACCESSORIES | Need a stylish gift for someone back home? You'll likely find something suitable at this cute boutique, where the shelves are lined with greeting cards, puzzles, kids' books, and locally designed wares like tea towels and jewelry. ⊠ *628 College St., Little Italy* ☎ *416/536–3872* ⊕ *redpegasus.ca* ⊙ *Closed Mon.* Ⓜ *Christie.*

MUSIC
Neurotica Records

RECORDS | Go crate-digging at this basement record store where new releases sit beside jazz, punk, and reggae oddities. Their buy-and-sell program accepts cassettes, CDs, DVDs, and even vintage studio gear—so if you're looking for something obscure, you just might stumble upon it here. ⊠ *567 College St., Little Italy* ✥ *Entrance off Manning* ☎ *416/603–7796* ⊕ *neurotica.ca* ⊙ *Closed Sun.–Tues.* Ⓜ *Bathurst.*

Chapter 10

YORKVILLE, CHURCH AND WELLESLEY, ROSEDALE, AND CABBAGETOWN

Updated by
Richard Trapunski

👁 Sights	🍴 Restaurants	🛏 Hotels	🛍 Shopping	🍸 Nightlife
★★★★☆	★★★★☆	★★★★★	★★★★★	★★★★☆

TORONTO'S FILM SCENE

So many films are shot in Toronto (the city has posed as everywhere from Paris to Moscow) that it's earned the nickname "Hollywood North." The highlight of the cinematic year is the world-renowned Toronto International Film Festival.

North America's third-largest film production center after L.A. and New York, Toronto keeps cameras rolling with its excellent local crews and production facilities, and plenty of filmmaker tax credits. It helps, too, that Toronto's chameleonic streets easily impersonate other cities and time periods. Credits include: the Distillery District as Prohibition-era Chicago (*Chicago*), Casa Loma as the school for young mutants (*X-Men*), and the U of T campus as Harvard (*Good Will Hunting*). Spotting Toronto "tells" in films is fun, but locals get even more jazzed when the city represents itself for a change, as in 2010's *Scott Pilgrim vs. the World* and 2013's *The F Word* (aka *What If*).

MORE FESTIVALS

Hot Docs. North America's largest documentary film festival. April–May. ✉ *The Annex* ⊕ *www. hotdocs.ca.*

Inside Out 2SLGBTQ+ Film Festival. This major event features films made by and about people in the LGBTQ+ community. May–June. ⊕ *www. insideout.ca.*

Toronto After Dark. Dedicated to horror, sci-fi, and thriller films. Late October. ✉ *Toronto* ⊕ *www. torontoafterdark.com.*

TORONTO INTERNATIONAL FILM FESTIVAL

Perhaps the most important film festival in the world after Cannes and Sundance, TIFF is open to the public and even the star-studded galas are accessible to the average Joe. More than 300 works by both acclaimed and lesser-known directors from around the world are shown. Movies that premiere at TIFF have won Academy Awards and launched the careers of emerging actors and directors—TIFF audiences have been among the first in the world to see movies like *La La Land*, *Slumdog Millionaire*, and *Juno*. The red carpet is rolled out for star-studded premieres, and actors and directors may be on hand afterward for Q&As. Along with the serious documentaries, foreign films, and Oscar contenders, TIFF has fun with its Midnight Madness program, screening campy horror films, comedies, and action movies. ⊠ *TIFF Bell Lightbox, 350 King St. W, at John St.* ☎ *416/599–2033, 888/258–8433* ⊕ *www.tiff.net* Ⓜ *St. Andrew.*

ATTENDING THE FESTIVAL

When: The 11-day festival begins in early September.

Where: Screenings and ticket booths are located throughout the city, but the festival HQ is the TIFF Bell Lightbox building. ⊠ *350 King St. W (at John St.).*

Tickets: If you plan to see 10 or more films, consider a festival ticket package (on sale starting in July). Individual tickets release four days before the start of the festival; if something sells out, keep checking daily at 8am. Ticket prices start at C$19 (C$29 for premium screenings). Ticket sales are final, but you can exchange without a fee. Plan to pick up your order an hour before the screening time to avoid lines, and arrive at least two hours early for rush tickets.

WHERE TO WATCH

Oddball series and theme nights: Revue, Royal

Documentaries: Hot Docs Ted Rogers Cinema

For pure cinephiles: TIFF Bell Lightbox

IMAX: Ontario Science Centre's Shoppers Drug Mart OMNIMAX Theatre (Toronto's only 70mm celluloid IMAX); Cineplex Cinemas Yonge-Dundas; Scotiabank Theatre; Cinesphere (the world's first permanent IMAX cinema)

3-D: Scotiabank Theatre; TIFF Bell Lightbox; Varsity and Varsity VIP; Cineplex Cinemas Yonge-Dundas (which also offers select films in 4DX, featuring motion seats and environmental effects like water and wind)

Summer films alfresco: Kew Gardens (Wednesday, free); Toronto Outdoor Picture Show (Fort York, Corktown Common, Bell Manor Park; Thursday and Sunday, free); Christie Pits (Sunday, free). Most screenings start at sunset (usually around 8:30 or 9 pm) and run through July and August.

NEIGHBORHOOD SNAPSHOT

TOP EXPERIENCES

■ **Get cultured:** Take in the Gardiner Museum or the Royal Ontario Museum, two of the city's finest.

■ **Discover the Village:** Experience LGBTQ+ culture in Church and Wellesley, better known to locals as the Village.

■ **Quirky shopping:** Browse a wide range of interesting indie boutiques in Church and Wellesley and Rosedale.

■ **Splurge on a few fancy threads:** Discover Canada's homegrown fashion houses along Yorkville's upscale "Mink Mile."

■ **Take in the extra-cozy scenery:** Meander through Cabbagetown, known for its beautiful cottages.

GETTING HERE

Church and Wellesley is located along Church Street, which runs parallel to Yonge Street a few blocks east. To get to the heart of the action, take the subway to Wellesley and walk east. You could also take the subway to College and walk north along Church Street, or take the subway to Bloor-Yonge and head south.

Yorkville runs along Bloor Street (and a few streets north) between the Bloor-Yonge (to the east) and St. George (to the west) subway stations.

For Rosedale, take the subway to Summerhill and walk south along Yonge Street, or take the subway to Rosedale and head north.

PLANNING YOUR TIME

Church and Wellesley tends to come alive on weekends, particularly in the summertime. Yorkville, thanks to its location near the center of the city at Yonge and Bloor, is perpetually buzzing. Rosedale is quieter and more residential.

FUN FACTS

■ Yorkville was once the heart of Toronto's folk scene, with coffee shops that played host to artists like Joni Mitchell, Gordon Lightfoot, and Buffy Sainte-Marie.

■ Toronto hosts one of the biggest Pride events in the world in the heart of the Gay Village.

■ The infamous Don Jail, near Riverdale Park in Cabbagetown, was partially active until 2013 before being turned into an outpost of the Bridgepoint Health rehab hospital.

■ Some of the country's most notable people are buried at Mount Pleasant Cemetery in Rosedale, including musician Glenn Gould, Prime Minister William Lyon Mackenzie King, and athlete Charlie Conacher.

Located a stone's throw from where two of Toronto's main drags (Yonge and Bloor) intersect, Yorkville and Church and Wellesley are close together, but their personalities are a study in contrasts.

Yorkville is one of the ritziest neighborhoods in town, where you'll often see luxury cars pulled up outside the Holt Renfrew department store, or slow-rolling past packed bistro patios. By contrast, Church and Wellesley is a casual, out-and-proud LGBTQ+ community where locals party late into the night (and then roll out of bed for brunch the next day). To the northeast, tony residential Rosedale is a place to window-shop for fantasy Victorian houses, and around cute clothing and home decor boutiques. Farther east, Cabbagetown offers nice houses and hidden-gem sightseeing.

Yorkville

Toronto's equivalent of 5th Avenue or Rodeo Drive, Yorkville—and Bloor Street in particular, cheekily called "Mink Mile"—is a dazzling spread of posh shops stocked with designer clothes, furs, and jewels, along with restaurants, galleries, and specialty boutiques. Though the screening hub has moved farther downtown, it's also where much of the excitement takes place in September during the annual Toronto International Film Festival, one of the world's largest and most people-friendly film festivals, where the public actually gets to see premieres and hidden gems and attend industry panels. Hotels offer luxury, cafés teem with the well heeled, and everyone practices air kisses. Beauty salons and plastic surgeons thrive, but so do gelato spots.

Sights

Gardiner Museum
ART MUSEUM | FAMILY | Dedicated to the art of clay and ceramics, this museum has more than 4,000 pieces in its permanent collection, from 17th-century English delftware and 18th-century European porcelain to Japanese Kakiemon-style pottery and Chinese blue-and-white porcelain. If your visit coincides with lunchtime, hit on-site bistro Clay for creative, locally oriented cuisine (and one of the best hidden patios in town). Free guided tours of the museum take place at 2 daily and there are drop-in sessions in the clay studio (*Wed.–Sun.*; C$18). ■ TIP→ **Admission is free on Wednesday after 4 (kids under 18 and students are always free).** ✉ *111 Queen's Park Crescent, Yorkville* ☎ *416/586–8080* ⊕ *www.gardinermuseum.on.ca* C$15 Ⓜ *Museum.*

★ Royal Ontario Museum
SCIENCE MUSEUM | FAMILY | The ROM (as the Royal Ontario Museum is known to locals), opened in 1914, is Canada's largest museum and has a reputation for making its science, art, and archaeology exhibits accessible and appealing. The architecture of the gigantic complex, which includes the ultramodern Michael Lee-Chin Crystal gallery—a series of interlocking prismatic shapes spilling out onto Bloor Street—helps exemplify this.

Other highlights include the Hyacinth Gloria Chen Crystal Court, a four-story atrium with aluminum bridges connecting the old and new wings, and an

angular pendant skylight through which light pours into the open space. A look through the windows reveals parts of the treasures inside, such as the daunting creatures from the Age of Dinosaurs exhibit standing guard. The Patricia Harris Gallery of Textiles and Costume angles out 80 feet over Bloor Street from its fourth-floor perch.

The Daphne Cockwell Gallery of Canada exhibits an impressive range of First Peoples historical objects and artifacts, from pre-contact time to the present. The Matthews Family Court of Chinese Sculpture Gallery displays monumental Buddhist sculpture dating from 200 BC through 1900; the Gallery of Korea has over 260 artifacts of Korean art and culture. The Sir Christopher Ondaatje South Asian Gallery houses the best objects of a 7,000-piece collection that spans 5,000 years, and includes items from Bangladesh, Bhutan, India, the Maldives, Nepal, Pakistan, Sri Lanka, and Tibet. ■TIP➜ **The main floor has free admission during the summer.** ☒ *100 Queen's Park, Yorkville* ☎ *416/586–8000* ⊕ *www.rom.on.ca* ☒ *C$23* Ⓜ *Museum.*

Toronto Reference Library
LIBRARY | Designed by one of Canada's most admired architects, Raymond Moriyama, who also created the Ontario Science Centre, this five-story library is arranged around a large atrium, which gives a wonderful sense of open space. One-third of the more than 6.2 million items—spread across 82 km (51 miles) of shelves—are open to the public. Audio carrels are available for listening to nearly 40,000 music and spoken-word recordings. There's an impressively large performing arts collection, and, lest you think libraries have to be quiet, listening stations and piano rooms are on the fifth floor—as is the Arthur Conan Doyle Room, which is of special interest to Baker Street fans. It houses the world's finest public collection of Holmesiana, including records, films, photos, books,

manuscripts, letters, and even cartoon books starring Sherlock Hemlock of *Sesame Street*. The new fourth-floor Jack Rabinovitch Reading Room opened in 2022, with collections from the man who founded Canada's most prestigious literary award, the Giller Prize. ☒ *789 Yonge St.* ☎ *416/395–5577* ⊕ *www.torontopubliclibrary.ca* Ⓜ *Bloor-Yonge.*

Village of Yorkville Park
CITY PARK | FAMILY | Yorkville is also home to a unique park on Cumberland Street, right outside Bay subway station, designed as a series of gardens along old property lines and reflecting both the history of the Village of Yorkville and the diversity of the Canadian landscape. The result of an international design competition, the park lines the street with a soothing waterfall fixture, tree-lined enclaves, and a big rock sculpture that children love to climb on. It's rare to find that kind of open public space in a retail area in the city that doesn't require you to buy something, though the ample outdoor seating often looks like a shared open-air café for nearby shops like Starbucks, Sorry Coffee Co., and vegan lunch spot Kupfert & Kim. ☒ *115 Cumberland St., Yorkville* ⊕ *toronto.ca/parks* Ⓜ *Bay.*

🍴 Restaurants

Home to the rich and fabulous, Yorkville is a prime spot for celebrity sightings, especially during the Toronto International Film Festival. Posh bars and lively patios all provide a chance to do a little people-watching, and to sample some of the city's best high-end cuisine.

★ Café Boulud
$$$$ | FRENCH | Spearheaded by world-renowned restaurateur Daniel Boulud, Café Boulud occupies the coveted dining room of the Four Seasons Hotel Toronto and presents itself as a serene, airy French brasserie decked out with sage-green banquettes and gilded accents. The café does simple, well-executed classic and

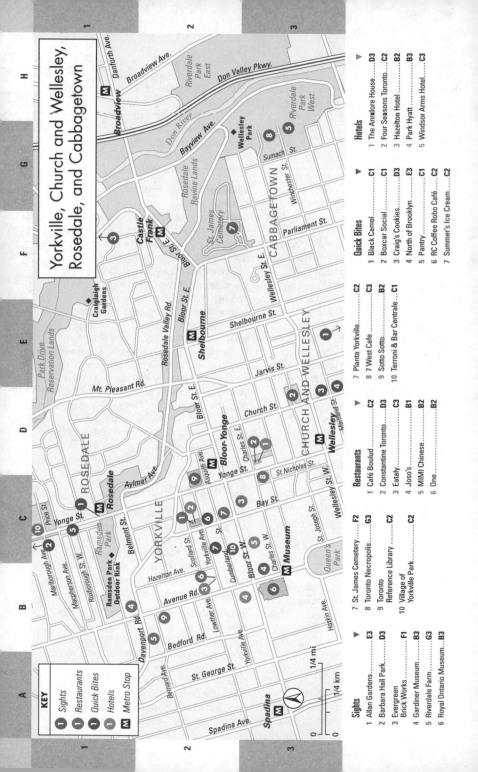

Yorkville, Church and Wellesley, Rosedale, and Cabbagetown

KEY
- **1** Sights
- **1** Restaurants
- **1** Quick Bites
- **1** Hotels
- **Ⓜ** Metro Stop

0 ¼ mi
0 ¼ km

Sights ▶
1 Allan Gardens E3
2 Barbara Hall Park D3
3 Evergreen
   Brick Works F1
4 Gardiner Museum B3
5 Riverdale Farm G3
6 Royal Ontario Museum ... B3
7 St. James Cemetery F2
8 Toronto Necropolis G3
9 Toronto
   Reference Library C2
10 Village of
   Yorkville Park C2

Restaurants ▶
1 Café Boulud C2
2 Constantine Toronto D3
3 Eataly C3
4 Joso's B1
5 MIMI Chinese B2
6 One B2
7 Planta Yorkville C2
8 7 West Cafe C3
9 Sotto Sotto B2
10 Terroni & Bar Centrale .. C1

Quick Bites ▶
1 Black Camel C1
2 Boxcar Social C1
3 Craig's Cookies D3
4 North of Brooklyn E3
5 Pantry C1
6 RC Coffee Robo Café C2
7 Summer's Ice Cream C2

Hotels ▶
1 The Anndore House D3
2 Four Seasons Toronto C2
3 Hazelton Hotel B2
4 Park Hyatt B3
5 Windsor Arms Hotel C3

contemporary French fare, like mouth-watering rotisserie duck, a signature Frenchie burger and cocktails like the French 55. **Known for:** classic French food; celebrity chef connection; inventive desserts. [$] *Average main: C$45* ✉ *60 Yorkville Ave., Yorkville* ☎ *416/963–6005* 🌐 *www.cafeboulud.com/toronto* [M] *Bay.*

Eataly

$$$ | **ITALIAN** | Eataly's wonderland of fresh Italian groceries can also be enjoyed on-site in seven different restaurants, bars, counters, and cafés. There's the Trattoria Milano for northern Italian dishes and aperitivo, La Piazza for shareable plates like salumi and cheese, La Pizza & La Pasta (pretty self-explanatory), Birroteca for fresh beer in partnership with Indie Alehouse, multiple big patios to sip drinks like Aperol spritzes and wines, plus multiple cafés for pastries, sandwiches, pizzas, chocolates, and gelatos. **Known for:** extensive Italian wine and cocktail list; fresh pasta and pizza made on-site; multiple options, from small cafés to sit-down eateries. [$] *Average main: C$22* ✉ *55 Bloor St.* ☎ *437/374–0250* 🌐 *eataly.ca* 🕒 *Hours vary, check website* [M] *Bay.*

Joso's

$$$$ | **SEAFOOD** | Sensuous paintings of nudes and the sea and signed celebrity photos line the walls at this two-story seafood institution. The kitchen prepares dishes from the Dalmatian side of the Adriatic Sea, and members of the international artistic community who frequent the place adore the unusual and healthy array of seafood and fish. **Known for:** eccentric, artistic decor; seafood-focused menu; the restaurant's cameo on Drake's Take Care album cover. [$] *Average main: C$45* ✉ *202 Davenport Rd., Toronto* ☎ *416/925–1903* 🌐 *www.josos.com* 🕒 *Closed Sun. and Mon. No lunch.* [M] *Dupont.*

★ MIMI Chinese

$$$$ | **CHINESE** | A good drive away from Toronto's two Chinatowns on the edge of Yorkville, MIMI Chinese offers a memorable dining experience built on regional dishes from the Guangdong, Sichuan, and Hunan regions of China. It's an upscale yet unpretentious room, with a dark red-and-black aesthetic, waiters in black bow ties, and one-way kitchen mirrors that give you a full view of bustling chefs plating dishes and slicing up glistening barbecue pork *char siu* (though they can't see you). **Known for:** old-school service from white-shirted waiters; well-executed versions of regional Chinese dishes; recommendations for other great Chinese restaurants on the menu and website. [$] *Average main: C$35* ✉ *265 Davenport Rd., Yorkville* ☎ *416/505–0799* 🌐 *mimichinese.com* 🕒 *Closed Mon. and Tues.* [M] *Dupont.*

★ One

$$$$ | **INTERNATIONAL** | The modern dining room at One, inside the Hazelton Hotel, is all rich woods, smoked glass, cowhide, and onyx—and thankfully the food lives up to all the razzle-dazzle. "Lobster spoons" with vermouth butter and miso-glazed black cod share space on a broad, varied menu with fresh pastas and exceptional house-aged steaks sourced from Prince Edward Island and Alberta. **Known for:** buzzy streetside patio; excellent seafood and steak; top-notch service. [$] *Average main: C$55* ✉ *The Hazelton Hotel Toronto, 118 Yorkville Ave., Yorkville* ☎ *416/961–9600* 🌐 *onerestaurant.ca* [M] *Bay.*

Planta

$$$ | **VEGETARIAN** | The upscale-yet-whimsical take on vegan food at Planta caused quite a stir when it opened in 2016, and the restaurant (now one of four in the city) is still a favorite of the Yorkville crowd. Menu standouts include satisfying thin-crust pizzas with plant-based mozzarella, an excellent veggie burger, and a queso dip that will fool

even the pickiest cheese lover. **Known for:** bold, trendy decor; fun cocktails and local beer; plant-based sushi. $ *Average main: C$23* ✉ *1221 Bay St., Yorkville* ☎ *647/812-1221* ⊕ *plantarestaurants.com* ⊗ *Closed Mon.* Ⓜ *Bay.*

★ Sotto Sotto

$$$$ | **ITALIAN** | This southern Italian hideaway has been a magnet for visiting celebrities and well-heeled Yorkville locals since the early 1990s, and it's still one of the city's most popular posh restaurants. The dozen or so pastas, including freshly made gnocchi, are reliably excellent, but the grilled seafood options, spanning yellowfin tuna to tiger shrimp to calamari, are stellar. **Known for:** low-lit, intimate setting; refined Italian dishes; wall of celebrity photos. $ *Average main: C$32* ✉ *120 Avenue Rd., Yorkville* ☎ *416/962-0011* ⊕ *www.sottosotto.ca* ⊗ *No lunch Sun.* Ⓜ *Bay.*

☕ Coffee and Quick Bites

RC Coffee Robo Café

$ | **CAFÉ** | If you want your latte made by a robot, this is the spot to get it. The first location of a new automated coffee kiosk concept that's slowly creeping across the city, the Robo Café makes the specialty espresso-based coffee drinks like cappuccinos, cortados, and flat whites—complete with ice or oat milk—you'll find at indie coffee shops throughout the city, but taking the barista out of the equation. **Known for:** iced drinks in the summertime; alternative milk options like almond and oat; high-quality coffee made by a robot. $ *Average main: C$4* ✉ *1255 Bay St., Yorkville* ⊕ *rccoffee.com* Ⓜ *Bay.*

Summer's Ice Cream

$ | **ICE CREAM** | **FAMILY** | Yorkville is filled with ice cream and gelato shops, but Summer's is the most beloved. A family-run shop since the '80s, this ice cream parlor doesn't do anything fancy or trendy but excels with the classic, made-in-house flavors. **Known for:** family-friendly service; prime location for people-watching; homemade ice cream with plenty of flavors. $ *Average main: C$6* ✉ *101 Yorkville Ave., Yorkville* ☎ *416/944-2637* ⊕ *summersicecream.com* ⊗ *Closed Mon.* Ⓜ *Bay.*

🛏 Hotels

★ Four Seasons Hotel Toronto

$$$$ | **HOTEL** | Luxury is the name of the game at this gleaming 55-story hotel, where the rooms are done in neutral tones and outfitted with soaking tubs, rain showers, and heated bathroom floors. **Pros:** on-site dining and nightlife hot spots; excellent on-site spa; top-notch service. **Cons:** hefty price tag; some rooms look onto residential building next door; modern decor can feel a bit austere. $ *Rooms from: C$750* ✉ *60 Yorkville Ave., Yorkville* ☎ *416/964-0411* ⊕ *www.fourseasons.com/toronto* ⇄ *259 rooms* ✵ *No Meals* Ⓜ *Bay.*

★ Hazelton Hotel

$$$$ | **HOTEL** | **FAMILY** | The Hazelton is a popular destination for visiting celebrities—and it looks the part, with clubby, modern furnishings, floor-to-ceiling windows or French balconies, and bathrooms wrapped in forest-green granite. **Pros:** outstanding service; favorite of Hollywood celebs; great on-site spa. **Cons:** high quality with the price tag to match; no hope of getting a room during TIFF; low-rise building means underwhelming views. $ *Rooms from: C$1,000* ✉ *118 Yorkville Ave., Yorkville* ☎ *416/963-6300* ⊕ *www.thehazeltonhotel.com* ⇄ *77 rooms* ✵ *No Meals* Ⓜ *Bay.*

★ Park Hyatt

$$$$ | **HOTEL** | One of Toronto's most historic and luxurious hotels, the Park Hyatt (originally the Park Plaza) has new life after a major 2021 renovation. **Pros:** iconic rooftop Writers Room bar with amazing views; relaxing and luxurious Stillwater

Spa on-site; sophisticated, homey feel. **Cons:** historic personality sanitized to fit Hyatt brand; some amenities require multiple elevators to get to; some perks, like breakfast, only included for Hyatt members. $ *Rooms from: C$750* ✉ *4 Avenue Rd.* ☎ *416/925–1234* ⊕ *hyatt.com* ⇨ *219 rooms* ❘◎❘ *No Meals* Ⓜ *Museum.*

Windsor Arms

$$$$ | HOTEL | Nestled on a side street near some of Yorkville's toniest shops, the Windsor Arms caters to a luxury clientele, and personalized service is a priority: there's a high guest-to-staff ratio and 24-hour butlers are on duty. **Pros:** high repeat business due to privacy and personalized service; luxurious, quiet atmosphere; good dining options, including afternoon tea service. **Cons:** high standards mean high prices; some fourth-floor rooms can be noisy if events are being hosted downstairs; rooms book up fast at peak times. $ *Rooms from: C$550* ✉ *18 St. Thomas St., Yorkville* ☎ *416/971–9666* ⊕ *www.windsorarms-shotel.com* ⇨ *28 rooms* ❘◎❘ *No Meals* Ⓜ *Bay.*

🍸 Nightlife

The trendy bars of Yorkville tend to draw a well-heeled clientele for excellent drinks, food, and views.

BARS
d|bar

COCKTAIL LOUNGES | This high-end lounge in the flagship Four Seasons Hotel Toronto is modern and chic, with top-notch cocktails, including the bourbon, absinthe, sherry, and coffee-infused vermouth–based Bon Vivant. The food is spearheaded by French chef Daniel Boulud, so the menu goes far above and beyond simple bar bites—the charcuterie is house-made, they take the burger very seriously, and there are fresh oysters at the raw bar. ✉ *60 Yorkville Ave., Toronto* ☎ *416/963–6010* ⊕ *www.dbartoronto. com* Ⓜ *Bay.*

Hemingway's

PUBS | Hemingway's is a homey bastion in a sea of Yorkville swank. The three-story complex, with indoor and outdoor spaces (including a heated rooftop patio), is a mishmash of booths, tables, several bars, mirrors, artsy posters, and books. The pub grub menu, which covers everything from brunch to late night, is a big draw for the regular-heavy crowd, too. A different kind of sports bar, it's also a good place to watch international events like soccer, rugby, and cricket. ✉ *142 Cumberland St., Toronto* ☎ *416/968–2828* ⊕ *www.hemingways.to* Ⓜ *Museum.*

★ Writers Room Bar

COCKTAIL LOUNGES | Such Canadian literary luminaries as Margaret Atwood and Mordecai Richler have used the 17th-floor Park Hyatt bar as a setting in their writings, and now it's been renamed the Writers Room. A popular date spot, it's also a good place to sip a glass of wine, scotch, or a cocktail and soak in the city. The chic bar has big, open windows and an impressive patio that offers some of the most breathtaking views of the city, including the nearby ROM and University of Toronto. Inventive, spirit-forward cocktails (presented with quotes from books) come with little bowls of nuts and olives. There are also adventurous sharing plates like foie gras doughnuts, beef tartare, and oysters. ✉ *Park Hyatt Hotel, 4 Avenue Rd., top fl., Toronto* ☎ *416/948–3140* ⊕ *hyatt.com* Ⓜ *Museum.*

🎭 Performing Arts

CLASSICAL MUSIC
★ Koerner Hall

MUSIC | This handsome 1,135-seat concert hall pleases performers and audiences with rich acoustics and undulating wood "strings" floating overhead. Acts have included such greats as Yo-Yo Ma, Chick Corea, Ravi Shankar, Midori, Taj Mahal, and Savion Glover. It's part of the TELUS Centre for Performance and

Learning. ⊠ *273 Bloor St. W, Yorkville* ☎ *416/408–0208* ⊕ *rcmusic.com* Ⓜ *St. George.*

Shopping

Back in the 1960s, Yorkville was Canada's hippie headquarters. Today it's an upscale shopping and dining destination: the place to find high-end everything. The pedestrian-friendly streets in the heart of Yorkville—north of Bloor, west of Bay—are full of designer stores that are fun to browse even if you're not buying, while Bloor Street, from Yonge Street to Avenue Road, is a virtual runway of world-renowned designer shops like Bulgari, Prada, Dolce & Gabbana, Chanel, and quality chains.

ANTIQUES

Wagman Antiques

ANTIQUES & COLLECTIBLES | Wagman carries a large selection of art deco pieces and lighting, along with Italian (and a few French) pieces from the '40s, '50s, and '60s. This is the place to find a show-stopping glass-veneered sideboard or a Murano glass lamp. Depending on the piece, Wagman can ship to the United States and beyond. ⊠ *224 Davenport Rd., at Avenue Rd., Toronto* ☎ *416/964–1047* ⊕ *wagmanantiques.com* ◔ *Closed weekends* Ⓜ *Dupont or St. George.*

ART GALLERIES

Loch Gallery

ART GALLERIES | This intimate gallery in an old Victorian house almost exclusively exhibits representational historic and contemporary Canadian painting and sculpture, and specializes in 19th- and 20th-century Canadian artists. ⊠ *16 Hazelton Ave., Toronto* ☎ *416/964–9050* ⊕ *www.lochgallery.com* ◔ *Closed Sun. and Mon.* Ⓜ *Museum.*

BOOKS

Indigo

BOOKS | This Canadian megachain bookstore has stores all over the country, but it's headquartered in Toronto. It has a huge selection of books, magazines, records, and gift items as well as a Starbucks and occasional live entertainment. Increasingly, it's becoming a "lifestyle" store with items such as housewares, mugs, pillows, blankets, and cookware taking up prime in-store real estate. ⊠ *55 Bloor St. W, Yorkville* ☎ *416/925–3536* ⊕ *www.chapters.indigo.ca* Ⓜ *Bay.*

CLOTHING

Chanel

OTHER ACCESSORIES | Located in one of the city's historic buildings, this boutique is one of the company's largest in North America. Most of the brand's latest offerings, including classic and seasonal bags and accessories, are here, and the staff is welcoming, knowledgeable, and helpful, just what you'd expect from a store of this caliber. ⊠ *98 Yorkville Ave., Toronto* ☎ *416/925–2577* ⊕ *www.chanel. com* Ⓜ *Bay.*

★ **George C**

MIXED CLOTHING | If you're put off by the anonymous uniformity of the big designers along Bloor but you have some money to spend and want a touch of originality, head to this three-story Victorian refurb for an inspired selection of bold, sophisticated shoes, bags, and clothes for men and women from French, Italian, American, and Australian designers that you won't find anywhere else. ⊠ *21 Hazelton Ave., Yorkville* ☎ *416/962–1991* ⊕ *georgec.ca* ◔ *Closed Mon.* Ⓜ *Bay.*

★ **Harry Rosen**

MEN'S CLOTHING | This five-floor department store is dedicated to the finest men's fashions, stocked to the gills with suits, shirts, outerwear, shoes, and accessories from designers such as Tom Ford, Armani, Dolce & Gabbana, and

Zegna (each with their own shop-within-a-shop). There's also plenty of preppy classics available for those who favor a more relaxed look. ⊠ *82 Bloor St. W, Toronto* ☎ *416/972–0556* ⊕ *www.harry-rosen.com* Ⓜ *Museum.*

Hermès

HANDBAGS | The Parisian design house caters to the upscale horse- and hound-loving set, with classic sportswear, handbags, and accessories. ⊠ *100 Bloor St. W, Toronto* ☎ *416/968–8626* ⊕ *www.hermes.com* Ⓜ *Museum.*

Motion

WOMEN'S CLOTHING | This Toronto-based boutique features unique, comfortable clothing in cottons, linens, and wools. Many pieces are designed and made in-house, but outside designers such as Rundholz and Oska are also featured. Bold, chunky accessories complement the earthy, arty look perfectly. ⊠ *106 Cumberland St., Yorkville* ☎ *416/968–0090* ⊕ *www.motionclothing.com* Ⓜ *Bay.*

119 Corbò

MIXED CLOTHING | Both legendary and of-the-moment designers—Balenciaga, The Row, Jacquemus, and Stella McCartney, to name a few—are gathered here under one roof, along with some of the finest footwear and accessories in town. ⊠ *119 Yorkville Ave., Toronto* ☎ *416/928–0954* ⊕ *www.119corbo.com* Ⓜ *Museum.*

Over the Rainbow

MIXED CLOTHING | Once located in a stand-alone shop in Yorkville and now in the Manulife Centre, this boutique for all things denim has been around since the 1970s. Over the Rainbow carries every variety of cut and flare: the trendy, the classic, and the questionable from lines like Fidelity, Nudie Jeans, and Naked & Famous fill the shelves. In winter, check out their extensive collection of Canada Goose jackets. ⊠ *Manulife Centre, 55 Bloor St. W, Toronto* ☎ *416/967–7448*

⊕ *www.rainbowjeans.com* ☾ *Closed Sun.* Ⓜ *Bay.*

Prada

MIXED CLOTHING | The avant-garde designs of this luxury Italian fashion house are overshadowed only by the gleaming interior of the store and the traffic-stopping window displays. ⊠ *131 Bloor St. W, Toronto* ☎ *416/975–4300* ⊕ *www.prada.com* Ⓜ *Bay.*

★ Roots

MIXED CLOTHING | The longtime favorite brand for leather jackets, varsity jackets, bags, and basics is crafted from tumbled leather and stamped with the country's national icon, the beaver. The homegrown company's impressive flagship store showcases the more modern styling possibilities of their laid-back offerings. ⊠ *80 Bloor St. W, Toronto* ☎ *416/323–3289* ⊕ *www.roots.com* Ⓜ *Bay.*

Shan

SWIMWEAR | Montréal designer Chantal Levesque founded this label in 1985, and now stocks locations in more than 25 countries with her creative couture swimwear, swimwear accessories, and wraps. There's a separate collection for men. ⊠ *38 Avenue Rd., Yorkville* ☎ *416/961–7426* ⊕ *www.shan.ca* Ⓜ *Bay or St. George.*

The Webster

MIXED CLOTHING | The first Canadian outpost of this ostentatious Miami-based fashion and design store is eye-catching from the moment you're welcomed in by the doorman. There's custom art throughout the shop, including a foosball table, plush bear, palm tree, and neon pink staircase that takes you between the three floors, each with its own personality. There are purses, women's clothes, shoes, perfumes, and men's streetwear from bold-named brands like Bottega Veneta, Givenchy, Mugler, Burberry, and Virgil Abloh, but each is carefully cherry-picked to fit the overall aesthetic. Off on a quiet street, it's an edgier, more gallery-like version of luxury Yorkville shopping. ⊠ *121 Scollard St., Yorkville* ☎ *416/922–0726* ⊕ *thewebster.us* Ⓜ *Bay.*

DEPARTMENT STORES AND SHOPPING CENTERS

★ Holt Renfrew

DEPARTMENT STORE | This multilevel national retail specialty store is the style leader in Canada. There are handbags, watches, cosmetics, and fragrances from London, New York, Paris, and Rome, plus footwear and clothing from boldface designers (including Fendi, Burberry, and Gucci) as well as items from contemporary designers. Gents can head a few steps west to 100 Bloor Street West to browse Holt's menswear collection at the two-floor Holt Renfrew Men.

■**TIP→ Concierge service and personal shoppers are available, but just browsing makes for a rich experience.** ⊠ *50 Bloor St. W, Yorkville* ☎ *416/922–2333* ⊕ *www. holtrenfrew.com* Ⓜ *Bay.*

Yorkville Village

MALL | Formerly known as Hazelton Lanes, this small upscale shopping mall is home to fashion-forward TNT (short for The Next Trend); structured womenswear by Judith & Charles; flower and gift shop Teatro Verde; and downtown Toronto's only Whole Foods Market. ⊠ *55 Avenue Rd., Yorkville* ☎ *416/968–8600* ⊕ *www. yorkvillevillage.com* Ⓜ *Bay.*

FOOD

★ Eataly Market

FOOD | Eataly is a sprawling and bustling monument to Italian food and cooking. Over three floors and 50,000 square feet within the Manulife Centre, the hybrid specialty food store/restaurant market is teeming with fresh Italian and locally sourced products from house-made cheese to fish, meat, bread, pastries, gelato, pasta, prepared meals, and more. There are also Italian wines

and house-brewed beer, made in the basement Birroteca by Indie Alehouse (one of seven on-site cafés, bars, and restaurants). ⊠ *55 Bloor St. W, Yorkville* ☎ *437/374–0250* ⊕ *eataly.ca* Ⓜ *Bay.*

Pusateri's

FOOD | From humble beginnings as a Little Italy produce stand, Pusateri's has grown into Toronto's favorite high-end supermarket, with in-house prepared foods, local and imported delicacies, and desserts and breads from the city's best bakers, among many other treats. This second location is among the most high-end, curated to meet the Yorkville neighborhood. ⊠ *57 Yorkville Ave., Yorkville* ☎ *416/925–0583* ⊕ *www.pusateris.com* Ⓜ *Bay.*

HOME DECOR

Hollace Cluny

HOUSEWARES | Though it's off the main shopping drag, Hollace Cluny is a must-visit for modern design aficionados looking for that special piece. Along with classics from brands like Knoll, they carry a huge array of pieces from contemporary designers, with everything from ceramics to eye-popping statement lighting fixtures. ⊠ *245 Davenport Rd., Toronto* ☎ *416/968–7894* ⊕ *www.hollace-cluny.ca* ۞ *Closed weekends* Ⓜ *Museum.*

William Ashley

HOUSEWARES | The gleaming 13,500-square-foot flagship of this 75-year established Toronto tableware and home decor store carries an extensive collection of dinnerware patterns and crystal glasses that range from Wedgwood to Denby to Baccarat. They're happy to pack and ship all over North America. Stop by the Teuscher of Switzerland chocolate boutique on the way out. ⊠ *131 Bloor St. W, Yorkville* ☎ *416/964–2900* ⊕ *www.williamashley. com* Ⓜ *Bay.*

JEWELRY AND ACCESSORIES

Cartier

JEWELRY & WATCHES | The Toronto location of this internationally renowned luxury jeweler caters to the city's elite. The glass cases feature a good selection of the jewelry designer's classic creations, including the triple-gold-band Trinity Ring and the striking nail-shape Juste Un Clou collection. ⊠ *131 Bloor St. W, Yorkville* ☎ *416/413–4929* ⊕ *www.cartier.com* Ⓜ *Bay.*

Lisa Gozlan Jewelry

JEWELRY & WATCHES | Young local designer Lisa Gozlan makes modern and fashionable jewelry that feels special but that you can wear every day. This bright showroom in Yorkville carries her signature rings, necklaces, hoops, and bracelets, all meant to be stacked and layered. The whimsical happy faces, "evil eyes," pearls, hearts, and gold and silver pieces often show up on the Instagram feeds of celebrities and influencers. ⊠ *87 Cumberland St., Yorkville* ☎ *416/818–8101* ⊕ *lisagozlan.com* Ⓜ *Bay.*

Royal De Versailles

JEWELRY & WATCHES | With a reputation as one of Toronto's most luxurious jewelers, Royal De Versailles stocks some of the most striking and elegant pieces in town. Watch aficionados will be particularly impressed by their huge collection of high-end timepieces (they have one of the largest Rolex selections in Canada). ⊠ *101 Bloor St. W, Yorkville* ☎ *416/967–7201* ⊕ *www.royaldeversailles.com* Ⓜ *Bay.*

Tiffany & Co.

JEWELRY & WATCHES | Good things come in little blue boxes, and this two-floor Tiffany location is filled with them—namely, rows and rows of classic, wearable fine jewelry designs. As at other Tiffany locations, the sales staff has a reputation for being patient, helpful, and friendly. ⊠ *150 Bloor St. W, Yorkville* ☎ *416/921–3900* ⊕ *www.tiffany.ca* Ⓜ *Bay.*

SPAS

Novo Spa

SPAS | A perennial favorite among Toronto's day-spa enthusiasts, this Yorkville hideaway offers massages (couples, prenatal), facials, manicures, pedicures, and various waxing treatments. The calming staff members always have soothing refreshments on hand. ⊠ *66 Avenue Rd., Yorkville* ☎ *416/926–9303* ⊕ *www.novospa.ca* Ⓜ *Bay.*

Church and Wellesley

Colorful rainbow flags fly high and proud in this vibrant neighborhood, just east of downtown. The area is energetic and boisterous any time of year, but absolutely frenetic during the annual Pride festival and parade in June. Given its long history, the area has evolved into a tight-knit, well-established community, with pharmacies, grocery stores, and dry cleaners rubbing shoulders with a mix of new and decades-old gay- and lesbian-centric nightspots. Glad Day, the world's oldest LGBTQ+ bookstore, is a must-visit.

Sights

Barbara Hall Park

CITY PARK | **FAMILY** | This pocket-size park is pleasant enough during the day, but at night it comes alive with strings of rainbow-color lights that symbolize the LGBTQ+ community. There's a mural of gay history on an adjacent building, and tucked away in one corner is the Toronto AIDS Memorial. ⊠ *519 Church St., Church–Wellesley* ⊕ *the519.org* Ⓜ *Wellesley.*

 Restaurants

Constantine

$$$ | **MEDITERRANEAN** | On the ground floor of the renovated Anndore House hotel, this sprawling spot's open kitchen turns out varied fare like Middle Eastern mezes, pastas, and gorgeously plated desserts. Grilled meats are great here—especially the lamb burger—but vegetarian options abound. **Known for:** buzzy, loungelike atmosphere; grilled Mediterranean specialties; daily afternoon happy hour specials. �$ *Average main: C$28* ✉ *15 Charles St. E, Church–Wellesley* ☎ *647/475–4436* ⊕ *www.constantineto. com* Ⓜ *Bloor-Yonge.*

7 West Cafe

$$ | **ECLECTIC** | No late-night craving goes unsatisfied at this decades-running 24-hour eatery specializing in lighter fare. Soups like Moroccan or vegetarian chili and sandwiches like sloppy joes and herbed chicken with honey mustard are comforting and filling. **Known for:** optimal socializing on the hidden rooftop patio; cozy atmosphere with lots of candles; home-style fare. �$ *Average main: C$18* ✉ *7 Charles St. W, Church–Wellesley* ☎ *416/928–9041* ⊕ *www.7westcafe.com* Ⓜ *Bloor-Yonge.*

☕ Coffee and Quick Bites

Craig's Cookies

$ | **BAKERY** | Actor-turned-baker Craig Pike started this local chain of cookie shops as a small pop-up, but they've since gone viral and then turned ubiquitous throughout the city. The signature is a simple but addictive chocolate chip cookie with a little bit of salt to balance out the sweet, though there are many, many more options in this Church Street location's glass display case. **Known for:** craft coffee drinks and "shots" of organic milk for a dollar; ice cream sandwiches made with freshly baked cookies; always changing cookie flavors. �$ *Average main: C$3* ✉ *483 Church St., Church–Wellesley* ☎ *416/519–5336* ⊕ *craigscookies.com* Ⓜ *Wellesley.*

North of Brooklyn

$$ | **PIZZA** | In hotly debated "best pizza in the city" barroom discussions, this local pizza chain is one of the top contenders. This location is a top spot in the Village for a tasty and crispy pie, slice, or handful of garlic knots. **Known for:** top-quality ingredients; specialty creations like kale-and-bacon and mushroom-and-truffles; hot and fresh classic New York–style slices. �$ *Average main: C$20* ✉ *269 Church St., Church–Wellesley* ☎ *647/980–7990* ⊕ *northofbrooklyn.com* Ⓜ *Wellesley.*

 ## 🛏 Hotels

The Anndore House

$$$$ | **HOTEL** | This hip boutique hotel above the popular restaurant Constantine caters to a young, plugged-in clientele with amenities like app-activated temperature control, an on-site barbershop, and record players in every room. **Pros:** great location between Yorkville and Church Street; good value for the area; beautiful common spaces. **Cons:** room design could feel more luxurious; walls are thin; in-room air-conditioning units can be loud. �$ *Rooms from: C$400* ✉ *15 Charles St. E, Church–Wellesley* ☎ *416/924–1222* ⊕ *www.theanndorehouse.com* ⤴ *115 rooms* ▮◎▮ *No Meals* Ⓜ *Bloor-Yonge.*

🍸 Nightlife

The "Gay Village," the "gayborhood," or just plain old "Church and Wellesley"—whatever you call it, this strip of bars, restaurants, shops, and clubs is a fun, always-hopping hangout for the LGBTQ+ crowd and their friends.

BARS
Bar Volo

BREWPUBS | Tucked down a cobblestone laneway across the street from its original location on Yonge Street, Bar Volo is one of the city's top destinations for beer lovers. Once specializing in rare and one-off brews from other breweries (still

Toronto Comedians

Toronto has long been a hub for emerging comedic talent. Gilda Radner, John Candy, Dan Aykroyd, Dave Thomas, Martin Short, Eugene Levy, Catherine O'Hara, and Rick Moranis all cut their teeth at Second City or on SCTV, a TV offshoot of the theater and precursor to *Saturday Night Live*. Of course, they all went on to even greater fame in movies and television. Toronto native Lorne Michaels created *SNL*, which itself laid the groundwork for countless comedy careers. A second golden age of Toronto comedy rose in the 1990s with Mike Myers and the *Kids in the Hall*'s Dave Foley, Bruce McCulloch, and Mark McKinney, all of whom got their start at the Rivoli. Canadian comedians Jim Carrey and Howie Mandel, on the other hand, debuted at Yuk Yuk's comedy club. Most recently, Samantha Bee frequented the Rivoli before becoming the host of *Full Frontal*, while Nathan Fielder and Mae Martin cut their teeth in the city's alternative comedy scene, which now centers around the Comedy Bar.

a major, the new location at the other two Volo locations in Little Italy), Bar Volo now has its own brewery on-site. That means you can get traditional English-style hand-pulled cask beers, highly drinkable German and Italian-style lagers, and some hoppy ales. It's a European style, which means the beers are all well-made, approachable classics and not too wacky (though you can find some of those on the beer list as well). For non-beer drinkers, there's also a full cocktail program and a full list of natural wines they import themselves. After pandemic-era changes to the city's liquor laws, those one-off wines and beers are all available to buy and take home. Or sip them alongside southern Italian tapas inside or on the sizable front patio. ✉ 17 Nicholas St. ☎ 416/928–0018 ⊕ www.barvolo.com ⊗ Closed Mon. Ⓜ Wellesley.

Boutique Bar
BARS | In comparison to the raucous, glittering scene you'll find nearby, Boutique Bar is a (relatively) low-key spot for a cocktail, whether you're feeling like a classic negroni, a martini, or one of the house creations. If you can, grab a spot on the tiny front patio and watch the comings and goings along Church Street. DJs bring the party on weekends. ✉ 506 Church St., Church–Wellesley ☎ 647/705–0006 ⊕ boutiquebar.ca Ⓜ Wellesley.

Woody's
BARS | A predominantly upscale crowd of men, mostly in their twenties to forties, frequents this cavernous pub and its brother bar Sailor where DJs mix nearly every night. The Toronto gay bar institution is known for Best Chest and Best Butt contests, which are hosted by some of the city's most beloved drag queens, as well as raucous dance parties. The exterior of Woody's was used on the television show *Queer as Folk*. ✉ 467 Church St., Church–Wellesley ☎ 416/972–0887 ⊕ www.woodystoronto.com Ⓜ Wellesley.

DANCE CLUBS
Crews and Tangos
DANCE CLUBS | Downstairs is Crews, a queer bar with a stage for karaoke, open mic, or drag shows (depending on the night), a dance floor in back with a DJ spinning house beats, and a sizable back patio. Upstairs, Tangos has a bar and a small dance floor that gets packed with

twenty- and thirtysomethings kicking it to old-school hip-hop and 1980s beats. The gender ratio is surprisingly balanced and the drag shows are lots of fun. ⊠ *508 Church St.* ☎ *647/349–7469* ⊕ *crewsandtangos.com* Ⓜ *Wellesley.*

 Performing Arts

THEATER
Buddies in Bad Times Theatre
THEATER | Canada's largest queer theater company presents edgy plays and festivals, as well as specialty events like parties, burlesque, and stand-up. ⊠ *12 Alexander St., Church–Wellesley* ☎ *416/975–8555* ⊕ *www.buddiesinbadtimes.com* Ⓜ *Wellesley.*

Shopping

BOOKS
Glad Day Bookshop
BOOKS | Glad Day is the world's oldest LGBTQ+ bookstore—no mean feat, especially in high-rent Toronto. In the Gay Village epicenter of Church Street, the store is packed with shelves featuring the latest and greatest in queer voices from across Canada and beyond; those shelves are frequently rolled aside to host readings, events, and even dance parties. The bar serves both coffee and alcohol, and the kitchen turns out homey diner-style eats (which are particularly appreciated during weekend drag brunches). ⊠ *499 Church St., Church–Wellesley* ☎ *416/901–6600* ⊕ *gladday.ca* Ⓜ *Wellesley.*

MUSIC
Dead Dog Records
RECORDS | Though Yonge Street is no longer a record store mecca, Dead Dog is an excellent indie shop in the nearby Gay Village. There are plenty of new vinyl records from hot up-and-coming indie bands, artists from a wide spectrum of genres, and box sets and reissues from legends like David Bowie, but regulars gravitate toward the constantly refreshing used bins to flip around for gems. There's also a good collection of DVDs, Blu-Rays, and band T-shirts, and this being the Village location, a good selection of queer artists as well. ⊠ *568 Church St.* ☎ *647/325–4575* ⊕ *deaddogrecords.com* Ⓜ *Wellesley.*

Rosedale

This posh residential neighborhood northeast of Yorkville has tree-lined curving roads (it's one of the few neighborhoods to have escaped the city's grid pattern), many small parks, and a jumble of oversized late-19th-century and early-20th-century houses in Edwardian, Victorian, Georgian, and Tudor styles. An intricate ravine system weaves through this picturesque corner of downtown, its woodsy contours lined with old-money and old-world majesty. The neighborhood is bounded by Yonge Street, the Don Valley Parkway, St. Clair Avenue East, and the Rosedale Ravine.

Sights

Evergreen Brick Works
PLAZA/SQUARE | Located within Toronto's ravine system and centered around a repurposed century-old industrial brick factory, this sustainable public space/social enterprise/nature preserve can be hard to categorize but offers plenty of unique experiences in one place. It offers beautiful trails, lookouts and wildlife (including well-loved snapping turtles), food and music in the summer, a public skating rink in the winter, and one of the city's favorite farmers' markets on Saturday year-round. There's also lots of public art and children's educational programming. ⊠ *550 Bayview Ave., Rosedale* ☎ *416/596–7670* ⊕ *evergreen.ca* Ⓜ *Free daily shuttle bus from outside Broadview subway station every day from 8 am to 6 pm or until 9 on Wednesday.*

🍴 Restaurants

Terroni and Bar Centrale

$$$ | ITALIAN | FAMILY | Local Italian mini-chain Terroni has several locations around the city but this one, with the ground-floor Bar Centrale wine bar inspired by Italian train stations, is especially popular. Head upstairs to the bi-level Terroni for locally beloved thin-crust pizzas, seafood spaghetti, and Italian cheeses and mushrooms, along with stunning views. **Known for:** excellent thin-crust pizzas; gluten-free and vegan options; bustling bar scene. [$] *Average main: C$23* ✉ *1095 Yonge St.* ☎ *416/925–4020* 🌐 *terroni.com* [M] *Summerhill.*

☕ Coffee and Quick Bites

Black Camel

$$ | SANDWICHES | This tiny café, just outside the Rosedale subway station, serves some of the city's favorite sandwiches. **Known for:** optional toppings of caramelized onions, sautéed mushrooms, and a variety of sauces; quick service, even during busy lunch rush; five-day roasted brisket and pulled pork. [$] *Average main: C$12* ✉ *4 Crescent Rd., Rosedale* ☎ *416/929–7518* 🌐 *blackcamel.ca* [M] *Rosedale.*

Boxcar Social

$ | CAFÉ | The original location of the artisan coffee shop/wine-and-spirit bar mini-chain that now has eclectic locations throughout the city, this Summerhill spot is a relaxed but lively spot from morning to evening. Located in a two-story Victorian home (and former dry cleaner), Boxcar Social has a bustling bar, a quiet and sophisticated upstairs lounge, a nice back patio, and a next-door bottle shop for those who prefer takeout. **Known for:** beers and wines to go from the bottle shop; an impressive list of whiskeys, wines, and craft beers; well-made espresso drinks and cold brew. [$] *Average main: C$6* ✉ *1208 Yonge St.* ☎ *844/726–9227* 🌐 *boxcarsocial.ca* ⏲ *Closed at night Sun.–Tues.* [M] *Summerhill.*

Pantry

$$ | ECLECTIC | This fast-casual takeout spot is an offshoot of one of the city's top catering companies, the Food Dudes—and though the salads and proteins here are produced in massive quantities, everything is handled with a deft, flavorful touch. Pick a combo size, then choose from the daily mix of multicultural offerings in the display case. **Known for:** quick service; rotating menu of takeout dishes; plenty of vegetarian-friendly options. [$] *Average main: C$15* ✉ *1094 Yonge St.* ☎ *416/792–1198* 🌐 *orderpantry.com* [M] *Rosedale.*

🎟 Performing Arts

CLASSICAL MUSIC

Toronto Mendelssohn Choir

MUSIC | This group of more than 120 singers and choristers was formed in 1894 and performs major classical choral works at various venues, including the lovely Koerner Hall and Yorkminster Park Baptist Church at Yonge and St. Clair. The choir often performs with the Toronto Symphony Orchestra, including at its annual Christmas performance of Handel's *Messiah.* ✉ *Yorkminster Park Baptist Church, 1585 Yonge St., Rosedale* ☎ *416/598–0422* 🌐 *www.tmchoir.org* [M] *St. Clair.*

🏃 Activities

Rosedale Ravine

HIKING & WALKING | FAMILY | Though you might not expect it from one of the toniest areas in downtown Toronto, Rosedale is home to a lovely nature trail running mostly below street level. It runs in a giant U shape, beginning on Heath Street East near Yonge and St. Clair (on the northern edge of Rosedale), swooping down to just east of Bloor and

Sherbourne, then ending at picturesque Mount Pleasant Cemetery. It's a relatively easy stroll, also popular with runners and cyclists. ⊠ *Heath St. E at Yonge St., Rosedale* ⊕ *toronto.ca/trails* Ⓜ *St. Clair.*

🛍 Shopping

One of Toronto's most exclusive neighborhoods, Rosedale has a strip of upscale antiques and home decor shops, as well as some other specialty shops.

ANTIQUES
Absolutely Inc.

ANTIQUES & COLLECTIBLES | Curios, from glass fishing floats to hand-beaded animal sculptures, are sold at this fascinating interiors shop. You'll also find an array of vintage jewelry, antique boxes made of materials ranging from marble to abalone, English campaign furniture, French architects' drafting tables, and all manner of furniture, light fixtures, and even handbags. ⊠ *1236 Yonge St., Rosedale* ☎ *416/922–6784* ⊕ *www.absolutelyinc. com* 🕙 *Closed Sun.* Ⓜ *Rosedale.*

Putti

ANTIQUES & COLLECTIBLES | This home decor shop is very romantic, and very turn-of-the-century. Everywhere you look, you'll see antiques, mid-century furniture, and home accessories piled so high that they scrape the chandeliers. There's an impressive array of French toiletries, as well as frilly frocks and fairy wings for children's flights of fancy. ⊠ *1104 Yonge St., Rosedale* ☎ *416/972–7652* ⊕ *www. putti.ca* Ⓜ *Rosedale.*

CLOTHING
Tuck Shop Trading Co.

MIXED CLOTHING |"Refined Canadiana" is the motto at this shop, which pairs cute, cheery clothing for men and women with home goods worthy of a hip Muskoka cottage. Tees, patterned swim trunks, and statement earrings sit alongside luxe scented candles and embroidered woven baskets. If any of Toronto's neighborhoods have particularly captured your

heart, grab one of the winter hats (or, as the locals call 'em, toques) from their house-made City of Neighbourhoods line. ⊠ *1226 Yonge St., Rosedale* ☎ *416/859– 3566* ⊕ *tuckshopco.com* Ⓜ *Summerhill.*

FOOD AND WINE
Summerhill LCBO

WINE/SPIRITS | Once a stately railway station, this unique, clock-tower-fronted location of Ontario's provincially owned chain of liquor stores is where oenophiles, scotch lovers, and other locals with a taste for the finer things go hunting for rare bottles. The store also frequently hosts tastings. ■ **TIP→ Keep customs limits on alcohol purchases, as well as whether you'll be checking a bag, in mind before you stock up.** ⊠ *10 Scrivener Sq.* ☎ *416/922–0403* ⊕ *lcbo.com* Ⓜ *Summerhill.*

Summerhill Market

FOOD | A neighborhood grocer that goes back more than a half century, Summerhill Market is now one of the bougiest shopping experiences you can have in the city. Not so much the "pop in for a couple of things" market unless your grocery budget is very high, it's the spot to get fancy culinary condiments, fish, meat, produce, and prepared foods. ⊠ *446 Summerhill Ave., Rosedale* ☎ *416/921–2714* ⊕ *summerhillmarket. com* Ⓜ *Rosedale.*

SHOES, HANDBAGS, AND LEATHER GOODS
Mephisto

SHOES | These French-made walking shoes have been around since the 1960s and are constructed entirely from natural materials. Passionate walkers swear by them and claim they never, ever wear out—even on cross-Europe treks. Styles, which include options for men and women, run the gamut from smart ankle boots to minimalist slides. ⊠ *1177 Yonge St., Rosedale* ☎ *416/968–7026* ⊕ *ca. mephisto.com* Ⓜ *Summerhill.*

In addition to producing numerous works by Canadian artists, the Toronto Dance Theatre collaborates with choreographers from throughout the United States and Europe.

Cabbagetown

Mockingly named by outsiders for the cabbages that grew on tiny lawns and were cooked in nearly every house by early Irish settlers in the 1840s, the term Cabbagetown is used with a combination of inverse pride and almost wistful irony today (as gentrification has increased real estate value here exponentially). It's fun to stroll around and enjoy the architectural diversity of this funky residential area, and there are a few attractions of interest, too. The enclave extends roughly from Parliament Street on the west—about 1½ km (1 mile) due east of Yonge Street—to the Don River on the east, and from Bloor Street on the north to Shuter Street on the south.

Sights

Allan Gardens

NATURE PRESERVE | FAMILY | Allan Gardens has been a green oasis in Toronto for well over a century. A domed indoor botanical garden and arboretum, the conservatory is filled with plant, flower, and tree species from around the world, preserved and cultivated in six different climate zones. If you're a nature lover you can easily spend hours among the succulents, vines, orchids, hibiscus, and weeping willows, and all for free. ✉ *19 Horticultural Ave., Cabbagetown* ☎ *416/392–7288* ⊕ *toronto.ca/parks* 🚉 *Free* Ⓜ *College.*

Necropolis Cemetery

CEMETERY | This nonsectarian burial ground, established in 1850, is the final resting place for many of Toronto's pioneers, including prominent turn-of-the-century black Canadian doctors, businessmen, and politicians. The cemetery's chapel, gate, and gatehouse date from 1872; the buildings constitute one of the most attractive groupings of small Victorian-era structures in Toronto. ✉ *200 Winchester St.* ☎ *416/923–7911* ⊕ *mountpleasantgroup.com* ❂ *Closed Sun. Open by appointment other days.* Ⓜ *10-minute walk from Gerrard and Sumach bus stop.*

Riverdale Farm

FARM/RANCH | FAMILY | This spot once hosted the city's main zoo, but it's now home to a rural community representative of a late 19th-century farm. Permanent residents include horses, cows, sheep, goats, pigs, donkeys, ducks, geese, and chickens. While it's not a petting zoo per se, kids get a real kick out of watching farmers go about their daily chores, which include feeding and bathing the animals. The adjacent playground has a wading pool. The nearby Riverdale Park offers some of the best skyline views in the city. ✉ *201 Winchester St., Cabbagetown* ☎ *416/392–6794* ⊕ *riverdalefarmtoronto.ca* 🎟 *Free* Ⓜ *505 Dundas streetcar, River St. stop.*

St. James Cemetery

CEMETERY | At the northeast corner of Parliament and Wellesley Streets, this cemetery contains interesting burial monuments of many prominent politicians, business leaders, and families in Toronto. The small yellow-brick Gothic Chapel of St. James-the-Less has a handsome spire rising from the church nave and was built in 1861. This National Historical Site is one of the most beautiful churches in the country. ✉ *635 Parliament St.* ☎ *416/964–9194* ⊕ *www.stjamescemetery.ca* Ⓜ *65 Parliament bus, Wellesley St. stop.*

 **Performing Arts**

★ Toronto Dance Theatre

MODERN DANCE | The oldest contemporary dance company in the city, TDT has created more than 100 original works since its beginnings in the 1960s, often using original scores by Canadian composers. Multiple pieces are performed each year in its home theater in Cabbagetown. ✉ *80 Winchester St., 1 block east of Parliament St., Cabbagetown* ☎ *416/967–1365* ⊕ *www.tdt.org* Ⓜ *Castle Frank.*

Chapter 11

GREATER TORONTO

11

Updated by
Daniel Otis

👁 Sights	🍴 Restaurants	🛏 Hotels	💼 Shopping	🍸 Nightlife
★★★★☆	★★★☆☆	★★☆☆☆	★★★☆☆	★★☆☆☆

NEIGHBORHOOD SNAPSHOT

TOP EXPERIENCES

■ **Wine and dine:** Starting at Eglinton station, wander down Yonge Street to experience midtown Toronto's most popular shopping and dining district.

■ **Indulge your inner animal lover:** See more than 5,000 creatures in natural-looking habitats at the Toronto Zoo, a long-standing family favorite.

■ **Discover Japan:** From martial arts to traditional dance, you never know what you're going to encounter at the Japanese Canadian Cultural Centre.

■ **Take a dip:** Swim in the cool waters of Lake Ontario beneath towering cliffs at Bluffers Park and Beach, which boasts some of the softest sand in the city.

■ **Enjoy green space:** Head out of the city center to the rolling hills and ravines of Don Mills or forested reserves at the Kortright Centre.

■ **Go back in time:** The Middle Eastern and Persian artifacts at the spectacular Aga Khan Museum transport you to another era.

GETTING HERE

Buses run from various subway stations to Edwards Gardens, the Ontario Science Centre, the Toronto Zoo, and Scarborough Bluffs; the subway goes directly to Black Creek Pioneer Village and Yonge and Eglinton. You'll need a car to visit the Kortright Centre and the McMichael Canadian Art Collection. Canada's Wonderland is most easily reached by car but is accessible by public transit.

PLANNING YOUR TIME

You can explore each Greater Toronto sight independently or combine a couple of sights in one trip. The Ontario Science Centre and Edwards Gardens are very close together, for example, and would make a manageable day trip; and, if you're driving from the city, you could visit Black Creek Pioneer Village and the Kortright Centre for Conservation on the way to the McMichael Canadian Art Collection. Families should reserve a full day at Canada's Wonderland.

FUN FACTS

■ What's known as the Greater Toronto Area, or GTA, encompasses Toronto and four surrounding regional municipalities: Durham, Halton, Peel, and York.

■ The GTA is home to about 6 million people; nearly half are immigrants to Canada from countries like India, China, Philippines, Pakistan, Sri Lanka, and Jamaica.

■ Before 1998, Toronto areas like Scarborough, North York, and Etobicoke were separate cities.

■ Scarborough in particular is one of the most diverse parts of this multicultural city, and you can take a tasty tour of the world in its otherwise unassuming strip malls.

You won't get a full Toronto experience if you don't tread far from the Harbourfront or the main drags along Queen and Bloor Streets.

The Greater Toronto Area is what has helped the city earn its unofficial title of the "most multicultural city in the world." To the north and particularly the east is where you'll find the ethnic enclaves, sprawling parks, fascinating museums, and one-of-a-kind attractions that make the region even more intriguing. Most of these must-sees are accessible by public transportation, although a car would make the journey to some of the more far-flung destinations more convenient.

North Toronto

North Toronto encompasses Yonge Street between Eglinton Avenue—the neighborhood's southern, more bold and youthful end, which has garnered the playful nickname "Yonge and Eligible"—and north to Lawrence Avenue, with its more refined restaurants and upscale boutiques. The streets to the east and west of Yonge Street are mainly leafy and residential, and at the eastern edge are major tourist attractions: the Ontario Science Centre, a never-ending source of entertainment for the young and young-at-heart; the regal Aga Khan Museum of Islamic Art; and Toronto Botanical Garden and Edwards Gardens, a phenomenal display of flowers and plants.

Sights

★ Aga Khan Museum
ART MUSEUM | More than 1,000 pieces of Islamic art from the collection of the family of renowned philanthropist

and religious leader Aga Khan are the focus of this museum. Here you'll find Middle Eastern and Persian artifacts and inscriptions, many so ancient that they are only displayed for a few months at a time to preserve their lifespan. It's worth making the trip for the stunning architecture, which includes a massive main building topped by a silver hexagonal dome and a park distinguished by a glass pyramid more intricate than the one at the Louvre. The museum's mandate is strictly secular, but it's hard not to have a spiritual moment staring into the central courtyard pond. Guided tours are available for C$10. Check their calendar for workshops and performances. ⊠ 77 Wynford Dr. ☎ 416/646–4677 ⊕ www.agakhanmuseum.org ☒ C$20, free Wed. 4–8. Parking C$10. ⊙ Closed Mon.

Japanese Canadian Cultural Centre
ARTS CENTER | FAMILY | Serving Toronto's Japanese community and thousands of lovers of Japanese culture, this space features a traditional garden and offers workshops and classes in martial arts, music, visual arts, traditional dance, cooking, and more. Visiting art shows are frequently in rotation, as well as artist talks and movie screenings; there's even a Japanese film festival each June. Plan a visit if checking out the nearby Aga Khan Museum. ⊠ 6 Garamond Ct., North York ☎ 416/441–2345 ⊕ www.jccc.on.ca.

Ontario Science Centre
SCIENCE MUSEUM | FAMILY | It has been called a museum of the 21st century, but it's much more than that—where else can you stroll through a real rain

The futuristic Ontario Science Centre engages visitors of all ages with hands-on exhibits and workshops.

forest and explore the boundaries of the human body? Even the building itself is extraordinary: three linked pavilions float gracefully down the side of a ravine and overflow with exhibits that make science and technology fascinating. The sprawling Weston Family Innovation Centre, rife with hands-on activities, is all about experience and problem solving. Younger visitors learn through play in KidSpark, a space specially designed for children eight and under to enjoy and explore. IMAX films and demonstrations of robotics, electricity, and more take place daily; check the schedule when you arrive. ⊠ *770 Don Mills Rd., at Eglinton Ave. E, North Toronto* ☎ *416/696–1000* ⊕ *www.ontariosciencecentre.ca* ✉ *C$22, parking C$12.*

Toronto Botanical Garden and Edwards Gardens

GARDEN | FAMILY | These beautiful themed botanical gardens and adjacent estate garden (once owned by industrialist Rupert Edwards) flow into one of the city's most visited ravines. Paths wind along colorful floral displays and exquisite rock gardens, which are incredibly popular with wedding photographers. There's also a signposted "teaching garden" for kids to touch and learn about nature. You can join a free 90-minute tour between May and early September, on most days except Mondays and Wednesdays; check online for times. Refreshments and baked goods are available on-site at the Bloom Cafe. The parking lot can get very busy on weekends in spring and autumn. For a long nature walk, head south through Wilket Creek Park and the winding Don Valley. After hours of walking (or biking or jogging) through almost uninterrupted parkland, you reach the southern tip of Taylor Creek Park on Victoria Park Avenue, just north of the Danforth—here you can catch a subway. ⊠ *777 Lawrence Ave. E, North Toronto* ⊹ *Entrance at southwest corner of Leslie St. and Lawrence Ave. E* ☎ *416/397–1341, 416/397–4145 tours* ⊕ *www. torontobotanicalgarden.ca.*

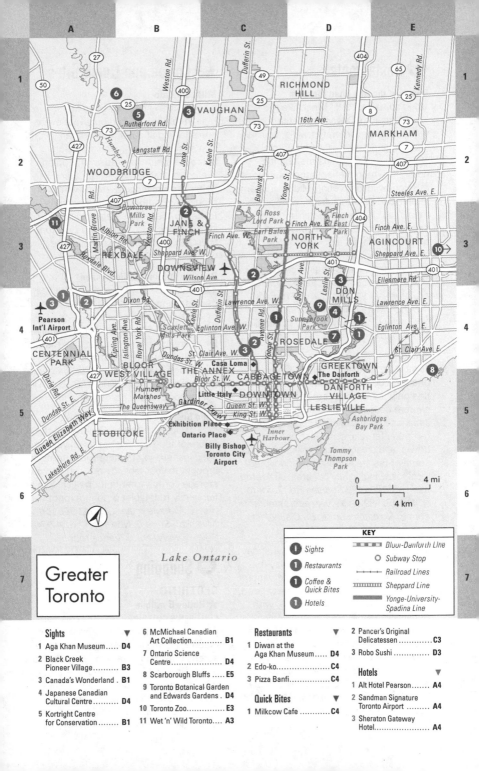

Greater Toronto

Lake Ontario

KEY

- **1** Sights
- **1** Restaurants
- **1** Coffee & Quick Bites
- **1** Hotels

- ▬▬ Bloor-Danforth Line
- ○ Subway Stop
- ├─┼─┤ Railroad Lines
- ▥▥▥ Sheppard Line
- ▬▬ Yonge-University-Spadina Line

Sights ▼

1 Aga Khan Museum..... **D4**
2 Black Creek Pioneer Village.......... **B3**
3 Canada's Wonderland . **B1**
4 Japanese Canadian Cultural Centre......... **D4**
5 Kortright Centre for Conservation........ **B1**
6 McMichael Canadian Art Collection............ **B1**
7 Ontario Science Centre..................... **D4**
8 Scarborough Bluffs **E5**
9 Toronto Botanical Garden and Edwards Gardens . **D4**
10 Toronto Zoo.............. **E3**
11 Wet 'n' Wild Toronto.... **A3**

Restaurants ▼

1 Diwan at the Aga Khan Museum **D4**
2 Edo-ko..................... **C4**
3 Pizza Banfi................ **C4**

Quick Bites ▼

1 Milkcow Cafe **C4**

2 Pancer's Original Delicatessen **C3**
3 Robo Sushi **D3**

Hotels ▼

1 Alt Hotel Pearson....... **A4**
2 Sandman Signature Toronto Airport **A4**
3 Sheraton Gateway Hotel...................... **A4**

🍴 Restaurants

Diwan at the Aga Khan Museum
$$$ | **MIDDLE EASTERN** | Much like the Aga Khan Museum, Diwan is an architectural wonder that incorporates walls, ceilings, and hanging lamps salvaged from a 19th-century Damascus merchant's home. The menu reflects the museum's mission by incorporating Middle Eastern, Indian, and Persian cuisine, with seasonal meat, seafood, and vegetarian dishes. **Known for:** impressive dishes like sweet onion bhaji fritters and kale coconut sambol; eye-popping mix of a modern building and antique details; crisp service. [$] *Average main: C$26* ✉ *Aga Khan Museum, 77 Wynford Dr.* ☎ *416/646–4670* 🌐 *diwan.agakhanmuseum.org* 🕒 *Closed Mon. and Tues. No dinner Sun., Wed., and Thurs.*

Edo-ko
$$ | **JAPANESE FUSION** | **FAMILY** | Open in one form or another since the 1980s, this neighborhood eatery strives to capture both contemporary and authentic Japanese *washoku*-style cooking. Think tempura, teriyaki, sushi, sashimi, poke bowls, and creative maki rolls. **Known for:** some of the area's best sushi; devoted local following; lovely bar area. [$] *Average main: C$17* ✉ *429 Spadina Rd., Toronto* ☎ *416/482–8973* 🌐 *www.edorestaurants.com* 🕒 *No lunch Sun.* [M] *St. Clair West.*

Pizza Banfi
$$ | **ITALIAN** | **FAMILY** | No matter what day or time, Pizza Banfi is usually busy for two reasons: it doesn't take reservations, and the classic Italian food is really good. While the decor is slightly cliché, with Renaissance-style wall paintings over light-color bricks, the pizzas are the real attraction. **Known for:** one of the neighborhood's favorites; generous servings of pasta; good-priced daily specials. [$] *Average main: C$20* ✉ *333B Lonsdale Rd., Yonge and Eglinton* ☎ *416/322–5231* 🕒 *Closed Sun.* [M] *St. Clair West.*

☕ Coffee and Quick Bites

Milkcow Cafe
$ | **DESSERTS** | Asian desserts are all the rage in Toronto, so find out what everyone's talking about at this Korean favorite that specializes in organic milk soft-serve ice cream layered with toppings like cotton candy, honeycomb, and jelly beans. **Known for:** soft serve with exciting toppings; mouth-watering macarons; loaded crepes. [$] *Average main: C$10* ✉ *2651 Yonge St., Yonge and Eglinton* ☎ *647/346–6669* 🌐 *www.milkcowcafe.ca* 🕒 *Closed Mon.* [M] *Eglinton.*

Pancer's Original Delicatessen
$ | **JEWISH DELI** | This legendary deli has been serving kosher-style kishkes, knishes, and oversize smoked-meat-on-rye sandwiches for four generations. **Known for:** shareable platters; traditional matzo ball soup; towering meat sandwiches. [$] *Average main: C$10* ✉ *3856 Bathurst St., North York* ☎ *416/636–1230* 🌐 *www.pancersoriginaldeli.com* [M] *Wilson.*

Robo Sushi
$$$ | **JAPANESE** | **FAMILY** | Experience the future of food service at this all-you-can-eat Japanese joint where most items are brought to your table by real robots with storage compartments for bellies. **Known for:** family fun; tablet ordering; robot waiters. [$] *Average main: C$30* ✉ *865 York Mills Rd., Suite 9, North York* ☎ *647/748–3675* 🌐 *www.enjoy2eat.ca/robo.*

🛍 Shopping

CLOTHING

★ Hatley Boutique
CHILDREN'S CLOTHING | **FAMILY** | This company began as a cottage business in rural Québec nearly 40 years ago with a line of aprons depicting cute farm animals. Now this mainly children's boutique is stocked with quirky and colorful nature-inspired clothing covered in insects, animals, trees, and flowers inspired by the Canadian wilderness. ✉ *2648 Yonge St.,*

Canada's Wonderland is the country's first theme park.

at Craighurst Ave., Yonge and Eglinton ☎ 416/486-4141 ⊕ www.hatley.com Ⓜ Lawrence or Eglinton.

OUTDOOR EQUIPMENT
Sporting Life

SPORTING GOODS | The first off the mark with the latest sportswear trends, this is the place to get hip, high-end outdoorsy labels like Canada Goose, the North Face, and Moncler—or to snag ski and snowboard gear, and poll the staff for advice on where to use it. ✉ 2665 Yonge St., north of Eglinton Ave. ☎ 416/485-1611 ⊕ www.sportinglife.ca Ⓜ Eglinton.

Northern and Eastern Suburbs

Toronto's cultural vibrancy extends beyond downtown, with pockets accessible deep in the GTA (Greater Toronto Area). The McMichael Canadian Art Collection, in the quaint suburb of Kleinburg, houses the stellar collection of Group of Seven pieces. Just minutes outside of downtown, Black Creek Pioneer Village is a living-history museum that is subway accessible and extremely kid friendly. Nearby is the enormous theme park Canada's Wonderland. The sprawling Toronto Zoo, set in the beautiful Rouge River Valley, is the perfect destination for a day trip, as is the Kortright Centre for Conservation … if you've got wheels.

Sights

Black Creek Pioneer Village

MUSEUM VILLAGE | FAMILY | A namesake subway station is a short walk from this living-history-museum village that makes you feel as though you've gone through a time warp. Black Creek Pioneer Village is a collection of over 40 buildings from the 19th century, including a town hall, a weaver's shop, a printing shop, a blacksmith's shop, and a one-room schoolhouse. The mill dates from the 1840s and has a massive wooden waterwheel that can grind up to 100 barrels of flour a day. As people in period costumes go about the daily routine of mid-19th-century Ontario life, they explain what they're doing and answer questions. Visitors can see farm animals, churn butter, take wagon rides and Victorian dance classes, and explore a hands-on discovery center. ⊠ *1000 Murray Ross Pkwy., near intersection of Jane St. and Steeles Ave., Toronto* ☎ *416/736–1733* ⊕ *www.blackcreek.ca* ⊠ *C$16, parking C$9* ⊘ *Closed Mon. and Tues.* Ⓜ *Pioneer Village Station.*

Canada's Wonderland

AMUSEMENT PARK/CARNIVAL | FAMILY | Canada's first and largest theme park, filled with more than 200 games, rides, restaurants, and shops, includes favorite attractions like Planet Snoopy, home of Charlie Brown and the rest of the *Peanuts* gang; Windseeker, which features 32 301-foot swings; and Skyhawk, where riders take control of their own cockpit. But Wonderland isn't just for the smallest members of the family; one of 17 roller coasters in the park, The Bat takes riders forward, and then back, through stomach-churning corkscrews and loops. Bring swim gear to take advantage of Splash Works, a 20-acre on-site water park, which boasts 17 waterslides, cliff jumping, and Canada's largest outdoor wave pool.
■ TIP➜ **Order tickets online in advance for discount prices.** ⊠ *1 Canada's Wonderland Dr.* ☎ *905/832–8131* ⊕ *www.canadaswonderland.com* ⊠ *From C$50* ⊘ *Closed Nov.–late May and weekdays in Sept. and Oct.*

Kortright Centre for Conservation

NATURE PRESERVE | Only 10 minutes north of the city, this delightful conservation center has more than 16 km (10 miles) of hiking trails through forest, meadow, and marshland, as well as a Bee Space where kids can see them up close and taste their honey, and an Innovation Trail that demonstrates how technology can reduce our impact on the wild. In the magnificent woods there have been sightings of foxes, coyotes, rabbits, deer, and a wide array of birds. Seasonal events include a spring sugar bush maple syrup festival and a honey harvest festival. To get here, drive 3 km (2 miles) north along Highway 400, exit west at Major Mackenzie Drive, and continue south 1 km (½ mile) on Pine Valley Drive to the gate. ⊠ *9550 Pine Valley Dr., Woodbridge* ☎ *905/832–2289* ⊕ *www.kortright.org* ⊠ *From C$8, parking C$4.*

McMichael Canadian Art Collection

ART MUSEUM | On 100 acres of lovely woodland in Kleinburg, 30 km (19 miles) northwest of downtown, the McMichael's permanent collection consists of more than 6,500 pieces by Canadian artists. The museum holds impressive works by Tom Thomson, Emily Carr, and the Group of Seven landscape painters, as well as their early-20th-century contemporaries. These artists were inspired by the wilderness and sought to capture it in bold, original styles. First Nations art and prints, drawings, and sculpture by Inuit artists are well represented. Strategically placed windows help you appreciate the scenery as you view art that took its inspiration from the vast outdoors. Inside, wood walls and a fireplace set a country mood. Free guided tours are offered from Thursday to Sunday at 12:30, and on Thursday and Friday at 2. ⊠ *10365 Islington Ave., west of Hwy. 400 and north of Major Mackenzie Dr., Kleinburg* ☎ *905/893–1121* ⊕ *www.mcmichael.com* ⊠ *C$18, parking C$7* ⊘ *Gallery closed Mon.–Wed.; grounds open 7 days a week.*

★ Scarborough Bluffs

HIKING & WALKING | Stretching over 9 miles along Toronto's eastern waterfront, the majestic Scarborough Bluffs tower more than 300 feet above the cool, clean waters of Lake Ontario. Visit any time of year for a nature walk; in summer, sandy beaches are a great way to beat the heat. You can access the bluffs from 11 city parks, including Bluffer's Park and Beach, which features one of the finest stretches of sand in the city, and Guild

The sandy beaches at Scarborough Bluffs are a great place to beat the summer heat.

Park and Gardens, which boasts sweeping views of the lake and tranquil gardens dotted with grand architectural relics and sculptures from demolished 19th- and early-20th-century buildings. While a car is the easiest way to visit, most Scarborough Bluffs parks are accessible by TTC bus or GO Transit train. ⊠ *1 Brimley Rd. S* 🖼 *416/392–2489* ⊕ *www.toronto.ca/ explore-enjoy/parks-gardens-beaches/ scarborough-bluffs* 🎫 *Free.*

Toronto Zoo

ZOO | FAMILY | With terrain ranging from river valley to dense forest, the Rouge Valley was an inspired choice of site for this 710-acre zoo in which 5,000 different mammals, birds, reptiles, and fish are grouped according to their natural habitats, in both indoor and outdoor enclosures. Daily activities might include chats with zookeepers and animal demonstrations. A visit takes at least three hours and includes the Africa, Americas, Australasia, Indo-Malaya, and Canadian Domain pavilions. In the spring and summer, the Zoomobile can take you through the outdoor exhibit area. The African Savanna is a fantastic walking safari; a dynamic reproduction that brings rare and beautiful animals and distinctive geological landscapes to the city's doorstep. Reserve ahead for a behind-the-scenes tour or to camp overnight in the Serengeti Bush Camp. ⊠ *2000 Meadowvale Rd., at Exit 389 off Hwy. 401, Scarborough* 🖼 *416/392–5900, 416/392–5947 for Serengeti Bush Camp reservations* ⊕ *www.torontozoo.com* 🎫 *C$28, parking C$14* 🕐 *Some areas closed in winter.*

Wet 'n' Wild Toronto

WATER PARK | FAMILY | This 100-acre water park has huge water slides, a lazy river, a fantastic wave pool, and Bear Footin' Bay, a delightful area for younger children to splash around in. You can also splurge on a group cabana or hang out at the Coconut Cove Bar. Arrive early on summer weekends. ⊠ *7855 Finch Ave. W, off Hwy. 427* 🖼 *416/369–0123* ⊕ *www. wetnwildtoronto.com* 🎫 *C$50, parking C$20* 🕐 *Closed late Sept.–late June.*

Pearson International Airport Area

It's certainly not the most exciting part of the city, but if you have an early-morning departure or late-night arrival at Pearson International Airport, staying nearby might be the best option. Sheraton Gateway Hotel and Alt Hotel are the easiest to access. There are many others in the area, and more than 30 hotels offer airport shuttle services.

Hotels

Alt Hotel Pearson
$$ | HOTEL | Not your average airport hotel, this hip lodging offers plush digs at affordable prices. **Pros:** minutes from all airport terminals; rooms have lots of high-tech touches; modern and minimalist decor. **Cons:** no fridges in rooms; few meal options nearby; location on the highway. [$] *Rooms from: C$200* ✉ *6080 Viscount Rd., Mississauga* ☎ *905/362–4337, 855/855–6080* 🌐 *www.germain-hotels.com/en/alt-hotel/toronto-airport* 🛏 *153 rooms* 🍴 *No Meals.*

Sandman Signature Toronto Airport
$$ | HOTEL | FAMILY | Reasonable prices, an indoor swimming pool and hot tub, and quiet, modern rooms are the advantages of this property just down the road from Pearson International Airport. **Pros:** roomy fitness center; excellent service; large rooms. **Cons:** restaurant can get very busy; some rooms need a refresh; little to do nearby. [$] *Rooms from: C$180* ✉ *55 Reading Ct., Greater Toronto* ☎ *416/798–8840* 🌐 *www.sandmanhotels.com/signature-toronto-airport* 🛏 *256 rooms* 🍴 *No Meals.*

Sheraton Gateway Hotel
$$$ | HOTEL | For quick layovers, it's hard to beat the location of this chain hotel right inside Terminal 3 of Pearson International Airport. **Pros:** you can't get closer to your gate than this; double-paned windows keep out airport sounds; attractive restaurant. **Cons:** pricey compared to nearby options; some noise from other rooms and hallways; little to do around hotel. [$] *Rooms from: C$350* ✉ *Terminal 3, Toronto AMF* ☎ *905/672–7000* 🌐 *www.marriott.com/en-us/hotels/yyzgs-sheraton-gateway-hotel-in-toronto-international-airport* 🛏 *474 rooms* 🍴 *No Meals.*

Chapter 12

SIDE TRIPS FROM TORONTO

Updated by
Jesse Ship

12

⊙ Sights	🍴 Restaurants	🛏 Hotels	🛍 Shopping	🍸 Nightlife
★★★★★	★★★★☆	★★★★☆	★★★☆☆	★★☆☆☆

WELCOME TO
SIDE TRIPS FROM TORONTO

TOP REASONS TO GO

★ **Take in Niagara Falls:** The Falls' amazing display of natural power is Ontario's top attraction. See them from both the U.S. and Canadian sides.

★ **Enjoy Shakespeare and Shaw:** A couple of long-dead British playwrights have managed to make two Ontario towns boom from May through October with the Shakespeare Festival in Stratford and the Shaw Festival in Niagara-on-the-Lake.

★ **Tour award-winning wineries:** The Niagara Peninsula has an unusually good microclimate for growing grapes; most of the more than 60 wineries have tastings.

★ **Explore the great outdoors:** Ski at resorts north of Toronto; canoe backcountry rivers in Algonquin Provincial Park; hike or bike the Niagara-to-Lake-Huron Bruce Trail or the Niagara Parkway along the Niagara River.

★ **Get a taste of Ontario:** Niagara-on-the-Lake and Stratford are both renowned for their skilled chefs who serve culinary masterpieces created with farm-fresh ingredients.

1 Niagara Falls. South of Toronto near the U.S. border, the thundering falls are an impressive display of nature's power. Taking a boat ride to the bottom of the falls is a thrilling experience, and one that's guaranteed to leave you soaked.

2 Niagara-on-the-Lake. This pretty Victorian-style town at the junction of Lake Ontario and the Niagara River is the hub of the Niagara wine region.

3 The Niagara Escarpment. The Niagara Peninsula north of St. Catharines offers wineries, hiking trails, and long stretches of country roads.

4 Stratford. An acclaimed Shakespeare Festival brings this rural town alive from April through October. Overwhelmingly popular, it has become Stratford's raison d'être, with a

multitude of inns and locavore restaurants growing up around it. Frequent outdoor music and arts festivals color the squares and parks all summer.

5 Midland and Penetanguishene. These quiet harbor towns provide a gateway to ski resorts and the Georgian Bay Islands National Park.

6 Gravenhurst. This small but lively (in summer) town in the rustic Muskoka region offers a wealth of outdoor adventures.

7 Huntsville. Travel to Algonquin Provincial Park for the best snow in southern Ontario and beautiful hiking, swimming, and wildlife.

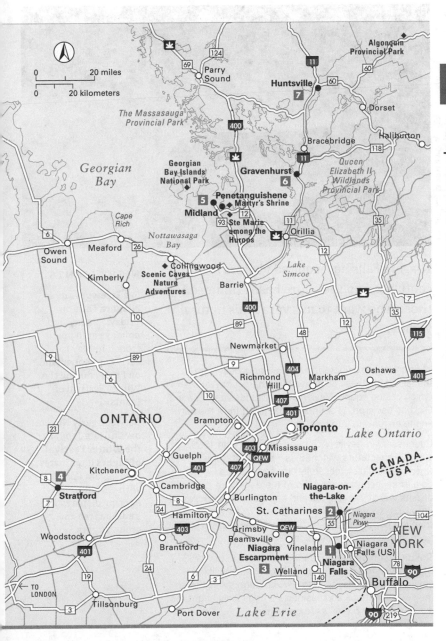

NIAGARA FALLS

Niagara Falls is as dramatic by night as by day.

Niagara Falls has inspired visitors for centuries, and the allure hasn't dimmed for those who want to marvel at this natural wonder.

Missionary and explorer Louis Hennepin described the falls in 1678 as "an incredible Cataract or Waterfall which has no equal." Nearly two centuries later, Charles Dickens declared, "I seemed to be lifted from the earth and to be looking into Heaven."

Countless daredevils have been lured here. In 1859, 100,000 spectators watched as French tightrope walker Charles Blondin successfully crossed Niagara Gorge on a three-inch-thick rope. From the early 18th century, dozens went over in boats and barrels. Nobody survived until 1901, when schoolteacher Annie Taylor emerged from her barrel and asked, "Did I go over the falls yet?" Such stunts were outlawed in 1912.

The depiction of the thundering cascades in the 1953 Marilyn Monroe film *Niagara* is largely responsible for creating modern-day tourism. And though the lights of the souvenir shops and casinos shine garishly bright for some, views of the falls are unspoiled.

NIGHT LIGHTS

See **Fireworks over Niagara Falls** on Friday, Sunday, and holidays at 10 pm from mid-May to early September (and on Friday during the Winter Festival of Lights).

Between early November and late January, the **Winter Festival of Lights** illuminates the Niagara Parkway, with 125 animated lighting displays and 3 million tree and ground lights.

WAYS TO EXPLORE

BY AIR

National Helicopters. National Helicopters has 20-minute tours over the falls and wine country, plus romance and other specialty tours. ✉ *Niagara District Airport, 468 Niagara Stone Rd., Niagara-on-the-Lake* ☎ *905/641–2222, 800/491–3117* ⊕ *www.nationalhelicopters.com.*

Niagara Helicopters. This company does 12-minute sightseeing flights over the whirlpool, gorge, and all three falls, plus winery trips. ✉ *3731 Victoria Ave., Niagara Falls* ☎ *905/357–5672* ⊕ *www.niagarahelicopters.com.*

The Whirlpool Aero Car cable car crosses the gorge over the Niagara River whirlpool.

BY BOAT

The Maid of the Mist is an oldie but a goodie, and still pulls in huge crowds. Adrenaline-fueled Whirlpool Jet Boat Tours in Niagara-on-the-Lake plow headfirst into the Class V Niagara River rapids on an hour-long ride.

BY BUS

Double Deck Tours. Take an authentic London double-decker bus tour with Double Deck Tours. Fares include admission to Journey Behind the Falls, Maid of the Mist, and the Whirlpool Aero Car; the four-hour tour also includes the Floral Clock and Niagara Glen. ✉ *5900 Falls Ave., Niagara Falls* ☎ *905/374–7423* ⊕ *www.doubledecktours.com* 🎫 *C$49.95 for 2-hour, C$149.95 for 4-hour.*

BY FOOT

Stroll the Niagara Parkway promenade, stand on the Table Rock Centre terrace, and walk over the Rainbow Bridge. The White Water Walk is the closest you'll get to the rapids from land; Journey Behind the Falls is a walk through tunnels behind the falls.

IN 1 DAY

If you have only a day at Niagara Falls, walk the waterfront promenade and go on a Maid of the Mist tour. (Plan for wet shins and shoes.) Also consider the Whirlpool Aero Car, a cable-car ride over the whirlpool, or the Whitewater Walk, to see the rapids up close. Dinner within view of the falls, which are colorfully lit at night, is a relaxing end to a full day.

THE AMERICAN SIDE

Canada has the superior views and a more developed waterfront, with better restaurants. In contrast, the American waterfront is lined with parks, ideal for hiking and picnicking. Because you're behind the falls here, rather than facing them, views are limited. Stick to Canada for most of your visit, but if you have more time, cross the Rainbow Bridge on foot to get close to Bridal Veil Falls on a Cave of the Winds tour from Goat Island.

12

Side Trips from Toronto NIAGARA FALLS

WINE REGION KNOW-HOW

Ontario may not be famed for its wines—yet—but the Niagara Peninsula alone has around 75 wineries and has been producing wine commercially since the early 1970s. Four decades on, the region is coming into its own with some of the world's best wines of origin.

The position of the Niagara appellation, wedged between Lake Ontario and the Niagara Escarpment, creates a microclimate that regulates ground and air temperature and allows for successful grape growing (today more than 30 varietals) in an otherwise too-cold province. Winds off of Lake Ontario are directed back by the escarpment, preventing cold air from settling. Heat stored in lake waters in summer keeps ground temperatures warmer longer into winter. In spring, the cold waters keep the grounds from warming too fast, protecting buds from late-spring frosts. Some say that the slightly colder climate means a more complex-tasting grape. Indisputably it *does* provide perfect conditions for producing some of the world's best ice wine.

WHAT'S IN A VQA

Canadian wine is regulated by the Vintners Quality Alliance. Many Niagara wineries proudly declare their vintages VQA; in fact, 65% of all VQA wines in Ontario are Niagara wines. To be deemed VQA wines must meet rigorous standards—they must be made entirely from fresh, quality-approved Ontario-grown grapes (no concentrates) and approved grape varieties, pass laboratory testing, and gain approval from an expert tasting panel. Look for the VQA stamp on the label.

NIAGARA WINE TOURING BASICS

THE ONTARIO WINE ROUTE

Niagara Grape & Wine Festival. The Niagara Grape & Wine Festival group organizes three big events in Niagara. The largest, with an annual half-million attendees, is the 10-day Niagara Wine Festival in September. The three-week Niagara Ice Wine Festival in January is a nod to Niagara's specialty, ice wine. The three-weekend Niagara New Vintage Festival, in June, is a wine and culinary event. ⊠ *Montebello Park, 64 Ontario St.* ☎ *905/688–0212* ⊕ *www.niagarawinefestival.com.*

TIMING AND COSTS

Most wineries are open year-round, with limited hours in winter. Tastings begin between 10 and noon. Reservations may be needed for tours in summer.

Tastings usually cost C$1–C$2 per wine, or up to C$10 for more expensive wines. The larger wineries do regular public tours; at smaller operations you may be able to arrange a tour in advance. Tasting and/or tour fees are often waived if you buy a bottle of wine.

ORGANIZED TOURS

Crush on Niagara. Crush on Niagara tour packages include overnight stays, meals, and winery tours. ⊠ *4101 King St.* ☎ *905/562–3373, 866/408–9463* ⊕ *www.crushtours.com.*

Grape and Wine Tours. Grape and Wine Tours runs day trips and one- or two-night packages from Toronto and Oakville. Pickup and drop-off at Niagara-on-the-Lake and Niagara Falls hotels is included. ⊠ *758 Niagara Stone Rd.* ☎ *905/562–4920, 855/682–4920* ⊕ *www.niagaragrapeandwinetours.ca.*

ONTARIO'S ICE WINES: SWEET SIPPING

Ontario is the world's leading producer of ice wine. It's produced from ripe grapes left on the vine into the winter. When grapes start to freeze, most of the water in them solidifies, resulting in a fructose-laden, aromatic, and flavorful center. Ice-wine grapes must be picked at freezing temperatures before sunrise and basket-pressed immediately. By nature ice wine is sweet, and when well made it smells of dried fruits, apricots, and honey and has a long, refreshing finish.

Vidal grapes are ideal for ice wine, due to their thick skin and resistance to cracking in sub-zero temperatures. The thin-skinned Riesling yields better results but is susceptible to cracking and ripens much later than Vidal.

Drink ice wine after dinner, with a not-too-sweet dessert, or alongside a strong cheese. Here in Niagara it also appears in unexpected places such as tea, martinis, chocolate, ice cream, French toast, and glazes for meat and seafood.

The rush of 700,000 gallons of water a second. The divinely sweet, crisp taste of ice wine. The tug of a fish hooked under a layer of ice. Sure, the big-city scene in Toronto delivers the hustle and bustle you came for, but escaping the city can transport you to another world. The struggle is choosing which world to visit first.

There's Niagara Falls, acres of local vineyards in Niagara-on-the-Lake and the surrounding wine region, or the whimsical "cottage country," with its quiet towns, challenging ski slopes, and lakefront resorts. Or you can hit the outdoors on Bruce Trail, Canada's oldest and longest footpath, which winds from Niagara Falls to Tobermory 885 km (550 miles) north.

If superlatives are what you seek, the mesmerizing and deservedly hyped Niagara Falls, one of—or more technically, three of—the most famous waterfalls in the world, is Ontario's most popular attraction. Worth seeing at least once, it is truly beautiful (say what you will about the showy town behind it).

Oenophile trailblazers should consider Niagara's rapidly developing wine trail. The Niagara Escarpment, hugging Lake Ontario's western shores, is one of the most fertile growing areas in Canada. A lakeshore drive southwest of Toronto yields miles of vineyards and farm-to-table restaurants, culminating in the Victorian white-picket-fence town of Niagara-on-the-Lake, known for its amazing five-star restaurants and hotels and nearly as luxurious bed-and-breakfasts.

Nourish your appreciation for the arts in and around Stratford. Two major theater events, the Stratford Festival and the Shaw Festival (in Niagara-on-the-Lake), have long seasons with masterfully orchestrated plays by William Shakespeare and George Bernard Shaw.

Both outdoors enthusiasts who want to rough it and soft-adventure seekers who yearn for a comfortable bed with the glow of a fireplace at night feel the lure of the nearly 3,000-acre Algonquin Provincial Park. Sunday drivers find solace near Georgian Bay and in the Muskokas, part of Ontario's lake-smattered cottage country.

Planning

When to Go

With the exception of destinations like wineries and ski resorts, June through September is prime travel season: the Stratford and Shaw Festivals are in full swing, hours of operation are longer for most attractions, the mist coming from Niagara Falls is at its most refreshing, and patios are open almost everywhere, not to mention the obvious abundance of water activities and amusement parks.

That said, there's fun to be had in wintertime as well. While Muskoka cottage country, Stratford, and some parks in Algonquin become inaccessible ghost towns between November and April (the time most resorts schedule renovations and maintenance), ski resorts and wineries offer many packages and activities. Enjoy tours and tastings of one of Ontario's most prized exports during Niagara's Ice Wine Festival, or enjoy the Canadian winter by snowboarding, skiing, ice fishing, and snowmobiling. Travel around the holiday season to take in the beautiful decorations, lights, and special events.

Getting Here and Around

AIR

Toronto's Pearson International Airport, 30 km (18 miles) north of downtown, is the obvious choice. Downtown Toronto's smaller Billy Bishop Toronto City Airport serves mostly Porter Airlines; it gets you Niagara-bound on the Gardiner Expressway in a matter of minutes. Hamilton International Airport is about halfway between Toronto and Niagara Falls. Buffalo Niagara International Airport is 30 miles from Niagara Falls, ON, but border crossings can add time to your trip.

CONTACTS Billy Bishop Toronto City Airport. ⊠ *1 Island Airport, Harbourfront* ☎ *416/203–6942* ⊕ *www.billybishopairport.com.* **Buffalo Niagara International Airport.** ⊠ *4200 Genesee St., Buffalo* ☎ *716/630–6000* ⊕ *www.buffaloairport. com.* **Hamilton International Airport.** ⊠ *9300 Airport Rd., Hamilton* ☎ *905/679–1999* ⊕ *flyhamilton.ca.* **Toronto Pearson International Airport.** ⊠ *6301 Silver Dart Dr., Mississauga* ✈ *Best accessed by UPX, direct train from Union subway station* ☎ *866/207–1690 toll free, 416/247–7678* ⊕ *www.torontopearson.com.*

CAR

Ontario's only toll road is the east–west Highway 407, north of Toronto. It's expensive (C22¢–C25¢ per kilometer) and has no tollbooths; you will be billed via mail if the system has your state's license plate information on file. Avoid Toronto-area highways during weekday rush hours (6:30 to 9:30 am and 3:30 to 6:30 pm). Traffic between Toronto and Hamilton might crawl along at any hour.

You can get by without a car in downtown Niagara Falls and Stratford if you book a hotel close to the action.

The Ministry of Transportation has updates for roadwork and winter road conditions.

CONTACT Ministry of Transportation. ☎ *416/235–4686, 800/268–4686* ⊕ *www. mto.gov.on.ca.*

TRAIN

VIA Rail connects Toronto with Niagara Falls and Stratford. GO Transit, Toronto's commuter rail, has summer weekend service to Niagara Falls. Ontario Northland's Northlander line travels between Toronto and Bracebridge, Gravenhurst, Huntsville, and other northern points.

CONTACTS GO Transit. ☎ *416/869–3200, 888/438–6646 toll free* ⊕ *www.gotransit. com.* **Ontario Northland.** ☎ *705/476–5598, 800/363–7512* ⊕ *www.ontarionorthland. ca.* **VIA Rail.** ☎ *888/842–7245* ⊕ *www. viarail.ca.*

Hotels

Make reservations well in advance during summer and at ski areas in winter. Prices are higher in peak season and nearer to the tourist centers. In Niagara Falls, for example, hotel rates are determined by proximity to the falls. Taxes are seldom included in quoted prices, but rates sometimes include food, especially in more remote areas such as Muskoka, where many resorts offer meal plans.

Restaurant and hotel reviews have been shortened. For full information, visit Fodors.com. Restaurant prices are the average cost of a main course at dinner or, if dinner is not served, at lunch. Hotel prices are the lowest cost of a standard double room in high season.

What It Costs in Canadian Dollars

	$	$$	$$$	$$$$
RESTAURANTS				
	under C$12	C$12– C$20	C$21– C$30	over C$30
HOTELS				
	under C$125	C$125– C$175	C$176– C$250	over C$250

Planning Your Time

Toronto is a great base to begin your explorations of Ontario.

1 day: In a long day you could see a matinee at the Shakespeare festival, hit a ski resort north of Toronto, visit a few Niagara Escarpment wineries, or—with some stamina—see Niagara Falls. All these destinations require about four hours of driving time round-trip, not accounting for rush-hour traffic jams.

2 days: A couple of days are sufficient to get a feel for Niagara Falls, Niagara-on-the-Lake, Stratford, or a Muskoka town or two. Alternatively, head up to Collingwood for an overnight snowboarding or skiing trip.

4 days: You can decide between an intensive outdoorsy trip in the Algonquin area hiking, biking, camping, canoeing, and exploring; or, a relaxing tour of Niagara Falls and Niagara-on-the-Lake, with some time spent at spas and wineries, biking, and hitting culinary hot spots.

1 week: Combine Stratford and Niagara, or really delve into the Niagara region. (A week is probably too much for just Niagara Falls or just Niagara-on-the-Lake.)

Alternatively, you could spend some serious time communing with nature in Algonquin Park and meandering through quaint Muskoka and Georgian Bay towns.

Restaurants

The dining in Stratford and Niagara-on-the-Lake is enough to boost a whole other genre of tourism, as there are a number of outstanding restaurants thanks to the area's many chefs being trained at the area's reputable culinary schools, and impeccably fresh ingredients from local farms. Produce, meats, cheeses, beers, and wine are all produced in Ontario, and some restaurants even have their own gardens, vineyards, or farms. In the immediate areas surrounding Niagara Falls, the dining is a little more lackluster, as views, convenience, and glamour take precedence over food, but there are some great pubs and upscale restaurants to be found among the tourist traps. Reservations are always encouraged, if not essential.

Visitor Information

CONTACTS Niagara Falls Tourism.
☎ 800/563–2557 ⊕ www.niagarafallstourism.com. **Ontario Parks.** ☎ 888/668–7275, 519/826–5290 ⊕ www.ontarioparks.com. **Ontario Snow Resorts Association.**
☎ 705/443–5450 ⊕ www.skiontario.ca. **Ontario Tourism.** ☎ 800/668–2746, 905/754–1958 ⊕ www.destinationontario.com/en-ca. **Tourism Niagara.** ✉ Niagara Falls ☎ 289/477–5344 ⊕ www.tourismniagara.com.

Niagara Falls

130 km (81 miles) south of Toronto.

Niagara Falls has inspired artists for centuries. English painter William H. Bartlett, who visited here in the mid-1830s, noted that "you may dream of Niagara, but words will never describe it to you." Although cynics have called it everything from "water on the rocks" to "the second major disappointment of American married life" (Oscar Wilde)—most visitors are truly impressed. Henry James recorded in 1883 how one stands there "gazing your fill at the most beautiful object in the world."

WHEN TO GO

Water-based falls tours operate only between mid-May and mid-September, and the summer weather combats the chilly falls mist. Fewer events take place in other seasons, and it's too cold in winter to linger on the promenade along the parkway next to the falls, but it's much easier to reserve a window-side table for two at a falls-view restaurant. Clifton Hill and most indoor attractions are open year-round. At any time of year it feels a few degrees cooler on the walkway near the falls.

GETTING HERE AND AROUND

Niagara Falls is easily accessible by car, bus, and train. VIA Rail and GO (summer only) trains serve Niagara Falls, both stopping at the main rail station, not far from the falls. WEGO is a Niagara-region bus system with four lines designed for tourists. The nearest airports are in Toronto, Hamilton, and Buffalo, NY.

If you want to explore on your own, a car is by far the best choice. The four- to eight-lane Queen Elizabeth Way—better known as the QEW—runs from the U.S. border at Fort Erie through the Niagara region to Toronto.

BORDER CROSSINGS

Everyone—including children and U.S. citizens—must have a passport or other approved travel document (e.g., a New York State–issued "enhanced" driver's license) to enter the United States. The Department of Homeland Security website (⊕ www.dhs.gov/cross-us-borders) has the latest information. Avoid crossing the border at high-traffic times, especially

First Things First

Start at the **Table Rock Welcome Centre** (✉ 6650 Niagara Pkwy., about 500 meters south of Murray Hill) for a close-up of Horseshoe Falls. Here you can buy a Niagara Parks Great Gorge Adventure Pass, tickets for the WEGO buses, and do the Journey Behind the Falls and Niagara's Fury. At the end of the WEGO line, it's easy to hop aboard and do all the falls-front sights in a northward direction. Starting with a Maid of the Mist or a Jet Boat Tour when you arrive is also a good way to get your feet wet—literally.

Friday and Saturday night. The Canada Border Agency and the U.S. Customs and Border Protection list border wait times into Canada and into the United States, respectively, online at ⊕ cbsa-asfc.gc.ca/bwt-taf/menu-eng.html and ⊕ www.cbp.gov/travel/advisories-wait-times. Crossings are at the Peace Bridge (Fort Erie, ON–Buffalo, NY), the Queenston–Lewiston Bridge (Queenston, ON–Lewiston, NY), and the Rainbow Bridge (Niagara Falls, ON–Niagara Falls, NY).

PARKING

In Niagara Falls, parking prices increase closer to the falls. It can be triple the price to park along the Niagara Parkway (C$26.55 per day) than it is up the hill near Victoria Street (usually C$5 per day). If you park up top, know that the walk down to the falls is a steep one. You might want to take a taxi back up, or hop aboard the Falls Incline Railway, a funicular that operates between the Table Rock Centre and Portage Road behind the Konica Minolta Tower. The trip takes about one minute and costs C$2.75 (day passes are available for C$7).

SHUTTLE

Available year-round, climate-controlled WEGO buses travel on a loop route on the Niagara Parkway between the Table Rock Centre and the Whirlpool Aero Car parking lot, about 9 km (6 miles) north and as far north as Queenston Heights Park, 15 km (9 miles) downriver. A day pass, available from welcome centers and at any booth on the system, is C$9 per person per day (get the second day free from late October to mid-April). You can get on and off as many times as you wish at well-marked stops along the route, and buses pick up frequently (every 20 minutes).

CONTACTS Niagara Falls VIA Rail Canada Train Station. ⊠ *4267 Bridge St.* 🕾 *888/842–7245* ⊕ *www.viarail. ca.* **WEGO.** 🕾 *905/356–1179* ⊕ *www. wegoniagarafalls.com.*

DISCOUNTS AND DEALS

■**TIP→ Many attractions have significant online discounts and combination tickets.**

Bundled passes are available through the tourism board, at welcome centers (foot of Clifton Hill and Murray Hill, near the Maid of the Mist ticket booth, or Table Rock Centre), and at most attractions' ticket windows.

The Clifton Hill Fun Pass incorporates entry to six of the better Clifton Hill attractions (including the SkyWheel and the Midway Combo Pass rides) for C$29.95. The Midway Combo Pass (C$9.99) includes two indoor thrill rides: Wild West Coaster Simulator and the Ghostblasters Dark Ride.

Available mid-April to late October, the Niagara Falls and Great Gorge Pass (C$65) covers admission to Journey Behind the Falls, Maid of the Mist, White Water Walk, and Niagara's Fury, plus a number of discounts and two days of unlimited use of both the WEGO buses and the Falls Incline Railway. From late October to mid-April, the Winter Magic Pass includes Niagara's Fury, the Butterfly Conservatory, Journey Behind the Falls, and discount coupons.

CONTACT Clifton Hill Fun Pass. ⊕ *www. cliftonhill.com.*

TOURIST INFORMATION

The main Niagara Falls Tourism center is on Robinson Street near the Skylon Tower.

Open June through August, welcome centers are run by Niagara Parks and have tickets for and information about Niagara Parks sights, including WEGO and Falls Incline Railway passes and the Niagara Falls and Great Gorge Adventure Pass. Welcome Centre kiosks are at the foot of Clifton Hill, foot of Murray Hill, and near the Maid of the Mist ticket booth; a welcome center booth is inside the Table Rock Centre.

CONTACTS Niagara Parks. ⊠ *Niagara Falls* 🕾 *905/356–2241, 877/642–7275* ⊕ *www. niagaraparks.com.* **Niagara Parks Commission.** 🕾 *905/371–0254, 877/642–7275* ⊕ *www.niagaraparks.com.* **Ontario Trails Council.** ⊠ *Niagara Falls* 🕾 *877/668–7245, 613/389–7678* ⊕ *www.ontariotrails.on.ca.*

 ## Sights

Battle Ground Hotel Museum

HISTORY MUSEUM | The region's only surviving example of a 19th-century tavern, this clapboard building originally opened to serve early visitors to the battleground of the War of 1812. There are displays of the lives of settlers during the war, native artifacts, and military attire. ⊠ *6137 Lundy's La.* 🕾 *905/358–5082* ⊕ *niagara-fallsmuseums.ca/visit/battle-ground-ho-tel-museum.aspx* 🖭 *Donations accepted* ⊘ *Closed Mon.–Thurs. Closed late Aug.–mid-May.*

Bird Kingdom

ZOO | FAMILY | A tropical respite from the crowds and Las Vegas–style attractions, Bird Kingdom is the world's largest indoor aviary, with more than 400 free-flying birds and more than 80 bird

Clifton Hill's food, shopping, games, rides, and other attractions will keep the whole family entertained.

species from around the world in the 50,000-square-foot complex. For creepy-crawly lovers, there are also spiders, lizards, and snakes—including a 100-pound python that you can hold. Parking is an additional C$3 per half hour, but there's a public lot on nearby Hiram Street that is C$10 per day. ✉ *5651 River Rd., Niagara Falls* ☎ *905/356–8888, 866/994–0090* ⊕ *www.birdkingdom.ca* ✉ *C$18.*

Casino Niagara
CASINO | Smaller and more low-key than Fallsview, Casino Niagara has slot machines, video-poker machines, and gambling tables for blackjack, roulette, and baccarat. There are also several lounges, a sports bar, and an all-you-can-eat buffet restaurant. ✉ *5705 Falls Ave., Niagara Falls* ☎ *905/374–3598, 888/946–3255* ⊕ *www.casinoniagara.com.*

Clifton Hill
AMUSEMENT PARK/CARNIVAL | **FAMILY** | This is undeniably the most crassly commercial district of Niagara Falls, with haunted houses, wax museums, and fast-food chains galore (admittedly, the Burger

King here is unique for its gigantic Frankenstein statue). Attractions are typically open as late as 2 am in summer or 11 pm the rest of the year, with admission ranging from about C$10 to C$16. One of the most popular attractions is the 175-foot SkyWheel (C$15) with enclosed, climate-controlled compartments. Next door, Dinosaur Adventure Golf (C$11.99) combines minigolf, ferocious mechanical dinosaurs, and an erupting mini-volcano. The Great Canadian Midway is a 70,000-square-foot entertainment complex with arcade games, a bowling alley, air hockey, and food. Ripley's Believe It or Not! Museum is creepily fascinating, while Movieland Wax Museum has such lifelike characters as Harry Potter and Barack and Michelle Obama. Hershey's Chocolate World is 7,000 square feet of truffles, fudge, and the trademark Kisses, marked by a six-story chocolate bar. ✉ *Clifton Hill, Niagara Falls* ☎ *905/358–3676* ⊕ *www.cliftonhill.com.*

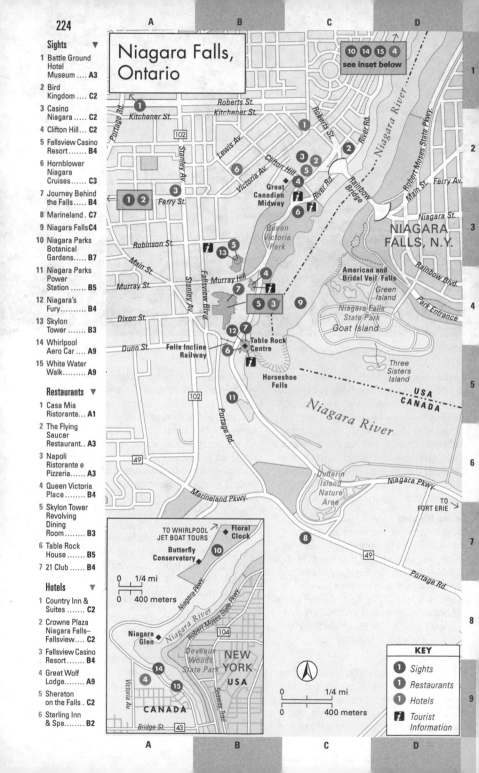

Niagara Falls, Ontario

Sights ▼

1 Battle Ground Hotel Museum **A3**
2 Bird Kingdom **C2**
3 Casino Niagara **C2**
4 Clifton Hill ... **C2**
5 Fallsview Casino Resort **B4**
6 Hornblower Niagara Cruises **C3**
7 Journey Behind the Falls **B4**
8 Marineland . **C7**
9 Niagara Falls **C4**
10 Niagara Parks Botanical Gardens **B7**
11 Niagara Parks Power Station **B5**
12 Niagara's Fury **B4**
13 Skylon Tower **B3**
14 Whirlpool Aero Car **A9**
15 White Water Walk **A9**

Restaurants ▼

1 Casa Mia Ristorante ... **A1**
2 The Flying Saucer Restaurant .. **A3**
3 Napoli Ristorante e Pizzeria **A3**
4 Queen Victoria Place **B4**
5 Skylon Tower Revolving Dining Room **B3**
6 Table Rock House **B5**
7 21 Club **B4**

Hotels ▼

1 Country Inn & Suites **C2**
2 Crowne Plaza Niagara Falls–Fallsview **C2**
3 Fallsview Casino Resort **B4**
4 Great Wolf Lodge **A9**
5 Sheraton on the Falls . **C2**
6 Sterling Inn & Spa **B2**

KEY

1 Sights
1 Restaurants
1 Hotels
ⓘ Tourist Information

Niagara Falls: Past and Future

The story begins more than 10,000 years ago as a group of glaciers receded, diverting the waters of Lake Erie north into Lake Ontario. The force and volume of the water as it flowed over the Niagara Escarpment created the thundering cataracts. Erosion has been considerable since then, more than 7 miles in all, as the soft shale and sandstone of the escarpment have been washed away and the falls have receded. Diversions of the water for power generation have slowed the erosion somewhat, spreading the flow more evenly over the entire crestline of Horseshoe Falls. The erosion is now down to 1 foot or less per year.

At this rate—given effects of power generation and change in riverbed composition—geologists estimate it will be some 50,000 years before the majestic cascade is reduced to rapids somewhere near present-day Buffalo, 20 miles to the south.

Fallsview Casino Resort

CASINO | Canada's largest gaming and resort facility crowns the city's skyline, overlooking the Niagara Parks with picture-perfect views of the falls. Within the 30-story complex are Canada's first casino wedding chapel, a glitzy theater, spa, shops, and plenty of restaurants. Gaming enthusiasts will find more than 100 gaming tables and 3,000 slot machines on one of the world's largest casino gaming floors. The Las Vegas–style Avalon Ballroom showcases a wide array of talents, from Al Pacino to Jon Stewart. ⊠ 6380 Fallsview Blvd., Niagara Falls ☎ 888/325–5788, 905/371–7505 ⊕ www.fallsviewcasinoresort.com.

★ Hornblower Niagara Cruises

AMUSEMENT RIDE | FAMILY | Operating since 1846, when they were wooden-hulled, coal-fired steamboats, the misty tour boats are now run by Hornblower. Double-deck steel vessels tow fun-loving passengers on 20-minute journeys to the foot of the falls, where the spray is so heavy that ponchos must be distributed. From the observation areas along the falls, you can see those boarding the boats in their blue slickers. The very similar Maid of the Mist boat tours operate from the American side.

■ TIP→ Unless you cower in the center of the boat, your shoes and pants *will* get wet: wear quick-drying items or bring spares. ⊠ 5920 Niagara Pkwy. ⊕ www.niagaracruises.com/voyage-to-the-falls-boat-tour ☎ C$35.84 ⊙ Closed Nov.–Apr.

Journey Behind the Falls

VIEWPOINT | FAMILY | This 30- to 45-minute tour starts with an elevator ride down to an observation deck that provides an eye-level view of the Canadian Horseshoe Falls and the Niagara River. From there a walk through tunnels cut into the rock takes you behind thunderous waterfalls, and you can glimpse the back side of the crashing water through two portals cut in the rock face. ⊠ Table Rock Welcome Centre, 6650 Niagara Pkwy., Niagara Falls ☎ 905/371–0254, 877/642–7275 ⊕ www.niagaraparks.com ☎ C$23.

Marineland

AMUSEMENT PARK/CARNIVAL | FAMILY | A theme park with a marine show, wildlife displays, and rides—as well as a beluga whale habitat with underwater viewing areas—Marineland is 1½ km (1 mile) south of the falls. The daily marine shows include performing killer whales, dolphins, harbor seals, and sea lions. Children can pet and feed deer at the Deer Park. Among the many rides are

Rides on the Maid of the Mist tour boats have been thrilling visitors to Niagara Falls since 1846.

Dragon Mountain, the world's largest nonstop roller coaster, and tamer fare like Ocean Odyssey for the kids. ✉ *7657 Portage Rd., off Niagara Pkwy., Niagara Falls* ☎ *905/356–9565* ⊕ *www.marineland.ca* 🎫 *C$51* 🕐 *Closed mid-Oct.–mid-May.*

★ Niagara Falls

WATERFALL | One of North America's most impressive natural wonders, the falls are actually three cataracts: the American and Bridal Veil Falls in New York State, and the Horseshoe Falls in Ontario. In terms of sheer volume of water—more than 700,000 gallons per second in summer—Niagara is unsurpassed compared to other bodies of water on the continent.

On the Canadian side, you can get a far better view of the American Falls and a close-up of the Horseshoe Falls. You can also park your car for the day in any of several lots and hop onto one of the WEGO buses, which run continuously to all the sights along the river. If you want to get close to the foot of the falls, the Maid of the Mist boats take you near enough to get soaked in the spray.

After experiencing the falls from the Canadian side, you can walk or drive across Rainbow Bridge to the U.S. side. On the American side you can park in the lot on Goat Island near the American Falls and walk along the path beside the Niagara River, which becomes more and more turbulent as it approaches the big drop-off of just over 200 feet.

The amusement parks and tacky souvenir shops that surround the falls attest to the area's history as a major tourist attraction. Most of the gaudiness is contained on Clifton Hill, Niagara Falls' Times Square. Despite these garish efforts to attract visitors, the landscaped grounds immediately bordering the falls are lovely and the beauty of the falls remains untouched.

One reason to spend the night here is to admire the falls illumination, which takes place every night of the year, from dusk until at least 10 pm (as late as 1 am during the summer). Even the most contemptuous observer will be mesmerized as the falls change from red to purple to blue to green to white, and finally all the colors of the rainbow in harmony. ⊠ *Niagara Falls.*

Niagara Parks Botanical Gardens

GARDEN | FAMILY | These 100 acres of immaculately maintained gardens are among the most captivating attractions around Niagara Falls. Here you'll find the Niagara Parks Butterfly Conservatory, housing one of North America's largest collections of free-flying butterflies—at least 2,000 butterflies from 50 species around the world are protected in a climate-controlled, rain forest–like conservatory. ■TIP→ **Between May and mid-October, for C$25 per person, you can tour the gardens in a horse and carriage.** ⊠ *2565 Niagara Pkwy., Niagara Falls* ☎ *905/356–8119, 877/642–7275* ⊕ *www. niagaraparks.com* ☑ *Parking C$5.*

Niagara Parks Power Station

OTHER MUSEUM | You can spend hours exploring North America's first green energy projects. Wander through turn-of-the-20th-century machinery, explore exhibits, get to know the history of AC and DC current through the eyes of inventor Nikola Tesla, and even take a glass-paneled elevator trip to the mouth of the dam. The station comes to life at night for *Currents: Niagara's Power Transformed,* an immersive, 40-minute interactive show of sound, light, and state-of-the-art 3-D projection mapping technology. ⊠ *7055 Niagara Pkwy., Niagara Falls* ☎ *877/642–7275* ⊕ *www. niagarafallstourism.com/play/attractions/ niagara-parks-power-station* ☑ *C$20.*

Niagara's Fury

OTHER ATTRACTION | FAMILY | Learn how Niagara Falls formed over thousands of years on this 20-minute simulation ride. Standing on a mesh platform surrounded by an uninterrupted 360-degree viewing screen, you feel snow falling, winds blowing, the floor rumbling, and waves crashing as you watch glaciers form, collide, and melt, creating the falls as we know them today. ■TIP→ **In certain spots you *will* get wet; ponchos are provided.** ⊠ *Table Rock Welcome Centre, 6650 Niagara Pkwy.* ☎ *905/356–2241, 877/642–7275* ⊕ *www.niagaraparks.com/ visit/attractions/niagaras-fury* ☑ *C$17.*

Skylon Tower

VIEWPOINT | FAMILY | Rising 775 feet above the falls, this is the best view of the great Niagara Gorge and the entire city. The indoor-outdoor observation deck has visibility up to 130 km (80 miles) on a clear day. Other reasons to visit include amusements for children, a buffet restaurant, a revolving dining room, and a 3-D theater that lets you experience the falls up close. ■TIP→ **Admission is free if you're enjoying a meal in the dining room.** ⊠ *5200 Robinson St., Niagara Falls* ☎ *905/356–2651, 800/814–9577* ⊕ *www. skylon.com* ☑ *C$17.*

Whirlpool Aero Car

OTHER ATTRACTION | FAMILY | In operation since 1916, this antique cable car crosses the Whirlpool Basin in the Niagara Gorge. This trip is not for the fainthearted, but there's no better way to get an aerial view of the gorge, the whirlpool, the rapids, and the hydroelectric plants. ⊠ *3850 Niagara Pkwy., 4½ km (3 miles) north of falls, Niagara Falls* ☎ *905/371–0254, 877/642–7275* ⊕ *www.niagaraparks. com/visit/attractions/whirlpool-aero-car* ☑ *C$17* ☉ *Closed early Nov.–mid-Mar.*

White Water Walk

NATURE SIGHT | FAMILY | A self-guided route involves taking an elevator to the bottom of the Niagara Gorge, the narrow valley created by the Niagara Falls and River, where you can walk along a 1,000-foot boardwalk beside the Class VI rapids of the Niagara River. The gorge is rimmed by sheer cliffs as it enters the giant whirlpool. ⊠ *4330 Niagara Pkwy., 3 km (2 miles) north of falls, Niagara Falls*

Did You Know?

In addition to fueling
tourism with their
natural beauty, the falls
have also provided power
to local residents and
industry for more than
270 years. Today, the
Niagara Power Plant is
the largest producer of
electricity in New York
State.

☎ *905/371–0254, 877/642–7275* 🌐 *www.niagaraparks.com* 🎫 *C$17* 🕒 *Closed mid-Nov.–early Apr.*

🍴 Restaurants

Dining in Niagara Falls is still a bit disappointing because of the lack of sophistication that usually comes with a tourist-heavy area (especially when compared with the neighboring foodie paradise Niagara-on-the-Lake). A view of the falls and a convenient location don't come cheap, so prices are rarely what one would consider reasonable. Thankfully, the landscape is slowly changing, and some falls-view restaurants, such as 21 Club, are hiring creative chefs who are stepping up the quality—though still at a pretty penny. But with views like these, it might be worth it.

★ Casa Mia Ristorante
$$$$ | **ITALIAN** | The best ingredients prepared simply and served in generous portions are what make this off-the-beaten-path restaurant such a find. A free shuttle service from Niagara Falls hotels whisks guests to this labor of love, owned and operated by the Mollica family. **Known for:** extreme popularity with local diners; wine cellar with more than 300 options; relaxed dining experience. [$] *Average main: C$35* ✉ *3518 Portage Rd., Niagara Falls* ☎ *905/356–5410, 888/956–5410* 🌐 *www.casamiaristorante.com* 🕒 *Closed Sun. No lunch Sat.*

The Flying Saucer Restaurant
$$ | **AMERICAN** | **FAMILY** | This kooky '50s-style diner is a hit with the kids—and with parents looking for ample portions and well-priced meals. Menus are dressed up like a tabloid newspaper and feature an extensive list of flame-broiled diner classics, and then some. **Known for:** over 50 years in business; getting a selfie with the aliens; big breakfasts. [$] *Average main: C$15* ✉ *6768 Lundy's La., Niagara Falls* ☎ *905/356–4553* 🌐 *flyingsaucerrestaurant.com.*

Napoli Ristorante e Pizzeria
$$ | **ITALIAN** | A five-minute drive from Clifton Hill, this local joint manages to be both casual and refined. Sit in the back room where exposed-brick columns and black-and-white photos of Naples on the walls set the scene for the southern Italian pasta dishes and thin-crust pizzas. **Known for:** family-operated establishment that's a local favorite; extensive Italian and Niagara-region wine selection; heavenly affogato. [$] *Average main: C$16* ✉ *5485 Ferry St., Niagara Falls* ☎ *905/356–3345* 🌐 *www.napoliristorante.ca* 🕒 *No lunch.*

Queen Victoria Place
$$$ | **CONTEMPORARY** | Inside a former refectory building dating from 1904, this gracious second-floor restaurant has a huge veranda overlooking the falls across Niagara Parkway. The kitchen is run by celebrated chef Sydney Krick, whose menu reflects high-quality contemporary cuisine like burgers with melted goat cheese, porcini-crusted lamb chops, and maple-brined pork chops. **Known for:** books up in advance for seating on the veranda; focus on locally sourced artisanal ingredients; smart wine and beer pairings. [$] *Average main: C$25* ✉ *6345 Niagara Pkwy., at Morrow St., Niagara Falls* ☎ *905/356–2217* 🌐 *www.niagaraparks.com/dining* 🕒 *Closed Tues.*

Skylon Tower Revolving Dining Room
$$$$ | **AMERICAN** | The big draw here is the revolving 360-degree view perched 520 feet above the Horseshoe Falls—it's simply breathtaking. The atmosphere puts it above those serving similar cuisine in the area, drawing an eclectic crowd of couples in cocktail attire and families in casual clothes. **Known for:** best spot for seasonal firework shows; revolving selection of special dishes; award-winning cuisine. [$] *Average main: C$55* ✉ *5200 Robinson St., Niagara Falls* ☎ *905/356–2651, 888/975–9566* 🌐 *www.skylon.com* 🕒 *Closed Nov.–Apr.*

Table Rock House

$$$$ | **CONTEMPORARY** | White tablecloth service and an up-close-and-personal view of the rushing Horseshoe Falls rapids amount to a stunning dining experience. Prix-fixe dinners are recommended to take advantage of the hearty menu. **Known for:** crème brûlée with Wayne Gretzky cream whiskey; the closest possible dining experience to the falls; Fogo Island shrimp ciabatta sandwich. [$] *Average main: C$45* ✉ *6650 Niagara Pkwy., Niagara Falls* ☎ *905/354–3631* 🌐 *www.niagarafallstourism.com/eat/fallsview-dining/table-rock-house-restaurant.*

21 Club

$$$$ | **STEAKHOUSE** | The best fine-dining-with-a-view in town, 21 Club plays up its casino locale without being kitschy. The high-ceiling modern space is inspired by roulette, in a profusion of red, black, and gold, and juxtaposes the traditional steakhouse menu. **Known for:** steak options spanning the continents; extensive wine list with more than 700 options; on-site sommeliers who know their stuff. [$] *Average main: C$40* ✉ *Fallsview Casino Resort, 6380 Fallsview Blvd., Niagara Falls* ☎ *905/358–3255, 888/325–5788* 🌐 *www.fallsviewcasinoresort.com/dining* ⏲ *Closed Mon. and Tues. No lunch.*

🛏 Hotels

A room with a view of the falls means staying in a high-rise hotel, usually a chain. Hotels with falls views are clustered near the two streets leading down to the falls: Clifton Hill (and adjacent Victoria Avenue) and Murray Street (and adjacent Fallsview Boulevard). Families gravitate toward Clifton Hill for its range of entertainment options. Murray Street, where the Fallsview Casino is located, is less ostentatious and closer to the falls.

Niagara Falls has plenty of B&Bs, but they're mediocre compared with those in Niagara-on-the-Lake, 20 km (12 miles) north. All the hotels here are within walking distance of the falls.

Country Inn & Suites

$$ | **HOTEL** | If you're on a budget but not willing to stay at a dingy motor lodge, this seven-story hotel is probably your best choice. **Pros:** high-speed Internet is among the amenities; within walking distance of Clifton Hill; breakfast is included. **Cons:** 15-minute walk down to the falls; crowded during peak season; no views. [$] *Rooms from: C$130* ✉ *5525 Victoria Ave., Niagara Falls* ☎ *905/374–6040, 800/830–5222* 🌐 *www.countryinns.com* 🛏 *108 rooms* 🍴 *Free Breakfast.*

Crowne Plaza Niagara Falls – Fallsview

$$ | **HOTEL** | Since it opened as the Hotel General Brock in 1929, this grande dame of Niagara hotels has hosted royalty, prime ministers, and Hollywood stars—including Marilyn Monroe, who stayed here while filming the potboiler film *Niagara*. **Pros:** central location near Clifton Hill; old-world sophistication; pool and hot tubs. **Cons:** even rooms with views have small windows; some of the decor is a bit tired; charge for Internet access. [$] *Rooms from: C$139* ✉ *5685 Falls Ave.* ☎ *905/374–4447, 800/263–7135* 🌐 *www.niagarafallscrowneplazahotel.com* 🛏 *234 rooms* 🍴 *No Meals.*

★ **Fallsview Casino Resort**

$$$$ | **HOTEL** | Thanks to its lofty perch, all 35 stories of the Fallsview Casino Resort overlook the Horseshoe, American, and Bridal Veil Falls. **Pros:** the most glamorous address in Niagara Falls; Avalon Ballroom is just steps away; excellent spa and pool. **Cons:** rates are as high-flying as the views; rooms fill up fast in high season; a bit like a shopping mall. [$] *Rooms from: C$349* ✉ *6380 Fallsview Blvd., Niagara Falls* ☎ *905/358–3255, 888/325–5788* 🌐 *www.fallsviewcasinoresort.com* 🛏 *374 rooms* 🍴 *No Meals.*

Great Wolf Lodge
$$$$ | RESORT | FAMILY | Instead of the usual casino-and-slot-machine ambience you find in other area hotels, you'll find a spectacular water park of 12 slides, seven pools, outdoor hot tubs, and other fun amenities at the Great Wolf Lodge. **Pros:** diversions for kids and adults in the water park; delightful themed suites; great for kids. **Cons:** open-concept rooms lack privacy for parents; many of the amenities cost extra; menus lack healthy options. [$] *Rooms from: C$379* ✉ *3950 Victoria Ave., Niagara Falls* ☎ *905/354–4888* 🌐 *www.greatwolf.com* 🛏 *406 suites* 🍴 *No Meals.*

Sheraton on the Falls
$$$ | HOTEL | Just steps from Niagara Parkway, this 22-story tower at the corner of Clifton Hill is the most polished option in that area. **Pros:** perfect location very close to local attractions; breakfast room overlooks all three falls; nicely renovated rooms. **Cons:** no views from below the sixth floor; expensive Wi-Fi and parking; chain hotel feel. [$] *Rooms from: C$239* ✉ *5875 Falls Ave., Niagara Falls* ☎ *905/374–4445, 888/229–9961* 🌐 *www.sheratononthefalls.com* 🛏 *670 rooms* 🍴 *No Meals.*

Sterling Inn & Spa
$$$$ | B&B/INN | Unique among the many options in Niagara Falls is this boutique hotel in a converted 1930s milk factory—hence the unusual bottle-shape tower near the entrance. **Pros:** on-site restaurant known for locally sourced cuisine; breakfast in bed is included in the rates; the quirky feel of a boutique hotel. **Cons:** low-slung building has no views of the falls; 20-minute walk to Clifton Hill; parking costs extra. [$] *Rooms from: C$302* ✉ *5195 Magdalen St., Niagara Falls* ☎ *289/292–0000, 877/783–7772* 🌐 *www.sterlingniagara.com* 🛏 *41 rooms* 🍴 *Free Breakfast.*

Activities

HIKING AND BIKING

Niagara Glen Nature Reserve
HIKING & WALKING | The 82.5-acre Niagara Glen nature reserve has 4 km (2½ miles) of hiking trails through forested paths that pass giant boulders left behind as the falls eroded the land away thousands of years ago. Some trails are steep and rough, and the elevation change is more than 200 feet. Guided hiking tours are available. ✉ *3050 Niagara Pkwy., Niagara Falls* 🌐 *www.niagaraparks.com.*

Niagara River Recreation Trail
BIKING | From Fort Erie to Niagara-on-the-Lake, this recreation trail is 56 km (35 miles) of bicycle trails along the Niagara River. The 29-km (18-mile) route between Niagara Falls and Niagara-on-the-Lake is paved. The trail is divided into four sections: Niagara-on-the-Lake to Queenston; Queenston to the Whirlpool Aero Car; Chippawa to Black Creek; and Black Creek to Fort Erie. ✉ *Niagara Falls* 🌐 *www.niagaraparks.com.*

Niagara-on-the-Lake

15 km (9 miles) north of Niagara Falls, 130 km (80 miles) south of Toronto.

The hub of the Niagara wine region is the town of Niagara-on-the-Lake (sometimes abbreviated NOTL). Since 1962 this town of 14,000 residents has been considered the southern outpost of fine summer theater in Ontario because of its acclaimed Shaw Festival. As one of the country's prettiest and best-preserved Victorian towns, Niagara-on-the-Lake has architectural sights, shops, flower-lined streets, and plentiful ornamental gardens in summer; quality theater nearly year-round; and some of the best chefs and hoteliers in the country.

WHEN TO GO

The town is worth a visit at any time of the year for its inns, restaurants, and proximity to the wineries (open year-round), but the most compelling time to visit is from April through November, during the Shaw Festival, and when the weather allows alfresco dining. Wine-harvesting tours and events take place in the fall and, for ice wine, in December and January. Be warned that the tiny town can get packed over Canadian and American holiday weekends in summer: parking will be scarce; driving, slow; and you might have to wait for tastings at wineries.

GETTING HERE AND AROUND

From Buffalo or Toronto, Niagara-on-the-Lake is easily reached by car via the QEW. NOTL is about a two-hour drive from Toronto, a bit far for just a day trip. From Niagara Falls or Lewiston, take the Niagara Parkway. There's no public transport in Niagara-on-the-Lake or to Niagara Falls, 15 km (9 miles) south.

Niagara-on-the-Lake is a very small town that can easily be explored on foot. Parking downtown can be nightmarish in peak season. Parking along the main streets is metered, at C$2.25 to C$2.75 per hour. On most residential streets parking is free but still limited.

TOURS

Sentineal Carriages conducts year-round tours in and around Niagara-on-the-Lake. Catch a carriage at the Prince of Wales hotel or make a reservation for a pickup. The private, narrated tours are C$95 for 30 minutes, C$140 for 45 minutes, and C$180 for one hour (prices are per carriage).

CONTACT Sentineal Carriages. ✉ *Niagara-on-the-Lake* ☎ *905/468–4943* ⊕ *www.sentinealcarriages.ca.*

VISITOR INFORMATION

CONTACT Niagara-on-the-Lake Chamber of Commerce and Visitor & Convention Bureau. ✉ *26 Queen St.* ☎ *905/468–1950* ⊕ *www.niagaraonthelake.com.*

Sights

Château des Charmes

WINERY | Founded in 1978, this is one of Niagara's first wineries, and one of the two largest family-owned wineries in Niagara (Peller is the other). Originally from France, the Bosc family were pioneers in cultivating European varieties of grapes in Niagara. Wines here consistently win awards, and the winery is particularly known for its chardonnay and Gamay Noir Droit, made from a grape variety that was accidentally created through a mutation. The wine is proprietary, and this is the only winery allowed to make it. ✉ *1025 York Rd., Niagara-on-the-Lake* ☎ *905/262–4219* ⊕ *www.chateaudescharmes.com* 🎫 *Tasting flights C$25; tours from C$10.*

Floral Clock

CLOCK | The 40-foot-in-diameter floral clock, one of the world's largest, is composed of 16,000 bedding plants. Its "living" face is planted in a different design twice every season—viola in the spring and Alternantheras and Santolina Sage in the summer and fall. ✉ *2405 Niagara Pkwy., Niagara-on-the-Lake* ☎ *905/356–8119* ⊕ *www.niagaraparks.com* 🎫 *Free.*

★ Fort George National Historic Site

MILITARY SIGHT | **FAMILY** | On a wide stretch of parkland south of town sits this fort that was built in the 1790s but lost during the War of 1812. It was recaptured after the burning of the town in 1813 and largely survived the war, only to fall into ruins by the 1830s. Thankfully, it was reconstructed a century later, and you can explore the officers' quarters, the barracks rooms of the common soldiers,

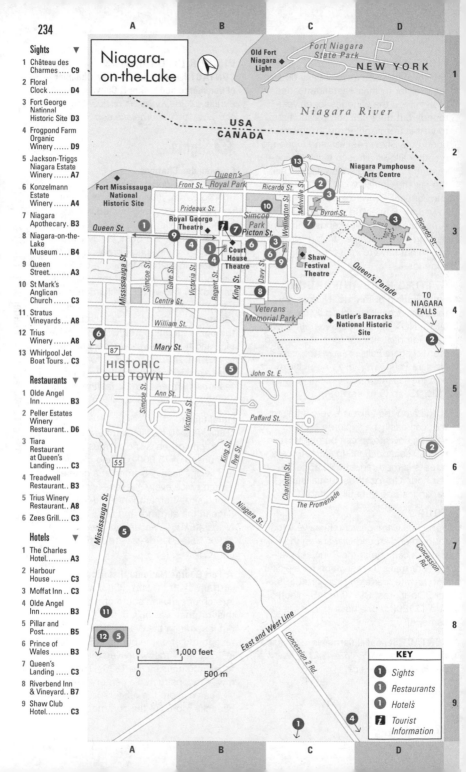

234

Sights ▼

1 Château des Charmes **C9**
2 Floral Clock **D4**
3 Fort George National Historic Site **D3**
4 Frogpond Farm Organic Winery **D9**
5 Jackson-Triggs Niagara Estate Winery **A7**
6 Konzelmann Estate Winery **A4**
7 Niagara Apothecary. **B3**
8 Niagara-on-the-Lake Museum **B4**
9 Queen Street........ **A3**
10 St Mark's Anglican Church **C3**
11 Stratus Vineyards... **A8**
12 Trius Winery **A8**
13 Whirlpool Jet Boat Tours.. **C3**

Restaurants ▼

1 Olde Angel Inn **B3**
2 Peller Estates Winery Restaurant.. **D6**
3 Tiara Restaurant at Queen's Landing **C3**
4 Treadwell Restaurant.. **B3**
5 Trius Winery Restaurant.. **A8**
6 Zees Grill.... **C3**

Hotels ▼

1 The Charles Hotel......... **A3**
2 Harbour House **C3**
3 Moffat Inn .. **C3**
4 Olde Angel Inn **B3**
5 Pillar and Post......... **B5**
6 Prince of Wales **B3**
7 Queen's Landing **C3**
8 Riverbend Inn & Vineyard.. **B7**
9 Shaw Club Hotel......... **C3**

Niagara-on-the-Lake

Old Fort Niagara Light

Fort Niagara State Park

NEW YORK

Niagara River

USA
CANADA

Niagara Pumphouse Arts Centre

Queen's Royal Park

Front St.
Ricardo St.
Melville St.
Ricardo St.
Byron St.
Wellington St.

Prideaux St.

Fort Mississauga National Historic Site

Royal George Theatre

Simcoe Park

Queen St.

Court House Theatre

Picton St.

Shaw Festival Theatre

Queen's Parade

TO NIAGARA FALLS

Mississauga St.
Simcoe St.
Gate St.
Victoria St.
Regent St.
King St.
Davy St.

Centre St.

Veterans Memorial Park

Butler's Barracks National Historic Site

William St.

Mary St.

HISTORIC OLD TOWN

John St. E.

Simcoe St.
Ann St.

Paffard St.

Victoria St.

King St.
Rye St.
Charlotte St.

The Promenade

Niagara St.

Concession 1 Rd.

Mississauga St.

East and West Line

Concession 2 Rd.

0   1,000 feet
0   500 m

KEY

● Sights
● Restaurants
● Hotels
ℹ Tourist Information

the kitchen, and more. Staff in period costumes conduct tours and reenact 19th-century infantry and artillery drills. ✉ *51 Queens Parade, Niagara-on-the-Lake* ☎ *905/468–6614* ⊕ *www.pc.gc.ca/ en/lhn-nhs/on/fortgeorge* 🎟 *C$12.50, C$6.25 parking* ⊙ *Closed weekdays Nov.–Apr.*

Frogpond Farm Organic Winery

WINERY | Ontario's first certified-organic winery is a small, family-owned affair with exclusively organic wines. The setting is truly farmlike: sheep and guinea hens mill about outside while you taste. With only eight varieties—all VQA and including a nice ice wine—you can become an expert in this label in one sitting. The wines are available on-site, online, and at selected restaurants in Ontario; many of the labels are available at the Liquor Control Board of Ontario. ✉ *1385 Larkin Rd., Niagara-on-the-Lake* ☎ *905/468–1079, 877/989–0165* ⊕ *www. frogpondfarm.ca* 🎟 *Free.*

Jackson-Triggs Niagara Estate Winery

WINERY | An ultramodern facility, this famous winery blends state-of-the-art wine-making technology with age-old, handcrafted enological savvy, as evidenced by the stainless steel trough by the entrance. A multitude of tours, workshops, and events are offered. The hourly public tour is a great introduction to winemaking and includes three tastings and a mini-lesson in wine tasting. Its award-winning VQA wines can be sipped in the tasting gallery and purchased in the retail boutique. ✉ *2145 Niagara Stone Rd., Niagara-on-the-Lake* ☎ *905/468–6173, 866/589–4637* ⊕ *www. jacksontriggswinery.com* 🎟 *Tastings C$10, tours C$30.*

Konzelmann Estate Winery

WINERY | An easygoing winery with a friendly staff and sociable tasting bar, Konzelmann has garnered praise for its fruitier wines in particular, and it's known for high-quality ice wines, one of which was the first Canadian wine to ever make *Wine Spectator's* top 100 wines list. Konzelmann's vineyards border Lake Ontario, and the winery has a viewing platform with vistas of the vines and water. The retail shop is well stocked with wine-related gifts. ✉ *1096 Lakeshore Rd., Niagara-on-the-Lake* ☎ *905/935–2866* ⊕ *www.konzelmann.ca* 🎟 *Tastings and tours from C$10.*

Niagara Apothecary

HISTORIC SIGHT | FAMILY | Restored to resemble a circa 1869 pharmacy, the apothecary has glass-fronted walnut cabinets that display vintage remedies such as Merrill's System Tonic, which "purifies the blood and builds up the system." Among the boxes and bottles is a rare collection of apothecary flasks. ✉ *5 Queen St.* ☎ *905/468–3845, 800/220–1921* ⊕ *www.niagaraapothecary.ca* 🎟 *Free* ⊙ *Closed Oct.–May.*

Niagara-on-the-Lake Museum

HISTORY MUSEUM | FAMILY | In connected side-by-side buildings—one the 1875 former Niagara High School building and the other the first building in Ontario to have been erected as a museum, in 1906—this extensive collection relates to the often colorful history of the Niagara Peninsula from earliest times through the 19th century. ■**TIP→ From June through September the museum offers guided walking tours of the town at 11 am on Saturday and Sunday.** ✉ *43 Castlereagh St.* ☎ *905/468–3912* ⊕ *www.notlmuseum. ca* 🎟 *C$5, tours C$10* ⊙ *Closed Dec. 18– Jan. 1 and some holidays.*

★ Queen Street

TOWN | You can glimpse the town's rich architectural history walking along this single street. At the corner of Queen and King Streets is Niagara Apothecary, a mid-Victorian building that was an apothecary from 1866 to 1964. The Court House situated across the street became the Town Hall in 1862. Presently, it houses a small 327-seat theater during Shaw Festival. At No. 209 is the handsome Charles Inn, formerly known as Richardson-Kiely House, built in 1832 for Charles Richardson, a barrister and member of Parliament. ■TIP→ **The 10 or so blocks of shopping include upscale restaurants and cafés, designer-label boutiques, old-fashioned ice-cream parlors, and a spa. You could easily spend an entire day in this area.**

St. Mark's Anglican Church

RELIGIOUS BUILDING | One of Ontario's oldest Anglican churches, St. Mark's was built in 1804, and its parish is even older, formed in 1792. The stone church still houses the founding minister's original library of 1,500 books, brought from England. During the War of 1812, American soldiers used the church as a barracks, and rifle pits dug in the cemetery are still visible. The church is open for concerts, lectures, and weekly services. ✉ *41 Byron St., Niagara-on-the-Lake* ☎ *905/468–3123* ⊕ *stmarksnotl.org.*

Stratus Vineyards

WINERY | Standing out from a vast landscape of single varietal wines, Stratus specializes in assemblage: combining multiple varieties of grapes to create unique blends. Established in 2000, and emerging on the Niagara wine scene in 2005, they continue to perfect what has traditionally been a recipe for disaster for winemakers. A fine example is the Stratus White, a mix of six grape varieties that's complex and unlike anything you've ever tasted (in a good way). Sip all three assemblage wines (white, red, and ice wine) and a handful of single varietals in the modern glass-walled tasting room, installed in the world's first LEED-certified winery. ■TIP→ **Tours must be reserved in advance and can include cheese and charcuterie.** ✉ *2059 Niagara Stone Rd.* ☎ *905/468–1806* ⊕ *www.stratuswines. com* 🍷 *Tastings C$20 (flight of 4).*

Trius Winery

WINERY | With more than 300 wine awards, this winery—one of Niagara's

first and largest—produces many excellent varieties. Its reds (especially Trius Red and Trius Cabernet Franc) are some of the best in Niagara, consistently taking top prizes at competitions; the Trius Brut is another gold medalist. The half-hour cellar and vineyard tour are set to the tune of bubbly social media–ready installations complete with generous complimentary samplings. Another dozen themed tours and regular events include a seminar where you can blend your own wine and an evening of chef-hosted meals at their terrific restaurant. ■TIP→ **Book in advance for tours.** ✉ *1249 Niagara Stone Rd.* ☎ *905/468–7123, 888/510–5537* ⊕ *www.triuswines.com* 🍷 *Tastings from C$2, tours from C$45.*

Whirlpool Jet Boat Tours

OTHER ATTRACTION | **FAMILY** | An hour-long thrill ride, these tours veer around and hurdle white-water rapids that follow Niagara canyons up to the wall of rolling waters, just below Niagara Falls. Children must be at least six years old for the open-boat Wet Jet Tour and four years old for the covered-boat (dry!) Jet Dome Tour; minimum height requirements also apply. Tours depart from Niagara-on-the-Lake or Niagara Falls, ON (June to August only) and Lewiston, NY. ✉ *61 Melville St., Niagara-on-the-Lake* ☎ *905/468–4800, 888/438–4444* ⊕ *www.whirlpooljet.com* 🍷 *C$73.95* ⊗ *Closed mid-Oct.–mid-Apr.*

Peller Estates Winery, known for its award-winning Rieslings and ice wines, provides visitors an elegant experience, from winery tours to tastings to fine dining.

🍴 Restaurants

George Bernard Shaw once said, "No greater love hath man than the love of food," and Niagara-on-the-Lake, which hosts a festival devoted to the playwright, is a perfect place to indulge your epicurean desires. Many eateries serve fine produce and wines from the verdant Niagara Peninsula, and the glut of high-end options fosters fierce competition. A number of inns and wineries here have restaurants. Especially in summer, make reservations whenever possible. Many restaurants serve dinner only until 9.

Olde Angel Inn
$$ | **BRITISH** | **FAMILY** | You can request a Yorkshire pudding to accompany any meal at this tavern just off Queen Street, which should tip you off to its British leanings, played out further in the decor: a warren of rooms with creaky floors and well-used wooden tables and chairs, low ceilings and exposed beams, and convivial chatter throughout. Ontario's oldest operating inn sets out pub fare such as shepherd's pie, bangers and mash, and steak-and-kidney pie. **Known for:** 24 domestic and imported brews on tap; operation since 1789; live music many evenings. [$] *Average main: C$20*
✉ *224 Regent St., Niagara-on-the-Lake*
☎ *905/468–3411* 🌐 *oldeangelinn.com.*

★ Peller Estates Winery Restaurant
$$$$ | **EUROPEAN** | Frequently cited as the best restaurant in Niagara-on-the-Lake—an impressive feat in a town with so many excellent restaurants—Peller Estates manages refinement without arrogance. The stately colonial revival dining room is anchored by a huge fireplace at one end and has windows running the length of the room overlooking a large patio and the estate vineyards. **Known for:** farm-to-table cooking with locally sourced ingredients; seasonal game entrées; gorgeous views. [$] *Average main: C$45*
✉ *290 John St. E, Niagara-on-the-Lake*
☎ *905/468–4678* 🌐 *www.peller.com.*

Tiara Restaurant at Queen's Landing

$$$$ | FRENCH | Niagara-on-the-Lake's only waterfront restaurant, the regal Tiara sits beside a marina with a view of the Niagara River beyond the sailboat masts. The elegant, amber-hue Georgian-meets-contemporary dining room is buttoned up but accented by a pretty stained-glass ceiling and near-panoramic windows that give nearly every table a water view. **Known for:** decadent weekend brunch buffet; prime views from the terrace; prime rib surf-and-turf dinner. [$] *Average main: C$50* ✉ *155 Byron St., Niagara-on-the-Lake* ☎ *905/468–2195, 888/669–5566* 🌐 *www.vintage-hotels.com/queens-landing/tiara-restaurant.*

★ Treadwell Restaurant

$$$$ | CANADIAN | This brainchild of chef-owner Stephen Treadwell (formerly of the prestigious Auberge du Pommier), his chef de cuisine Matthew Payne, and his son, wine sommelier James Treadwell, Treadwell embodies the farm-to-table philosophy. Sit down for dinner on the sidewalk patio or in the sleek dining room and indulge in some of the best that southern Ontario has to offer. **Known for:** lobster club sandwich rules the brunch menu; prestigious Ontario-focused wine list; bread from nearby Treadwell Bakery. [$] *Average main: C$41* ✉ *114 Queen St., Niagara-on-the-Lake* ☎ *905/934–9797* ✍ *orders@treadwellcuisine.com* 🌐 *www.treadwellcuisine.com.*

★ Trius Winery Restaurant

$$$$ | INTERNATIONAL | Niagara-on-the-Lake's first winery restaurant is still one of its best. After a complimentary winery tour and tasting, you can indulge in the spacious, light-filled dining room with big double doors framing vineyards almost as far as the eye can see. **Known for:** excellent seasonal dinner selections; the bar has its own tasting menu; farm-to-table cooking. [$] *Average main: C$66* ✉ *1249 Niagara Stone Rd., at Hwy. 55, Niagara-on-the-Lake* ☎ *905/468–7123, 888/510–5537* 🌐 *www.triuswines.com/trius-winery-restaurant.html.*

Zees Grill

$$$ | ECLECTIC | For alfresco dining, it's hard to beat Zees Grill for its huge wraparound patio with heat lamps across from the Shaw Festival Theatre. More informal than most similarly priced restaurants in town, its seasonal menu brings panache to homegrown comfort foods such as grilled swordfish with purple potato hash and buttered baby bok choy or beef ribs with shallot, garlic, and fingerling potato hash. **Known for:** brined turkey breast sandwich with cranberry-infused aioli; banana bread French toast; one of the best local places for outdoor dining. [$] *Average main: C$30* ✉ *92 Picton St.* ☎ *905/468–5715* 🌐 *www.niagarasfinest.com/restaurants/zees* ⏲ *No lunch Dec.–mid-Apr.*

Hotels

Niagara-on-the-Lake may be Canada's B&B capital, with more than 100 to its name. Their service and quality can rival some of the priciest hotels. In terms of superior lodging, you're spoiled for choice in Niagara-on-the-Lake and it's hard to go wrong with any of the properties within the town's historic center. Prices are high, but hotels sometimes offer significant deals online.

The Charles Hotel

$$$$ | B&B/INN | An air of old-fashioned civility permeates this 1832 Georgian gem, with a nice location on the main street. **Pros:** historic design updated with modern touches; highly lauded restaurant; cozy building. **Cons:** some quirks like variable water temperature; some verandas are shared with neighbors; rooms are smaller than you'd expect. [$] *Rooms from: C$265* ✉ *209 Queen St., Niagara-on-the-Lake* ☎ *905/468–4588, 866/556–8883* 🌐 *www.niagarasfinest.com/charles* 🛏 *12 rooms* 🍴 *Free Breakfast.*

★ **Harbour House**

$$$$ | HOTEL | The closest hotel to the waterfront is this luxurious and romantic boutique hotel with a gently sloping gambrel roof and handsome cedar shingles. **Pros:** the ideal spot to pamper yourself; luxury without a stuffy feeling; full breakfast included. **Cons:** virtually no public spaces; gym and spa are off-site; some rooms lack water views. $ *Rooms from: C$310* ⊠ *85 Melville St., Niagara-on-the-Lake* ☎ *905/468–4683, 866/277–6677* ⊕ *www.harbourhousehotel.ca* ➦ *31 rooms* ▯⊙▯ *Free Breakfast.*

Moffat Inn

$$$ | HOTEL | A central location, reasonable prices, and expert management make this 1835 stucco inn a real find. **Pros:** perfect location on Picton Street; reasonable rates; free Wi-Fi access. **Cons:** not as posh as other area hotels; dated decor and worn carpets; no elevator. $ *Rooms from: C$240* ⊠ *60 Picton St., Niagara-on-the-Lake* ☎ *905/468–4116, 888/669–5566* ⊕ *www.vintage-hotels.com* ➦ *24 rooms* ▯⊙▯ *No Meals.*

Olde Angel Inn

$$$ | B&B/INN | Steeped in military history, the Olde Angel is one of the oldest lodgings in Ontario. **Pros:** excellent price for a hotel in the heart of town; on-site English-style tavern; perfect for history buffs. **Cons:** poor soundproofing, which is a problem for rooms over the pub; dedicated parking for cottages only; no housekeeping in cottages. $ *Rooms from: C$225* ⊠ *224 Regent St., Niagara-on-the-Lake* ☎ *905/468–3411* ⊕ *www.angel-inn.com* ➦ *7 rooms* ▯⊙▯ *No Meals.*

★ **Pillar and Post**

$$$$ | HOTEL | A two-story hotel six blocks from the heart of town, this building has been a cannery, barracks, and basket factory in its 100-plus-year history. **Pros:** unaffected mix of historic and modern; free parking and high-speed Internet; excellent service. **Cons:** not as central as some other hotels; no elevator to second-floor rooms; resort fee for outdoor pool.

$ *Rooms from: C$400* ⊠ *48 John St., Niagara-on-the-Lake* ☎ *905/468–2123, 888/669–5566* ⊕ *www.vintage-hotels.com* ➦ *122 rooms* ▯⊙▯ *No Meals.*

Prince of Wales

$$$$ | HOTEL | A visit from the Prince of Wales in 1901 inspired the name of this venerable hostelry that still welcomes the occasional royal guest or film star. **Pros:** over-the-top-elegant public spaces; relaxing array of spa treatments; highly trained staff. **Cons:** some views of the parking lot; rabbit warren of corridors; breakfast not included. $ *Rooms from: C$370* ⊠ *6 Picton St., Niagara-on-the-Lake* ☎ *905/468–3246, 888/669–5566* ⊕ *www.vintage-hotels.com* ➦ *110 rooms* ▯⊙▯ *No Meals.*

Queen's Landing

$$$$ | HOTEL | About half of the rooms at this Georgian-style mansion have knockout views of the fields of historic Fort George or the placid waters of the marina—ask for one when making a reservation. **Pros:** service is taken seriously and staff goes above and beyond to please; the tropical indoor pool has a lovely skylight; five-minute walk to city center. **Cons:** historic feel is only skin deep; thin walls between rooms; breakfast not included. $ *Rooms from: C$400* ⊠ *155 Byron St., Niagara-on-the-Lake* ☎ *905/468–2195, 888/669–5566* ⊕ *www.vintage-hotels.com* ➦ *142 rooms* ▯⊙▯ *No Meals.*

Riverbend Inn & Vineyard

$$$$ | B&B/INN | Surrounded by its own private vineyard, this beautifully restored, green-shuttered 1820 mansion is formal in style: it's fronted by a grand portico with four massive columns, and an enormous original 19th-century crystal chandelier greets you in the lobby. **Pros:** five rooms have private balconies over the vineyards; great location for wine lovers; inexpensive breakfasts. **Cons:** furnishings could use an upgrade; far from downtown attractions; no elevator. $ *Rooms from: C$350* ⊠ *16104 Niagara Pkwy.,*

Niagara-on-the-Lake, in the heart of the Niagara wine region, has gained fame for its fine wines and food, beautiful setting, and the annual summer Shaw Festival.

Niagara-on-the-Lake ☎ 905/468–2270, 888/955–5553 🌐 www.riverbendinn.ca ⇨ 21 rooms 🍴 No Meals.

Shaw Club Hotel

$$$$ | **HOTEL** | In a town that's largely Georgian or Victorian in style, modern elements like steel and glass give the Shaw Club an edgy and hip vibe. **Pros:** ideal location near the Shaw Festival Theatre; contemporary style in a handsome building; easygoing staff. **Cons:** annex rooms lack the main building's wow factor; some plastic room furnishings; little local charm. *$ Rooms from: C$295 ✉ 92 Picton St., Niagara-on-the-Lake ☎ 905/468–5711, 800/511–7070 🌐 www.shawclub.com ⇨ 30 rooms 🍴 Free Breakfast.*

Performing Arts

ARTS FESTIVALS

★ Shaw Festival

FESTIVALS | Niagara-on-the-Lake remained a sleepy town until 1962, when local lawyer Brian Doherty organized eight weekend performances of two George Bernard Shaw plays, *Don Juan in Hell* and *Candida.* The next year he helped found the festival, whose mission is to perform the works of Shaw and his contemporaries, including Noël Coward, Bertolt Brecht, J. M. Barrie, J. M. Synge, and Anton Chekhov. Now, the festival has expanded to close to a dozen plays, running from April to October, including some contemporary plays by Canadian playwrights and one or two musicals. All are staged in one of four theaters within a few blocks of one another. The handsome Festival Theatre, the largest of the three, stands on Queen's Parade near Wellington Street and houses the box office. The Court House Theatre, on Queen Street between King and Regent Streets, served as the town's municipal offices until 1969 and is a national historic site. At the corner of Queen and Victoria Streets, the Royal George Theatre was originally built as a vaudeville house in 1915. The Studio Theatre, the smallest of the four, hosts mostly contemporary performances. The festival is one of the biggest events in the summer. ■TIP→ **Regular-price tickets cost C$32 to C$135, but discounts abound.** ✉ *10 Queen's Parade, Niagara-on-the-Lake* ☎ *905/468–2172, 800/511–7429* ⊕ *www. shawfest.com.*

Shopping

Niagara-on-the-Lake's historic Queen Street is lined with Victorian storefronts with everything from art galleries to gourmet food stores selling olives, marinades, and vinaigrettes.

FOOD
Alitura Fine Foods & Market
FOOD | There are many fruit stands and produce markets along the streets of Niagara-on-the-Lake, but just outside of the area is the mother lode that dwarfs the others. Alitura Fine Foods & Market, in a barn with a red-and-white-striped awning, sells regional fruits and vegetables and tempts with its fresh-baked goods: sausage rolls, bread, and fruit pies. ✉ *1822 Niagara Stone Rd., Niagara-on-the-Lake* ☎ *905/468–3224.*

Greaves Jams & Marmalades
FOOD | This shop has been making jams, jellies, and marmalades from mostly local produce, using family recipes, since the company began in 1927. The spreads are free from preservatives, pectin, or additives. The jams are often served for afternoon tea in upscale hotel restaurants. ✉ *55 Queen St., Niagara-on-the-Lake* ☎ *905/468–7831* ⊕ *www. greavesjams.com.*

The Niagara Escarpment

102 km (63 miles) southeast of Toronto, 41 km (25 miles) west of Niagara-on-the-Lake.

The Niagara Peninsula north of St. Catharines is known as Niagara Escarpment or the Twenty Valley, for the huge valley where the region's main towns of Jordan,

Vineland, and Beamsville are. This area is much less visited than Niagara-on-the-Lake, and the wineries more spread out. Peach and pear trees, hiking trails, and long stretches of country road are the lay of the land. Aside from wine tasting, you can also visit the cute-as-a-button town of Jordan.

WHEN TO GO
Unlike Niagara-on-the-Lake, this area doesn't get overcrowded in summer, the ideal season for puttering along the country roads. Many restaurants, cafés, and shops have abbreviated hours between mid-September and late May. Most wineries do open for tastings in winter, but call ahead to be sure and to check on driving conditions, as some of these spots are on steep or remote rural roads.

GETTING HERE AND AROUND
Aside from booking a structured winery tour, getting behind the wheel yourself is the only way to visit the attractions in this region. This area is about 75 minutes from Toronto and 45 minutes from Niagara-on-the-Lake and is a feasible day trip.

VISITOR INFORMATION
CONTACT Twenty Valley Tourism Association. ✉ *4890 Victoria Ave. N* ☎ *905/562–3636* ⊕ *www.twentyvalley.ca.*

⊙ Sights

★ Cave Spring Vineyard
WINERY | On Jordan's Main Street, Cave Spring is one of the leading wine producers in Canada, with Ontario's oldest wine cellars, in operation since 1871. Go for the Riesling, Chardonnay, and ice wine. It shares ownership with the Inn on the Twenty and Inn on the Twenty Restaurant (next door) and produces custom blends for the latter. ■TIP→ **There are public tours every day at 1:30 between June and September (only Friday and weekends the rest of the year).** ✉ *3836 Main St.* ☎ *905/562–3581* ⊕ *www.cavespring.ca* 🥂 *Wine flights from C$20.*

★ **Dillon's Small Batch Distillers**

DISTILLERY | A nice break from the steady pace of Niagara-area wineries, Dillon's set up its celebrated small-batch gin and spirits operation in the Beamsville area, prized for its clean water sources and high-quality produce. But they can't get away from grapes completely, which make up the base of the distinctly flavored gins and vodkas (rosehip, strawberry, cherry, and more). Take a tour (C$15) for an in-depth understanding of the distillation process that includes apothecarian exotics like cassis, bitters, and absinthe. The gift and liquor store could double as a design museum. Outdoor picnic tables are used for summer Sunday food-truck brunches. ✉ *4833 Tufford Rd., Beamsville* ☎ *905/563–3030* ⊕ *www.dillons.ca.*

Fielding Estate Winery

WINERY | Muskoka chairs beside the cedar-framed entrance set the tone for the warm and charming winery within. Inside the modern West Coast–style cedar building with a corrugated tin roof and massive stone chimney, Fielding Estate has envious views of vineyards and Lake Ontario from huge picture windows and a big stone fireplace for chilly days. A young team—husband-and-wife owners and two winemakers—has been making quick strides here. The mostly Chardonnay- and Riesling-producing vineyard has a low yield that enables flavors to be concentrated. ✉ *4020 Locust La.* ☎ *888/778–7758, 905/563–0668* ⊕ *www.fieldingwines.com* 🍷 *Tastings from C$9.*

Jordan Village

TOWN | Charming Main Street Jordan, also known as Jordan Village, is a small enclave of cafés and shops selling everything from antiques to artisanal foods. The Inn on the Twenty, the Inn on the Twenty Restaurant, and Cave Spring Cellars are also here. Just a few blocks long, Jordan Village can be fully explored in a morning or afternoon. Home store Chic by Janssen is worth a wander to gawk at items like Siberian fox throws, a bronze bear the size of an actual bear cub, and a C$4,000 cedar canoe. Irongate Garden Elements is a favorite with gardeners. ✉ *Jordan Rd., off QEW Exit 55, Jordan* ⊕ *www.jordanvillage.ca.*

Tawse Winery

WINERY | Eco-friendly Tawse Winery is so committed to producing top-notch Pinot Noir that it installed a six-level gravity-flow system to avoid overhandling the delicate grapes. The investment seems to be paying off, especially considering it's been voted "Winery of the Year" multiple years at the Canada Wine Awards. The rural hillside winery is modern, its big stainless-steel vats visible from the tasting room. ■ **TIP→ Don't leave empty-handed, because tasting fees are waived if you buy two or more bottles.** ✉ *3955 Cherry Ave.* ☎ *905/562–9500* ⊕ *www.tawsewinery.ca* 🍷 *Tastings C$8 (3 wines), tour C$50.*

Vineland Estates Winery

WINERY | One of Ontario's most beautiful wineries occupies 75 acres that were once a Mennonite homestead established in 1845. The original buildings have been transformed into the visitor center and production complex. Several tour and tasting options are available, including packages that include chocolate, ice wine, and specialty cocktails. The excellent restaurant on-site serves lunch and dinner, and you can find a guesthouse and a B&B on the property. ✉ *3620 Moyer Rd., Vineland* ✚ *40 km (25 miles) west of Niagara-on-the-Lake* ☎ *905/562–7088, 888/846–3526* ⊕ *www.vineland.com* 🍷 *Tastings C$16* ⊙ *Closed Mon. and Tues.*

🍽 Restaurants

★ **Inn on the Twenty Restaurant**

$$$$ | **EUROPEAN** | The huge windows framing the Twenty Valley conservation area are reason enough to dine at this restaurant, regarded as one of

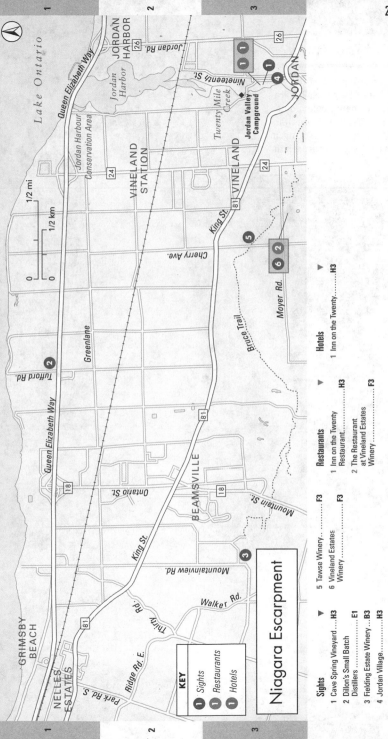

Lake Ontario

JORDAN HARBOR

Jordan Harbor

Jordan Harbour Conservation Area

Queen Elizabeth Way

Jordan Rd.

Nineteenth St.

Twenty Mile Creek

Jordan Valley Campground

JORDAN

VINELAND STATION

VINELAND

Cherry Ave.

King St.

Bruce Trail

Moyer Rd.

GRIMSBY BEACH

NELLES ESTATES

Queen Elizabeth Way

Tufford Rd.

Greenlane

BEAMSVILLE

Ontario St.

Mountain St.

King St.

Mountainview Rd.

Walker Rd.

Ridge Rd. E.

Thirty Rd.

Park Rd. S.

0   1/2 mi
0   1/2 km

Niagara Escarpment

KEY
- 1 Sights
- 1 Restaurants
- 1 Hotels

Sights ▶
1 Cave Spring Vineyard.....**H3**
2 Dillon's Small Batch
  Distillers.................**E1**
3 Fielding Estate Winery....**B3**
4 Jordan Village............**H3**
5 Tawse Winery..............**F3**
6 Vineland Estates
  Winery...................**F3**

Restaurants ▶
1 Inn on the Twenty
  Restaurant...............**H3**
2 The Restaurant
  at Vineland Estates
  Winery...................**F3**

Hotels ▶
1 Inn on the Twenty........**H3**

Did You Know?

Numerous waterfalls trickle along the Niagara Escarpment's beloved Bruce Trail. At more than 890 km (550 miles) long, it is the longest footpath in Canada.

the best around Toronto, on Jordan's boutique-lined Main Street. Regional specialties and local and organic produce are emphasized on a seasonal menu that has included Wellington County boneless rib-eye steak served with mushroom-and-onion fricassee and blue cheese butter. **Known for:** special menus that highlight local produce; unbeatable views of the countryside; Québec foie gras on brioche. $ *Average main: C$32* ✉ *3836 Main St., off QEW Exit 55 or 57, Jordan* ☎ *905/562–7313* ⊕ *www.vintage-hotels. com/inn-on-the-twenty.*

★ The Restaurant at Vineland Estates Winery

$$$$ | **CANADIAN** | Exquisite progressive Canadian food and venerable wines are served by an enthusiastic staff on this bucolic property with three 19th-century Mennonite stone buildings. Sit on the large outdoor patio overlooking vineyards and Lake Ontario beyond or in the glassed-in restaurant, where many of the tables have a similar panoramic view. **Known for:** desserts are the perfect demonstration of simplicity and innovation; daily five-course table d'hote menu shows off local dishes; artisanal charcuterie and cheese platters. $ *Average main: C$40* ✉ *3620 Moyer Rd., Vineland* ☎ *905/562–7088, 888/846–3526* ⊕ *vineland.com/the-restaurant* ۞ *Closed Mon. and Tues.*

Hotels

Inn on the Twenty

$$$$ | **B&B/INN** | Seven of the 24 suites in the main building of this Main Street Jordan inn are two-story affairs with plenty of space, but the rooms to book—in nice weather at least—are the five ground-level suites with very private garden patios. **Pros:** top-notch cuisine at the sophisticated Inn on the Twenty Restaurant; impeccably decorated rooms; central location for wineries. **Cons:** not as much to do in Jordan as in surrounding areas; rooms lack amenities like TVs; breakfast

a little lackluster. $ *Rooms from: C$340* ✉ *3845 Main St., off QEW Exit 55 or 57* ☎ *905/562–5336, 800/701–8074* ⊕ *www. innonthetwenty.com* ⇆ *28 suites* ۞ *Free Breakfast.*

Activities

HIKING
Bruce Trail

HIKING & WALKING | Canada's oldest and longest footpath, the Bruce Trail stretches 890 km (550 miles) along the Niagara Escarpment, with an additional 400 km (250 miles) of side trails. It takes in scenery from the orchards and vineyards of the Niagara Escarpment—one of Canada's 15 UNESCO World Biosphere Reserves—to the craggy cliffs and bluffs at Tobermory, 370 km (230 miles) north of Niagara-on-the-Lake. You can access the hiking trail at just about any point along the route; the main trail is marked with white blazes, the side trails with blue blazes. Northern parts of the trail are remote. ✉ *14184 Niagara Pkwy., Niagara-on-the-Lake* ☎ *905/529–6821, 800/665–4453* ⊕ *brucetrail.org.*

Stratford

145 km (90 miles) west of Toronto.

In July 1953 Alec Guinness, one of the world's greatest actors, joined with Tyrone Guthrie, probably the world's greatest Shakespearean director, beneath a hot, stuffy tent in a quiet town about a 90-minute drive from Toronto. This was the birth of the Stratford Shakespeare Festival, which now runs from April to late October or early November and is one of the most successful and admired festivals of its kind.

Today Stratford is a city of 32,000 that welcomes more than 500,000 visitors annually for the Stratford Shakespeare Festival alone. But Shakespeare is far from the only attraction. The Stratford

Summer Music Festival (July and August) is another highlight, shopping in the enchanting city core is a favorite pastime, and with more amazing restaurants than you could hope to try in one visit, dining out in Stratford could be a reason to return.

WHEN TO GO

The festival runs from mid-April through late October or early November. Most visitors choose their travel dates based on the plays they want to see. About half of the city's restaurants and B&Bs close off-season; the city is quiet in the colder months, but shops and art galleries stay open, hotels have reduced rates, and you'll rub elbows with locals rather than visitors.

GETTING HERE AND AROUND

Ontario's main east–west highway, the 401, which traverses the province all the way from Michigan to Québec, is the main route from Toronto to Kitchener-Waterloo; from there, Highway 7/8 heads to Stratford. Traffic-free driving time is about two hours. VIA Rail has daily service to downtown Stratford from Toronto's Union Station; the trip is about two hours.

CONTACT Stratford VIA Rail Train Station. ⊠ *101 Shakespeare St.* ☎ *888/842–7245.*

VISITOR INFORMATION

CONTACT Stratford Tourism Alliance. ⊠ *47 Downie St.* ☎ *519/271–5140, 800/561–7926* ⊕ *www.visitstratford.ca.*

Sights

Gallery Stratford

ART GALLERY | Operating since 1967 in a historic pump house, Gallery Stratford exhibits high-profile Canadian visual artists all year and, in summer, local up-and-coming artists. ⊠ *54 Romeo St., Stratford* ☎ *519/271–5271* ⊕ *www.gallerystratford.on.ca.*

Stratford Perth Museum

HISTORY MUSEUM | You can brush up on Stratford and Perth County history with

Stratford Walking Tours

The Stratford Tourism Alliance produces several themed, self-guided walking tours, such as the Bacon and Ale Trail (C$39.55, including five coupons that can be redeemed along the way), Historic Downtown, Local Landmarks, and Shakespearean Gardens. Pick one up from the tourism office at 47 Downie Street.

permanent displays and changing exhibits that cover such topics as hockey in Stratford, the city's railroad, the settlement of the area in the early 1800s, and of course an exhibit paying tribute to one of Stratford's most famous locals, Justin Bieber. The museum's open-air Players Backstage theater now hosts its own plays and occasional concerts from the likes of Canadian talent such as Ron Sexsmith by night, and there are hiking trails and picnic areas to explore by day. ⊠ *4275 Huron Rd., Stratford* ☎ *519/393–5311* ⊕ *www.stratfordperthmuseum.ca* ⊠ *C$7.*

🍴 Restaurants

For a tiny town, Stratford is endowed with an unusual array of excellent restaurants. Perth County is a locavore's dream of farmers' markets, dairies, and organic farms. The proximity of the Stratford Chefs School (which also offers day courses to visitors) supplies a steady stream of new talent, and the Shakespeare festival ensures an appreciative audience.

The Alley

$$$ | **ASIAN FUSION** | This local favorite with an Asian-fusion angle offers fresh, locally sourced ingredients in a minimalist and modern dining room. The alley patio,

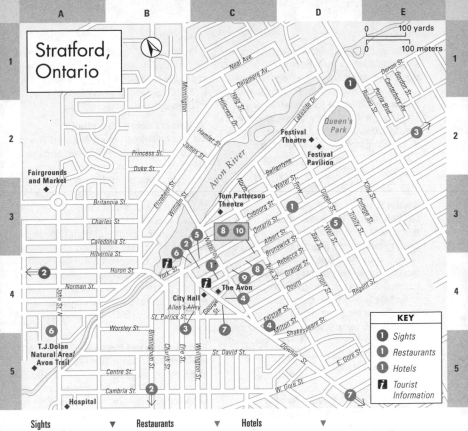

Stratford, Ontario

0 ... 100 yards
0 ... 100 meters

KEY

1 Sights

1 Restaurants

1 Hotels

🛈 Tourist Information

Sights ▼	Restaurants ▼	Hotels ▼
1 Gallery Stratford **D1**	1 The Alley.................**C4**	1 Avery House.............**D3**
2 Stratford Perth Museum **A4**	2 Bentley's.................**C4**	2 Birmingham Manor B&B **B5**
	3 Bijou.......................**C4**	3 Festival Inn **E2**
	4 Brch & Wyn **C4**	4 Foster's Inn **C4**
	5 Mercer Kitchen + Beer Hall.................**C4**	5 Queen and Albert B&B **D3**
	6 Pazzo Taverna and Pizzeria **C4**	6 Stewart House Inn......**A4**
	7 The Planet Diner.........**C4**	7 Swan Motel **D5**
	8 The Prune.................**C3**	8 The Three Houses Bed & Breakfast Inn.....**C4**
	9 Revival House............**C4**	
	10 YSK Bistro **C3**	

partially covered against the elements, is a reliable spot for wholesome creations like a refreshing cold soba noodle bowl loaded with shrimp from Fogo Island. **Known for:** omakase food boards for sharing; giant homemade steamed bao (stuffed Asian buns); tucked-away terrace filled with greenery. $ *Average main: C$25* ⊠ *34 Brunswick St., Stratford* ☎ *519/271–5645* ⊕ *www.keystonealley. com* ☼ *Closed Sun.–Tues.*

Bentley's

$$ | CANADIAN | The well-stocked bar at this casual pub with booth and patio seating divides the room into two equal halves, with the locals converging on the east side. The pub fare includes quintessentials such as fish-and-chips, grilled steak and fries, burgers, and finger food. **Known for:** roast prime rib draws a crowd on Friday; easygoing staff and clientele; 20 beers on tap. $ *Average main: C$15* ⊠ *99 Ontario St.* ☎ *519/271–1121* ⊕ *www.bentleysbarinn.com.*

★ Bijou

$$$ | EUROPEAN | A husband-and-wife team, both Stratford Chefs School grads, operates this small culinary gem. The chalkboard menu changes daily, and nearly everything on it is locally sourced. **Known for:** desserts like ricotta cheesecake with sea buckthorn sauce and orange sorbet; farm-to-table cooking at its finest; caters to dietary restrictions. $ *Average main: C$30* ⊠ *74 Wellington St.* ☎ *519/273–5000* ⊕ *www.bijourestaurant.com* ☼ *Closed Mon.*

Brch & Wyn

$$ | CONTEMPORARY | You can't always please everyone but Brch & Wyn does a solid job of catering to both the strong-coffee-and-brunch crowd and the theatergoers looking to prolong an intimate evening. The mood of the converted industrial space is airy with exposed brick and beam, contrasted by tropical garden wall coverings and plush couches and bar tables. **Known for:** highly curated wine and beer list; hearty grilled "toastie" sandwiches; charcuterie and artisan cheese boards. $ *Average main: C$12* ⊠ *245 Downie St., Stratford* ☎ *519/305–5996* ⊕ *www.brchandwyn.ca* ☼ *Closed Mon.*

★ Mercer Kitchen + Beer Hall

$$$ | ASIAN FUSION | In an elevated French bistro setting, Mercer Kitchen engages chefs who have no interest in doing anything that's been done before. Wash down the innovative pan-Asian cuisine— think crispy arctic char with a sweet and spicy papaya salad—with a pint from one of a dozen rotating local craft beer taps. **Known for:** rotating selection of steamed bao; delicious smoked meat yaki soba noodles; locally sourced ingredients, all dishes made from scratch. $ *Average main: C$28* ⊠ *104–108 Ontario St., Stratford* ☎ *519/271–9202* ⊕ *www.mercerhall. ca.*

Pazzo Taverna and Pizzeria

$$$ | ITALIAN | Located where several important streets come together, Pazzo Taverna and Pizzeria is home to one of the city's best and most convivial Italian restaurants. Have a drink and people-watch at the bar or on the patio. **Known for:** locals flock to the downstairs pizzeria; lasagna with lobster, shrimp, and crab; streetside seating. $ *Average main: C$22* ⊠ *70 Ontario St., Stratford* ☎ *519/273–6666* ⊕ *www.pazzo.ca* ☼ *Closed Mon.*

The Planet Diner

$$ | DINER | Don't be surprised if you end up licking your fingers or reaching for a fork and knife to polish off your burger at this polka-dotted eatery. The vegan-friendly favorites are made messy, saucy, and decadent, a respite for plant eaters who have forsaken meats but still crave the soothing comfort that only items like a creamy mac and cashew cheese can bring. **Known for:** brightly decorated vegan doughnuts and cinnamon buns; gluten-free buns available for most dishes; cashew ice-cream banana split.

[$] *Average main: C$17* ✉ *118 Downie St., Stratford* 🌐 *www.theplanetdiner.com.*

The Prune

$$$$ | **CANADIAN** | Chef Bryan Steele, who is also senior cookery instructor at Stratford Chefs School, coaxes fresh local ingredients into innovative dishes with the best of what's available globally. Dishes change with the harvest, but have included Lake Huron whitefish meunière with asparagus and cinnamon cap mushrooms; and spring risotto with Parmesan, crispy egg, and wild leek pesto. **Known for:** themed prix-fixe Sunday lunches in the summer on the patio; sommelier oversees extensive Ontario-grown wine list; desserts made by in-house pastry chef. [$] *Average main: C$40* ✉ *151 Albert St., Stratford* ☎ *519/271–5052* 🌐 *theprune.com* 🕒 *Closed Sun.–Tues. and Nov.–mid-May.*

Revival House

$$$ | **FRENCH** | Reimagined French classics like steak frites with root vegetables are hearty productions created with local ingredients. Constructed in 1873 as a congregational church, the building has most of the original architecture in place, but today snowy white table linens gleam in the afternoon light that pours through the stained-glass windows. **Known for:** lively summertime patio; French comfort food; fantastic Sunday brunch. [$] *Average main: C$28* ✉ *70 Brunswick St., Stratford* ☎ *519/273–3424* 🌐 *www.revival.house* 🕒 *Church closed Mon.–Wed. and Jan.–Mar. Belfry closed Sun.–Mon. and Jan.–Mar.*

YSK Bistro

$$ | **CAFÉ** | Locals come to this jazzed-up eatery for the signature wraps and hot drippy sandwiches loaded with toppings like Black Forest ham and melted brie. But the daily breakfast is a special treat; favorites are the French toast with homemade apple compote and the Mennonite sandwich with homemade summer sausage, cheddar, corn relish, and honey mustard. **Known for:** vibrant-patterned tablecloths; brilliant build-your-own-sandwich menu; picnic baskets to go. [$] *Average main: C$15* ✉ *151 Albert St.* ☎ *519/273–7041* 🌐 *www.yorkstreetkitchen.com* 🕒 *Closed Sun. and Mon.*

Hotels

Stratford has a wide range of atmospheric B&Bs, motels on the outskirts of downtown, and inns around the center. Room rates are discounted substantially in winter, sometimes by more than 50%.

Avery House

$$$ | **B&B/INN** | This 1874 Gothic revival home has been transformed into an impeccably decorated B&B with an eclectic interior. **Pros:** continually updated decor; affable host loves her job; big breakfasts. **Cons:** communal dining not everyone's cup of tea; located on a busy road; ground-floor unit's bathroom isn't en suite. [$] *Rooms from: C$179* ✉ *330 Ontario St., Stratford* ☎ *519/273–1220, 800/510–8813* 🌐 *www.averyhouse.com* 🕒 *Closed Nov.–May* 🛏 *6 rooms* 🍴 *Free Breakfast.*

★ **Birmingham Manor B&B**

$$$ | **B&B/INN** | This gorgeous Victorian home is filled with artifacts of theater history from Italian commedia dell'arte to Shakespearean histories. **Pros:** breakfast made with herbs and vegetables picked fresh from the garden; endless supply of home-baked biscotti; the garden attracts lots of butterflies and birds. **Cons:** some noise from street; uneven flooring upstairs; breakfast coffee on the weak side. [$] *Rooms from: C$215* ✉ *240 Birmingham St., Stratford* ☎ *519/273–6545* 🌐 *birminghammanor.com* 🛏 *5 rooms* 🍴 *Free Breakfast.*

Festival Inn

$$ | **HOTEL** | Stratford's largest hotel—about 10 minutes by car east of town—offers an unusually wide range of accommodations, from motel-style rooms to beautifully decorated suites with their own jetted tubs. **Pros:** breakfast is served

every morning; modern rooms with many amenities; exceptional staff. **Cons:** except for the swooping annex building, architecture is bland; uninspired location on a commercial strip; dated decor. $ *Rooms from: C$154* 1144 Ontario St., Stratford 519/273–1150, 800/463–3581 www.festivalinnstratford.com 169 rooms *Free Breakfast.*

Foster's Inn

$$$ | B&B/INN | Two doors down from the Avon and Studio theaters, this brick storefront building dates back to 1906 and has an interesting bit of history—it once housed the International Order of Odd Fellows, a fraternal organization that started in the United Kingdom. **Pros:** excellent location in downtown Stratford; the most delicious steaks in town; great deals in winter. **Cons:** fills up fast in the summer season; two-night minimum stay often required; lobby attached to restaurant. $ *Rooms from: C$250* 111 Downie St., Stratford 519/271–1119, 888/728–5555 www.fostersinn.com 9 rooms *No Meals.*

Queen and Albert B&B

$$ | B&B/INN | A 1901 storefront enlivened with a striped awning is the unique facade of this residential-neighborhood B&B. **Pros:** ginger-mango crepes and other delights served in the sunny breakfast room; large rooms with fun and funky decor; two rooms share a balcony. **Cons:** decor is a bit of a hodgepodge; no elevator to upstairs rooms; cramped parking lot. $ *Rooms from: C$175* 174 Queen St., Stratford 519/272–0589 www.queenandalbert.com Closed Nov.–Apr. 4 rooms *Free Breakfast.*

Stewart House Inn

$$$$ | B&B/INN | The interior of this elegant 1870s home retains a Victorian feel but is filled with modern conveniences. **Pros:** exceptional service; outdoor swimming pool; complimentary espresso. **Cons:** not as central as some other inns; ground-floor room available only in summer; not recommended for families with

young kids. $ *Rooms from: C$289* 62 John St. N, Stratford 519/271–4576, 866/826–7772 stewart-house-inn.ontariocahotel.com 6 rooms *Free Breakfast.*

Swan Motel

$$ | HOTEL | The original 1960s motel sign still marks this single-story motel 3 km (2 miles) south of downtown, where you'll find clean-as-a-whistle, albeit utilitarian, rooms at good prices. **Pros:** little extras like muffins set out in the morning; quiet location backed by farmland; best deal in town. **Cons:** basic rooms with parking-lot views; not walkable to downtown; motorlodge layout. $ *Rooms from: C$145* 960 Downie St., Stratford 519/271–6376 www.swanmotel.ca Closed Nov.–May 24 rooms *No Meals.*

The Three Houses Bed & Breakfast Inn

$$$ | B&B/INN | On a quiet residential street, this elegant and tastefully decorated trio of Edwardian and Victorian homes has been frequented by movie stars like Julie Andrews and Christopher Plummer. **Pros:** popular with couples on honeymoon; exquisite decorative taste; heated saltwater pool. **Cons:** irregular hours in the winter; often rented out to film crews; some steps to climb. $ *Rooms from: C$225* 100 Brunswick St., Stratford 519/272–0722 www.thethreehouses.com 6 suites *Free Breakfast.*

Performing Arts

ARTS FESTIVALS

★ Stratford Festival

FESTIVALS | FAMILY | One of the two largest classical repertory companies in the world—England's Royal Shakespeare Company is the other—the Festival presents not only Shakespeare plays, but also works by other dramatists (including new plays) and popular musicals and musical revues in its four theaters.

The 1,800-seat **Festival Theatre** (55 Queen St.), with its hexagonal wooden

Bringing the Bard to Ontario

Stratford's origins are modest. After the War of 1812, the British government granted a million acres of land along Lake Huron to the Canada Company, headed by a Scottish businessman. Surveyors came to a marshy creek surrounded by a thick forest and named it "Little Thames," noting that it might make a good millsite. It was Thomas Mercer Jones, a director of the Canada Company, who renamed the river the Avon and the town Stratford. The year was 1832, 121 years before the concept of a theater festival would take flight and change Canadian culture.

For years Stratford was considered a backwoods hamlet. Then came the first of two saviors of the city, both of them also Thomases. In 1904 an insurance broker named Tom Orr transformed Stratford's riverfront into a park. He also built a formal English garden, where flowers mentioned in the plays of Shakespeare—monkshood to sneezewort, bee balm to bachelor's button—bloom grandly to this day.

Next, Tom Patterson, a fourth-generation Stratfordian born in 1920, looked around; saw that the town wards and schools had names like Hamlet, Falstaff, and Romeo; and felt that some kind of drama festival might save his community from becoming a ghost town. The astonishing story of how he began in 1952 with C$125 (a "generous" grant from the Stratford City Council), tracked down Tyrone Guthrie and Alec Guinness, and somehow, in little more than a year, pasted together a longstanding theater festival is recounted in his memoir, *First Stage: The Making of the Stratford Festival.*

Soon after it opened, the festival wowed critics worldwide with its professionalism, costumes, and daring thrust stage. The early years brought giants of world theater to the tiny town of some 20,000: James Mason, Alan Bates, Christopher Plummer, Jason Robards Jr., and Maggie Smith. Stratford's offerings are still among the best of their kind in the world—the next-best thing to seeing the Royal Shakespeare Company in Stratford-upon-Avon in England.

thrust stage and permanent wooden stage set, is the largest and the oldest of the theaters—in its first incarnation in 1953 it was just a stage under a tent. The 1,100-seat **Avon Theatre** (✉ *99 Downie St.*) has a traditional proscenium stage, while the **Tom Patterson Theatre** (✉ *111 Lakeside Dr.*) has a long, runway-style thrust stage and 600 seats. The petite **Studio Theatre** (✉ *34 George St. E*), with only 260 seats, is the go-to space for experimental and new works. It has a modern appearance and a hexagonal thrust stage.

Throughout the season, 12 to 16 productions are mounted, always with at least a couple of family-friendly productions. At the height of the festival in July and August you may be able to choose from among eight performances. The festival also offers numerous concerts, workshops, tours, lectures, and talks, such as Meet the Festival, where the public can ask questions of actors and artists. The festival has both matinees and evening performances (and many visitors do see two plays per day). ✉ *55 Queen St.* ☎ *519/273–1600, 800/567–1600* ⊕ *www. stratfordfestival.ca.*

★ Stratford Summer Music

FESTIVALS | For five weeks in July and August, Stratford Summer Music brings musicians—from elegant string quartets to folky bluegrass bands—to indoor and outdoor venues around town. Outdoor performances, like those sounding from a barge on the Avon River, are free. Series may include Friday night cabarets at Revival House and classical music lunches. Some performances sell out, so get tickets in advance. ⊠ *Stratford* ☎ *519/271–2101* ⊕ *www.stratfordsummermusic.ca.*

Nightlife

The Relic Lobby Bar

COCKTAIL LOUNGES | The Relic could easily sub in for the stage of a festival production with its minimalist, rustic design that harkens back to Old Havana. Like in the Cuban capital, rum is the spirit of choice with an extensive cocktail list featuring classic tiki drinks and modern mixology wizardry. Guest bartenders and acoustic jazz ensembles are also known for making appearances. ⊠ *6 Ontario St., Stratford* ☎ *519/273–4763* ⊕ *therelicbar.ca* ♥ *Closed Sun. and Mon.*

Activities

BIKING

Totally Spoke'd

BIKING | Stratford is an ideal town for cruising via bicycle. Totally Spoke'd rents cruisers, mountain bikes, and tandem bikes. Rates are C$35 to C$47 per day. ⊠ *29 Ontario St.* ☎ *519/273–2001* ⊕ *www.totallyspoked.ca* ♥ *Closed Mon.*

Shopping

Downtown Stratford is a great place for daytime distractions and is utterly devoid of chain stores. Ontario Street alone is lined with quaint bookstores stocking great local reads, chocolatiers, myriad

Discount Tickets

Regular Stratford Festival tickets are around C$55 to C$110, but there are many ways to pay less. Spring previews and some fall performances are heavily discounted. Savings of up to half off can be had for students and seniors, and theatergoers aged 16 to 29 can buy seats online for C$25 for select performances two weeks prior. Also available are early-ordering discounts, rush seats, half-price Tuesdays, two-for-one Thursdays, and family and group discounts.

colorful housewares and women's clothing shops, and catch-all gift stores.

GIFTS

Stratford Festival Shop

SOUVENIRS | In two locations (at the Avon and Festival theaters), this is the place for Shakespeare finger puppets, every Shakespeare play ever written, original costume sketches, soundtracks to musicals, quotable aprons, and Bard-themed children's books. ⊠ *Avon Theatre, 99 Downie St., Stratford* ☎ *519/271–0055* ⊕ *store.stratfordfestival.ca.*

Watson's Chelsea Bazaar

SOUVENIRS | At this brimming curio shop you might find a cat curled up among the reasonably priced china, glassware, French soaps, kitchen gadgets, and other bric-a-brac. The Bradshaw family has owned a store at this location in various forms (it used to be a high-end china hall) since the 1800s. ⊠ *84 Ontario St., Stratford* ☎ *519/273–1790* ⊕ *www.watsonsofstratford.com.*

The award-winning Festival Theatre, the largest of the Stratford Shakespeare Festival's four venues, has been staging great drama for theater lovers since 1957.

Midland and Penetanguishene

150 km (90 miles) north of Toronto.

Southern Georgian Bay's largest city is Barrie, but much more interesting are the quiet towns of Midland and Penetanguishene (also called Penetang by locals), occupying a small corner of northern Simcoe County known as Huronia, on a snug harbor at the foot of Georgian Bay's Severn Sound. These are docking grounds for trips to the Georgian Bay Islands National Park. To the west, the attractive harbor town of Collingwood, on Nottawasaga Bay, is at the foot of Blue Mountain, the largest ski hill in the province.

WHEN TO GO

Few tourist attractions apart from ski resorts are open between Labour Day (early September) and Victoria Day weekend (late May).

GETTING HERE AND AROUND

Georgian Bay towns and attractions are west of Highway 400, either via Highway 26 toward Collingwood or well marked off Highway 400 north of Barrie. These towns and regions are two and a half to four hours from Toronto and are generally long-weekend or even weeklong trips from the city.

■ TIP→ **If you are heading here in winter, go with a four-wheel-drive vehicle.**

Resorts, especially, are usually well off the highway and may require navigating twisting backcountry routes.

VISITOR INFORMATION

CONTACTS Georgian Bay Coastal Route. ⊕ *www.visitgeorgianbay.com.* **Visit Southern Georgian Bay.** ☎ *705/445–7722, 888/227–8667* ⊕ *www.visitsouthgeorgianbay.ca.*

● Sights

Georgian Bay Islands National Park
NATIONAL PARK | A series of 63 islands in Lake Huron's Georgian Bay, the park can be visited only via boat. Organized boat tours with the park or private companies operate from the weekend closest to May 24 through mid-October, weather permitting. To explore one of the islands on foot, book a trip on the park's *DayTripper* boat, bring your own boat, or take a water taxi in Honey Harbour.

The park's own boat, the *DayTripper* (C$15.70 June–early Oct.), makes the 15-minute trip to Beausoleil Island, which has hiking trails and beaches, from Honey Harbour, 15 km (9 miles) north of Port Severn at Highway 400 Exit 156.

Two companies do cruises through the Georgian Bay but don't allow you to disembark on any of the islands. The 300-passenger *Miss Midland,* operated by Midland Tours (C$36), leaves from the Midland town dock and offers 2½-hour sightseeing cruises daily at 2 mid-May to mid-October. The company can arrange departures from Toronto, which includes time to explore the town of Midland. From the Penetanguishene town dock, Penetanguishene 30,000 Island Cruises takes passengers on Penetanguishene Harbour and the Georgian Bay islands tours, including 1½- and 2½-hour cruises of Penetanguishene Harbour and 3½-hour cruises of the 30,000 islands of Georgian Bay, on the 200-passenger MS *Georgian Queen.* Lunch (C$55) and dinner (C$63) cruises are available with reservations. Captain Steve Anderson, the owner and your tour guide, has operated these tours—a family business—since 1985. Cruises depart one to three times daily in July and August; less frequently (but usually Saturday, Sunday, and Wednesday) in May, June, September, and October. ⊠ *2611 Honey Harbour Rd., off Hwy. 400 Exit 153 or 156* ☎ *705/526–9804* ⊕ *www.pc.gc.ca/ en/pn-np/on/georg* ⌨ *C$6.25* ⊗ *Closed early Oct.–late May.*

Huronia Museum and Huron Ouendat Village
INDIGENOUS SIGHT | Nearly 1 million artifacts on Native and maritime history are on display at the museum building, and there's also a replica Native American village. Visitors can expect contemporary art and extensive photography pieces, in addition to traditional Native art and archaeological collections. ⊠ *549 Little Lake Park Rd., Midland* ☎ *705/526–2844, 800/263–7745* ⊕ *huroniamuseum.com* ⌨ *C$7.*

Martyrs' Shrine
RELIGIOUS BUILDING | On a hill overlooking Ste.-Marie among the Hurons, a twin-spired stone cathedral was built in 1926 to honor the eight missionaries stationed in Huronia who were martyred between 1642 and 1649. In 1930, all eight were canonized by the Roman Catholic Church. The shrine is still active as a pilgrimage site and has daily services. ⊠ *16163 Hwy. 12 W, Midland* ☎ *705/526–3788* ⊕ *www. martyrs-shrine.com* ⌨ *C$10* ⊗ *Closed mid-Oct.–mid-May.*

Ste.-Marie Among the Hurons
HISTORIC SIGHT | FAMILY | A Jesuit mission was originally built on this spot in 1639. The reconstructed village, which was once home to a fifth of the European population of New France, was the site of the first European community in Ontario; it had a hospital, farm, workshops, and a church. Workers also constructed a canal from the Wye River. A combination of disease and Iroquois attacks led to the mission's demise. More than 20 structures, including two native longhouses and two wigwams, have been faithfully reproduced from a scientific excavation. Staff members in period costume demonstrate 17th-century trades, share Native stories and legends, and grow vegetables—keeping the working village alive. ⊠ *16164 Hwy. 12 W, 5 km (3 miles) east of Hwy. 93, Midland*

☎ 705/526–7838 🌐 *www.saintemarieamongthehurons.on.ca* 🎟 *C$12* ⏲ *Closed Oct.–Mar.*

Scenic Caves Nature Adventures

CAVE | FAMILY | Explore ancient caves, hike along craggy hilltop trails, get a thrill on zip line rides, or brave the suspension footbridge—25 meters (82 feet) above the ground with amazing views of the bay 300 meters (985 feet) below. Hiking boots or sneakers are required. ✉ *260 Scenic Caves Rd., Collingwood* ☎ *705/446–0256* 🌐 *www.sceniccaves.com* 🎟 *C$32* ⏲ *Closed Nov.–Apr.*

Hotels

Horseshoe Resort

$$ | RESORT | FAMILY | Modern accommodations at this lodge on a 1,600-acre property come in a variety of shapes and sizes: choose from two-level lofts, spacious hotel rooms, or condos. **Pros:** nearly endless list of outdoor activities; lots of different lodging options; suites with amazing amenities. **Cons:** scenic but isolated location; uncomfortable sofa beds; off-season dining options limited. [$] *Rooms from: C$169* ✉ *1101 Horseshoe Valley Rd., Barrie* ☎ *705/835–2790, 800/461–5627* 🌐 *www.horseshoeresort.com* 🛏 *101 rooms* 🍴 *No Meals.*

★ Westin Trillium House

$$$$ | RESORT | FAMILY | Whether you're looking for a luxurious winter ski getaway or a summer escape into the biking and hiking trails of the Niagara Escarpment, the Westin Trillium House really does have something for every season and for everyone (including your four-legged friends, who get beds in every unit). **Pros:** dozens of dining options outside your door; in-room gas fireplaces keep things cozy; plenty of nearby activities. **Cons:** some rooms have parking lot views; free parking is a long walk from resort; a bit of a chain hotel feeling. [$] *Rooms from: C$409* ✉ *220 Gord Canning Dr., Blue Mountains* ☎ *705/443–8080* 🌐 *www.marriott.com/hotels/travel/yyzth-the-westin-trillium-house-blue-mountain* 🛏 *227 rooms* 🍴 *No Meals.*

Activities

SKIING AND SNOWBOARDING

★ Blue Mountain Ski Resort

SKIING & SNOWBOARDING | The largest ski resort in Ontario, this huge property near Collingwood revolves around its brightly painted Scandinavian-style alpine "village" with several blocks of shops, restaurants, bars, a grocery, and a plaza with live music. Ontario's most extensively developed and frequented ski area has 42 trails, 22 of which are available after dark for night skiing, served by high-speed six-person lifts; quad, triple, and double lifts; and magic carpets. Aside from the slopes, it has a mountaintop skating rink and beer garden, an outstanding 18-hole golf course, mountain biking, a lakeside beach, an aquatic park, and even a roller coaster that winds down the mountain. ✉ *108 Jozo Weider Blvd.* ☎ *705/445–0231, 416/869–3799 from Toronto* 🌐 *www.bluemountain.ca.*

Mount St. Louis Moonstone

SKIING & SNOWBOARDING | FAMILY | Skiers and snowboarders can take advantage of 40 runs at Mount St. Louis Moonstone, 26 km (16 miles) north of Barrie. The majority of slopes are for beginner and intermediate skiers, though there's a sprinkling of advanced runs. The resort's Kids Camp, a day-care and ski-school combination, attracts families. Inexpensive cafeterias within the two chalets serve decent meals. **■ TIP→ No overnight lodging is available.** ✉ *24 Mount St. Louis Rd., off Hwy. 400 Exit 131* ☎ *705/835–2112, 877/835–2112* 🌐 *www.mountstlouis.com* 🎟 *C$66* ⏲ *Closed Mar.-Nov.*

Gravenhurst

74 km (46 miles) north of Barrie.

Outcroppings of pink and gray granite, drumlins of conifer and deciduous forest, and thousands of freshwater lakes formed from glaciers during the Ice Age characterize the rustic Muskoka region north of Toronto. Called Muskoka for Lake Muskoka, the largest of some 1,600 lakes in the area, this region is a favorite playground of those who live in and around Toronto. Place names such as Orillia, Gravenhurst, Haliburton, Algonquin, and Muskoka reveal the history of the land's inhabitants, from Algonquin tribes to European explorers to fur traders.

Gravenhurst is a town of approximately 10,000 and the birthplace of Norman Bethune, a surgeon, inventor, and political activist who is a Canadian hero. The heart of town is the colorful Muskoka Wharf, with its boardwalk along the water, restaurants, steamship docks, vacation condos, and a plaza that hosts festivals and a Wednesday farmers' market from mid-May to early October. Still, Gravenhurst is a tiny town and can be seen in a day or even an afternoon.

WHEN TO GO

As with everywhere in Muskoka, Gravenhurst comes alive in the summer months, with many attractions opening only after Victoria Day and closing sometime between Labour Day and mid-October, as the weather dictates. Nevertheless, area resorts do plan winter activities—snowshoeing, sleigh rides, and the like—and restaurants are open (with shorter off-season hours) year-round.

GETTING HERE AND AROUND

From Toronto, take Highway 400 north, which intersects with the highly traveled and often congested Highway 11. Gravenhurst is about 70 km (40 miles) north of the junction on Highway 11.

Driving time in good traffic is a bit over two hours. Ontario Northland buses and trains operate six days a week between Toronto's Union Station and downtown Gravenhurst.

CONTACTS Gravenhurst Bus and Railway Station. ⊠ *1–150 2nd St. S, Gravenhurst* ☎ *705/687–2301* ⊕ *ontarionorthland.ca/en/station/gravenhurst.* **Ontario Northland.** ⊠ *Gravenhurst* ☎ *800/461–8558* ⊕ *www.ontarionorthland.ca.*

VISITOR INFORMATION

CONTACTS Haliburton County Tourism. ☎ *705/286–1333, 800/461–7677* ⊕ *www.haliburtoncounty.ca.* **Muskoka Tourism.** ☎ *705/689–0660, 800/267–9700* ⊕ *www.discovermuskoka.ca.*

 # Sights

Bethune Memorial House

HISTORIC HOME | An 1880-vintage frame structure, this National Historic Site honors the heroic efforts of field surgeon and medical educator Henry Norman Bethune (1830–1939), who worked in China during the Sino-Japanese War in the 1930s and trained thousands to become medics. There are rooms that evoke the period and an exhibit tracing the highlights of his life. ⊠ *235 John St. N, Gravenhurst* ☎ *705/687–4261* ⊕ *www.pc.gc.ca/en/lhn-nhs/on/bethune* ⊠ *C$8.50* ⊙ *Closed Nov.–May.*

Casino Rama

CASINO | The largest First Nations–run gambling emporium in Canada, Casino Rama lures visitors to the Orillia area. A short jaunt from the ski resort areas around Barrie, the 192,000-square-foot complex has 2,500 slot machines, more than 110 gambling tables, eight restaurants, a lounge, and an adjoining 300-room all-suites luxury hotel. Catch acts like Trooper, Russell Peters, and Aqua here. ⊠ *5899 Rama Rd., Rama* ☎ *705/329–3325, 800/832–7529* ⊕ *www.casinorama.com.*

The Muskoka region north of Toronto is a popular destination for people wanting to escape the faster pace of city life.

Muskoka Discovery Centre

OTHER MUSEUM | Learn about steamboat history in this museum with a rotating collection of historic boats that have included a 1924 propeller boat, a 30-foot 1894 steamboat, and gleaming wooden speedboats. ⊠ *Muskoka Wharf, 275 Steamship Bay Rd., Gravenhurst* ☎ *705/687–2115, 866/687–6667* ⊕ *realmuskoka.com* ✉ *C\$20* ✆ *Closed Sun. and Mon. in late Oct.–mid-June.*

Muskoka Steamships

NAUTICAL SIGHT | **FAMILY** | In warm weather, the best way to experience Muskoka Lake is aboard one of these historic vessels. The restored 128-foot-long, 99-passenger RMS *Segwun* (the initials stand for Royal Mail Ship) is North America's oldest operating steamship, built in 1887, and is the sole survivor of a fleet that provided transportation through the Muskoka Lakes. The 200-passenger *Wenonah II* is a 1907-inspired vessel with modern technology. Reservations are required. ⊠ *Muskoka Wharf, 185 Cherokee La.* ☎ *705/687–6667, 866/687–6667* ⊕ *realmuskoka.com* ✉ *Sightseeing cruises C\$39* ✆ *Closed weekends Nov.–May.*

Stephen Leacock Museum

HISTORY MUSEUM | Readers of Canada's great humorist Stephen Leacock may recognize Orillia as "Mariposa," the town he described in *Sunshine Sketches of a Little Town.* Leacock's former summer home is now the Stephen Leacock Museum, a National Historic Site. Among the rotating exhibits are books, manuscripts, and photographs depicting Leacock, his family, and the region that inspired his writings. In the Mariposa Room, characters from the book are matched with the Orillia residents who inspired them. ⊠ *50 Museum Dr., off Hwy. 12B* ☎ *705/329–1908* ⊕ *www.orillia.ca/en/visiting/leacock-museum.aspx* ✉ *C\$5* ✆ *Closed Mon. and Tues.*

🍴 Restaurants

★ Blue Willow Tea Shop

\$\$\$ | **CAFÉ** | The dozen or so petite tables are set with blue-willow-pattern china in this quaint restaurant serving traditional English fare on the Muskoka Wharf. High tea—a three-tier platter of shortbread, scones with Devonshire cream, and savory finger sandwiches, plus a pot of tea per person—is served every afternoon. **Known for:** gift shop selling a variety of 27 loose leaf teas; quaint waterfront views; rotating seasonal high tea menus. $ *Average main: C$27* ✉ *Muskoka Wharf, 900 Bay St.* ☎ *705/687–2597* 🌐 *www.bluewillowteashop.ca* 🕒 *Closed Mon. and Tues. No dinner.*

Boathouse Restaurant
$$$ | **CONTEMPORARY** | Consistent with the aesthetics of Taboo Resort, the Boathouse offers luxurious and contemporary international cuisine in a subdued dining room with sleek furnishings, hardwood floors, and a wall of lakefront windows. The kitchen has oriented the menu to appeal to a health-conscious crowd. **Known for:** waterfront barbecues with roast pork and lamb; lovely views of the water; fresh seafood dishes. $ *Average main: C$24* ✉ *Taboo Muskoka, 1209 Muskoka Beach Rd., Gravenhurst* ☎ *866/369–9672* 🌐 *www.taboomuskoka.com/dine/boathouse-restaurant.*

The Oar
$$$ | **MODERN AMERICAN** | A cut above the rest, The Oar entertains guests with its beautiful pinewood floors and rustic cabin-like interiors. Burgers and steaks can be had but the upscale tavern menu has been known to include specials like quinoa-stuffed portobellos on a layer of avocado chimichurri and pan-fried locally caught pickerel, plated with root veggies and pecans. **Known for:** all-you-can-eat spaghetti nights; live music on the patio; locally sourced ingredients. $ *Average main: C$23* ✉ *530 Muskoka Rd. N, Gravenhurst* ☎ *705/687–8618* 🌐 *www.theoar.ca* 🕒 *Closed Sun. and Mon.*

Sawdust City Brewing Co.
$$ | **AMERICAN** | Stock up on hoppy brews fresh from the source when visiting Sawdust City, which owes its name to the former local logging trade. There's a full kitchen on-site serving hearty gastropub fare like cheesy truffled burgers and duck wings, with regular live music scheduling. **Known for:** inside bar, patio, and kitchen areas with separate menus; beer flight samplings; eight rotating taps. $ *Average main: C$15* ✉ *397 Muskoka Rd. N, Gravenhurst* ☎ *705/681–1100* 🌐 *sawdustcitybrewing.com.*

Hotels

Bayview Wildwood Resort
$$$$ | **RESORT** | **FAMILY** | A 20-minute drive south of Gravenhurst, this all-inclusive lakeside resort dates to 1898 and is particularly geared to outdoor types and active families. **Pros:** for privacy there are cottages with decks; casual, carefree atmosphere; free activities for kids. **Cons:** noisy trains pass by day and night; rustic feel isn't for everyone; strict meal times. $ *Rooms from: C$449* ✉ *1500 Port Stanton Pkwy.* ☎ *705/689–2338, 800/461–0243* 🌐 *www.bayviewwildwood.com* 🛏 *73 rooms* 🍴 *All-Inclusive.*

★ **Taboo Muskoka**
$$$ | **RESORT** | A magnificent 1,000-acre landscape of rocky outcrops and evergreen trees typical of the region surrounds this alpine lodge-style resort. **Pros:** fantastic golf course; forest and lake views; excellent spa. **Cons:** expensive rates in high season; no bar or food service at the pool; lots of corporate events. $ *Rooms from: C$225* ✉ *1209 Muskoka Beach Rd., Gravenhurst* ☎ *705/687–2233, 800/461–0236* 🌐 *www.tabooresort.com* 🛏 *62 rooms* 🍴 *Free Breakfast.*

Shopping

BEER

Muskoka Brewery
WINE/SPIRITS | It's a real treat to visit this brewery, tasting room, and retail store for one of the most popular beers in Ontario, especially if you come for the free tour. While you're here, taste beers like the

cream ale and Mad Tom IPA, or seasonal ales like the Peach of Mind kölsch, the Dry Hopped Wit Out a Paddle, or the Hollow Cane Vienna lager. It's halfway between Gravenhurst and Bracebridge, off Highway 11. ✉ *1964 Muskoka Beach Rd.* ☎ *705/646–1266* ⊕ *www.muskoka-brewery.com.*

Huntsville

51 km (32 miles) north of Gravenhurst.

Muskoka's Huntsville region is filled with lakes and streams, stands of virgin birch and pine, and deer—and no shortage of year-round resorts. It is usually the cross-country skier's best bet for an abundance of natural snow in southern Ontario. All resorts have trails.

Huntsville is a major gateway to Algonquin Provincial Park. Most people go to Algonquin in the summer, but the many winter attractions—ice fishing, cross-country skiing, dogsled tours—make it a popular destination in cold months as well. The only time to avoid is the notorious blackfly season, usually sometime in May. The mosquito population is healthy all summer, so pack repellent, pants, and long-sleeved shirts. Algonquin Provincial Park can be done in a weekend, but four days is the average stay; the park is huge and there's a lot of ground to cover.

WHEN TO GO
Summer is high season for vacationers in Huntsville, but the town is also ideal for cross-country skiing, ice fishing, and other backcountry winter adventures.

GETTING HERE AND AROUND
From Toronto, take Highway 400 north just past Barrie and then take Highway 11 north about 120 km (75 miles). Without traffic, the trip is about three hours. At least four Ontario Northland buses operate between Toronto's Union Station and Huntsville daily; travel time is four

hours, and the station is in the north of the city, a short walk to Main Street. From Gravenhurst, Huntsville is about 55 km (35 miles) north on Highway 11, a 45-minute drive.

A good four-hour drive from Toronto, Algonquin Provincial Park is most readily reached via Highway 400 north to Highway 60 east. The huge park has 29 different access points, so call to devise the best plan of attack for your visit based on your interests. The most popular entry points are along the Highway 60 corridor, where you'll find all the conventional campgrounds. If you're heading into the park's interior, spring for the detailed Algonquin Canoe Routes Map (C$4.95), available from the park's website. The visitor centers at the park gates or on the Highway 60 corridor—43 km (27 miles) east of the west gate—have information on park programs, a bookstore, a restaurant, and a panoramic-viewing deck.

■ **TIP→ In winter, go with a four-wheel-drive vehicle.**

CONTACT Huntsville Bus Station. ✉ *225 Main St. W, Huntsville* ☎ *705/789–6431* ⊕ *ontarionorthland.ca/en/station/huntsville.*

VISITOR INFORMATION
CONTACT Huntsville/Lake of Bays Chamber of Commerce. ✉ *37 Main St. E, Huntsville* ☎ *705/789–4771* ⊕ *www.lakeofbays.on.ca.*

Sights

★ Algonquin Provincial Park
NATIONAL PARK | Stretching across 7,650 square km (2,954 square miles) and containing nearly 2,500 lakes, Algonquin Provincial Park logs 272 bird species, 45 species of mammals, and 50 species of fish. Many visitors are hikers, canoeists, or campers, but don't be put off if you're not the outdoorsy sort; about a third of Algonquin's visitors come for the day to walk one of the 17 well-groomed

Highway 60 takes drivers on a scenic route through Ontario's famed Algonquin Provincial Park.

and well-signed interpretive trails or to enjoy a swim or a picnic. Swimming is especially good at the Lake of Two Rivers, halfway between the west and east gates along Highway 60. Spring, when the moose head north, is the best time to catch a glimpse of North America's largest land mammal. Getting up at the crack of dawn gives you the best chance of seeing the park's wildlife. Park naturalists give talks on area wildflowers, animals, and birds, and you can book a guided hike or canoe trip. Expeditions to hear wolves howling take place in late summer and early autumn. The park's Algonquin Logging Museum (late June–mid-October, daily 9–5) depicts life at an early Canadian logging camp. The east gate is west of the town of Whitney, and the west gate is east of the town of Dwight. ✉ *Hwy. 60, Algonquin Provincial Park* ☎ *705/633–5572* 🌐 *www.algonquinpark.on.ca* 🎟 *C$21 per vehicle.*

🍴 Restaurants

★ Arowhon Pines Restaurant

$$$$ | **CANADIAN** | A meal at this breathtaking hexagonal restaurant in the heart of Algonquin Provincial Park is the highlight of many visits. A view of the lake is a great accompaniment to the food, as is the towering stone fireplace in the center of the log-walled dining room. **Known for:** children's menus and babysitting service; limited seating for non-resort guests; weekend lunch buffet. [$] *Average main: C$95* ✉ *Algonquin Provincial Park West Entrance, 8 km (5 miles) north of Hwy. 60, Algonquin Provincial Park* ☎ *705/633–5661, 866/633–5661* 🌐 *www.arowhonpines.ca* 🕒 *Closed mid-Oct.–late May.*

Bartlett Lodge Restaurant

$$$$ | **CANADIAN** | In the original 1917 lodge building, this small lakeside pine dining room offers an ever-changing prix-fixe menu of contemporary Canadian cuisine, which might kick off with fennel and mustard-rubbed pork belly and

Adventure Tours Near Algonquin

If planning an Algonquin Provincial Park adventure seems daunting, leave it to the pros. Transport from Toronto, meals, and accommodations are included. You might, for example, do a multiday paddle-and-portage trip, catered with organic meals. Most companies have cabins, some quite luxurious, in Algonquin Park for tour participants; other tours may require backcountry tent camping.

Call of the Wild. Call of the Wild offers guided trips of different lengths—dogsledding and snowmobiling in winter, canoeing and hiking in summer—deep in the park away from the more touristy areas. The tour company's in-park Algonquin Eco Lodge is powered only by waterfall. A popular package is a four-day canoe trip and three days relaxing at the lodge. ✉ *Algonquin Eco Lodge, 3594 Elephant Lake Rd.* ☎ *905/471–9453, 800/776–9453* 🌐 *www.callofthewild.ca.*

Northern Edge Algonquin. Northern Edge Algonquin eco-adventure company provides adventurous learning vacations and retreats with activities such as moose tracking (via canoe), forest meditations, stand-up paddle-boarding, and women-only weekends. Home-cooked comfort food is local and organic; lodging ranges from new cabins to tents. ✉ *Algonquin Park Access Point 1* ☎ *888/383–8320* 🌐 *www. northernedgealgonquin.com.*

Voyageur Quest. Voyageur Quest has a variety of adventure wilderness canoe trips year-round in Algonquin Provincial Park and throughout northern Ontario, including a number of family-geared vacations. ✉ *Round Lake, Algonquin Park Access Point 1* ☎ *416/486–3605, 800/794–9660* 🌐 *www. voyageurquest.com.*

Winterdance Dogsled Tours. Winterdance Dogsled Tours takes you on half-day, full-day, multiday, and moonlight Siberian husky–led dogsledding adventures in and near Algonquin Provincial Park. Canoe tours are available in summer, as are kennel visits with the sled dogs. ✉ *6577 Haliburton Lake Rd.* ☎ *705/457–5281* 🌐 *www. winterdance.com.*

move on to pistachio and cherry-crusted Australian rack of lamb or the house specialty, beef tenderloin. Fish and vegetarian options, such as sweet-potato gnocchi with shaved Gruyère, are always available. **Known for:** bring your own wine; four-course prix-fixe dinners; complimentary water taxi pickup. [$] *Average main: C$72* ✉ *Boat from Algonquin Provincial Park Cache Lake Landing, south of Hwy. 60, Huntsville* ☎ *705/633–5543, 866/614–5355* 🌐 *www.bartlettlodge.com* ⏲ *Closed late Oct.–mid-May. No lunch.*

Hotels

★ Arowhon Pines

$$$$ | **RESORT** | The stuff of local legend, Arowhon is a family-run wilderness retreat deep in Algonquin Provincial Park known for an unpretentious rustic atmosphere and superb dining. **Pros:** all-inclusive rate includes a wide range of activities; excellent restaurant; secluded feel. **Cons:** pricey considering its lack of frills; road can be tricky at night; limited cell phone service. [$] *Rooms from: C$410* ✉ *Algonquin Provincial Park West Entrance, 8 km (5 miles) north of Hwy. 60* ☎ *705/633–5661, 866/633–5661*

🌐 *www.arowhonpines.ca* ⏲ *Closed mid-Oct.–May* 🛏 *50 rooms* 🍴 *All-Inclusive.*

Bartlett Lodge

$$$$ | RESORT | Smack in the center of Algonquin Provincial Park, this impressive 1917 resort is reached by a short boat ride across Cache Lake. **Pros:** completely quiet and peaceful; breakfast and dinner included; some rooms have wood stoves. **Cons:** gratuity included for groups of eight or more; no phones or TVs in the cabins; lots of mosquitoes in the summer. [$] *Rooms from: C$272* ✉ *Boat from Algonquin Provincial Park Cache Lake Landing, south of Hwy. 60, Algonquin Provincial Park* ☎ *705/633–5543, 905/338–8908* 🌐 *www.bartlettlodge.com* ⏲ *Closed late Oct.–early May* 🛏 *14 rooms* 🍴 *Free Breakfast.*

Deerhurst Resort

$$$ | RESORT | FAMILY | This golf-focused resort along Peninsula Lake is a 780-acre, self-contained community with restaurants and lodgings to fit every budget and occasion, from weddings to corporate events. **Pros:** resort arranges various Algonquin Park tours; summer and winter activities for everyone; affordable hike-and-stay packages. **Cons:** size can sometimes be overwhelming; busy check-in and checkout lines; getting enough towels can be a challenge. [$] *Rooms from: C$219* ✉ *1235 Deerhurst Dr., south of Rte. 60, Huntsville* ☎ *705/789–6411, 800/461–4393* 🌐 *www.deerhurstresort.com* 🛏 *400 rooms* 🍴 *No Meals.*

Walker Lake Resort

$$$$ | RESORT | FAMILY | Rustic two- and three-bedroom furnished cottages overlook Walker Lake at this resort, and many come with whirlpool tubs and fireplaces. **Pros:** very peaceful setting; free fishing boat rentals; easy access to Algonquin Park. **Cons:** no on-site restaurant; cottages require weekly rentals; bring your own bottled water. [$] *Rooms from: C$375* ✉ *1040 Walker Lake Dr., Huntsville* ☎ *705/635–2473, 800/565–3856* 🌐 *www.walkerlakeresort.com* 🛏 *7 cottages* 🍴 *No Meals.*

Activities

SKIING AND SNOWBOARDING

Hidden Valley Highlands Ski Area

SKIING & SNOWBOARDING | FAMILY | The ski area has 35 skiable acres with 13 hills and three quad lifts. It's great for beginner and intermediate skiers, with a couple of black-diamond runs for daredevils. ✉ *1655 Hidden Valley Rd., off Hwy. 60, Huntsville* ☎ *705/789–1773, 800/398–9555* 🌐 *www.skihiddenvalley.on.ca* 🎟 *C$59.*

SPORTS OUTFITTERS

Algonquin Outfitters

CANOEING & ROWING | The most well-known outfitter in the area has multiple locations in and around the park, specializing in canoe trip packages and rentals, outfitting and camping services, sea kayaking, and a water-taxi service to the park's central areas. Stores are at Oxtongue Lake (the main store—near the west Highway 60 park entrance), Huntsville, Opeongo Lake, Bracebridge, Haliburton, and Brent Base on Cedar Lake. ✉ *Oxtongue Lake store, 1035 Algonquin Outfitters Rd., R.R. 1, just north of Hwy. 60, Dwight* ☎ *705/635–2243, 800/469–4948* 🌐 *algonquinoutfitters.com.*

★ **Portage Store**

CANOEING & ROWING | If you plan to camp in the park, contact the Portage Store, which provides extensive outfitting services and guided canoe trips. It rents canoes and sells self-guided canoe packages that include all the equipment you need for a canoeing-and-camping trip in the park. Also available are bike rentals, maps, detailed information about routes and wildlife, and an on-site general store and casual restaurant. ✉ *Hwy. 60, Canoe Lake, Algonquin Provincial Park* ☎ *705/633–5622* 🌐 *www.portagestore.com.*

Index

A

Abraham's Trading Inc. (shop), 130
Absolutely Inc. (shop), 198
Adventure tours, 261
Aga Khan Museum, 203
Against the Grain Urban Tavern ✕, 88
AGO Bistro ✕, 117
Air tours, 215
Air travel, 38, 56, 219
Alexandros ✕, 157
Algonquin Provincial Park, 259–260
Alitura Fine Foods & Market, 241
Allan Gardens, 199
Allen's ✕, 155–156
Alley, The ✕, 246, 248
Alo ✕, 127
Alt Hotel Pearson 🖫, 210
Amsterdam BrewHouse, 70
Angus Glen Golf Club, 32
Anndore House, The 🖫, 194
Annex, The, 19, 28, 164–165, 169–174
dining, 170–172
lodging, 172
nightlife and the arts, 172–173
shopping, 173–174
transportation, 164
Annex Hotel, The 🖫, 172
Annie Aime (shop), 144
Aquariums, 67
Arowhon Pines 🖫, 261–262
Arowhon Pines Restaurant ✕, 260
Art Gallery of Ontario, 115, 117
Arts, 24–25. ⇨ See also Nightlife and the arts under specific areas
Arts Market, 155
ATMs, 43
Avery House 🖫, 249
Avling (bar), 154
Avoca ✕, 157
Avon Theatre, 261
Axis Club, 177

B

Bakka Phoenix (shop), 173
Balfour Books (shop), 178
Bang Bang ✕, 142
Banh Haus ✕, 117
Banh Mi Boys ✕, 127
Banks, 43
Bar Hop Brewco, 129
Bar Raval ✕, 175
Bar Volo, 194–195
Barbara Hall Park, 193
Barberian's Steak House ✕, 105, 107
BarChef, 129

Bars, pubs, and lounges, 70, 78–79, 87, 96, 100, 110, 129, 138–139, 143–144, 154, 157, 172, 177, 189, 194–195, 252
Bartlett Lodge 🖫, 262
Bartlett Lodge Restaurant ✕, 260–261
Baseball, 32
Basketball, 32
Bata Shoe Museum, 170
Battle Ground Hotel Museum, 222
Bau-Xi Gallery, 120
Bayview Wildwood Resort 🖫, 258
Beach, The (neighborhood), 19, 28, 150–151, 159–162
Beach Hill Smokehouse ✕, 156
Beaches, 159, 161
Beaches International Jazz Festival, 54
Beast Pizza ✕, 72
Beer Bistro ✕, 85
Bellwoods Brewery, 143
Bentley's ✕, 248
Bentway, The, 21, 61, 64
Berczy Park, 91
Bethune Memorial House, 256
Betty's (bar), 96
Bicycling and bicycle tours, 38–39, 56, 70, 252
Bier Markt (bar), 96
Big Carrot, The (shop), 158
Big Chill, The ✕, 175
Bijou ✕, 248
Bindia Indian Bistro ✕, 93
Bird Kingdom, 222–223
Birmingham Manor B&B 🖫, 249
Birreria Volo (bar), 177
Bisha Hotel Toronto 🖫, 76–77
Black Camel ✕, 197
Black Creek Pioneer Village, 207–208
Black Market, 131
Black Pony, The ✕, 159
Blackbird Baking Co. ✕, 123
Blue Mountain Ski Resort, 255
Blue Willow Tea Shop ✕, 257–258
BMV (shop), 174
Boat and ferry travel, 39, 56
Boat tours, 46, 215, 225, 236
Boathouse Restaurant ✕, 258
Bobbette and Belle ✕, 153
Border crossings, 221
Boutique Bar, 195
Boxcar Social ✕, 197
Brch & Wyn ✕, 248
Breweries and brewpubs, 70, 79, 98, 100, 143, 258–259
Brick Street Bakery ✕, 100
Broadview Hotel, The 🖫, 154
Bruce Trail, 245
Buca ✕, 72
Buddies in Bad Times Theatre, 196
Budweiser Stage, 70
Bungalow (shop), 124

Burger's Priest ✕, 75
Bus tours, 46, 215
Bus travel, 39, 56
Bymark ✕, 85

C

Cabbagetown, 19, 182–183, 199–200
Cactus Club Cafe ✕, 85
Café Boulud ✕, 185, 187
Café Diplomatico ✕, 175
Cafe Neon ✕, 136
Café Pamenar ✕, 123
Caledonian, The (bar), 177
Call of the Wild (tours), 261
Cambridge Suites 🖫, 86
Campbell House Museum, 125
Canada's Wonderland, 208
Canadian National Exhibition, 54–55
Canadian Stage, 97
Canoe ✕, 85
Canoeing, 162, 262
Car rentals and travel, 39–41, 219
Carbon Bar, The ✕, 93
Cartier (shop), 190
Casa Loma (historic house), 170
Casa Mia Ristorante ✕, 230
Casino Niagara, 223
Casino Rama, 256
Cave Spring Vineyard, 241
C'est What (bar), 96
Chanel (shop), 190
Charles Hotel, The 🖫, 238
Chase, The ✕, 85
Château des Charmes (winery), 233
Chelsea Hotel 🖫, 108
Chiado ✕, 175
Chica ✕, 72
Children, attractions for, 34
Chinatown, 18, 27, 114–121
dining, 117, 119–120
nightlife and the arts, 121
shopping, 120–121
transportation, 114
Church and Wellesley, 19, 29, 102–103, 193–196
City Hall, 125, 127
Classical music, 79–80, 169, 173, 189–190, 197, 252
Clifton Hill, 223
Climate, 236
CN Tower, 64
Cocktail Bar, 143
Comedy Bar, 173
Comedy clubs, 79, 173, 195
Common Sort (shop), 174
Communist's Daughter (bar), 142
Constantine ✕, 193–194
Consulates, 43, 56
Contact Photography Festival, 54
Contacts, 56
Corkin Gallery, 101

Corktown Designs (shop), *101*
Country Inn & Suites ⌂ , *231*
Courage My Love (shop), *124*
Craft Ontario Shop, *139*
Craig's Cookies ✕ , *194*
Credit cards, *43–44*
Crews and Tango (dance club), *195–196*
Crowne Plaza Niagara Falls – Falls-
view ⌂ , *231*
Crush on Niagara, (tour), *217*
Cuisine, *22–23, 72*
Currency and exchange, *44*

D

D & E Lake Ltd. (shop), *87*
Dakota Tavern, *143*
Dance, *130, 200*
Dance clubs, *144, 177, 195–196*
Danforth Music Hall, *157*
Dead Dog Records (shop), *196*
Dear Grain ✕ , *142*
Deerhurst Resort ⌂ , *262*
Delta Hotel Toronto ⌂ , *69*
Descendant ✕ , *153*
Dillon's Small Batch Distillers, *242*
Dining, *45*
cuisine, *22–23, 72*
price categories, *45, 220*
Dipped Donuts ✕ , *123*
Discounts and deals, *222, 252*
Distillery District, *18, 26, 90–91,
98–101*
dining, *98, 100*
nightlife and the arts, *100*
shopping, *101*
transportation, *90*
Distillery Winter Festival, The, *55*
Diwan at the Aga Khan Museum
✕ , *206*
Djbar, *189*
Doll Factory by Damzels (shop), *155*
Don Valley Golf Course, *33*
DoubleTree by Hilton Downtown
⌂ , *108*
Drake Hotel, The ⌂ , *138*
Drake Underground, The (bar), *138*
Drom Taberna, *129*
Duer (shop), *132*
Duff's Famous Wings ✕ , *175*
Dumpling House ✕ , *119*
Durumi (shop), *131*
Dynasty Pot Shop, *140*

E

Eat Nabati ✕ , *122*
Eataly ✕ , *187*
Eataly Market, *192*
Ed Mirvish Theatre, *112*
Edo-ko ✕ , *206*
Ed's Real Scoop ✕ , *161*
Edulis ✕ , *73*

Egg Club ✕ , *107*
El Catrin ✕ , *98, 100*
El Mocambo (music venue), *121*
Elgin and Winter Garden Theatre
Centre, *110, 112*
Elmwood Spa, *112*
E11even ✕ , *68*
Embassies/consulates, *43, 56*
Emergencies, *41, 56*
Entertainment District, *18, 26, 71–81*
dining, *72–76*
lodging, *76–78*
nightlife and the arts, *78–80*
shopping, *80–81*
Evergreen Brick Works, *196*
Evviva ✕ , *73*
Executive Hotel Cosmopolitan ⌂ ,
86–87

F

Factory Theatre, *80*
Fairmont Royal York ⌂ , *87*
Fallsview Casino Resort ⌂ , *225, 231*
Fat Pasha ✕ , *170*
Feheley Fine Arts, *97*
Festival Inn ⌂ , *249–250*
Festival Theatre, *250–251*
Festivals and seasonal events, *54–55,
180–181, 214, 217, 240–241, 250–252*
Fielding Estate Winery, *242*
Film, *54, 55, 71–72, 173, 177–178,
180–181*
Film Cafe ✕ , *122*
Financial District, *18, 26, 81–88*
dining, *85–86*
lodging, *86–87*
nightlife, *87*
shopping, *83, 88*
Fireworks over Niagara Falls, *214*
Flatiron Building, *91–92*
Flatiron's Christmas Market, *98*
Flock ✕ , *169*
Flying Saucer Restaurant, The
✕ , *230*
Food tours, *46*
Floral Clock, *233*
Football, *32*
Fort George National Historic Site,
233, 235
Fort York, *64, 66*
Foster's Inn ⌂ , *250*
Four Seasons Hotel Toronto ⌂ , *188*
401 Richmond (gallery), *130–131*
416 Snack Bar ✕ , *128*
Foxley ✕ , *141*
Frans ✕ , *169*
Free Times Cafe (music club), *177*
Fresh on Spadina ✕ , *73*
Freshii ✕ , *75*
Frogpond Farm Organic Winery, *235*
Future Bistro ✕ , *170–171*

G

Gadabout (shop), *154–155*
Gallery Stratford, *246*
Gardiner Museum, *183*
Garrison, The (music venue), *143–144*
GB Hand-Pulled Noodles ✕ , *107–108*
George C (shop), *190*
Georgian Bay Islands National
Park, *254*
Gerrard India Bazaar, *158*
Getoutside (shop), *132*
GG's Burgers ✕ , *161*
Giulietta ✕ , *175*
Glad Day Bookshop, *196*
Gladstone House ⌂ , *138*
Gladstone Melody Bar, *138–139*
Glen Abbey Golf Club, *33*
Golf, *32–33*
Good Egg (shop), *125*
Good Neighbor (shop), *155*
Gotstyle (shop), *101*
Graffiti Alley, *127*
Grape and Wine Tours, *217*
Gravenhurst, *212, 256–259*
Gravitypope (shop), *140*
Great Hall, The, *139*
Great Wolf Lodge ⌂ , *232*
Greater Toronto, *19, 202–210*
dining, *206*
lodging, *210*
shopping, *206–207*
transportation, *202*
Greaves Jams & Marmalades
(shop), *241*
Greektown, *19, 28, 150–151, 155–158*

H

Hammam Spa, *81*
Harbour House ⌂ , *239*
Harbour Sixty Steakhouse ✕ , *68*
Harbourfront, *18, 26, 58–71*
dining, *68–69*
lodging, *69*
nightlife and the arts, *69–70*
outdoor activities and sports, *70*
shopping, *71*
transportation, *60*
Harbourfront Centre, *66–67*
Harry Rosen (shop), *190–191*
Hart House, *165, 167*
Hart House Theatre, *169*
Harvey's ✕ , *75*
Hatley Boutique, *206–207*
HAVEN (shop), *98*
Hazelton Hotel ⌂ , *188*
Health concerns, *43*
Heel Boy (shop), *141*
Helicopter tours, *215*
Hemingway's (bar), *189*
Hermès (shop), *191*
High Park, *145*

Hiking, 46, 197–198, 208–209, 232, 245
Hilton Toronto ⌘, 77
History (music venue), 161
Hockey, 33
Hockey Hall of Fame, 81, 83
Hollace Cluny (shop), 192
Holt Renfrew (department store), 192
Honda Indy (festival), 55
Hong Shing ✕, 107
Hornblower Niagara Cruises, 225
Horses Atelier (shop), 140–141
Horseshoe Resort ⌘, 255
Horseshoe Tavern, 129
Hot Docs (film festival), 54, 180
Hot Docs Ted Rogers Cinema, 173
Hôtel Le Germain Toronto ⌘, 77
Hotel Ocho ⌘, 128
Hotels, 43. ⇨ See also lodging under
  specific areas
price categories, 43, 220
Huntsville, 212, 259–262
Huronia Museum and Huron Ouendat
  Village, 254
Hyatt Regency Toronto ⌘, 77

I

I Miss You Vintage (shop), 144
Ice-skating, 33
Ice wine, 217
Icha Tea ✕, 138
ImPerfect Fresh Eats ✕, 75
In Vintage We Trust (shop), 147
Indigo (shop), 190
Inn on the Twenty ⌘, 245
Inn on the Twenty Restaurant ✕,
  242, 245
Inside Out 2SLGBTQ+ Film Festival,
  180
Insomnia (bar), 172
InterContinental Toronto Centre
  ⌘, 77
IQ Living (shop), 158
Itinerary suggestions, 52–53, 220

J

Jackson-Triggs Niagara Estate
  Winery, 235
Japanese Canadian Cultural Centre,
  203
Jazz Bistro, 110
John Fluevog (shop), 101
Jordan Village, 242
Joso's ✕, 187
Journey Behind the Falls (tour), 225

K

Kayaking, 162
Kensington Market, 18, 27, 114–115,
  121–125
Kew-Balmy Beach, 159

Khao San Road ✕, 73
Kid Icarus (shop), 125
Kimpton Saint George ⌘, 172
King's Café ✕, 122
Kinka Izakaya ✕, 107
Kinka Izakaya Bloor (bar), 172
Koerner Hall, 189–190
Konzelmann Estate Winery, 235
Kortright Centre for Conservation,
  208

L

La Carnita (bar), 177
La Palette ✕, 128
Lady Marmalade ✕, 153
Lahore Tikka House ✕, 158
Lai Wah Heen ✕, 107
Lake Inez ✕, 158–159
Lapinou ✕, 73
Le Germain Hotel Maple Leaf Square
  ⌘, 69
Le Paradis ✕, 171
Le Sélect Bistro ✕, 73–74
Le Swan ✕, 136
Lee's Palace (music venue), 172
Leslieville, 19, 28, 150–155
Leslieville Pumps ✕, 153
Lillian H. Smith Branch of the
  Toronto Public Library, 167
Lilliput Hats (shop), 178
Lisa Gozlan Jewelry (shop), 193
Little India, 19, 28, 150–151, 158–159
Little Italy, 19, 29, 164–165, 174–178
dining, 174, 177
nightlife and the arts, 177–178
shopping, 178
transportation, 164
Little Pebbles ✕, 123–124
Lobby Lounge at Shangri-La, 78
Loch Gallery, 190
Lodging, 43. ⇨ See also under specific
  areas
price categories, 43, 220
Loga's Corner ✕, 147
Louix Louis ✕, 86
Lula Lounge (dance club), 144
Lululemon Athletica (shop), 131
Luma ✕, 74
Luminato Festival, 54

M

MacMillan Theatre, 169
Mademoiselle ✕, 74
Madrina Bar y Tapas ✕, 100
Maha's ✕, 159
Maid of the Mist (tour), 226
Mamakas Tavern ✕, 141–142
Marbl ✕, 74
Marineland (theme park), 225–226
Market 707 ✕, 122
Marriott Eaton Centre ⌘, 110

Martin Goodman Trail, 70
Martyrs' Shrine, 254
Massey Hall (music venue), 112
Mattachioni ✕, 159
Matty's Pattys ✕, 143
McMichael Canadian Art Collection,
  208
MEC (shop), 132
Mephisto (shop), 198
Mercatto ✕, 169
Mercer Kitchen + Beer Hall ✕, 248
Merchant of York (shop), 71
Meridian Hall, 96–97
Mezes ✕, 156
Midland and Penetanguishene, 212,
  253–255
Milkcow Cafe ✕, 206
Mill Street Brewery, 100
MIMI Chinese ✕, 187
Mira Mira ✕, 161
Miss Thing's ✕, 147
Moffat Inn ⌘, 239
Money matters, 43–44
Moores Clothing for Men (shop), 88
Motion (shop), 191
Mount St. Louis Moonstone (ski
  resort), 255
Mountain Equipment Co-op (shop), 81
Museum of Contemporary Art
  (MOCA), 145
Museum of Illusions, 92
Museums and art galleries, 81, 83,
  92, 97, 101, 105, 115, 117, 120, 125,
  130–131, 139, 144, 145, 155, 170, 183,
  185, 190, 203–204, 207–208, 222, 227,
  235, 246, 254, 256, 257
Music, 24–25, 54, 55, 70, 79–80, 96–97,
  112, 121, 129–130, 139, 143–144, 154,
  157, 161, 169, 172, 173, 177, 189–190,
  197, 252
Muskoka Brewery, 258–259
Muskoka Discovery Centre, 257
Muskoka Steamships, 257

N

Nadège ✕, 138
Nami Japanese Restaurant ✕, 93, 95
Napoli Ristorante e Pizzeria ✕, 230
Nathan Phillips Square Rink, 33
National Ballet of Canada, 130
National Bank Open, 55
Natrel Rink, 33
Necropolis Cemetery, 199–200
Neighborhoods, 26–29
Nella Cucina (shop), 174
NEO COFFEE BAR (Old Town) ✕, 95
NEO COFFEE BAR (Queen's Park) ✕, 169
Neurotica Records (shop), 178
Niagara Apothecary (museum), 235
Niagara Escarpment, The, 212,
  241–245

Niagara Falls, *212, 214–215, 220–232*
border crossings, *221*
dining, *230–231*
lodging, *231–232*
outdoor activities and sports, *232*
transportation, *215, 221*
visitor information, *221, 222*
Niagara Glen Nature Reserve, *232*
Niagara Grape & Wine Festival, *217*
Niagara-on-the-Lake, *212, 232–241*
dining, *237–238*
lodging, *238–240*
nightlife and the arts, *240–241*
shopping, *241*
tours, *233, 236*
transportation, *233*
Niagara-on-the-Lake Museum, *235*
Niagara Parks Botanical Gardens, *227*
Niagara Parks Power Station, *227*
Niagara River Recreation Trail, *232*
Niagara Wine Region, *216–217*
Niagara's Fury (interactive exhibit), *227*
Night Baker, The ✕, *175, 177*
Nightlife, *24–25.* ⇨ *See also Nightlife and the arts under specific areas*
Noonan's (bar), *157*
North of Brooklyn ✕, *194*
North Toronto, *203–206*
Northern and Eastern Suburbs, *207–209*
Northern Edge Algonquin (tours), *261*
Novo Spa, *193*
Nuit Blanche (festival), *55*
Nutty Chocolatier (shop), *162*

O

Oar, The ✕, *258*
Old City Hall, *127*
Old Town, *18, 26, 90–98*
dining, *93, 95*
lodging, *95–96*
nightlife and the arts, *96–97*
shopping, *92, 97–98*
transportation, *90*
Olde Angel Inn ✕▦, *237, 239*
Oliver & Bonacini Cafe Grill, *87*
Omni King Edward Hotel, The ▦, *95–96*
One ✕, *187*
One King West Hotel and Residence ▦, *87*
119 Corbò (shop), *191*
Only Cafe, The (bar), *157*
Ontario Legislative Building, *167*
Ontario Science Centre, *203–204*
Ontario Spring Water Sake Company (IZUMI Brewery), *98*
Ontario Wine Route, *217*
Opera House The (music club), *154*
Original (shop), *131*
Ossington, *19, 27, 134–135, 141–145*
Othership (spa), *81*
Otto's Berlin Döner ✕, *122*

Outdoor activities and sports, *32–33.*
⇨ *See also under specific areas*
Over the Rainbow (shop), *191*
Oyster Boy ✕, *136*

P

Packing, *44–45*
Pancer's Original Delicatessen ✕, *206*
Pantages Hotel ▦, *110*
Pantry ✕, *197*
Papyrus ✕, *157*
Paradise Theatre, *173*
Park Hyatt ▦, *188–189*
Parkdale, *19, 27, 134–135, 145–148*
Parks, gardens, and ravines, *20–21, 61, 64, 67–68, 91, 135, 145, 151, 185, 193, 197–198, 199, 204, 208–209, 227, 232, 254, 259–260*
Passports, *45*
PATH (shopping complex), *83*
Patois ✕, *142*
Pazzo Taverna and Pizzeria ✕, *248*
Pearl Diver ✕, *95*
Pearl Harbourfront ✕, *69*
Pearson International Airport area, *210*
Peller Estates Winery Restaurant ✕, *237*
Penetanguishene, *212, 253–255*
Performing arts, *24–25.* ⇨ *See also Nightlife and the arts under specific areas*
PG Cluck's ✕, *177*
Pho Pasteur ✕, *119*
Piano Piano ✕, *171*
Pillar and Post ▦, *239*
Pilot Coffee Roasters ✕, *153–154*
Pink Sky ✕, *74*
Pizza Banfi ✕, *206*
Pizza Libretto (Entertainment District) ✕, *74*
Pizza Libretto (Ossington) ✕, *142*
Pizza Pizza ✕, *75*
PJ O'Brien ✕, *95*
Planet Diner, The ✕, *248–249*
Planta ✕, *187–188*
Portage Store, *262*
Poutine, *72*
Pow Wow Cafe ✕, *122*
Prada (shop), *191*
Pravda Vodka Bar, *96*
Price categories, *43, 45, 220*
Pride Toronto (festival), *54*
Prince of Wales ▦, *239*
Princess of Wales (theater), *80*
Province of Canada (shop), *155*
Prune, The ✕, *249*
Public transportation, *41–42*
Pusateri's (shop), *192*
Putti (shop), *198*

Q

Quasi Modo (shop), *141*
Queen and Albert B&B ▦, *250*
Queen and Beaver Public House, The, *110*
Queen Margherita Pizza ✕, *153*
Queen Mother Cafe ✕, *128*
Queen Street (Niagara-on-the-Lake), *235–236*
Queen Victoria Place ✕, *230*
Queen West, *18, 27, 114–115, 125–132*
dining, *127–128*
lodging, *128–129*
nightlife and the arts, *129–130*
shopping, *130–132*
transportation, *114*
Queen's Landing ▦, *239*
Queen's Park, *19, 28, 164–178*
dining, *167, 169*
nightlife and the arts, *169*
transportation, *164*

R

R&D ✕, *119*
Radisson Hotel Admiral Toronto-Harbourfront ▦, *69*
Ration ✕, *128*
RC Coffee Robo Café ✕, *188*
Real Sports Bar & Grill, *70*
Red Pegasus (shop), *178*
Reds Wine Tavern ✕, *86*
Relic Lobby Bar, The, *252*
Reposado (bar), *144*
Residence Inn Toronto Downtown ▦, *77–78*
Restaurant at Vineland Estates Winery ✕, *245*
Restaurant 20 Victoria ✕, *95*
Restaurants, *45.* ⇨ *See also dining under specific areas*
price categories, *45, 220*
Revival House ✕, *249*
Rex Hotel Jazz and Blues Bar, The, *130*
Rideshares, *42, 56*
Ripley's Aquarium of Canada, *67*
Risqué (shop), *174*
Ritz-Carlton, Toronto ▦, *87*
Riverbend Inn & Vineyard ▦, *239–240*
Riverdale Farm, *200*
Riverdale Park, *21*
Rivoli, The, *130*
Robo Sushi ✕, *206*
Rodney's Oyster House ✕, *74–75*
Rogers Centre, *67*
Rooftop at the Broadview Hotel, The (bar), *154*
Roots (shop), *191*
Rosedale, *19, 29, 182–183, 196–198*
Rosedale Ravine, *20, 197–198*
Roselle Desserts ✕, *95*
Rotate This (shop), *145*

Rouge National Urban Park, *21*
Rowing, *262*
Roy Thomson Hall, *80*
Royal Agricultural Winter Fair, *55*
Royal Alexandra (theater), *80*
Royal Cinema, The, *177–178*
Royal De Versailles (shop), *193*
Royal Ontario Museum, *183, 185*
Rustle and Still ✕, *171*
Ryu's Noodle Bar ✕, *156*

S

Safety, *43*
St. James Cathedral, *92*
St. James Cemetery, *200*
Saint James Hotel ⬚, *110*
St. Lawrence Hall, *92*
St. Lawrence Market, *92*
St. Mark's Anglican Church, *236*
St. Regis Toronto, The ⬚, *87*
Ste.-Marie among the Hurons, *254–255*
Salad King ✕, *107*
Sam James Coffee Bar ✕, *147*
Sandman Signature Toronto Airport ⬚, *210*
Sawdust City Brewing Co. ✕, *258*
Scarborough Bluffs, *208–209*
Scenic Caves Nature Adventures, *255*
Schmaltz Appetizing ✕, *172*
Scooped by Demetres ✕, *100*
Scotiabank Arena, *70*
Scribe, The (shop), *157*
Seagull Classics Ltd. (shop), *162*
Second Cup ✕, *75*
Secrets from Your Sister (shop), *174*
Seven Lives Tacos y Mariscos ✕, *123*
7 West Cafe ✕, *194*
Shakespeare Festival, *54, 250–251*
Shan (shop), *191*
Shangri-La Hotel Toronto ⬚, *129*
Shangri-La Toronto ⬚, *78*
Shaw Club Hotel ⬚, *240*
Shaw Festival, *54, 240–241*
Sheraton Centre ⬚, *78*
Sheraton Gateway Hotel ⬚, *210*
Sheraton on the Falls ⬚, *232*
Shoney's Clothing (shop), *124*
Shook ✕, *75–76*
ShopAGO, *120*
Shopping. ⇨ See under specific areas
Side trips from Toronto, *212–262*
  dining, *220, 230–231, 237–238, 242, 245, 246, 248–249, 257–258, 260–261*
  lodging, *219–220, 231–232, 238–241, 245, 249–250, 255, 258, 261–262*
  nightlife and the arts, *240–241, 250–252*
  outdoor activities and sports, *232, 245, 252, 255, 262*
  prices, *220*
  shopping, *241, 252, 258–259*

tours, *215, 217, 225, 233, 236, 246, 261*
transportation, *215, 219*
visitor information, *220, 221, 222*
Silver Snail (shop), *139*
Skiing, *255, 262*
Sky Dragon Chinese Restaurant ✕, *119*
Skyline Restaurant, The ✕, *147*
Skylon Tower, *227*
Skylon Tower Revolving Dining Room ✕, *230*
Snowboarding, *255, 262*
Soccer, *33*
Socco Annex (shop), *174*
SoHo Hotel and Residences, The ⬚, *78*
Soma Chocolatemaker (shop), *101*
Sonic Boom (shop), *131*
Soos ✕, *142*
Sotto Sotto ✕, *188*
Soulpepper Theatre Company, *100*
Spadina Avenue, *117*
Spas, *81, 112, 132, 193*
Sporting Life (shop), *207*
Sports. ⇨ See outdoor activities and sports under specific areas
Stand-up paddleboarding, *162*
Steam Whistle Brewery, *79*
Stephen Bulger Gallery, *144*
Stephen Leacock Museum, *257*
Sterling Inn & Spa ⬚, *232*
Stewart House Inn ⬚, *250*
Stratford, *212, 245–252*
  dining, *246, 248–249*
  lodging, *249–250*
  nightlife and the arts, *250–252*
  outdoor activities and sports, *252*
  shopping, *252*
  tours, *246*
  transportation, *246*
Stratford Festival, *54, 250–251*
Stratford Festival Shop, *252*
Stratford Perth Museum, *246*
Stratford Summer Music (festival), *252*
Stratford Walking Tours, *246*
Stratus Vineyards, *236*
Studio Brillantine (shop), *148*
Studio Theatre, *251*
Sultan's Tent and Cafe Moroc, *96*
Summer/Works Performance Festival, *55*
Summerhill LCBO (shop), *198*
Summerhill Market, *198*
Summerlicious (festival), *55*
Summer's Ice Cream ✕, *188*
Super Natural Market, *124*
Swan Motel ⬚, *250*
Swatow ✕, *119*
Swipe Design | Books + Objects (shop), *131*
Swiss Chalet Rotisserie and Grill ✕, *75*

T

Table Rock House ✕, *231*
Table Rock Welcome Centre, *221*
Taboo Muskoka ⬚, *258*
Tabülè ✕, *153*
Tafelmusik, *173*
Tap Phong Trading Co. Inc. (shop), *121*
Tarragon Theatre, *173*
Tawse Winery, *242*
Taxi travel, *42, 56*
Tefelmusik (music venue), *173*
Ten Spot, The (spa), *132*
Terroni ✕, *86*
Terroni and Bar Centrale ✕, *197*
Textile Museum of Canada, *105*
Textile Museum Shop, *121*
Theater, *55, 80, 97, 100, 110, 112, 130, 139, 154, 169, 173, 196, 240–241*
Theatre Centre, The, *139*
Théâtre Français de Toronto, *97*
Theatre Passe Muraille, *130*
Three Houses Bed & Breakfast Inn, The ⬚, *250*
Tiara Restaurant at Queen's Landing ✕, *238*
Tibet Kitchen ✕, *147*
TIFF Bell Lightbox, *71–72*
TIFF Next Wave Film Festival, *54*
TIFF Shop, *81*
Tiffany & Co. (shop), *193*
Tim Horton's ✕, *75*
Tiny Record Shop, *155*
Tipping, *45*
TOCA ✕, *76*
Tom Patterson Theatre, *251*
Tommy Thompson Park, *20, 151*
Tom's Place (shop), *124*
Toronto After Dark (film festival), *180*
Toronto Antiques on King, *80*
Toronto Argonauts (football team), *32*
Toronto Blue Jays (baseball team), *32*
Toronto Botanical Garden and Edwards Gardens, *204*
Toronto Caribbean Carnival, *55*
Toronto Dance Theatre, *200*
Toronto-Dominion Centre, *83*
Toronto Eaton Centre (mall), *112*
Toronto FC (soccer team), *33*
Toronto Fringe Festival, *55*
Toronto International Buskerfest, *55*
Toronto International Film Festival, *55, 181*
Toronto Island Park, *67–68*
Toronto Islands, *20*
Toronto Jazz Festival, *54*
Toronto Maple Leafs (hockey team), *33*
Toronto Marlies (hockey team), *33*
Toronto Marriott City Centre ⬚, *78*
Toronto Mendelssohn Choir, *197*
Toronto Raptors (basketball team), *32*
Toronto Reference Library, *185*
Toronto Symphony Orchestra, *79–80*

Toronto Zoo, *209*
Toronto's First Post Office, *92–93*
Tours and guides, *38–39, 46, 56, 70,*
  215, 217, 225, 233, 236, 246, 252, 261
Town Moto (shop), *144*
Train travel, *42, 219*
Transportation, *38–42, 56.* ⇨ *See also*
  under specific areas
Treadwell Restaurant ✕ , *238*
Tribal Rhythm (shop), *131*
Trinity Bellwoods Park, *20, 135*
Trius Winery Restaurant ✕ , *238*
TSUJIRI Dundas ✕ , *108*
Tuck Shop Trading Co., *198*
21 Club ✕ , *231*
Type Books (shop), *139–140*

U

Udupi Palace ✕ , *159*
Uncle Tetsu's Japanese Cheesecake
  ✕ , *108*
Union Station, *83*
University of Toronto, *167*
Urban Modo (shop), *141*

V

Via Mercanti ✕ , *123*
Victor ✕ , *76*
Village of Yorkville Park, *185*
Vineland Estates Winery, *242*
Visas, *45*
Visitor information, *56, 220, 221, 222*
Voyageur Quest (tours), *261*
VSP Consignment (shop), *144–145*

W

Waddington's (auction house), *97*
Wagman Antiques (shop), *190*
Wah Sing Seafood Restaurant ✕ ,
  119–120
Walker Lake Resort , *262*
Walking tours, *46, 215, 246*
Walrus Pub & Beerhall ✕ , *86*
Water sports, *162*
Waterfront, The, *20*
Watson's Chelsea Bazaar, *252*
Weather, *236*
Webster, The (shop), *191–192*
West Queen West, *19, 27, 134–141*
  dining, *136, 138*
  lodging, *138*
  nightlife and the arts, *138–139*
  shopping, *139–141*
  transportation, *134*
Westin Harbour Castle , *69*
Westin Trillium House , *255*
Wet 'n' Wild Toronto, *209*
Wheatsheaf Tavern, The ✕ , *76*
Whirlpool Aero Car, *227*
Whirlpool Jet Boat Tours, *236*
White Water Walk, *227, 230*
Wilbur Mexicana ✕ , *76*
William Ashley (shop), *192*
Windsor Arms , *189*
Wine Region, *216–217*
Wine tours, *217*
Wineries, *216–217, 233, 235, 236,*
  241, 242
Winter Festival of Lights, *214*
Winterdance Dogsled Tours, *261*
Winterlicious (festival), *54*

Woodbine Beach, *21, 159, 161*
Woody's (bar), *195*
World Food Market ✕ , *108*
Writers Room Bar, *189*
WVRST ✕ , *76*

X

Xola ✕ , *161*

Y

Yonge-Dundas Square Area, *18, 26,*
  104–112
  dining, *105, 107–108*
  lodging, *108, 110*
  nightlife and the arts, *110, 112*
  shopping, *112*
  transportation, *104*
Yorkville, *19, 29, 182–193*
  dining, *185, 187–188*
  lodging, *188–189*
  nightlife and the arts, *189–190*
  shopping, *190–193*
  transportation, *182*
Yorkville Village (mall), *192*
Young People's Theatre, *97*
YSK Bistro ✕ , *249*
Yuk Yuk's (comedy club), *79*

Z

Zane (shop), *141*
Zees Grill ✕ , *238*
Zoos, *200, 209, 222–223*

Photo Credits

Front Cover: William Berry / Alamy Stock Photo [Description: Toronto Ontario skyline as seen from Hanlans Point on the Toronto Islands, Toronto Ontario Canada]. Back cover, from left to right: Vadim Rodnev/Shutterstock. Javen/Shutterstock. Canadapanda/Shutterstock. Spine: Jiawangkun / Shutterstock. Interior, from left to right: Steven_Kriemadis/iStockphoto (1). Elijah-Lovkoff/iStockphoto (2-3). **Chapter 1: Experience Toronto:** TylersJourney/Shutterstock (6-7). Aqnus Febriyant/Shutterstock (8-9). Kiev. Victor/Shutterstock (9). Diego Grandi/ Shutterstock (9). Jesse Milns/Tourism Toronto (10). Philip Lange/ Shutterstock (10). JHVEPhoto/Shutterstock (10). Royal Ontario Museum (11). Spiroview Inc/Shutterstock (12). typhoonski/iStockphoto (12). EQRoy/Shutterstock (13). GuruXOOX/iStockphoto (14). Jferrer/iStockphoto (14). GTS Productions/Shutterstock (14). Flickr_BetterThanBacon (15). JHVEPhoto/Shutterstock (15). Edgar Bullon/iStockphoto (16). Bellwoods Brewery (16). ValeStock/Shutterstock (16). Reimar/Shutterstock (16). Vivian Lynch (17). Destination Toronto (20). PENA2020/Shutterstock (21). Jo-Anne McArthur/Village of Dreams Productions (22). Opticalmealfinder/Koi Koi (22). Fuwa Fuwa (22). Pai (23). Barb Simkova/Patois (23). Philip Lange/Shutterstock (24). Sockagphoto/Shutterstock (25). **Chapter 3: Harbourfront, Entertainment District, and the Financial District:** Jon Bilous/Shutterstock (57). Jon Bilous/Shutterstock (58). Loozrboy/Flickr (59). Courtesy of Tourism Toronto (59). Mdmworks/ iStockphoto (65). MagicBones/ Shutterstock (66). JL IMAGES/Shutterstock (71) Eskystudio/Shutterstock (79). Courtesy of Marc Bruxelle (84). **Chapter 4: Old Town and the Distillery District:** Cafe/Tourism Toronto (89). Inspired by Maps/ Shutterstock (93). Courtesy of Tourism Toronto (99). **Chapter 5: Yonge-Dundas Square Area:** Courtesy of Tourism Toronto (103). V.Ben/iStockphoto (109). Courtesy of Toronto Eaton Centre (111). **Chapter 6: Chinatown, Kensington Market, and Queen West:** Mikecphoto/Shutterstock (113). Jphilipg/Flickr, [CC BY 2.0] (116). Sampete/Dreamstime (120). Alastair Wallace/Shutterstock (126). **Chapter 7: West Queen West, Ossington, and Parkdale:** Courtesy of Tom Arban (133). Roy Harris/Shutterstock (136). Emily Sheff/Queen St West (140). Diegograndi/iStockphoto (146). **Chapter 8: Leslieville, Greektown, Little India, and The Beach:** Cedric Swaneck/Radical Road Brewing (149). Courtesy of OTMP (156). Amalia Ferreira Espinoza/Shutterstock (160). **Chapter 9: Queen's Park, the Annex, and Little Italy:** Courtesy of Liberty Group (163). Mikecphoto/Dreamstime (168). Joshua Davenport/Shutterstock (171). Cafe Diplomatico (176). **Chapter 10: Yorkville, Church and Wellesley, Rosedale, and Cabbagetown:** Courtesy of Tourism Toronto (179). George Pimentel/Wirelmage (180). Joshua Jensen/Flickr (181). Jesse Milns/Tourism Toronto (181). Javen/Shutterstock (184). David Hou (199). **Chapter 11: Greater Toronto:** Vvital/Shutterstock (201). Courtesy of Ontario Science Centre (204). Jay Thaker/Shutterstock (207). Andy.M/Shutterstock (209). **Chapter 12: Side Trips from Toronto:** Janifest/iStockphoto (211). Nitin Sanil Photography (214). Willem Dijkstra/Dreamstime (215). Courtesy of Niagara Falls Tourism (215). Elena Elisseeva/ Shutterstock (216). Tasting Room by Craig Hatfield (217). Elena Elisseeva/Shutterstock (217). Paulmckinnon/Dreamstime (223). Janifest/iStockphoto (226). CPU/Shutterstock (228-229). Tourism Toronto (237). Eskystudio/Shutterstock (240). Vvital/Shutterstock (244). Kerry Hayes/Stratford Shakespeare Festival (253). Markspowart/Dreamstime (257). Elenathewise/Dreamstime (260). About Our Writers: All photos are courtesy of the writers except for the following: Daniel Otis, courtesy of Aurora Portraits/Marcus Oleniuk.

*Every effort has been made to trace the copyright holders, and we apologize in advance for any accidental errors. We would be happy to apply the corrections in the following edition of this publication.

Fodor's TORONTO

Publisher: Stephen Horowitz, *General Manager*

Editorial: Douglas Stallings, *Editorial Director;* Jill Fergus, Amanda Sadlowski, *Senior Editors;* Kayla Becker, Brian Eschrich, Alexis Kelly, *Editors;* Angelique Kennedy-Chavannes, *Assistant Editor*

Design: Tina Malaney, *Director of Design and Production;* Jessica Gonzalez, *Senior Designer;* Erin Caceres, *Graphic Design Associate*

Production: Jennifer DePrima, *Editorial Production Manager;* Elyse Rozelle, *Senior Production Editor;* Monica White, *Production Editor*

Maps: Rebecca Baer, *Senior Map Editor;* Mark Stroud (Moon Street Cartography), David Lindroth, *Cartographers*

Photography: Viviane Teles, *Senior Photo Editor;* Namrata Aggarwal, Neha Gupta, Payal Gupta, Ashok Kumar, *Photo Editors;* Eddie Aldrete, *Photo Production Intern;* Kadeem McPherson, *Photo Production Associate Intern*

Business and Operations: Chuck Hoover, *Chief Marketing Officer;* Robert Ames, *Group General Manager*

Public Relations and Marketing: Joe Ewaskiw, *Senior Director of Communications and Public Relations*

Fodors.com: Jeremy Tarr, *Editorial Director;* Rachael Levitt, *Managing Editor*

Technology: Jon Atkinson, *Director of Technology;* Rudresh Teotia, *Associate Director of Technology;* Alison Lieu, *Project Manager*

Writers: Kimberly Lyn, Natalia Manzocco, Daniel Otis, Jesse Ship, Richard Trapunski

Editor: Brian Eschrich

Production Editor: Monica White

27th Edition

ISBN 978-1-64097-562-0

ISSN 1044-6133

SPECIAL SALES
This book is available at special discounts for bulk purchases for sales promotions or premiums. For more information, e-mail SpecialMarkets@fodors.com.

PRINTED IN CANADA

10 9 8 7 6 5 4 3 2 1

About Our Writers

Kimberly Lyn is a digital editor and freelance writer who proudly calls Toronto home. For more than a decade she has covered fashion, lifestyle, and travel topics for publications such as *Global News*, HuffPost Canada, and *Travel + Leisure*. When she's not on a mobile device, you'll find her dining at the latest restaurants, traveling the globe, or practicing yoga. For this edition, she updated Old Town and the Distillery District, and the Yonge-Dundas Square Area.

Natalia Manzocco is a writer and editor based in Toronto. Previously the food writer at *NOW* Magazine, Toronto's longest-running alt-weekly, Natalia has written about news, life, and culture for the *Toronto Star*, the *Globe and Mail*, *Postmedia*, and many others. She is also the founder of Pink Market, Toronto's LGBTQ+ craft fair, and plays in the band Weak Hands. She lives in Toronto's east end with her spouse and cat. She updated Leslieville, Greektown, Little India, and The Beach; and Queen's Park, the Annex, and Little Italy.

Daniel Otis is a Toronto-based journalist who covers travel, trials, and (almost) everything in-between. Reporting from across Canada and countries like Cambodia and Myanmar, Daniel's news and feature stories have appeared in more than two dozen publications, including the *Toronto Star*, the *Globe and Mail*, *Vice*, *Sunset* Magazine, and Slate. Visit ⊕ *danielotis.ca* to learn more. He updated Travel Smart and Greater Toronto.

Jesse Ship found his calling while teaching English in Taipei. A Belgian national who grew up in Toronto and Paris, it only made sense for him to professionally pursue the passions he was raised on: the arts, culture, and travel. If he's not out interviewing the latest experimental band or legendary DJ, or working in the Toronto film and TV industry, he can be found in Kensington Market writing copy or planning social media campaigns while dreaming of his next Southeast Asian adventure. He updated the Harbourfront, Entertainment District, and the Financial District; Chinatown, Kensington Market, and Queen West; and Side Trips from Toronto.

Richard Trapunski is an editor and journalist who lives and breathes Toronto. Most recently the music, tech, and local business editor for *NOW* Magazine, he also has a bustling freelance career contributing to publications like the *Toronto Star*, *The Walrus*, and *Toronto Life*. When he's not out at concerts, he's eating his way through his home city and traveling to others. He updated Experience Toronto; West Queen West, Ossington, and Parkdale; and Yorkville, Church and Wellesley, Rosedale, and Cabbagetown.

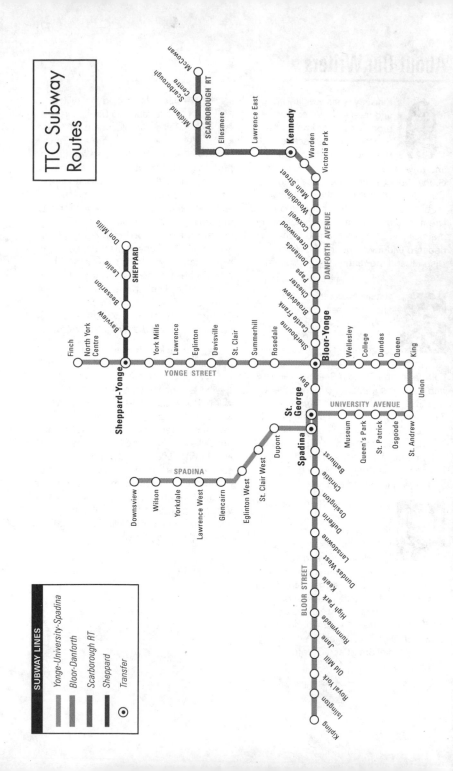

TTC Subway Routes

SUBWAY LINES
Yonge-University-Spadina
Bloor-Danforth
Scarborough RT
Sheppard
⊙ Transfer

SCARBOROUGH RT
McCowan
Scarborough Centre
Midland
Ellesmere
Lawrence East
Kennedy

Don Mills
Leslie
Bessarion
Bayview
SHEPPARD
Sheppard-Yonge

Finch
North York Centre
York Mills
Lawrence
Eglinton
Davisville
St. Clair
Summerhill
Rosedale
YONGE STREET

Warden
Victoria Park
Main Street
Woodbine
Coxwell
Greenwood
Donlands
Pape
Chester
Broadview
Castle Frank
Sherbourne
DANFORTH AVENUE

Bloor-Yonge
Wellesley
College
Dundas
Queen
King
Union

St. George
Bay
Spadina
Bathurst
Christie
Ossington
Dufferin
Lansdowne
Dundas West
Keele
High Park
Runnymede
Jane
Old Mill
Royal York
Islington
Kipling
BLOOR STREET

UNIVERSITY AVENUE
Museum
Queen's Park
St. Patrick
Osgoode
St. Andrew

Downsview
Wilson
Yorkdale
Lawrence West
Glencairn
Eglinton West
St. Clair West
Dupont
SPADINA